CALIFORNIA REAL ESTATE PRINCIPLES

7th Edition
YEAR 2003

Sherry Shindler Price

ASHLEY CROWN SYSTEMS, INC.

2003

This publication is designed to provide accurate and current information regarding the subject matter covered. The principles and conclusions presented are subject to local, state and federal laws and regulations, court cases and revisions of same. If legal advice or other expert assistance is required, the reader is urged to consult a competent professional in that field.

Project Manager: Charli Hislop
Editor: Cynthia Simone Communications
Legal Reviewer: Evelyn W. Winkel
Interior Design: Rebecca Thompson, Diversified Technigraphics, Inc.
Cover Design: Dria Kasunich

Printed in the United States of America

TABLE OF CONTENTS

Section Three — Financial Aspects of Real Estate

Section Four — Economic and Political Aspects of Real Estate

Section Five — Real Estate Practice

Section Six — Specialization

USE OF INTERNET WEB SITES

California Real Estate Principles has changed. It has grown to include more information than could ever be included in one book that someone could carry. This seventh edition just looks like it contains only 514 pages. The size has actually jumped to probably more than 6,000 pages at the very least. Because of the numerous references to web sites for nearly every topic in the book, the student can now continue to search for more facts on any subject about which he or she is curious.

Instructors can use the web sites for enrichment exercises or extra credit. Students can share knowledge gained from accessing the web sites and the links that will lead them to additional sites.

One caution, however. You must be *very* careful when typing the web site address. If it is not *completely* accurate, you will not be successful in finding the site. If you have any problem, please e-mail me at SShindler@aol.com for help.

Two search engines that will be helpful to you in researching beyond what you find in this text are http://www.ask.com and http://www.dogpile.com.

Good Luck,

Sherry

PREFACE

Whether your purpose is to increase your knowledge as a buyer or seller, or to pass the California Real Estate Licensing Exam, you will find the information presented in this book to be useful. Our intent is to help you reach your goal. While the book is written with the beginning student of real estate in mind, inquiring consumers also will find answers to their real estate questions. Use this book as an entry to the exciting world of real estate.

Each chapter begins with a Pre-Test to help you gauge your current knowledge of the material to be presented. Take it without studying, then read the text. Take the identical Post-Test at the end of the chapter and check your improvement. To reinforce your understanding of real estate terminology, review the Terms at the beginning of each chapter and take the Vocabulary matching exercise at the end. The complex world of real estate is presented in simple language with real-world examples to guide each student toward passing the California Real Estate Licensing Exam. After completing the reading assignments and exercises, you will be ready for the serious study required to pass the state exam.

Each real estate licensee has an obligation to his or her customers and clients to achieve knowledge and excellence. *California Real Estate Principles* is your first step.

ABOUT THE AUTHOR

Sherry Shindler Price brings a rich background in real estate and education to the creation and production of this book. Her twenty-five years in the real estate profession include eight years of specialization in investment properties and residential sales.

A California Community College Real Estate Instructor since 1986, Sherry has also used her extensive knowledge to write test questions for state licensing examinations in Nevada, Wisconsin, Minnesota, Maryland and Iowa. She has authored *Escrow Principles and Practices*, reviewed numerous real estate textbooks for major publishers and has written a series of continuing education courses for private real estate schools.

Sherry holds a bachelor of science degree in education from Long Beach State College, a California Real Estate Broker's License and a California Community College Lifetime Instructor's Credential.

AUTHOR'S ACKNOWLEDGMENTS

Many thanks to those hard working community college instructors who have made contributions to this seventh edition of California Real Estate Principles. You are the reason I keep on trying to make it better.

AUTHOR'S ACKNOWLEDGMENTS

All of the following people deserve thanks for helping this project come together.

Jeff Tiss (Continental Lawyers Title Company) — Thanks for taking the time to drop off all the forms supplied by your company and for your always helpful manner.

Tom Dahl (Ed Becker and Associates) — Thanks for your willingness to find the answers to my endless questions and share a good laugh.

Carol Gerber — Thanks for all the research and helpful information you gathered for me.

Bob Hunt (Re/Max, South County) — Your capable answers to my unexpected questions were always given with good will and humor. Thank you for your input on what was "really" happening in the real estate world. You are the one I always call to find out if yet another round of endless revision to real estate forms has been concluded. Your help in acquiring the most up-to-date information/forms is gratefully accepted.

Evelyn Winkel — Who would have ever thought that Evelyn Wood and Sherry Hurlock would write a book together? Thanks for being a friend all these years and for being the "smart" person on this project. Your eagle eye about legal matters saved me on more than one occasion, and you even did it without bruising my ego.

Talk about a bruised ego! The next two people must stand together as my principal tormentors during the writing of this book. *Carol Harris* and *Cynthia Simone*, the Countess of Corrections and the Duchess of Diction, respectively, must take credit for making me re-organize, re-write, and certainly re-explain subject after subject, chapter after chapter, until they were happy. If there is a heaven for editors, you two have certainly done your jobs and deserve special places reserved for those who insist on nothing but the best.

Becky Thompson — Thank you for your graphic creativity and cheerful translations of my obscure "doodles". I knew what I meant, but only a genius could figure out what it was from my talentless drawings.

Jay Achenbach — And special thanks to you, Jay, for your positive attitude and encouragement throughout this project. The finished product is a result of your desire for an excellent book that truly reflects your high personal standards.

Dedicated to Norn and G.P.

*T*HE REGULATION OF REAL ESTATE PRACTICE

1

CALIFORNIA
DEPARTMENT
OF REAL ESTATE

Focus

- **Government regulation in brokerage transactions**
- **Operations of the Department of Real Estate**
- **Types of licenses, requirements for obtaining broker and salesperson licenses and the licensing exams**
- **Continuing education**
- **Violations of Real Estate Law**
- **Trade and professional organizations**

Pre-Test

The following is a self test to determine how much you know about the California Department of Real Estate before reading this chapter. Take it without studying, then read the material presented in the text. At the end of the chapter you will find a repeat of this exam. Test your knowledge by answering the questions again, then check your improvement. (The answers are at the end of this chapter.) Good luck!

1. The term "Real Estate Law" refers to:
    a. contract law affecting real estate transactions
    b. law of agency   c. real property law   d. licensing law

2. The Real Estate Law is enforced by:
    a. the Real Estate Commissioner   c. local boards of realtors
    b. the civil courts   d. Code of Ethics

3. The Real Estate Commissioner is appointed by the:
    a. president of the board of realtors
    b. governor
    c. members of the California Department of Real Estate (CAR)
    d. Real Estate Advisory Commission

4. The fine for payment of a fee to an unlicensed person is:
    a. $50   c. $200
    b. $1000   d. $100

5. A real estate broker license is valid for:
    a. four years   c. three years
    b. two years   d. life

6. An applicant for a real estate salesperson license must be at least:
    a. 21 years old   c. 18 years old
    b. 16 years old   d. 20 years old

7. Who pays the salesperson?
    a. seller   c. escrow holder
    b. buyer   d. broker

8. How many hours of continuing education are required for a salesperson license renewal?
    a. 8   c. 25
    b. 45   d. 55

9. Which of the following continuing education classes are required every four years after the first renewal for both the salesperson and broker license renewal?
    a. consumer protection, agency   c. real estate practice, agency
    b. ethics, agency, trust funds, fair housing   d. ethics, real estate principles

10. When a broker's license is suspended, what is the status of all salespersons' licenses held by that broker?
    a. suspended   c. revoked
    b. nothing changes   d. temporarily cancelled

Terms

The following items are the keys to your success in real estate. Refer to them as you study this chapter for greater understanding of subjects presented here.

Ethics

A set of principles or values by which an individual guides his or her own behavior and judges that of others

Police Power

The power of the state to pass laws, within lawful limits, that promote the order, safety, health, morals and general welfare of its citizens

Real Estate Agent

Someone licensed by the Department of Real Estate, holding either a broker or salesperson license, who negotiates sales for other people

Real Estate Broker

Someone holding a broker license and permitted by law to employ those holding a salesperson license, who may negotiate sales for other people

Real Estate Law

The law that affects the licensing and conduct of real estate agents

Real Estate Salesperson

Someone holding a salesperson license who must be employed by a real estate broker, for pay, to perform any of the activities of a real estate broker

Real Estate Sales Associate

The same as a real estate salesperson, holding a salesperson license, employed by a broker

Revoke

Recall and make void

Suspend

Temporarily make ineffective

Trade Association

A voluntary nonprofit organization of independent and competing business units engaged in the same industry or trade, formed to help solve industry problems, promote progress and enhance service

Introduction

The earliest known real estate transactions were about as basic as you could get: People simply transferred property ownership from one to the other by exchanging symbolic clumps of dirt for something of value. As life became more complicated, however, and the population expanded—particularly in cities, there clearly was a need for a more sophisticated way to transfer real property.

At the same time, the need for some kind of regulation emerged—of the practice and the practitioners. Scoundrels and schemers, with their own perception of fairness and honesty, were taking advantage of the average citizen's lack of knowledge about real estate and the law.

Today, as a consumer, your interests are protected by the California Department of Real Estate. You are assured that your real estate agent is licensed and may be held accountable for his or her actions while conducting any real estate business. Because of the department's regulation of real estate licensing, you can be confident that your agent is at least 18 years of age, has passed a qualifying examination, has completed required real estate courses, and is honest and truthful. Your broker must also have met the department's required years of experience or education to qualify.

As a licensee, you are regulated by the Department of Real Estate, known as the DRE. When you apply for a real estate license, you accept legal responsibility for your actions while practicing real estate. You also promise to be honest and truthful in all your dealings with clients and customers.

The following discussion of the DRE and its related activities serves as the foundation for your career as a real estate agent. By its very nature, the material may seem a little difficult to get through, but *it is one of the most important chapters in your textbook.*

Every time you get involved in any way with a brokerage transaction, you will be affected by these consumer-friendly government regulations. It is in your best interest to learn them. Also, if you are sitting for the state exam, you will find it heavily tilted toward the information presented here.

Government Regulation in Brokerage Transactions

http://www.dre.ca.gov
Reference Book, Ch. 1

California has long been a leader in real estate trends. As a matter of fact, the nation's first real estate licensing law was passed in California in 1917. As time went by, however, new legislation was needed because of weaknesses in existing laws or abuses in real estate practice. As a result, the state passed new legislation to modernize real estate law and make it more responsive to consumers. This power of government to regulate and supervise the Real Estate Law is called **Police Power**.

The power of the state to pass laws, within lawful limits, that promote the order, safety, health, morals and general welfare of its citizens is known as police power. Whenever the police power of the state is used as a tool to enact new laws to protect the public interest, the use of that power must be justified as a benefit to the common good and not an arbitrary use of authority.

This power to pass such laws is given to the states by the United States Constitution, and to each county and city in California by the State Constitution. Thus, all citizens of California benefit from this empowerment of government to regulate the law.

The following examples of regulation by police power are reasonable uses of legislation to promote general well-being in communities: zoning in cities so that neighborhoods may be kept free of objectionable businesses; limitation of districts in which cemeteries, slaughterhouses, factories and the like may be located; controls for speeding and other careless driving on the highways; prohibiting adulteration or selling of impure goods; garbage disposal; vaccination of school children; regulation or prohibition of liquor, prostitution and gambling; requiring safety devices at places of employment. Even though some laws may seem to be restrictive on the conduct of private persons, their measure is in their worth to the common good.

The Real Estate Law, as an extension of the state's police power, is designed mainly for the protection of the public in real estate transactions where an agent is involved. In an attempt to create and maintain higher professional standards, and develop greater trust from the public in general, the real estate industry has supported legislation that protects consumer interests.

http://www.leginfo.ca.gov

Real estate brokers and salespersons are entrusted with people's hopes, dreams and money. Consumers must have a great deal of confidence in the real estate industry to place their trust in a broker or salesperson. With that in mind, the state uses its police power to place strict requirements on those who wish to practice real estate—in the form of real estate licensing.

When you hear the term **Real Estate Law**, it means the law that affects the licensing and conduct of real estate agents. It must be seen separately from what is known as real property law, law of agency, contract law or other legal aspects of real estate ownership and transfer.

Remember

Real Estate Law Affects:

1. Licensing of Real Estate Agents

2. Conduct of Real Estate Agents

The Real Estate Law, or license law, is not upheld in a court of law, but is enforced by the Real Estate Commissioner at special hearings.

The Two Main Purposes of the Real Estate Law are:

1. Protecting consumers from loss because of dishonest and incompetent agents

2. Protecting the good standing of ethical agents from the adverse publicity caused by unprincipled licensees

---

Operations of the Department of Real Estate

http://www.dre.ca.gov

The Real Estate Commissioner, appointed by the governor, determines administrative policy and enforces the provisions of the Real Estate Law. To be appointed, the designee must have been a real estate broker for five years, and be actively engaged in the real estate business in California.

http://www.ca.gov

Responsibilities of the Real Estate Commissioner

- Examine complaints against licensees
- Regulate specific aspects of the sale of subdivisions
- Monitor real property securities transactions
- Manage prepaid rental listing services
- Screen and qualify applicants for license
- Investigate non-licensees alleged to be performing acts for which a license is required

One of the jobs *not* assigned to the Commissioner: settling commission disputes. That issue falls under the power of a court of law, and must be handled through an attorney if the matter cannot be settled agreeably by the parties involved.

The Commissioner appoints a Real Estate Advisory Commission for consultation and advice on matters pertinent to the DRE. The Commission is made up of 10 members: six licensed real estate brokers and four public members. None but the Commissioner receive payment for tenure on the Commission, which meets at least four times yearly.

Real Estate Licensing

http://www.dre.gov
Reference Book, Ch. 1

As we have seen, the purpose of a real estate license is to protect both the consumer and the licensee. It is important for both to understand the obligations and restrictions of the different licenses that may be held.

The two main types of real estate licenses are the broker's license and the salesperson's license. The terms agent, broker, sales agent, salesperson and sales associate are all used to identify individuals holding either a broker or salesperson license.

A real estate salesperson does not have to be employed by a real estate broker, but must be so employed in order to engage in activities requiring a real estate license. Also, a salesperson must be employed by a broker to get paid any commissions. The broker is paid by the escrow company when an escrow closes, according to instructions from the brokers involved. The broker then pays the salesperson according to their commission split agreement. A salesperson may never get paid a commission directly by a buyer, seller or through escrow.

Under section 10131 Business and Professions Code (California Civil Code), a real estate broker is someone who, for compensation, does or negotiates to perform one or more of the following activities. A salesperson, if employed by a real estate broker, may also do any of the following activities.

Acts Requiring a Real Estate License

- Soliciting buyers

- Soliciting sellers

- Negotiating sales

- Negotiating exchanges

- Negotiating leases

- Negotiating sales contracts

- Negotiating a promissory note secured by real property

- Soliciting for tenants or rentals

- Negotiating loans

This diagram shows the relationship between the two categories of agents. Both the broker and the salesperson are licensees, but the salesperson must work under the broker.

Licensees (also known as Agents)

Broker (the boss)

Salesperson (the employee)

Terminology

http://www.leginfo.ca.gov

Real Estate Agent

A real estate agent is someone who is licensed by the Department of Real Estate to negotiate sales for other people. An agent can be either a broker or a salesperson

Real Estate Broker

A real estate broker is someone who holds a broker license issued by the Department of Real Estate. The broker is permitted by law to employ someone who holds a salesperson license, and to negotiate sales for other people.

Real Estate Salesperson

A real estate salesperson is someone who holds a salesperson license issued by the Department of Real Estate. The salesperson must be employed by a real estate broker in order to perform any of the activities that require a license.

Real Estate Sales Associate

A real estate sales associate is the same as a real estate salesperson. The sales associate holds a salesperson license and must be employed by a broker.

Exemptions to the License

Certain exemptions from licensing requirements are allowed. A real estate license is not needed by:

- a person who deals only with his or her own property
- a corporation that performs any of the specified activities through one of its regular officers, who must receive no special compensation for doing so
- anyone holding a duly executed power of attorney from the owner of property
- an attorney at law performing services in the regular course of business as an attorney

- any receiver, trustee in bankruptcy or person acting under order of any court
- any trustee selling under a deed of trust
- an employee of lending institutions, pension trusts, credit unions or insurance companies, in connection with loans secured by liens on real property or a business opportunity
- escrow agents collecting funds in connection with loans secured by liens on real property when the funds are deposited in the escrow agent's trust account

A broker may operate a business as a corporation as long as one officer of the corporation is a qualified real estate broker and acts as the chosen broker-officer. Salespersons may be employed by a corporate real estate broker as long as they are supervised by the responsible corporate broker-officer.

No unlicensed person may receive payment for any act requiring a real estate license, nor may any unlicensed person pose as a broker or salesperson. The fine for paying a fee to an unqualified person is $100 for each offense. The punishment for an individual falsely claiming to be broker or salesperson is a fine of up to $10,000 or imprisonment up to six months, or both. A corporation is subject to a criminal fine not to exceed $50,000.

Both broker and salesperson licenses are valid for four years and may be renewed at that time upon payment of a fee and evidence that the requirements for continuing education have been met. An applicant who fails to pass the state exam may apply for reexamination any number of times by filing an application and paying the fee. The person must take the exam within two years or file a new application and pay a new fee. Upon passing the state exam, the applicant may request a four-year license.

Along with an application and fee, a set of official fingerprints is required to obtain a real estate license. If a license is obtained by fraud, misrepresentation or deceit, the Commissioner may suspend the license, without a hearing, within 90 days after issuance.

Remember

Titles and Licenses

Brokers and salespersons are known as agents.

Brokers and salespersons are both licensees.

A salesperson must be employed by a broker to get paid.

The broker pays the salesperson.

The fine is $100 for paying a fee to an unlicensed person who performs an act requiring a real estate license.

Real Estate Examination

The purpose of the real estate license examination is to make sure consumers are protected in all transactions where they are to be represented by an agent. The exam tests an applicant's general knowledge of real estate, appraisal, finance, forms and other fundamentals of the industry. The subject matter covered in the examination is based on laws and procedures appropriate within the state of California.

Broker License Requirements

An applicant for an original real estate broker license must meet specific standards.

http://www.dre.ca.gov
Reference Book, Ch. 1

Basic Requirements: Broker

Be at least 18 years old
Have previous experience and education as required by law
Apply on a form prescribed by the Commissioner
Pass the qualifying examination
Be honest and truthful

The law requires two years of previous full-time experience as a real estate salesperson, or graduation from a four-year college. In addition, a broker applicant must successfully pass the following:

http://www.brokerlicense.com

College Level Courses

Accounting or Real Estate Economics
Legal Aspects of Real Estate
Real Estate Appraisal
Real Estate Finance
Real Estate Practice

The applicant must also complete three courses from the following group:

Additional Courses for Broker License

Advanced Legal Aspects of Real Estate
Advanced Real Estate Appraisal
Advanced Real Estate Finance
Business Law • Escrows
Mortgage Loan Brokering and Lending
Property Management
Real Estate Office Administration
Real Estate Principles

Note: Fees as of 7/1/01. (Check with the DRE for any changes.)

http://www.dre.ca.gov
Examiners

The examination fee for the broker license is $95 and it is valid for two years. An applicant who passes the written test must apply for a broker license within one year of the examination date. The fee for the four-year license is $218. On August 1, 1998, the DRE began enforcing a federal law which requires all applicants for an original or renewal real estate license to submit proof that they are either a United States Citizen, or a legal resident alien who is entitled to receive a public benefit. The document that is submitted to establish legal presence must be accompanied by a completed State Public Benefits Statement (RE 205).

Broker License Examination

The DRE prepared the following outline with the importance of each subject on the state examination to help you prepare for the broker exam.

REAL ESTATE BROKER LICENSING EXAMINATION	Content Weightings
Real Property and Laws Relating to Ownership Ownership of property, encumbrances and public power over property	Approx. **9%**
Tax Implications of Real Estate Ownership Knowledge of current tax laws affecting real estate ownership	Approx. **8%**
Valuation/Appraisal of Real Property Methods of appraising and valuing property factors which may influence value estimate	Approx. **15%**
Financing Real Estate Sources of financing Common clauses in mortgage instruments Types of loans, terms and conditions	Approx. **16%**
Transfer of Property Titles, escrows and reports	Approx. **9%**
Real Estate Practice Listing of real property, sales contracts and marketing	Approx. **21%**
Broker's Responsibility for Agency Management State real estate laws and regulations Laws relating to fair practices Knowledge of trends and developments Knowledge of commonly used real estate forms and math calculations	Approx. **22%**

Examination Rules and Grading: Broker

5 hours (2 1/2 hours morning, 2 1/2 hours afternoon)

200 multiple choice questions

Must answer 75% correct

Salesperson License Requirements

A person operating as a real estate agent under the supervision of a licensed broker must have earned a salesperson license by meeting the following requirements. A salesperson must be employed by a licensed broker to perform acts regulated by a salesperson license.

http://www.dre.ca.gov
Reference Book, Ch. 1

Basic Requirements: Salesperson

Be at least 18 years old

Apply on a form prescribed by the Commissioner

Pass a qualifying examination as required

Complete the real estate principles course

Be honest and truthful

Prior to-or within 18 months of-issuance of a conditional salesperson license, two additional courses must be completed from the following list:

http://www.
licenserenewal.com

Additional Courses for Salesperson License

Accounting • Business law • Escrow

Legal Aspects of Real Estate

Mortgage Loan Brokering and Lending

Property Management

Real Estate Appraisal

Real Estate Economics

Real Estate Finance

Real Estate Office Administration

Real Estate Practice

The examination fee for the salesperson's license is $60. An applicant who passes the salesperson examination may apply for a four-year license by submitting, within one year of the examination date, an application for the salesperson license with a $129 license fee, a set of fingerprints, a fingerprint processing fee of $32, and transcripts showing completion of the remaining required courses.

On August 1, 1998, the DRE began enforcing a federal law which requires all applicants for an original or renewal real estate license to submit proof that they are either a United States Citizen, or a legal resident alien who is entitled to receive a public benefit. The document that is submitted to establish legal presence must be accompanied by a completed State Public Benefits Statement (RE 205).

http://www.dre.ca.gov

The license fee is $178 if the applicant chooses to take up to 18 months to complete the required courses after being awarded a conditional real estate license. This license is then subject to automatic suspension if evidence of coursework completion is not submitted.

The salesperson's license must be held by the employing broker in the broker's principal office, not a branch office.

Salesperson License Examination

The DRE prepared the following outline with the importance of each subject on the state examination to help you prepare for the salesperson exam.

http://www.
dre.ca.gov
Reference
Book, Ch. 2

REAL ESTATE SALESPERSON LICENSING EXAMINATION	
	Content Weightings
Real Property and Laws Relating to Ownership Ownership of property, encumbrances and public power over property	Approx. **11%**
Tax Implications of Real Estate Ownership Knowledge of current tax laws affecting real estate ownership	Approx. **8%**
Valuation/Appraisal of Real Property Methods of appraising and valuing property factors which may influence value estimate	Approx. **15%**
Financing Real Estate Sources of financing Common clauses in mortgage instruments Types of loans, terms and conditions	Approx. **17%**
Transfer of Property Titles, escrows and reports	Approx. **10%**
Real Estate Practice Listing of real property, sales contracts and marketing	Approx. **22%**
Broker's Responsibilities and Functions of Salesperson State real estate laws and regulations Laws relating to fair practices Knowledge of trends and developments Knowledge of commonly used real estate forms and math calculations	Approx. **17%**

Examination Rules and Grading: Salesperson

3 1/4 hours

150 multiple choice questions

Must answer 70% correct

License Renewals: Brokers and Salespersons

Every four years, both brokers and salespersons must renew their real estate licenses. Both must present evidence of completing the required continuing education courses. A two-year grace period for renewal is allowed as long as all real estate activity has ceased during that time and a late fee is paid at the time of renewal. There is no provision for an inactive license status.

eLicensing Transactions

The DRE now offers elicensing, an interactive online system that lets you complete license renewal and change transactions via the Internet. Available transactions include:

- eLicensing registration
  License renewals
- Duplicate license requests
- Salesperson changes of employing broker
- mailing address changes

User-friendly features include customized menus, email confirmations, status tracking of online transactions, and clear instructions. eLicensing is available on the DRE website at www.dre.ca.gov.

Continuing Education

http://www.dre.ca.gov
Reference Book, Ch. 1

Each time brokers and salespersons renew their licenses—every four years—they must have completed 45 hours of approved continuing education courses. Here are the category requirements.

http://www.
licenserenewal.com

http://www.dre.ca.gov

License Renewals — 45 Hours

- every four years
- first four-year renewal requires only 3 hours each of ethics, agency, fair housing, trust funds
- 45 hours of approved continuing education required after first renewal
  - 3 hrs. ethics, professional conduct, legal aspects
  - 3 hrs. agency
  - 3 hrs. fair housing
  - 3 hrs. trust funds
  - 33 hrs. consumer protection
- renewal fees
  - *broker license — $218 on time, $327 late
  - *sales license — $129 on time, $193 late

Fee increase as of 7/1/01. Check with the DRE for correct information. Fees are always subject to change.

When a salesperson is discharged for a violation of any of the provisions of the Real Estate Law, the employing broker must immediately file a certified written statement of the facts with the Commissioner.

If a real estate broker license is revoked or **suspended** by the DRE, any salesperson licenses held by that broker are cancelled until the license is transferred to a new employing broker.

Violations of the Real Estate Law

http://www.leginfo.ca.gov

http://www.dre.ca.gov
Reference Book, Ch. 1

Most violations of Real Estate Law occur under sections 10176 and 10177 of the Business and Professions Code. Section 10176 generally refers to actions committed while conducting business under a real estate license. Section 10177 may refer to circumstances when a licensee is not necessarily acting as an agent.

Section 10176
Actions Committed While Conducting Business Under a Real Estate License

Misrepresentation (Section 10176a)
A great majority of the complaints received are about misrepresentation on the part of the broker or salesperson. The failure of a broker or salesperson to disclose to his or her principal material facts of which the principal should be made aware is included as a cause for discipline under this section.

False Promise (Section 10176b)
A false promise and a misrepresentation are not the same thing. A misrepresentation is a false statement of fact. A false promise is a false statement about what someone is going to do in the future.

Continued Misrepresentation (Section 10176c)
The Commissioner has the right to discipline a licensee for a continued and flagrant course of misrepresentation or making of false promises.

Dual Agency (Section 10176d)
A licensee must inform all principals if the licensee is acting as agent for more than one party in a transaction.

Commingling (Section 10176e)
This is mixing the funds of principals with the broker's own money. Commingling is not the same thing as conversion. Conversion is misappropriating and using principal's funds.

Definite Termination Date (Section 10176f)

A specified termination date is required on all exclusive listings relating to transactions for which a real estate license is required.

Secret Profit (Section 10176g)

Secret profit cases usually arise when the broker, who already has a higher offer from another buyer, makes a low offer, usually through a "dummy" purchaser. The broker then sells the property to the interested buyer for the higher price. The difference is the secret profit.

Listing-Option (Section 10176h)

A licensee who has both a listing and an option to buy on a property must inform the principal of the amount of profit the licensee will make, and to obtain the written consent of the principal approving the amount of such profit, before the licensee may exercise the option.

Dishonest Dealing (Section 10176i)

"Dishonest dealing" is a catch-all section similar to Section 10177(f). The difference is that under Section 10176(i) the acts must have been those requiring a license, while there is no such need under Section 10177(f).

Signatures of Prospective Purchasers (Section 10176j)

Brokers must obtain a written authorization to sell from a business owner before securing the signature of a prospective purchaser to any such agreement.

Section 10177
Circumstances When a Licensee Is Not Acting As An Agent

Obtaining a License by Fraud (Section 10177a)

The Commissioner may proceed against a licensee for misstatements of fact in an application for a license, and in those instances where licenses have been procured by fraud, misrepresentation or deceit.

Convictions (Section 10177b)

This section permits proceeding against a licensee after a criminal conviction for either a felony or a misdemeanor which involves moral turpitude and is substantially related to the qualifications, functions or duties of a real estate licensee.

False Advertising (Section 10177c)

Licensees who are parties to false advertising are subject to disciplinary action.

http://www.leginfo.ca.gov

Violations of Other Sections (Section 10177d)

This section is the Department's authority to proceed against the licensee for violation of any of the other sections of the Real Estate Law, the Regulations of the Commissioner and the subdivision laws.

Misuse of Trade Name (Section 10177e)

Only active members of the National Association of Realtors may use the term "Realtor".

Conduct Warranting Denial (Section 10177f)

This is a general section of the Real Estate Law. Almost any act involving a crime or dishonesty will fall within this section including the denial or suspension of a license issued by another government agency.

Negligence or Incompetence (Section 10177g)

Demonstrated negligence or incompetence, while acting as a licensee, is cause for disciplinary action.

Supervision of Salespersons (Section 10177h)

A broker is subject to disciplinary action if the broker fails to exercise reasonable supervision over the activities of the broker's salespersons.

Violating Government Trust (Section 10177i)

A licensee may not use government employment to violate the confidential nature of records thereby made available.

Other Dishonest Conduct (Section 10177j)

Any other conduct which constitutes fraud or dishonest dealing may subject the one so involved to license suspension or revocation.

Restricted License Violation (Section 10177k)

Violations of the terms, conditions, restrictions and limitations contained in any order granting a restricted license are grounds for disciplinary action.

Inducement of Panic Selling (Section 10177l)

A licensee may not solicit or induce the sale, lease or the listing for sale or lease, of residential property on the grounds of loss of value, increase in crime or decline in the quality of schools due to the present or prospective entry into the neighborhood of a person or persons of another race, color, religion, ancestry or national origin.

Violation of Franchise Investment Law (Section 10177m)

Violates any of the provisions of the Franchise Investment Law or any regulations of the Corporations Commissioner.

Violation of Corporations Code (Section 10177n)

Violates any of the provisions of the Corporations Code or of the regulations of the Commissioner of Corporations relating to securities as specified by the Corporations Code.

Recovery Account

http://www.dre.ca.gov
Reference Book, Ch. 1

A Real Estate Recovery Fund, created through collection of a fixed amount from each license fee, assures the payment of otherwise uncollectible court judgments against licensees who have committed fraud, misrepresentation, deceit or conversion of trust funds in a transaction.

Real Estate Education and Research Fund

The real estate industry depends on the public's trust to perform its job. In order to better serve the consumer, the Real Estate Education and Research Fund was created for the advancement of real estate education. Like the Real Estate Recovery Fund, money is collected from license fees for the Education and Research Fund.

Trade and Professional Organizations

http://www.dre.ca.gov
Reference Book, Ch. 3

http://www.car.org

http://www.realtor.com

http://www.creea.org

http://www.reea.org

http://www.nareb.com

A **Trade Association** is a voluntary nonprofit organization of independent and competing business units engaged in the same industry or trade, formed to help solve industry problems, promote progress and enhance service.

A real estate board or association is made up of members who share an interest in the business of real estate. Usually, members who join a local association of realtors automatically become members of the California Association of Realtors (CAR) and the National Association of Realtors (NAR). The purpose of a real estate association is to bring together those engaged in the real estate business; to encourage the highest ideals of professional conduct; to protect its members and the public from irresponsible, unprincipled or dishonest licensees; to promote the passing of laws for the protection of property rights and interests in general; and to do anything in its power to upgrade the reputation and dignity of the real estate business.

NAR brings together all licensees who share a common interest in promoting the real estate industry. A member of NAR is known as a Realtor, is subject to its rules and standards of conduct, and is entitled to its benefits. It is only through this membership that the right to use the term Realtor is granted. Members then operate their businesses using the Code of Ethics of NAR as a guideline for their actions.

CAR performs the same function as NAR, but on the state level. Licensees, by operating within the guidelines of NAR's Code of Ethics, bring to the real estate industry the highest ideals in dealing with the consumer.

Code of Ethics

http://www.realtor.com

Ethics is a set of principles or values by which an individual guides his or her own behavior and judges that of others. The professional behavior set forth in real estate law is a course which a licensee must follow. By observing the code of ethics, members of local, state and national trade associations promote good will and harmony, and further the interests of the real estate industry as well as the public.

Copies of the NAR Code of Ethics and the Commissioner's Regulations are in Chapter 13 of this book.

Post Test

The following self test repeats the one you took at the beginning of this chapter. Now take the exam again—since you have read all the material—and check your knowledge of real estate regulation.

1. The term "Real Estate Law" refers to:
   a. contract law affecting real estate transactions
   b. law of agency   c. real property law   d. licensing law

2. The Real Estate Law is enforced by:
   a. the Real Estate Commissioner   c. local boards of realtors
   b. the civil courts   d. Code of Ethics

3. The Real Estate Commissioner is appointed by the:
   a. president of the board of realtors
   b. governor
   c. members of the California Department of Real Estate (CAR)
   d. Real Estate Advisory Commission

4. The fine for payment of a fee to an unlicensed person is:
   a. $50   c. $200
   b. $1000   d. $100

5. A real estate broker license is valid for:
   a. four years   c. three years
   b. two years   d. life

6. An applicant for a real estate salesperson license must be at least:
   a. 21 years old   c. 18 years old
   b. 16 years old   d. 20 years old

7. Who pays the salesperson?
   a. seller   c. escrow holder
   b. buyer   d. broker

8. How many hours of continuing education are required for a salesperson license renewal?
   a. 8   c. 25
   b. 45   d. 55

9. Which of the following continuing education classes are required every four years after the first renewal for both the salesperson and broker license renewal?
   a. consumer protection, agency   c. real estate practice, agency
   b. ethics, agency, trust funds,   d. ethics, real estate principles
      fair housing

10. When a broker's license is suspended, what is the status of all salespersons' licenses held by that broker?
    a. suspended   c. revoked
    b. nothing changes   d. temporarily cancelled

Vocabulary

Read the definition, find the matching term and write the corresponding term number on the line provided.

Terms

1. Ethics
2. Police Power
3. Real Estate Agent
4. Real Estate Broker
5. Real Estate Law

6. Real Estate Salesperson
7. Real Estate Sales Associate
8. Revoke
9. Suspend
10. Trade Association

Definitions

1. ____ Someone holding a real estate license and employed by a real estate broker, for pay, to perform any of the activities of a real estate broker

2. ____ Someone permitted by law to employ those holding a salesperson license, and who may also negotiate sales

3. ____ The same as a real estate salesperson, holding a real estate license, employed by a broker

4. ____ Recall and make void

5. ____ A set of principles or values by which an individual guides his or her own behavior and judges that of others

6. ____ A voluntary nonprofit organization of independent and competing business units engaged in the same industry or trade, formed to help solve industry problems, promote progress and enhance service

7. ____ Temporarily make ineffective

8. ____ The law that affects the licensing and conduct of real estate agents

9. ____ The power of the state to pass laws, within lawful limits, that promote the order, safety, health, morals and general welfare of its citizens

10. ____ Someone licensed by the Department of Real Estate, holding either a broker or salesperson license, who negotiates sales for other people

Answers

Pre-Test/Post Test

1. d
2. a
3. b
4. d
5. a
6. c
7. d
8. b
9. b
10. d

Vocabulary

1. 6
2. 4
3. 7
4. 8
5. 1
6. 10
7. 9
8. 5
9. 2
10. 3

SECTION TWO

LEGAL ASPECTS OF REAL ESTATE

REAL PROPERTY

Focus

- **Bundle of Rights**
- **Types of estates in real property**
- **Real property vs. personal property**
- **Real property—a definition**
- **Fixtures**
- **Trade fixtures**
- **Land descriptions**

Pre-Test

The following is a self test to determine how much you know about Real Property before reading this chapter. Take it without studying, then read the material presented in the text. At the end of the chapter you will find a repeat of this exam. Test your knowledge by answering the questions again, then check your improvement. (The answers are at the end of this chapter.) Good luck!

1. The rights that go along with ownership of real property are called:
   - a. Bill of Rights
   - b. Bundle of Rights
   - c. Cradle of Rights
   - d. Deeded Rights

2. Which kind of estate may be willed?
   - a. less-than-freehold
   - b. leasehold
   - c. freehold
   - d. life estate

3. Craig and Sharon bought a new home and received a grant deed from the seller. What kind of estate do they possess?
   - a. estate of inheritance
   - b. less-than-freehold estate
   - c. an estate in common
   - d. a community estate

4. Sheila deeded a house she owned to her mother, Janet, with the condition that title to the house return to Sheila upon the death of her mother. What kind of estate does Janet hold?
   - a. less-than-freehold
   - b. estate of inheritance
   - c. fee simple defeasible
   - d. life estate

5. Another name for a leasehold estate is:
   - a. fee simple absolute
   - b. fee simple qualified
   - c. less-than-freehold
   - d. freehold

6. Personal property is:
   - a. immovable
   - b. a house
   - c. a built-in jacuzzi
   - d. movable

7. Chattel is:
   - a. real property
   - b. personal property
   - c. neither real nor personal
   - d. both real and personal

8. When real property is sold, anything that has become attached to it:
   - a. goes to the buyer
   - b. goes with the seller
   - c. is divided between buyer and seller
   - d. goes to the broker

9. Under the doctrine of correlative user:
   - a. a riparian owner may take all the water he or she needs
   - b. a riparian owner does not have access to underground water
   - c. a riparian owner must negotiate with non-riparian owners for water rights
   - d. an owner may take only his or her share of underground water

10. The method of land description most likely to be used in a city is:
    - a. U.S. Government Section and Township Survey
    - b. Recorded Lot, Block and Tract System
    - c. Metes and Bounds
    - d. common address

Terms

The following items are the keys to your success in real estate. Refer to them as you study this chapter for greater understanding of subjects presented here.

Appurtenance

Those rights, privileges and improvements that belong to and pass with the transfer of real property but are not necessarily a part of the actual property

Base Line

A survey line running east and west, used as a reference when mapping land

Bill of Sale

A written agreement used to transfer ownership in personal property

Bundle of Rights

An ownership concept describing all the legal rights that attach to the ownership of real property

Chattel

Personal property

Chattel Real

An item of personal property which is connected to real estate; for example, a lease

Condition Precedent

A condition which requires something to occur before a transaction becomes absolute and enforceable; for example, a sale that is contingent on the buyer obtaining financing

Condition Subsequent

A condition which, if it occurs at some point in the future, can cause a property to revert to the grantor; for example, a requirement in a grant deed that a buyer must never use the property for anything other than a private residence

Doctrine of Correlative User

Owner may use only a reasonable amount of the total underground water supply for his or her beneficial use

Emblements

Annual crops produced for sale

Estate

A legal interest in land; defines the nature, degree, extent and duration of a person's ownership in land

Estate in Fee

The most complete form of ownership of real property; a freehold estate that can be passed by descent or by will after the owner's death; also known as estate of inheritance or fee simple estate

Estate of Inheritance

See estate in fee

Fee

See estate in fee or fee simple absolute

Fee Simple Absolute

The largest, most complete ownership recognized by law; an estate in fee with no restrictions on its use

Fee Simple Estate

See estate in fee

Fee Simple Defeasible

Also known as fee simple qualified

Fee Simple Qualified

An estate in which the holder has a fee simple title, subject to return to the grantor if a specified condition occurs

Fixture

Personal property that has become affixed to real estate

Freehold Estate

An estate in real property which continues for an indefinite period of time

Less-Than-Freehold Estate

A leasehold estate, considered to exist for a definite period of time or successive periods of time until termination

Life Estate

An estate that is limited in duration to the life of its owner or the life of some other chosen person

Linear Foot

A measurement meaning one foot or 12 inches in length as contrasted to a square foot or a cubic foot

Littoral

Land bordering a lake, ocean or sea—as opposed to land bordering a stream or river (running water)

Meridian

A survey line running north and south, used as a reference when mapping land

Metes and Bounds

A method of land description in which the dimensions of the property are measured by distance and direction

Monument

A fixed landmark used in a metes and bounds land description

Personal Property

Anything movable that is not real property

Plat Map

A map of a town or subdivision showing the location and boundaries of individual properties, used in the recorded tract system to describe land

Property

The rights or interests which an owner has in something owned

Range

A land description used in the U.S. government survey system consisting of a strip of land located every six miles east and west of each principal meridian

Real Property

Land, anything affixed to the land, anything appurtenant to the land, anything immovable by law

Riparian Rights

The rights of a landowner whose land is next to a natural watercourse to reasonable use of whatever water flows past the property

Section

An area of land, as used in the government survey method of land description; a land area of one square mile or 640 acres; 1/36 of a township

Township

A land description used in the U.S. government survey system consisting of a six-by-six mile area containing 36 sections, each one mile square

Trade Fixture

An article of personal property affixed to leased property by the tenant as a necessary part of business; may be removed by tenant as personal property upon termination of the lease

Introduction

Ownership is the basic element in the whole subject of real estate. That precious, desirable, seemingly out-of-reach dream most of us share is considered a basic right in our culture. It has not always been that way.

Our laws of property ownership had their beginnings in English common law. Originally, all property was owned by the monarch at the time, or an appointed noble. As time went by, people became annoyed by their lack of rights regarding property ownership.

Their discontent set powerful forces of change in motion, so that eventually each owner of real property—or real estate, as it is now called—acquired certain rights along with property ownership.

Bundle of Rights

Known collectively as the Bundle of Rights, this very important package includes: the right to own, possess, use, enjoy, borrow against and dispose of real property.

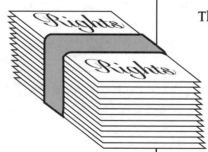

Bundle of Rights

Possession

The right to live on the property and the right to keep others out

Use

The right to use property, within the law, in any way, or for any purpose

Enjoyment

The right to peace and quiet without being bothered by others

Encumber

The right to borrow money and use property as security for the loan

Transfer

The right to sell property, give it as a gift or dispose of it in any way permitted by law

Types of Estates in Real Property

http://www.dre.ca.gov
Reference Book, Ch. 4

An **Estate** is the ownership interest or claim a person has in real property. There are two types of estates that may be owned: **Freehold** and **Less-than-Freehold**. The type of estate determines how much of a claim exists. Each type of estate is described in terms of its duration and the rights that accompany it.

Freehold Estates

The word freehold comes from feudal England. When the land owner was not subject to demands of the overlord and held the land freely, he held a freehold estate. This type of estate continues for an indefinite period of time and may be the estate of a homeowner or a landlord. It includes the Bundle of Rights.

Today, when we think of a freehold estate, we must consider the two types: **Estates in Fee** and **Life Estates**.

Estates in Fee

Sometimes known as a **Fee Simple** estate or a **Fee**, this is the most complete form of ownership. Since an owner of an estate in fee may dispose of it in his or her lifetime or after death by will, it is also known as an **Estate of Inheritance**.

This is commonly the kind of estate that is transferred in a normal real estate transaction. If the property is transferred or sold with no conditions or limitations on its use, it is known as an estate in **Fee Simple Absolute**.

If a seller imposes qualifications or conditions, the buyer then holds a **Fee Simple Qualified** or **Fee Simple Defeasible** estate. For example, a seller may require the property to be used for a specified purpose such as a church or a rehabilitation center. The owner sells the property with the condition that this requirement be met. If the buyer breaches this **Condition Subsequent** after the sale, the seller may take possession of the property and regain title. In another example of a condition subsequent, the seller may place special limitations on the use of the property after the sale. A buyer may be denied the right to sell alcoholic beverages on the property or allow a board and care use. If either of those events occurs, ownership of the property reverts to the seller or his or her heirs.

The parties to a contract may also impose a restriction known as a **Condition Precedent**. In this case, something must occur before a transaction becomes absolute and final. For example, a sale may be contingent on the buyer obtaining financing or qualifying for a VA or FHA loan.

Life Estates

A **Life Estate** is one that is limited in duration to the life of some designated person.

- Amy grants to Bill a life estate with the provision that upon Bill's death, the property reverts to Amy. Bill is then the life tenant, or the designated party on whom the life estate is based. Amy holds an **Estate in Reversion**.

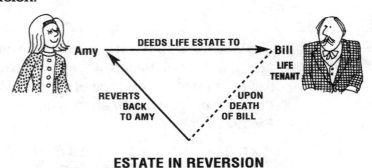

ESTATE IN REVERSION

- Greg grants to Linda a life estate, with the provision that upon Linda's death, the property goes to a third party, Charles. The interest that Charles holds is known as an **Estate in Remainder**.

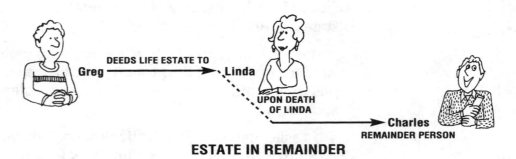

ESTATE IN REMAINDER

- Lowell grants to Verna a life estate for the life of Elizabeth, with the provision that it goes to Laura when Elizabeth dies. Verna may enjoy the benefits of the life estate as long as Elizabeth is alive. Upon Elizabeth's death, the estate goes to Laura or her heirs. That is called **Reserving a Life Estate.**

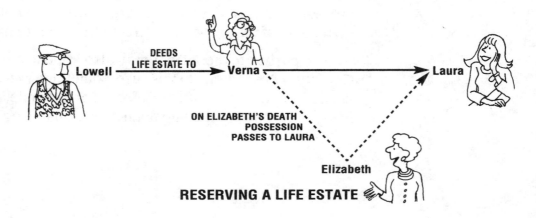

RESERVING A LIFE ESTATE

Since a life estate is a type of freehold, or fee estate, the holder of a life estate has all the rights that go with fee ownership except disposing of the estate by will. Remember, the life estate is tied to a designated life, and when that party dies, the estate goes either to the person in reversion or the person in remainder, or their heirs.

Life estate holders must pay the taxes and maintain the property. They may collect all rents and keep all profits for the duration of the life estate. They may encumber the property or dispose of it in any way except by will. Any interest the life estate holders may create in the property — extending beyond the life of the person used to measure the estate—will become invalid when that designated person dies.

A Life Estate Holder

1. Must pay the taxes and maintain the property

2. May collect all rents and keep all profits for the duration of the life estate

3. May encumber the property or dispose of it in any way except by will

---

Less-Than-Freehold Estates

We have just discussed estates in real property. A freehold estate, as we have seen, is the most complete form of ownership, the one that includes the most rights. The less-than-freehold estate is sometimes known as a leasehold estate or a lease. Renters or tenants hold this kind of an estate.

Leasehold estates are personal property or **Chattel Real**, and include the right to use property for a fixed period of time. Renters, or lessees, have the right of possession and quiet enjoyment. That means they have the right to the exclusive use of the rented property and the right to live quietly without privacy invasion.

Those rights are as legally secure as the rights of a landlord or lessor. For now, make sure you thoroughly understand the less-than-freehold estate. You will learn more about this subject in Chapter 6.

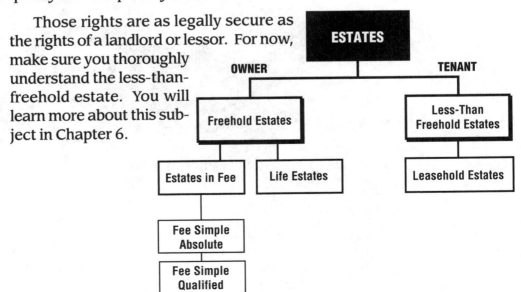

Real Property vs. Personal Property

Something that may be owned is known as **Property**. It can be real or personal. Anything that is not **Real Property** is **Personal Property**. Personal property includes money, movable goods and evidences of debt—such as a promissory note. Real property is immovable and is usually transferred or sold by a deed.

When real property is sold, *anything that has become attached* to it goes to the *buyer* as part of the sale unless other arrangements have been made. Personal property, sometimes known as **Chattel**, is movable and transferred or sold using a **Bill of Sale**. When real property is sold, items of personal property go with the seller unless other arrangements have been made. (Remember this thought. Later it will be clear why it is so important to know the difference between real and personal property.)

Real and personal property can change from one to the other. A tree is real property until it is cut as timber; then it becomes the personal property of whomever cut it. If that timber is milled into lumber, sold and used to build a house, it becomes real property. As the house ages and deteriorates, is torn down and hauled away as scrap lumber, it becomes personal property once again.

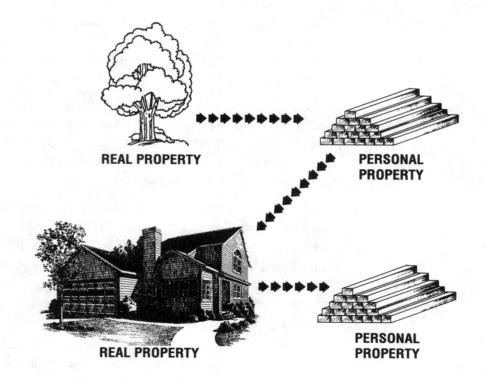

REAL PROPERTY

PERSONAL PROPERTY

REAL PROPERTY

PERSONAL PROPERTY

Real Property — A Definition

http://www.dre.ca.gov
Reference Book, Ch. 4

Real property may be described as land, anything permanently attached to the land, anything appurtenant (we'll define that word shortly) to the land or anything immovable by law.

Land

Let's look at the land we walk on. This is the soil and the rocks that extend to the center of the earth. Included in the definition of land as real property is *airspace, mineral rights* and *water rights*.

Land As Real Property

- Airspace
- Mineral Rights
- Water Rights

AIR SPACE

SURFACE RIGHTS

MINERAL & WATER RIGHTS

CENTER OF THE EARTH

Airspace is considered real property to a reasonable height. A good example of the efficient use of airspace is the building of high rise condominiums. An owner/developer may sell this airspace as real property.

Minerals are owned as real property unless they are non-solid, migratory minerals such as oil or gas. These may not be owned until taken from the ground, at which time they become the personal property of whomever removed them.

Certain *water rights* go with the land and are considered real property. Because of the many disputes over the use of underground (percolating) water and surface water, the law is very clear about the rights of owners. Water cannot be owned, nor can it be channeled or dammed for the benefit of one landowner. Under the **Doctrine of Correlative User**, an owner may take only a reasonable share of underground waters. The owner of property bordering on a stream or river has what is known as **Riparian Rights** (a riparian owner).

Owners may use the water to their benefit in a reasonable amount not to exclude adjoining owners. Owners of land bordering a lake **(Littoral Owners)** generally own to the average low water mark or the edge of the lake. The boundary line of land touching the ocean is the ordinary high-tide mark.

When there is a need for the government to divert water for public use, its Right of Appropriation is applied.

Anything Permanently Attached to the Land

Those items that are permanently attached to the land are also considered real property and belong to the owner. Houses, garages, fences, swimming pools or anything resting on the land to become permanent are owned as a part of the property. Anything permanently attached to the building, such as a **Fixture**, is owned as real property, as is anything attached by roots, such as trees, shrubs and flowers.

The exception to this is crops that are growing and are cultivated annually for sale—such as peaches in a commercial orchard or avocados in a commercial grove. These are known as **Emblements** and are personal property. Emblements may be owned by tenants as well as fee owners. Remember, the crops are the personal property, not the trees or plants they grow on.

Anything Appurtenant to the Land

Anything used with the land for its benefit is known as an **Appurtenance**. Easements and stock rights in a mutual water company are the two most common appurtenances to real property. An easement is a right-of-way across a parcel of land, and is transferred automatically with the property whenever it is sold. The easement is appurtenant to the property.

Stock in a mutual water company is owned by water users who have organized to form a water company for their mutual benefit. The shares in this water company are appurtenant to the land and go with the sale of the property.

Anything Immovable by Law

Established crops and trees are considered immovable by law and must be sold with the property. A seller may not sell the property and exclude the orange grove from the sale. The seller may have sold the crop resulting from the trees as personal property, but the trees remain real property and may not be excluded from the sale.

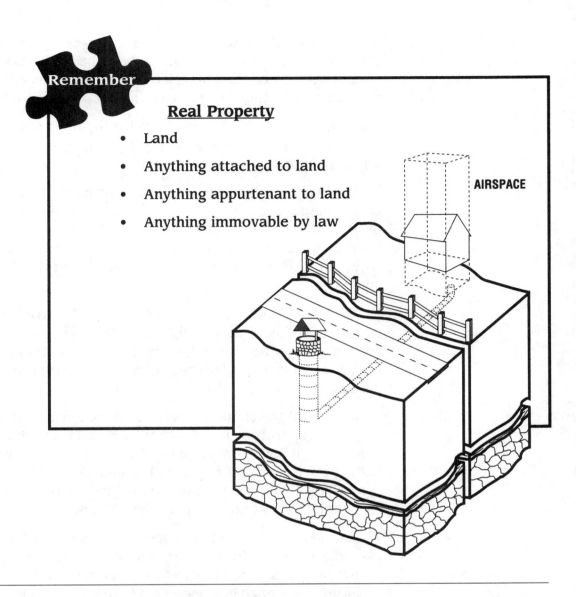

Remember

Real Property

- Land
- Anything attached to land
- Anything appurtenant to land
- Anything immovable by law

AIRSPACE

Fixtures

A fixture is an item of real property that used to be personal property. It has become a fixture because it is permanently attached to real property.

Now that you know what real property is—and is not— let's examine what that means to the consumer. Imagine that you are a prospective buyer. You walk into a house and fall in love with the chandelier hanging from the ceiling in the dining room. You make an offer to buy the house, it is accepted and the escrow goes through smoothly. The sellers get their money and you get the deed to the house.

When you arrive with your moving van, your anticipation turns to hostility when you discover a lonely light bulb hanging where the elegant chandelier had been. The former owners wonder why you are annoyed when you call to arrange the return of your chandelier. They tell you it is not your chandelier; it has been in the family for generations. They never intended it to go with the house.

If you didn't know the difference between real and personal property, you might think the sellers had a right to the chandelier.

Part of a real estate agent's job is to make sure all parties involved in a sale know what goes and what stays. In the above case, the listing agent should have asked the sellers if they wanted to keep the chandelier, and notified prospective buyers that it did not go with the house.

Since it was not excluded from the listing, it was reasonable for the buyer to assume it was real property. It had become a fixture and therefore should have gone with the sale.

When a buyer makes an offer on a property, there is a section in the offer-to-purchase contract where he or she may request any item of real or personal property such as the chandelier, washer/dryer, a refrigerator or a bedspread that matches the custom drapes. The buyer should always put an intention in writing to make sure the seller is informed and agrees.

Disputes about real and personal property have caused the courts to adopt a set of five tests to help them decide who is in the right when two parties disagree about what are fixtures: method of attachment, adaptation, relationship of the parties, intent of the parties and agreement of the parties.

<u>Method of attachment:</u> How is the disputed item attached to the property? If it is permanently attached, it is real property. In the case of the chandelier, it had been wired into the electrical system, which made it a fixture, or real property. It would be included in the sale of the house as something attached or affixed to the land unless the sellers specifically mentioned they wanted to take it with them.

<u>Adaptation:</u> Has the item been made especially for the property? For example, have the drapes been custom-made for the windows? Has the carpet been cut especially to fit the rooms? Is the stove built into the counter? If so, each has become a fixture and has lost its status as personal property.

<u>Relationship of the parties</u>: In a dispute about fixtures, when there is no convincing evidence of the right of one party, courts will look at whether the parties are landlord-tenant, lender-borrower, or buyer-seller. The court then makes a decision based on the relationship of the parties in the case.

<u>Intention:</u> If apparent, either in writing or by the actions of either party involved, this is considered to be the *most* important test of a fixture. Let's look at the tenant who wired special cosmetic lights into the bathroom wall, telling the landlord he intended the lights to remain his personal property. He said he would repair the wall when he moved and would take the lights with him. This was a clear case of a tenant's intention to keep the lights as his personal property. A fixture may remain personal property if all parties are informed. Intention should always be put in writing, however.

Agreement of the parties: When there has been a clear agreement between the parties in a dispute about fixtures, the courts will apply this test to determine who is in the right.

Five Tests of a Fixture:

	M	ethod of attachment
memory	**A**	daptation
aid	**R**	elationship of the parties
"MARIA"	**I**	ntention
	A	greement of the parties

Trade Fixtures

Items of personal property—such as shelves, cash registers, room partitions or wall mirrors—are known as **Trade Fixtures** when used to conduct a business. Tenants retain ownership of the items as personal property when they vacate the premises, but are responsible for repairing any damage that results from placing the trade fixtures.

Land Descriptions

http://www.dre.ca.gov
Reference Book, Ch. 4

Exploring new land captured the imagination of the hardy individuals and families who opened up the U.S. frontier. As they moved west and improved the land on which they settled, these pioneers created a need for systematic property description.

A street address was adequate for social contacts and for delivering mail, but it was not precise enough to identify a particular property.

Today, a legal description is required before a deed may be recorded to transfer title to a new owner. There are three common ways to describe property.

Three Ways to Identify Property:

- U.S. Government Section and Township Survey
- Recorded Lot, Block and Tract System
- Metes and Bounds

U.S. Government Section and Township Survey

http://www.csuchico.edu/lbib/
maps/townships.html

By the late 19th Century, the U.S. government had established a system of land description for new territories, states and other public lands. The rectangular survey system, also known as the U.S. Government Section and Township Survey, uses imaginary lines to form a grid to locate land. North-south longitude lines, called **Meridians**, and east-west latitude lines called **Base Lines**, intersect to form a starting point from which distances are measured.

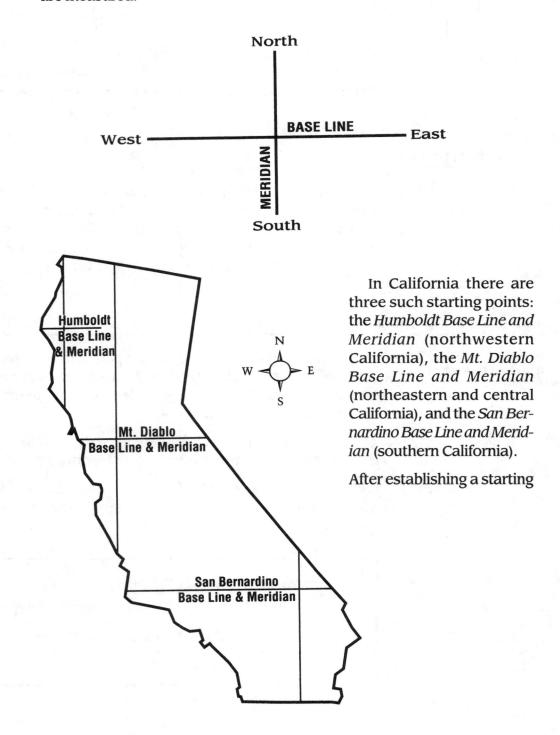

In California there are three such starting points: the *Humboldt Base Line and Meridian* (northwestern California), the *Mt. Diablo Base Line and Meridian* (northeastern and central California), and the *San Bernardino Base Line and Meridian* (southern California).

After establishing a starting

point at the intersection of a chosen principal meridian and base line, government surveyors drew imaginary lines called range lines every six miles east and west of the meridian to form columns called ranges. Each **Range** was numbered either east or west of the principal meridian. For example, the first range east of the meridian was called Range 1 East (R1E), and the first range west of the meridian was called Range 1 West (R1W).

Range Lines

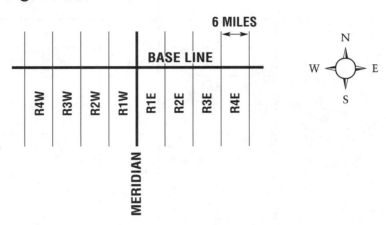

Imaginary township lines were drawn every six miles north and south of the base line to form a row or tier of **Townships**. Then these rows were numbered according to their distance from the base line. For example, the first row of townships north of the base line was called Township 1 North (T1N) and the first row of townships south of the base line was called Township 1 South (T1S).

Township Lines

Thus, a grid of squares, called townships—each six miles by six miles (36 square miles)—appears.

Townships

Each township is described by its location, relative to the intersection of the base line and meridian we have just discussed. A particular township in the fourth tier north of the base line and in the third range west of the meridian—with "T" for township and "R" for range—would be described as follows: T4N,R3W, San Bernardino Base Line and Meridian.

Township and Range

Range Lines - every 6 miles east and west of meridian

Township Lines - every 6 miles north and south of base line

The way to locate T4N,R3W is to start at the intersection of the base line and meridian and count up—or north—four rows and then count to the left—or west—three rows. On the following page is an exercise to test your understanding.

Exercise 1: Locating Townships and Ranges

1. Locate the following areas on the "Townships" diagram, page 44.

   T2S,R5E

   T3S,R2W

   T5S,R4E

   T4S,R1W

2. How far in miles is the west side of T4N,R3W from the principal meridian?

3. How far in miles is the east side of T2S,R5E from the principal meridian?

4. How many miles from the base line is the south side of T5S, R4E?

5. How many miles from the base line is the north side of T4S, R1W?

Answers

1. See Townships diagram, page 44
2. 18 miles
3. 30 miles
4. 30 miles
5. 18 miles

You have learned how to use the intersection of the base line and meridian as a starting point to locate a particular township. Now look at a township, which is divided into 36 **Sections**—each measuring one mile by one mile. The sections are numbered, starting with Section 1 in the northeast corner, and continuing in a snake-like manner to Section 36 in the southeast corner.

36 Sections in One Township

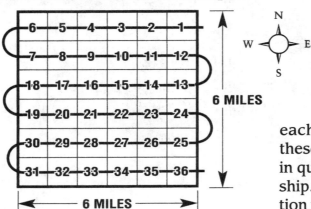

Make no mistake about the numbering of sections. On the state exam you may be asked questions like "Which section is directly west of Section 7?". Remember, each township contains 36 of these sections and the township in question is not the only township. There will always be a section next to it, and that is the one to which the question refers.

Neighboring Townships

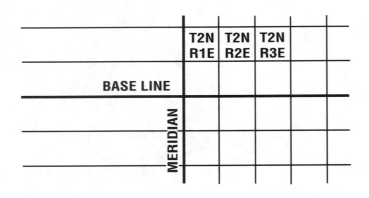

6	5	4	3	2	1	6	5	4	3	2	1	6	5	4	3	2	1
7	8	9	10	11	12	7	8	9	10	11	12	7	8	9	10	11	12
18	17	16	15	14	13	18	17	16	15	14	13	18	17	16	15	14	13
19	20	21	22	23	24	19	20	21	22	23	24	19	20	21	22	23	24
30	29	28	27	26	25	30	29	28	27	26	25	30	29	28	27	26	25
31	32	33	34	35	36	31	32	33	34	35	36	31	32	33	34	35	36

◄—— T2N,R1E ——► ◄—— T2N,R2E ——► ◄—— T2N, R3E ——►

Here is an exercise to help you understand sections.

Exercise 2: Locating Sections

1. Which section is directly west of Section 6 in T2N,R2E?
2. Which section is directly east of Section 36 in T2N,R1E?
3. Which section is directly west of Section 19, T2N,R3E?

Answers

1. Section 1, T2N,R1E
2. Section 31, T2N,R2E
3. Section 24, T2N,R2E

As you see from the Section diagram below, each section is one mile by one mile and contains 640 acres.

Section

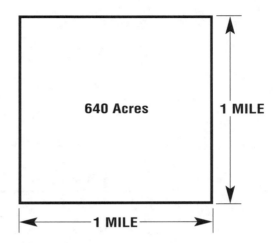

A section may then be divided further into quarter sections containing 160 acres each, and then divided into smaller and smaller parcels. These parcels are identified by their compass direction (NE, SE, NW, SW).

Quarter Sections

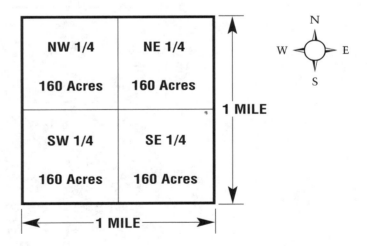

Armed with this knowledge, a student may locate any size parcel, no matter how large or small, by simply dividing the section. Another important number for you to know is 5,280, the number of feet in a mile. You may be asked to calculate an answer on the state exam regarding **Linear Feet** around a section. (Linear refers to length rather than area.)

The illustration on the following page shows how a section may be divided and each parcel described. It is followed by an exercise that tests your ability to locate sections and determine acreage.

Section Divisions

Section 3

| 320 Acres | 320 Acres |

Section 2

40 Acres	40 Acres	160 Acres
40 Acres	40 Acres	
160 Acres		160 Acres

N
W — E
S

Section 10

80 Acres	80 Acres	160 Acres		
160 Acres		40 Acres	10	10
			10	10
		40 Acres	40 Acres	

Section 11

160 Acres	160 Acres		
160 Acres	40 Acres	10	2.5 2.5 / 2.5 2.5
			10	10
	40 Acres	40 Acres	

Exercise 3: Figuring Acreage *(use Section Divisions diagram above)*

1. Locate the E 1/2 of Section 3. How many acres?
2. Locate the SE 1/4 of Section 2. How many acres?
3. Locate the E 1/2 of the NW 1/4 of Section 10. How many acres?
4. Locate the NW 1/4 of the SE 1/4 of Section 11. How many acres?
5. How many feet are there around 1/4 section?
6. Bonus question: Can you find the SW 1/4 of the NE 1/4 of the SE 1/4 of Section 11? How many acres?

(Hint: Always read the description backwards to locate a particular parcel, starting with the last and largest part, proceeding to the first and smallest part of the description. Then you will have located the property in question.)

Answers

1. 320 acres
2. 160 acres
3. 80 acres
4. 40 acres
5. 10,560 feet
6. Bonus answer: 10 acres

Here is a summary of the basic facts about U.S. Government Section and Township Survey. Use it as a reference to calculate land measurement.

Three Base Line and Meridians in California

    Humboldt Base Line and Meridian

    Mt. Diablo Base Line and Meridian

    San Bernardino Base Line and Meridian

Remember

System for Locating Land

- <u>Meridians</u> run north and south

- <u>Base Lines</u> run east and west

- <u>Range Lines</u> run north and south, parallel to the principal meridian, every six miles

- <u>Township Lines</u> run east and west, parallel to the base line, every six miles

- <u>Townships</u> are six miles by six miles, 36 square miles

- <u>Sections</u> are one mile by one mile, 36 in each township and contain 640 acres

- 5,280 feet = one mile

- 43,560 square feet = one acre

- 640 acres = one square mile

- 16.5 feet = one rod

- Four miles = distance around a section/square mile

Recorded Lot, Block and Tract System

Another land description method is the Recorded Lot, Block and Tract System. When developers divide parcels of land into lots, they are required by the California Subdivision Map Act to prepare and record a **Plat Map.**

http://www.ftbc.com/
platmap.htm

This shows the location and boundaries of each separate new lot in the subdivision, and must be recorded in the County Recorder's Office. It is the most convenient and easily understood method of land description.

After the subdivision map has been filed or recorded, it is public knowledge and is available to anyone. Each lot in a subdivision is identified by number, as is the block in which it is located; each lot and block is in a referenced tract. Recorded map descriptions of land are most likely to be found in cities where developers have planned communities and commercial growth areas.

Metes and Bounds

http://www.flatsurv.com/
legaldes.htm

A **Metes and Bounds** description of land delineates boundaries and measures distances between landmarks (or **Monuments**) to identify property. This is a method of land description in which the dimensions of the property are measured by distance and direction. Land that is irregular in shape or cannot be described using either of the two other methods may have a Metes and Bounds description.

Think of measuring when you think of metes, and boundaries when you think of bounds. Generally, you will only need to recognize this type of description when you see it. A surveyor will measure the distances and establish the legal description.

A Metes and Bounds description starts at a well-marked point of beginning, and—following the boundaries of the land—measures the distances between landmarks, then returns to the beginning.

Here is a description of an uneven, hilly parcel of land with an avocado grove in Vista, California:

Beginning at the intersection of the east line of Buena Creek Road and the south line of Cleveland Trail; thence east along the south line of Cleveland Trail 300 feet; thence south 657.5 feet to the center line of Buena Creek; thence northwesterly along the center line of Buena Creek to its intersection with the east line of Buena Creek Road; thence north 325 feet along the east line of Buena Creek road to the place of beginning.

A Metes and Bounds description of city property might begin as follows:

Beginning at a point on the southerly side of Del Cerro Street, 200 feet easterly from the intersection of the southerly side of Del Cerro Street and the easterly side of Vista Las Lomas; thence...

A Metes and Bounds description of land in Section and Township areas might begin as follows:

That part of lots 20, 21, 22 in the Harbor Lights Subdivision in the NW1/4 of the SE1/4 of Section 35, Township 24 north, Range 22 east of the San Bernardino Base Line and Meridian described as follows, beginning...

As a real estate agent, you will not be required to be an expert in any of the three land description methods. You will find it helpful to be adequately informed, however, about which method is used for the type of property you most frequently sell.

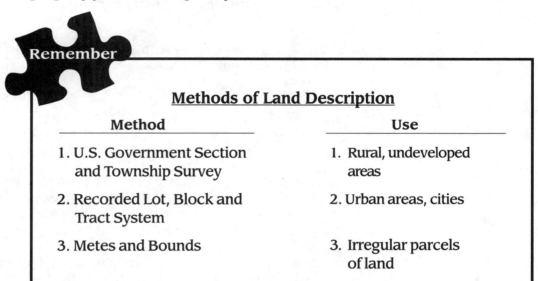

Remember

Methods of Land Description

Method	Use
1. U.S. Government Section and Township Survey	1. Rural, undeveloped areas
2. Recorded Lot, Block and Tract System	2. Urban areas, cities
3. Metes and Bounds	3. Irregular parcels of land

Post Test

The following self test repeats the one you took at the beginning of this chapter. Now take the exam again—since you have read all the material—and check your knowledge of real property.

1. The rights that go along with ownership of real property are called:
   - a. Bill of Rights
   - b. Bundle of Rights
   - c. Cradle of Rights
   - d. Deeded Rights

2. Which kind of estate may be willed?
   - a. less-than-freehold
   - b. leasehold
   - c. freehold
   - d. life estate

3. Craig and Sharon bought a new home and received a grant deed from the seller. What kind of estate do they possess?
   - a. estate of inheritance
   - b. less-than-freehold estate
   - c. an estate in common
   - d. a community estate

4. Sheila deeded a house she owned to her mother, Janet, with the condition that title to the house return to Sheila upon the death of her mother. What kind of estate does Janet hold?
   - a. less-than-freehold
   - b. estate of inheritance
   - c. fee simple defeasible
   - d. life estate

5. Another name for a leasehold estate is:
   - a. fee simple absolute
   - b. fee simple qualified
   - c. less-than-freehold
   - d. freehold

6. Personal property is:
   - a. immovable
   - b. a house
   - c. a built-in jacuzzi
   - d. movable

7. Chattel is:
   - a. real property
   - b. personal property
   - c. neither real nor personal
   - d. both real and personal

8. When real property is sold, anything that has become attached to it:
   - a. goes to the buyer
   - b. goes with the seller
   - c. is divided between buyer and seller
   - d. goes to the broker

9. Under the doctrine of correlative user:
   - a. a riparian owner may take all the water he or she needs
   - b. a riparian owner does not have access to underground water
   - c. a riparian owner must negotiate with non-riparian owners for water rights
   - d. an owner may take only his or her share of underground water

10. The method of land description most likely to be used in a city is:
   - a. U.S. Government Section and Township Survey
   - b. Recorded Lot, Block and Tract System
   - c. Metes and Bounds
   - d. common address

Vocabulary

Read the definition, find the matching term and write the corresponding term number on the line provided.

Terms

1. Appurtenance
2. Base Line
3. Bill of Sale
4. Bundle of Rights
5. Chattel
6. Condition Precedent
7. Condition Subsequent
8. Doctrine of Correlative User
9. Emblements
10. Estate
11. Estate in Fee
12. Fee Simple Absolute
13. Fee Simple Defeasible
14. Fee Simple Qualified
15. Fixture
16. Freehold Estate
17. Less-Than-Freehold Estate
18. Life Estate
19. Linear Foot
20. Littoral
21. Meridian
22. Monument
23. Personal Property
24. Property
25. Range
26. Real Property
27. Riparian Rights
28. Section
29. Township
30. Trade Fixture

Definitions

1. ___ An ownership concept describing all the legal rights that attach to the ownership of real property

2. ___ A legal interest in land; defines the nature, degree, extent and duration of a person's ownership in land

3. ___ An estate in real property which continues for an indefinite period of time

4. ___ A leasehold estate; considered to exist for a definite period of time or successive periods of time until termination

5. ___ The most complete form of ownership of real property; a freehold estate that can be passed by descent or by will after the owner's death; also known as estate of inheritance or fee simple estate

6. ___ The largest, most complete ownership recognized by law; an estate in fee with no restrictions on its use

7. ___ An estate in which the holder has a fee simple title, subject to return to the grantor if a specified condition occurs; also called a fee simple defeasible

8. ___ Also known as fee simple qualified

9. ___ Condition which requires something to occur before a transaction becomes absolute and enforceable; for example, a sale that is contingent on the buyer obtaining financing

10. ___ A condition which, if it occurs at some point in the future, can cause a property to revert to the grantor; for example, a requirement in a grant deed that a buyer must never use the property for anything other than a private residence

11. ___ An estate that is limited in duration to the life of its owner or the life of some other chosen person

12. ___ The rights or interests which an owner has in something owned

13. ___ Anything movable that is not real property

14. ___ Personal property

15. ___ A written agreement used to transfer ownership in personal property

16. ___ Land, anything affixed to the land, anything appurtenant to the land, anything immovable by law

17. ___ An owner may use only a reasonable amount of the total underground water supply for his or her beneficial use

18. ___ The rights of a landowner whose land is next to a natural watercourse to reasonable use of whatever water flows past the property

19. ___ Annual crops produced for sale

20. ___ Those rights, privileges and improvements that belong to and pass with the transfer of real property but are not necessarily a part of the actual property

21. ___ Personal property that has become affixed to real estate

22. ___ An article of personal property affixed to leased property by the tenant as a necessary part of business; may be removed by tenant as personal property upon termination of the lease

23. ___ A survey line running east and west, used as a reference when mapping land

24. ___ A survey line running north and south, used as a reference when mapping land

25. ___ A land description used in the U.S. Government Survey System consisting of a strip of land located every six miles east and west of each principal meridian

26. ___ A land description used in the U.S. Government Survey System consisting of a six-by-six mile area containing 36 sections, each one mile square

27. ___ A fixed landmark used in a Metes and Bounds land description

28. ___ Land bordering a lake, ocean, or sea—as opposed to land bordering a stream or river (running water)

29. ___ A measurement meaning one foot or 12 inches in length as contrasted to a square foot or a cubic foot

30. ___ An area of land, as used in the government survey method of land description; a land area of one square mile, or 640 acres; 1/36 of a township

Answers

Pre-Test/Post Test

1. b
2. c
3. a
4. d
5. c
6. d
7. b
8. a
9. d
10. b

Vocabulary

1.	4	16.	26	
2.	10	17.	8	
3.	16	18.	27	
4.	17	19.	9	
5.	11	20.	1	
6.	12	21.	15	
7.	14	22.	30	
8.	13	23.	2	
9.	6	24.	21	
10.	7	25.	25	
11.	18	26.	29	
12.	24	27.	22	
13.	23	28.	20	
14.	5	29.	19	
15.	3	30.	28	

CHAPTER

3

LAND TITLES AND ESTATES

Focus

- Background of land title in California

- California adopts a recording system

- Ownership of real property

- Limitations on real property: encumbrances

- Declared homestead

- Assuring marketability of title

- Title insurance

Pre-Test

The following is a self test to determine how much you know about titles and estates before reading this chapter. Take it without studying, then read the material presented in the text. At the end of the chapter you will find a repeat of this exam. Test your knowledge by answering the questions again, then check your improvement. (The answers are at the end of this chapter.) Good luck!

1. Which of the following is benefited by an easement appurtenant?
   - a. dominant tenement
   - b. servient tenement
   - c. the easement
   - d. the owner of the servient tenement

2. Vesting refers to:
   - a. co-ownership
   - b. how property is owned
   - c. something to wear
   - d. syndication

3. Debby and Jeff, brother and sister, want to buy a property together. Which of the following vestings would not be considered?
   - a. joint tenants
   - b. tenants in common
   - c. community property
   - d. tenancy in partnership

4. How does a corporation take title to real property?
   - a. joint tenancy
   - b. community property
   - c. tenancy in common
   - d. severalty

5. If the interest each person has in a tenancy in common is not stated in the deed:
   - a. it is presumed to be a joint tenancy
   - b. it is understood that each owner has an equal interest
   - c. it is voidable
   - d. it is invalid

6. All of the following are liens against real property except:
   - a. a judgment
   - b. a trust deed
   - c. property taxes
   - d. encroachments

7. Agreements affecting the use of real property are known as:
   - a. Covenants, Conditions and Restrictions
   - b. trust deeds
   - c. lis pendens
   - d. liens

8. Deed restrictions are imposed on a property by:
   - a. the legislature
   - b. the developer
   - c. Board of Equalization
   - d. city council

9. Which of the following is a legal, non-exclusive use of someone else's property?
   - a. adverse possession
   - b. trespassing
   - c. an easement
   - d. condemnation

10. A claimant has how many days to bring foreclosure action after a mechanic's lien is recorded?
    - a. 40
    - b. 50
    - c. 90
    - d. 120

Terms

The following terms are the keys to your success in learning about real estate. Refer to them as you study this chapter for greater understanding of subjects presented here.

A.L.T.A. Owner's Policy

American Land Title Association policy of extended title insurance policy, can be purchased by lender or buyer

Abstract of Title

A full summary of all consecutive grants, conveyances, wills, records and judicial proceedings affecting title to a specific parcel of real estate

Abstractor

A person who, historically, searches out anything affecting the title to real property and summarizes the information in the findings

Acknowledgment

A formal declaration to a public official (notary) by a person who has signed an instrument which states that the signing was voluntary

Actual Notice

Knowledge gained based on an actual observance, as opposed to Constructive Notice

California Land Title Association

A trade organization of the state's title companies

Chain of Title

The recorded history of matters such as conveyances, liens and encumbrances affecting title to a parcel of real estate

Condition Precedent

Requires that a certain event, or condition, occur before title can pass to a new owner

Condition Subsequent

A restriction, placed in a deed at the time of conveyance, upon future use of the property

Constructive Notice

Recordation of deed or possession of property

Conveyance

The transfer of title to land from one person to another by use of a written instrument

Declaration of Homestead

The recorded document that protects a homeowner from foreclosure by certain judgment creditors

Dominant Tenement

The property that benefits from an easement

Easement

The right to use another's land for a specified purpose, sometimes known as a right-of-way

Easement in Gross

An easement that is not appurtenant to any one parcel; for example, public utilities

Encroachment

The placement of permanent improvements on adjacent property owned by another

Expedientes

Land grants recorded by the Mexican government in California

Extended Policy

An extended title insurance policy

Guarantee of Title

An assurance of clear title

Instrument

A written legal document setting forth the rights and liabilities of the parties involved

Judgment

The final legal decision of a judge in a court of law regarding the legal rights of parties to disputes

License

Permission to use a property, which may be revoked at any time

Lien

A claim on the property of another for the payment of a debt

Lis Pendens

A recorded notice that indicates pending litigation affecting title on a property, preventing a conveyance or any other transfer of ownership until the lawsuit is settled and the lis pendens removed

Marketable Title

Good or clear saleable title reasonably free from risk of litigation over possible defects

Partition Action

A court action to divide a property held by co-owners

Patents

Deeds used by the U.S. government when confirming or transferring ownership to private parties

Servient Tenement

The property that is burdened by an easement

Severalty

Ownership of real property by one person or entity

Standard Policy

A policy of title insurance covering only matters of record

Title

Evidence of land ownership

Title Insurance

An insurance policy that protects the insured against loss or damage due to defects in the property's title

Title Plant

The storage facility of a title company in which it has accumulated complete title records of properties in its area

Treaty of Guadalupe Hidalgo

Ended the war with Mexico in 1848, and California became a possession of the United States

Undivided Interest

That interest a co-owner has in property, which carries with it the right to possession and use of the whole property, along with the co-owners

Vested

Owned by

Introduction

Historically, the question has been, "Who owns this property, and what is their interest in it?" As a real estate agent, you will find yourself explaining to your clients (sellers) and customers (buyers) ways property may be owned, what kind of ownership may be taken, how it is measured, what is the duration of that ownership and how much is owned.

http://www.californiahistory.com

This section answers such questions on titles and estates, with pretty basic information. You will use this knowledge every time you are involved in the transfer of real property. You will also need to know this material well for the state licensing exam. So let's start with who owned the land in the first place.

Background of Land Title in California

Ownership of land in California began with Spanish explorers who claimed it for the king of Spain in the early 16th Century. Since the king technically owned everything, all land was granted to private parties by the military representatives of Spanish rule. Ownership and transfer of land and property rights were determined by local authorities operating under a strict set of civil laws that were given to them by the Spanish king.

This continued until 1822, when Mexico began colonizing California and took over governing the territory. Mexican governors totally controlled who received grants of land during this time, and recorded the grants, known as **Expedientes**, in the government archives. Even so, the land descriptions were vague and evidence of title may or may not have been in the actual possession of the owner. This led to many disputes over ownership in later years, after California became a state.

In 1848, the **Treaty of Guadalupe Hidalgo** ended the war with Mexico, and California became a possession of the United States. Land claims that had been granted by Mexico were honored, and confirmed with **Patents** to the land, by the U.S. government, to those with proven ownership. Even though Spain or Mexico granted ownership, according to the Roman Civil Law they followed, the laws changed after California became a state in 1850. England's Common Law principles now governed the title of real property.

California Adopts A Recording System

http://www.dre.ca.gov
Reference Book, Ch. 5

In a move that was strictly an American device for safeguarding the ownership of land, the California legislature adopted a system of recording evidence of title or interest. This system meant records could be collected in a convenient and safe public place, so that those purchasing land would be more fully informed about the ownership and condition of the title. Even then, California was a leader in consumer friendly legislation. Citizens were protected against secret **Conveyances** and liens, and title to real property was freely transferable.

Recording Specifics

The Recording Act of California provides that, after **Acknowledgment** or being signed before a notary or certain public officials, any **Instrument** or **Judgment** affecting the title to—or possession of—real property may be recorded. Recording permits, rather than requires, the filing of documents that affect title to real property.

The process consists of copying the instrument to be recorded in the proper index, and filing it in alphabetical order, under the names of the parties, without delay. The document must be recorded by the county recorder in the county within which the property is located to be valid there.

When the recorder receives a document to be filed, he or she notes the time and date of filing and at whose request it was filed. After the contents of the document are copied into the record, the original document is marked "filed for record," stamped with the proper time and date of recording, and returned to the person who requested the recording.

The Effect: Public Notice

This process gives **Constructive Notice** of the content of any instrument recorded to anyone who cares to look into the records. Recording is considered to be public notice of the information filed there. Possession is also considered Constructive Notice. A buyer should always check to be sure there is no one living on the property who might have a prior claim to ownership. It is the buyer's duty to conduct proper inquiry before purchasing any property. Failure to do so does not relieve the buyer of that responsibility.

Ann bought a property through her broker, sight unseen. The escrow closed and the deed was recorded. When Ann tried to move into her new home, however, she found George living there. He told her he had bought the property a year ago and had not bothered to record the deed, but had moved in and considered it his home. When she consulted her attorney, Ann found that indeed George—because he was in possession of the property—had given notice to anyone who might inquire. One remedy for the situation would be legal action against the grantor who sold the property to both George and Ann. However, at the moment, George does not have legal title because of his possession of the property.

Priorities in Recording

As we have seen, recording laws are meant to protect citizens against fraud and to give others notification of property ownership. Other information that might influence ownership can be recorded also, such as liens and other encumbrances. To obtain priority through recording, a buyer must be a good faith purchaser, for a valuable consideration, and record the deed first.

Priority means the order in which deeds are recorded. Whether or not it is a grant deed, trust deed or some other evidence of a lien or encumbrance, the priority is determined by the date stamped in the upper right-hand corner of the document by the county recorder.

If there are several grant deeds recorded against the property, the one recorded first is valid. In a case where there are several trust deeds recorded against a property, no mention will be made about which one is the first trust deed, which is the second, and so forth.

A person inquiring about the priority of the deeds should look at the time and date the deed was recorded for that information. You will see, as we proceed in our study, the importance of the date and time of recording.

Here are examples of trust deeds. Study them to determine their order of priority.

Date of Recording Determines Priority

There are certain instruments that are not affected by the priority of recording rule, however. Certain liens, such as tax liens, and mechanic's liens take priority even though they are recorded after a deed. We will discuss liens and encumbrances later in detail, but it is helpful to note here the impact of the recording laws on this subject.

Ownership of Real Property

http://www.dre.ca.gov
Reference Book, Ch. 5

All property has an owner, either the government or a private institution or an individual. **Title** is the evidence that the owner of land is in lawful possession. It is the proof of ownership. Separate ownership and concurrent ownership are the two ways real estate may be owned.

Separate Ownership

Property owned by one person or entity is known as sole and separate, or ownership in **Severalty**. A corporation is known to hold title in severalty, because it is a sole entity.

Concurrent Ownership

When property is owned by two or more persons or entities at the same time, it is known as concurrent ownership, or co-ownership. Concurrent ownership comes in several forms such as *joint tenancy, tenancy in common, community property* and *tenancy in partnership.*

Four types of Concurrent Ownership

- Joint tenancy
- Tenancy in common
- Community property
- Tenancy in partnership

Joint Tenancy

When two or more parties own real property as co-owners, with the right of survivorship, it is called joint tenancy. The right of survivorship means that if one of the joint tenants dies, the surviving joint tenant automatically becomes sole owner of the property. The deceased's share does not go to his or her estate or heirs, but becomes the property of the co-tenant without becoming involved in probate. Also, the surviving joint tenant is not liable to creditors of the deceased who hold liens on the joint tenancy property.

In order to have a joint tenancy, there are four unities that must be in existence: *time, title, interest and possession.*

Remember

The Four Unities of Joint Tenancy

Time
All parties must become joint tenants at the same time.

Title
All parties must take title on the same deed.

Interest
All parties must have an equal **Undivided Interest** in the property.

Possession
All parties have equal right of possession.

memory	**T**	ime
aid	**T**	itle
"T-Tip"	**I**	nterest
	P	ossession

All four items must occur to have a joint tenancy. If any one of the unities is broken, the joint tenancy is dissolved.

Co-owners may sell their interest, give it away or borrow money against it, without consent of the other joint tenants. Because of the right of survivorship, a joint tenant may not will his or her share, unless there are no surviving joint tenants.

> *Audrey, Bob, Carol and David are joint tenants. David dies and his interest automatically goes to Audrey, Bob and Carol as joint tenants with equal one-third interests.*

> *Kelly and Roger own a house as joint tenants. Roger dies and Kelly now owns the house as her sole and separate property without probate. Roger's heirs are not entitled to his share because of the right of survivorship.*

Tenancy in Common

When two or more persons, whose interests are not necessarily equal, are owners of undivided interests in a single estate, a tenancy in common exists. Whenever some other form of ownership or vesting is not mentioned specifically, and there are co-owners, title is assumed to be a tenancy in common.

The only requirement of unity for tenants in common is the equal right of possession or undivided interest—as it is called. That means each owner has a certain equitable interest in the property (such as one-half interest, or one-fourth interest), but has the right to use the whole property. None of the owners may exclude any co-owner from the property, nor claim any portion of the property for exclusive use.

http://www.investorwords.com/t2.htm

Remember

The Four Characteristics of Tenants in Common

- Tenants in common may take title at different times.
- Tenants in common may take title on separate deeds.
- Tenants in common may have unequal interests.
- Tenants in common have an undivided interest or equal right of possession.

Any tenant in common may sell, encumber or will his or her interest, with heirs simply becoming a tenant in common among the others. A tenant in common must pay a proportionate share of any expenses incurred on the property, including money spent for repairs, taxes, loan payments and insurance.

When tenants in common do not agree on matters pertaining to the property, any of the co-owners may file a **Partition Action** which asks the court to decide the fate of the investment.

Stacey, Ken, Catherine and Dan are joint tenants. Dan sells his interest to Eva. The joint tenancy has been broken regarding the interest Dan had in the property. The new vesting, after the sale of Dan's interest, is Stacey, Ken and Catherine as joint tenants with equal interests, and the right of survivorship, with Eva as a tenant in common.

Stacey, Ken, Catherine and Eva, in the above property, wish to restore a joint tenancy with each of the four having the right of survivorship. Eva holds a tenancy in common, so she will have to be added to the joint tenancy. Since all joint tenants must take title at the same time, on the same document, Stacey, Ken, Catherine and Eva must sign a new deed that lists Stacey, Ken and Catherine as joint tenants and Eva as a tenant in common. Then the property can be deeded to all four parties as joint tenants. All requirements for a joint tenancy—time, title, interest and possession—will then be fulfilled.

Community Property

All property acquired by a husband and wife during a valid marriage—except for certain separate property—is called community property.

> ## Separate Property Includes:
> - All property owned before marriage
> - All property acquired by either of the parties during marriage by gift or inheritance
> - All income derived from separate property

If spouses want to maintain the status of their separate property, they must be very careful not to commingle it with their community property. Separate property (such as an apartment building with a negative cash flow) may not be supported with community property funds, nor can the income of either spouse be used in any way to maintain separate property. Any income, including wages from either spouse, is considered community property.

Community property cannot be sold or encumbered by only one of the partners. Either spouse may *buy* real or personal property without the consent of the other; both are bound by the contract made by either one, unless the new property is bought specifically as separate property, with funds from a separate property account.

However, a married couple in California has three choices when it comes to how they may take title. The first is *joint tenancy*, which includes the right of survivorship if one of the spouses dies but also may include a tax liability for the surviving spouse. The second is *community property*, which does include the right of survivorship, but also includes probate after a spouse dies and all the costs involved in that process. The third type of vesting is *community property with the right of survivorship*, which includes the best of the first two types of vesting. There is no particular tax liability because of the death of a spouse and there is also no probate with its seemingly endless costs.

When title is taken simply as *community property*, either party may will one-half of the community property. When vesting is *community property*, if there is no will, the surviving spouse inherits all community property. This is important to know, particularly with multiple marriages, for estate planning. Property may be owned with the intention that it go to one's children, only to learn after the parent's death that children of the first marriage are no longer natural heirs. If there is a subsequent husband or wife and no will has been made, the new spouse will become the natural heir to any property owned or community property.

Regarding separate property, if there is no will, the surviving spouse gets one-half and one child gets one-half. If there is more than one child, the surviving spouse gets one-third and the children get two-thirds.

Do All States Recognize Community Property Law?

Nine states - Arizona, California, Idaho, Louisiana, Nevada, New Mexico, Texas, Washington, and Wisconsin - use the community property system to determine the interest of a husband and wife in property acquired during marriage. If you now live or previously lived in one of these states, you should be aware that some special rules apply to community property. Any property you may have acquired while living in one of these nine states is probably community property even today.

Tenancy in Partnership

Ownership by two or more persons who form a partnership for business purposes is known as tenancy in partnership. Each partner has an equal right of possession for partnership.

Remember

Concurrent Ownership

	Joint Tenancy	Tenancy in Common	Community Property	Tenancy in Partnership
Parties	Any number	Any number	Spouses only	Any number
Interest	Must be equal	Equal or unequal	Must be equal	Determined by Agreement
Possession	Equal right	Equal right	Equal right	Equal right
Death	Survivorship	No survivorship	Survivorship (If no will)	No survivorship

Limitations on Real Property: Encumbrances

http://www.knowx.com/free/liens.htm

http://www.dre.ca.gov Reference Book, Ch. 5

An encumbrance is an interest in real property that is held by someone who is not the owner. Anything that affects the title or the use of the property is an encumbrance. A property is encumbered when it is burdened with legal obligations against the title.

Encumbrances fall into two categories: those that affect the title, known as money encumbrances, and those that affect the use of the property, known as non-money encumbrances. The encumbrances that create a legal obligation to pay are known as liens. A lien uses real property as security for the payment of a debt.

Common types of liens are trust deeds and mortgages; mechanic's liens; tax liens; and special assessments, attachments and judgments. Those types of encumbrances that affect the physical use of the property are easements, building restrictions, and zoning requirements and encroachments.

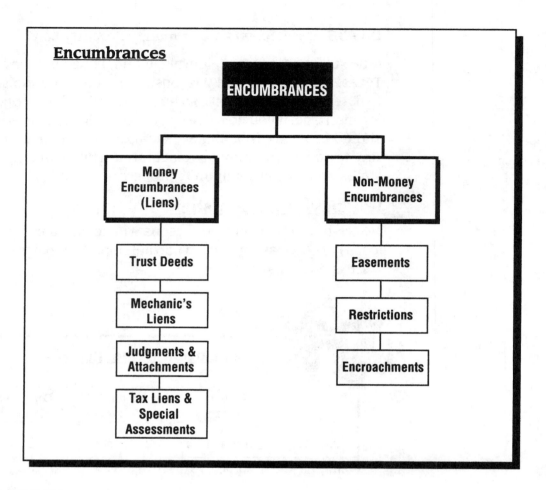

Money Encumbrances (Liens)

http://investorwords.com/
t2.htm

A lien is an obligation to pay a money encumbrance that may be voluntary or involuntary. An owner may choose to borrow money, using the property as security for the loan, creating a voluntary lien.

On the other hand, if the owner doesn't pay taxes or the debt owed, a lien may be placed against his or her property without permission.

A lien may be specific or general. A specific lien is one that is placed against a certain property, while a general lien affects all property of the owner.

Trust Deeds and Mortgages are both instruments used in real estate financing to create voluntary, specific liens against real property. They will be discussed in detail later.

Mechanic's Liens may be placed against a property by anyone who supplies labor or materials used for improvements on the property and does not get paid. A contractor, a subcontractor, a laborer on a job, or any person who furnishes materials such as lumber, plumbing or roofing is eligible to file a mechanic's lien.

A Mechanic's Lien must be verified and recorded. The law is very time specific about the recording, however. The statutory procedure must be followed exactly if the mechanic's lien is to be valid. Here are the four steps to be taken:

1. *Preliminary Notice:* This is a written notice that must be given to the owner within 20 days of first furnishing labor or materials for a job by anyone eligible to file a mechanic's lien. This document gives owners notice that their property may be liened if they do not pay for work completed.

2. *Notice of Completion:* If the owner files a notice of completion within 10 days after finishing the project, the original contractors have 60 days after the notice is filed, and all others have 30 days after the notice is filed, to record a mechanic's lien.

3. *No Notice of Completion:* If the owner does not file a notice of completion, all claimants have 90 days from the day work was finished to record a mechanic's lien.

4. Foreclosure Action: After a mechanic's lien is recorded, the claimant has 90 days to bring foreclosure action to enforce the lien. If he or she does not bring action, the lien will be terminated and the claimant loses the right to foreclose.

If an owner discovers unauthorized work on the property, he must file a *Notice of Non-Responsibility.* This is a notice that must be recorded and posted on the property to be valid, stating the owner is not responsible for work being done. This notice releases the owner from liability for work done without permission. The owner must file this notice within 10 days after discovering the unauthorized work. The notice normally is posted with a commercial lease at the beginning of a job, if a tenant is ordering the job.

Mechanic's Lien Time Line:

Here are the major events to be followed, in a timely manner, whenever improvement of real property is done.

- **Work Commences**
- **Preliminary 20-Day Notice**
- **Work Completed**
- **Notice of Completion Recorded**
- **Lien Recorded**
- **Foreclosure Action and Lis Pendens Recorded**
- **Service of Process**
- **Court Decision**
    - Judgment
    - Release of Lien
    - Dismissed
    - Foreclosure

Determining the starting time for a mechanic's lien is *very* important. A mechanic's lien has priority over any other liens filed *after* the commencement of labor or delivery of materials. That means if there is a foreclosure action, the mechanic's lien would be paid before any other liens that were recorded after work started on the job.

That includes trust deeds or mortgages recorded prior to the filing of the mechanic's lien, but after the start of the work. Lenders will make a physical inspection of the property to determine that no materials have been delivered and no work has been done before recording a construction loan to assure the priority of their trust deed or mortgage.

In the following example, note the mechanic's lien has the priority.

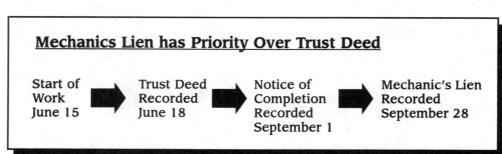

Mechanics Lien has Priority Over Trust Deed

Start of Work June 15 → Trust Deed Recorded June 18 → Notice of Completion Recorded September 1 → Mechanic's Lien Recorded September 28

Tax Liens and Special Assessments: If any government taxes, such as income or property taxes are no paid, they become a lien against the property. Special assessments are levied against property owners to pay for local improvements, such as underground utilities, street repair, or water projects. Payment for the projects is secured by a special assessment which becomes a lien against real property. Property taxes and special assessments are specific liens, whereas other government taxes are general liens.

Attachments and Judgments: An attachment is the process by which the court holds the property of a defendant pending outcome of a lawsuit. An attachment lien is valid for three years and may be extended in certain cases.

A judgment is the final determination of the rights of parties in a lawsuit by the court. A judgment does not automatically create a lien. A summary of the court decision, known as an abstract of judgment, must be filed with the county recorder. When the abstract is filed, the judgment becomes a general lien on all property owned or acquired by the judgment debtor for 10 years, in the county in which the abstract is filed.

Liz Pendens: A **Liz Pendens** is a recorded notice that indicates pending litigation affecting the title on a property. It clouds the title, preventing the sale or transfer of the property until removed.

Non-Money Encumbrances

http://www.dre.ca.gov
Reference Book, Ch. 5

A non-money encumbrance is one that affects the use of property such as an easement, a building restriction or an encroachment.

Easements: An **Easement** is the right to use another's land for a specified purpose, sometimes known as a right-of-way. An interest in an easement is non-possessory. That means the holder of an easement can use it only for the purpose intended and may not exclude anyone else from using it. The right to enter onto a property using an easement is called Ingress. Exit from a property using an easement is called Egress.

The party giving the easement is known as the servient tenement. The servient tenement is the one encumbered by the easement. The party receiving the benefit of the easement is known as the dominant tenement. An easement is appurtenant to the dominant tenement.

As you recall, the definition of real property included anything appurtenant to the land. Anything used for the benefit of the land is appurtenant to it. An easement appurtenant automatically goes with the sale of the dominant tenement.

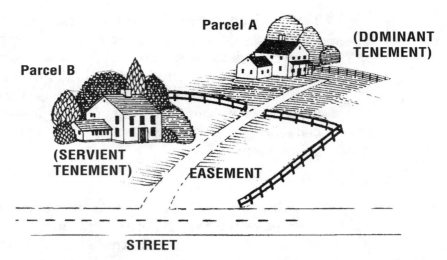

STREET

It is possible to have an easement that is not appurtenant to any particular land. Thus, Jacob—who owns no land—may have an easement over Salvadore's land for the purpose of getting to the stream where he regularly fishes. Or a commercial camping enterprise may use an easement over private property to take clients to remote sites, which might be inaccessible otherwise.

Public utilities also have easements that are not appurtenant to any one parcel. These easements are known as **Easements in Gross**. Make sure you understand the difference between an easement in gross and a **License**. An easement may not be terminated arbitrarily, as you will see in the following section. However, a license to use may be revoked at any time.

Easements are create in various ways - commonly by express grant or reservation in a grant deed or by a written agreement between owners of adjoining land. An easement always should be recorded to assure its continued existence. It is recorded by the party benefiting from the easement as the dominant tenement.

There are five ways to create an easement:

1. *Express Grant:* The servient tenement, or the giver of the easement, grants the easement by deed or express agreement.

2. *Express Reservation:* The seller of a parcel who owns adjoining land reserves an easement or right-of-way over the former property. It is created at the time of the sale with a deed or express agreement.

3. *Implied Grant or Reservation:* The existence of an easement is obvious and necessary at the time a property is conveyed, even though no mention is made of it in the deed.

4. Necessity: An easement created when a parcel is completely land locked and has no access. It is automatically terminated when another way to enter and leave the property becomes available.

5. *Prescription:* An easement by prescription may be created by continuous and uninterrupted use, by a single party, for a period of five years.

The use must be against the owner's wishes and be open and notorious. The party wishing to obtain the prescriptive easement must have some reasonable claim to the use of the property.

Easements may be terminated or extinguished in the following seven ways:

1. *Express Release:* The only one who can release an easement is the dominant tenement

2. *Legal Proceedings:* Quiet title action to terminate the easement brought by the servient tenement against the dominant tenement

3. *Merger:* This joins the dominant tenement and the servient tenement

4. *Non-Use:* When applied to a prescriptive easement for a period of five years, this terminates the easement

5. *Abandonment:* Obvious and intentional surrender of the easement

6. *Destruction of the Servient Tenement:* If the government takes the servient tenement for its use, as in eminent domain, the easement is terminated

7. *Adverse Possessions:* The owner of the servient tenement may, by his or her own use, prevent the dominant tenement from using the easement for a period of five years, thus terminating the easement

Restrictions: Another type of encumbrance is a restriction. A restriction is a limitation placed on the use of property and may be placed by a private owner, a developer or the government. It is usually placed on property to assure that land use is consistent and uniform within a certain area.

Restrictions are created in the deed at the time of sale or in the general plan of a subdivision by the developer. For example, a developer may use a height restriction to ensure views from each parcel in a subdivision.

When there is a conflict between local minimum building requirements and subdivision regulations, the developer must comply with whichever is the most restrictive.

Private restrictions are placed by a present or past owner and affect only a specific property or development, while zoning is an example of government restrictions that benefit the general public.

Restrictions are commonly known as C.C.& R.'s or Covenants, Conditions and Restrictions. A covenant is a promise to do or not do certain things. The penalty for a breach of a covenant is usually money damages. An example of a covenant might be that the tenant agrees to make some repairs, or that a property may be used only for a specific purpose.

A condition is much the same as a covenant, a promise to do or not do something (usually a limitation on the use of the property), except the penalty for breaking a condition is return of the property to the grantor.

A **Condition Subsequent** is a restriction, placed in a deed at the time of conveyance, upon future use of the property. Upon breach of the condition subsequent, the grantor may take back the property. A **Condition Precedent** requires that a certain event, or condition, occur before title can pass to the new owner.

Encroachments: The placement of permanent improvements on adjacent property owned by another is known as an **Encroachment**. Fences, walls or buildings can encroach on adjoining land and limit its use. An owner has three years to remove an unauthorized encroachment.

Common Encroachments

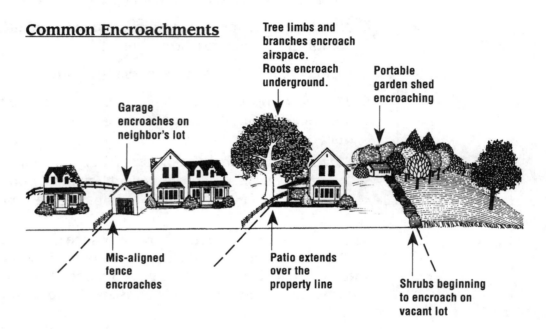

Tree limbs and branches encroach airspace.
Roots encroach underground.

Portable garden shed encroaching

Garage encroaches on neighbor's lot

Mis-aligned fence encroaches

Patio extends over the property line

Shrubs beginning to encroach on vacant lot

Declared Homestead

http://www.dre.ca.gov
Reference Book, Ch. 5

A homestead is not truly an encumbrance, but it does limit the amount of liability for certain debts against which a home can be used to satisfy a judgment. A **Declaration of Homestead** is the recorded document that protects a homeowner from foreclosure by certain judgment creditors.

The first $75,000 of a home's value may not be used to satisfy a judgment against the head of a household. A mentally or physically disabled person or someone over the age of 65 is entitled to protection up to $100,000. All others have a homestead exemption of $50,000. A homestead does not protect an owner against foreclosure on a trust deed, mechanic's lien or lien recorded prior to the filing of the homestead.

There are certain requirements that must be met before a homestead is valid. The claimant must be living on the property at the time of filing, must state his or her status as head of household or other, must describe the property and give an estimate of value.

Only one homestead can be valid at any one time. An owner must file an Abandonment of Homestead in order to obtain a homestead on a new property. Sale of the property automatically causes the homestead to terminate. However, if the owner moves from the homesteaded property and does not wish to file a new one, the original homestead remains valid. Destruction of the property does not terminate the homestead.

Homestead Declaration

RECORDING REQUESTED BY

AND WHEN RECORDED MAIL TO

NAME
STREET
ADDRESS
CITY
STATE
ZIP

(SPACE ABOVE THIS LINE FOR RECORDER'S USE)

HOMESTEAD DECLARATION

I, _____
(Full Name of Declarant)

do hereby certify and declare as follows:

(1) I hereby claim as a declared homestead the premises located in the City of _____,
County of _____, State of _____ commonly known as
_____
(Street Address)

and more particularly described as follows: [Give complete legal description]

(2) I am the declared homestead owner of the above declared homestead.

(3) I own the following interest in the above declared homestead:

(4) The above declared homestead is [strike inapplicable clause] my principal dwelling, the principal dwelling of my spouse, and
[strike inapplicable clause] I am / my spouse is currently residing on that declared homestead.

(5) The facts stated in this Declaration are true as of my personal knowledge.

Dated: _____, 19___ _____
(Signature of Declarant)

STATE OF _____
} ss.
COUNTY OF _____

On _____ before me, _____
(Name, title of officer–i.e., "Jane Doe, Notary Public")

personally appeared _____

personally known to me (or proved to me on the basis of satisfactory evidence) to be the person(s) whose name(s) is/are subscribed to the within instrument and acknowledged to me that he/she/they executed the same in his/her/their authorized capacity(ies), and that by his/her/their signature(s) on the instrument the person(s), or the entity upon behalf of which the person(s) acted, executed the instrument.

WITNESS my hand and official seal.

_____
Signature

(Seal)

This standard form is intended for the typical situations encountered in the field indicated. However, before you sign, read it, fill in all blanks, and make whatever changes are appropriate and necessary to your particular transaction. Consult a lawyer if you doubt the form's fitness for your purpose and use.

Assuring Marketability of Title

A **Marketable Title** does not means a perfect title. It means that the title is one a reasonable person would accept as clear and free from likely challenge. The documentary record of ownership, or the **Chain of Title** in the recorder's office in the county where the property is located, becomes very important in determining who actually owns what.

Before reliable histories of properties came into existence, **Abstractors** investigated the status of title to property. They searched available records and pertinent documents, and prepared a summary called an **Abstract of Title**. This listed all the conveyances and any other facts relating to the property for a prospective buyer or lender to inspect. This chain of title, along with an attorney's opinion, was the original basis for establishing marketable title.

In time, these records—kept in a **Title Plant**—were used to supply interested parties with a Certificate of Title. This stated that the property was found to be properly **Vested** in the present owner, subject to noted encumbrances. The next step was the **Guarantee of Title** under which the title insurance company provided written assurances about the title to real property, insuring against loss.

Title Insurance

http://www.bob-taylor.com/
title.htm

http://www.caltitle.com/
titleins.htm

http://www.dre.ca.gov
Reference Book, Ch. 5

Finally, title insurance companies, responding to the public need, began issuing policies of **Title Insurance**. The main benefit: Title insurance extends protection against matters of record and many non-recorded types of risks, depending on the type of policy purchased.

A **Standard Policy** of title insurance, in addition to matters of record, protects against:

- Off-record hazards such as forgery, impersonation, or failure of a party to be legally competent to make a contract

- The possibility that a deed of record was not in fact delivered with intent to convey title

- The loss which might arise from the lien of federal estate taxes, which is effective without notice upon death

- The expense incurred in defending the title

A standard policy does *not* protect against:

- Defects in the title known to the holder to exist at the date of the policy, but not previously disclosed to the title insurance company

- Easements and liens which are not shown by the public records

- Rights or claims of persons in physical possession of the land, but whose claims are not shown by the public records

- Rights or claims not shown by public records, yet which could be discovered by physical inspection of the land

- Mining claims

- Reservations in patents or water rights

- Zoning ordinances

Most of these risks are covered by a policy that may be purchased at added cost called an **Extended Policy**. The American Land Title Association offers an owner's extended coverage policy known as **A.L.T.A. Owner's Policy** that includes the same coverage as a standard policy, with the following additions:

- Protection against claims of parties in physical possession of the property, but no recorded interest

- Reservations in patents

- Unmarketability of title

Lenders may also purchase an A.L.T.A. policy, with the same extended coverage, to protect against loss of their investment in the property because of a defective title.

Policies of title insurance are now commonly used throughout California, usually in the standardized forms prepared by the **California Land Title Association**, which is the trade organization of the title companies in the state.

Every title insurer must adopt and make available to the public a schedule of fees and charges for title policies. In addition, each title insurance company must have on deposit with the Insurance Commissioner a guarantee fund for the protection of title insurance policy holders.

Post Test

The following self test repeats the one you took at the beginning of this chapter. Now take the exam again—since you have read all the material— and check your knowledge of titles and estates.

1. Which of the following is benefited by an easement appurtenant?
   a. dominant tenement
   b. servient tenement
   c. the easement
   d. the owner of the servient tenement

2. Vesting refers to:
   a. co-ownership
   b. how property is owned
   c. something to wear
   d. syndication

3. Debby and Jeff, brother and sister, want to buy a property together. Which of the following vestings would not be considered?
   a. joint tenants
   b. tenants in common
   c. community property
   d. tenancy in partnership

4. How does a corporation take title to real property?
   a. joint tenancy
   b. community property
   c. tenancy in common
   d. severalty

5. If the interest each person has in a tenancy in common is not stated in the deed:
   a. it is presumed to be a joint tenancy
   b. it is understood that each owner has an equal interest
   c. it is voidable
   d. it is invalid

6. All of the following are liens against real property except:
   a. a judgment
   b. a trust deed
   c. property taxes
   d. encroachments

7. Agreements affecting the use of real property are known as:
   a. Covenants, Conditions and Restrictions
   b. trust deeds
   c. lis pendens
   d. liens

8. Deed restrictions are imposed on a property by:
   a. the legislature
   b. the developer
   c. Board of Equalization
   d. city council

9. Which of the following is a legal, non-exclusive use of someone else's property?
   a. adverse possession
   b. trespassing
   c. an easement
   d. condemnation

10. A claimant has how many days to bring foreclosure action after a mechanic's lien is recorded?
    a. 40
    b. 50
    c. 90
    d. 120

Vocabulary

Read the definition, find the matching term and write the corresponding term number on the line provided.

Terms

1. A.L.T.A. Owner's Policy
2. Abstract of Title
3. Abstractors
4. Acknowledgment
5. Actual Notice
6. California Land Title Association
7. Chain of Title
8. Condition Precedent
9. Condition Subsequent
10. Constructive Notice
11. Conveyance
12. Declaration of Homestead
13. Easement
14. Easement in Gross
15. Encroachment
16. Expedientes
17. Extended Policy
18. Guarantee of Title
19. Instrument
20. Judgment
21. License
22. Lis Pendens
23. Marketable Title
24. Partition Action
25. Patents
26. Severalty
27. Standard Policy
28. Title
29. Title Insurance
30. Title Plant
31. Treaty of Guadalupe Hidalgo
32. Undivided Interests
33. Vested

Definitions

1. ___ Land grants recorded by the Mexican government in California

2. ___ Ended the war with Mexico in 1848, and California became a possession of the United States

3. ___ Deeds used by the U.S. government when confirming or transferring ownership to private parties

4. ___ The transfer of title to land from one person to another by use of a written instrument

5. ___ A formal declaration to a public official (notary) by a person who has signed an instrument which states that the signing was voluntary

6. ___ A written legal document setting forth the rights and liabilities of the parties

7. ___ The final legal decision of a judge in a court of law regarding the legal rights of parties to disputes

8. ___ Recordation of deed or possession of property

9. ___ Knowledge gained based on an actual observance, as opposed to Constructive Notice

10. ___ Good or clear saleable title reasonably free from risk of litigation over possible defects

11. ___ The recorded history of matters such as conveyances, liens and encumbrances affecting title to a parcel of real estate

12. ___ A person who, historically, searches out anything affecting the title to real property and summarizes the information in the findings

13. ___ A full summary of all consecutive grants, conveyances, wills, records and judicial proceedings affecting title to a specific parcel of real estate

14. ___ The storage facility of a title insurance company in which it has accumulated complete title records of properties in its area

15. ___ Owned by

16. ___ An assurance of clear title

17. ___ An insurance policy that protects the insured against loss or damage due to defects in the property's title

18. ___ A policy of title insurance covering only matters of record

19. ___ An owner's extended title insurance policy

20. ___ An extended title insurance policy

21. ___ Trade organization of the title companies of the state

22. ___ Requires that a certain event, or condition, occur before title can pass to a new owner

23. ___ A restriction, placed in a deed at the time of conveyance, upon future use of the property

24. ___ The recorded document that protects a homeowner from foreclosure by certain judgment creditors

25. ___ The right to use another's land for a specified purpose, sometimes known as a right-of-way

26. ___ The placement of permanent improvements on adjacent property owned by another

27. ___ An easement that is not appurtenant to any one parcel; for example, public utilities

28. ___ A recorded notice that indicates pending litigation affecting title on a property, preventing a conveyance or any other transfer of ownership until the lawsuit is settled and the lis pendens removed

29. ___ Permission to use a property which may be revoked at any time

30. ___ A court action to divide a property held by co-owners

31. ___ Ownership of real property by one person or entity

32. ___ Evidence of ownership of land

33. ___ That interest a co-owner has in property, which carries with it the right to possession and use of the whole property, along with the co-owners

Answers

Pre-Test/Post Test

1. a
2. b
3. c
4. d
5. b
6. d
7. a
8. b
9. c
10. c

Vocabulary

1.	16		19.	1
2.	31		20.	17
3.	25		21.	6
4.	11		22.	8
5.	4		23.	9
6.	19		24.	12
7.	20		25.	13
8.	10		26.	15
9.	5		27.	14
10.	23		28.	22
11.	7		29	21
12.	3		30.	24
13.	2		31.	26
14.	30		32.	28
15.	33		33.	32
16.	18			
17.	29			
18.	27			

CHAPTER

4

CONTRACTS

Focus

- **Contracts in general**
- **Basic elements of a contract**
- **Statute of Frauds**
- **Performance of contracts**
- **Discharge of contracts**
- **Statute of Limitations**
- **Remedies for Breach of Contract**
- **Liquidated damages**
- **Real estate contracts**

Pre-Test

The following is a self test to determine how much you know about contracts before reading this chapter. Take it without studying, then read the material presented in the text. At the end of the chapter you will find a repeat of this exam. Test your knowledge by answering the questions again, then check your improvement. (The answers are found at the end of this chapter.) Good luck!

1. Which of the following is an example of a unilateral contract?
   a. listing
   b. option
   c. offer to purchase
   d. rental agreement

2. Escrow instructions were signed by a buyer and seller, stating the selling price for a property, along with several other agreements. As part of the contract, the buyer could cancel the sale if the house did not sell within 45 days. The contract between the buyer and seller is:
   a. voidable
   b. invalid
   c. executory
   d. void

3. Adam, age 17, inherited a farm from his uncle. He sold it immediately, but later changed his mind and decided to cancel the sale. On what grounds could he do that?
   a. as a minor, the contract is void
   b. as a minor, the contract is voidable
   c. as a minor, the contract is unenforceable
   d. he cannot cancel the sale

4. A contract is only valid if:
   a. it is executory
   b. it is unilateral
   c. it is for a legal purpose
   d. it is bilateral

5. A written contract takes precedence over oral agreements. This principle is expressed by:
   a. the parol evidence rule
   b. the Statute of Limitations
   c. the Statute of Frauds
   d. the rule of previous evidence

6. An agreement to do or not to do a certain thing is called:
   a. negotiation
   b. a contract
   c. mutual consent
   d. forbearance

7. When a promise is given by one party with the expectation of performance by the other party, it is known as:
   a. a bilateral contract
   b. a unilateral contract
   c. implied contract
   d. express contract

8. Which of the following is no contract at all?
   a. void contract
   b. voidable contract
   c. unenforceable contract
   d. contract under duress

9. A contract that has been approved is said to be:
   a. rescinded
   b. revoked
   c. ratified
   d. executory

10. Another name for mutual consent is:
    a. implied agreement
    b. executory agreement
    c. unilateral agreement
    d. meeting of the minds

Terms

The following terms are the keys to your success in learning about real estate. Refer to them as you study this chapter for greater understanding of subjects presented here.

Acceptance

An unqualified agreement to the terms of an offer

Action

A lawsuit brought to court

Assignee

The person to whom a claim, benefit or right in property is made

Assignment

The transfer of a claim, benefit or right in property from one person to another

Assignor

The person transferring a claim, benefit or right in property to another

Attorney-in-Fact

A person holding the power of attorney

Bilateral Contract

A contract in which each party to the contract promises to perform some act or duty in exchange for the promise of the other party

Breach of Contract

A failure to perform on part or all of the terms and conditions of a contract

Consideration

Something of value—such as money, a promise, property or personal services

Contract

An agreement to do or not to do a certain thing

Contractual Intent

Intention to be bound by an agreement, thus preventing jokes and jests from becoming valid contracts

Counteroffer

The rejection of an original offer that becomes a new offer

Definite and Certain

Precise acts to be performed are to be clearly stated

Deposit Receipt

Also known as a sales contract; the primary document used to present an offer on real property

Duress

The use of force to get agreement in accepting a contract

Emancipated Minor

Someone who is legally set free from parental control/ supervision

Execute

To perform or complete; to sign

Executed Contract

A contract in which the obligations have been performed on both sides of the contract and nothing is left to be completed

Executory Contract

A contract in which obligation to perform exists on one or both sides of the contract

Express Contract

The parties declare the terms and put their intentions in words, either oral or written

Forbearance

Refraining from action by a creditor against the debt owed by a borrower after the debt has become due

Fraud

An act meant to deceive in order to get someone to part with something of value

Good Consideration

Gifts such as real property based solely on love and affection

Implied Contract

Agreement is shown by acts and conduct rather than words

Liquidated Damages

Sets in advance a specified amount of money as a penalty in the event of a breach of contract

Listing

A contract by which a principal employs an agent to do certain things for the principal

Menace

Using threat of violence to get agreement in accepting a contract

Minor

Someone under 18 years of age

Misrepresentation

An innocent or negligent misstatement of a material fact causing someone loss or harm

Mistake

An error or misunderstanding

Mutual Consent

Agreement to the provisions of a contract by the parties involved; a mutual willingness to enter into a contract

Novation

The substitution by agreement of a new obligation for an existing one

Offer

A presentation or proposal for acceptance to form a contract

Offeree

The party receiving an offer

Offeror

The party making an offer

Option

A right—given for consideration—to a party (optionee) by a property owner (optionor)

Parol Evidence

Oral or written negotiations made prior to a dispute about an executed contract

Power of Attorney

A written instrument giving a person legal authority to act on behalf of another person

Ratified

Approved

Rescission

Legal action taken to repeal a contract either by mutual consent of the parties or by one party when the other party has breached a contract

Revocation

The cancelling of an offer to contract by the person making the original offer

Specific Performance

An action brought in a court to compel a party to carry out the terms of a contract

Statute of Frauds

A state law which requires that certain contracts must be in writing and contain certain essential elements in order to be enforceable

Statute of Limitations

The period of time limited by statute within which certain court actions may be brought by one party against another

Tender

An offer by one of the parties to a contract to carry out his or her part of the contract

Timely Manner

An act must be performed within certain time limits described in a contract

Undue Influence

Using unfair advantage to get agreement in accepting a contract

Unenforceable

A contract that was valid when made but either cannot be proved or will not be enforced by a court

Unilateral Contract

An agreement in which one party promises to pay consideration or to do something in return for the performance of an act by another party; the party making the promise is not legally obligated to act unless the other party performs (a promise for an act)

Unilateral Rescission

Legal action taken to repeal a contract by one party when the other party has breached a contract

Valid

Legally binding

Valuable Consideration

Each party to a contract must give up something to make the agreement binding

Void

An agreement which is totally absent of legal effect

Voidable

An agreement which is valid and enforceable on its face, but may be rejected by one or more of the parties

Introduction

So far, we have studied the nature of real property, how it is described and how it may be owned. This chapter explains what a contract is and how contracts are used to assure the understanding and approval of all parties to an agreement.

Every time you are involved in a real estate transaction, you will use some kind of contract that transfers or indicates an interest in the property. It is important that you understand the nature of legal agreements, so you are able to explain them to your clients and customers as part of your role as a real estate agent.

Contracts in General

http://www.lawguru.com

http://www.dre.ca.gov
Reference Book, Ch. 6

A **Contract** is an agreement, enforceable by law, to do or not to do a certain thing. It may be an **Express Contract**, where the parties declare the terms and put their intentions in words, either oral or written. A lease or rental agreement, for example, is an express contract. The landlord agrees to allow the tenant to live in the apartment and the renter agrees to pay rent in return. An **Implied Contract** is one where agreement is shown by act and conduct rather than words. This type of contract is found every day when we go into a restaurant and order food, go to a movie or have a daily newspaper delivered. By showing a desire to use a service, we imply that we will pay for it.

Contracts may be **Bilateral** or **Unilateral**. A bilateral contract is one in which the promise of one party is given in exchange for the promise of the other party. In other words, both parties must keep their agreement for the contract to be completed. An example might be a promise from a would-be aviatrix to pay $2,500 for flying lessons, and a return promise from the instructor to teach her to fly.

A unilateral contract is one where a promise is given by one party with the expectation of performance by the other party. The second party is not bound to act, but if he or she does, the first party is obligated to keep the promise. An example might be a radio station offering $1,000 to the 100th caller. Some lucky person makes the call and the station pays the money. An option is another example of a unilateral contract.

A contract may be **Executory** or **Executed**. In an executory contract, something remains to be done by one or both parties. An escrow that is not yet closed or a contract not signed by the parties are examples of executory contract. In an executed contract, all parties have performed completely. One of the meanings of **Execute** is to sign, or complete in some way. An executed contract may be a sales agreement that has been signed by all parties.

Also, contracts may be **Void**, **Voidable**, **Unenforceable** or **Valid**.

Types of Contracts

Void contract

No contract at all; no legal effect *(Example: due to lack of capacity, illegal subject matter)*

Voidable contract

One which is valid and enforceable on its face, but may be rejected by one or more of the parties *(Example: induced by fraud, menace, duress)*

Unenforceable contract

Valid, but for some reason cannot be proved by one or both of the parties *(Example: an oral agreement which should be in writing because of Statute of Frauds)*

Valid contract

Binding and enforceable; has all the basic elements required by law

Basic Elements of a Contract

http://www.legaltools.com

For a contract to be legally binding and enforceable, the following requirements must be met:

Remember

Elements of a Contract

- Legally competent parties

- Mutual consent

- Lawful objective

- Sufficient consideration

- Contract In Writing (when required by law)

Legally Competent Parties

Parties entering into a contract must have legal capacity to do so. Almost anyone is capable, with a few exceptions. A person must be at least 18 years of age, unless married, in the military or declared **Emancipated** by the Court.

A **Minor** is not capable of appointing an agent, or entering into an agency agreement with a broker to buy or sell. Brokers dealing with minors should proceed cautiously and should seek an attorney's advice. A contract with a minor is considered voidable by the minor.

When it has been determined judicially that a person is not of sound mind, no contract can be made with that incompetent person. Also, if it is obvious that a person is completely without understanding, even without declaration, there can be no contract. In the case of an incompetent, a court appointed guardian would have legal capacity to contract.

Both minors and incompetents may acquire title to real property by gift or inheritance. Any conveyance of acquired property, however, must be court approved.

A contract made by a person who is intoxicated or under the influence of legal or illegal drugs may be cancelled when the individual sobers up. It may be **Ratified**—or also approved, depending on the parties.

Any person may give another the authority to act on his or her behalf. The document that does this is called a **Power of Attorney**. The person holding the power of attorney is called an **Attorney-in-Fact**. When dealing with real property, a power of attorney must be recorded to be valid, and is good for as long as the principal is competent. A power of attorney can be cancelled by the principal at any time by recording a **Revocation**. A power of attorney is useful, for example, when a buyer or seller is out of town and has full trust in that agent to operate in his or her behalf.

Mutual Consent

In a valid contract, all parties must mutually agree. **Mutual Consent**, or mutual assent, is sometimes called a meeting of the minds. It is an offer by one party and acceptance by the other party.

Offer

One party must offer and another accept, without condition. An **Offer** shows the **Contractual Intent** of the **Offeror**, or the person making the offer, to enter into a contract. That offer must be communicated to the **Offeree**, or the person to whom the offer is being made. Unconditional acceptance of the offer is necessary for all parties to be legally bound. The offer must be **Definite and Certain** in its terms, and the agreement must be genuine or the contract may be voidable by one or both parties.

Acceptance

An **Acceptance** is an unqualified agreement to the terms of an offer. The offeree must agree to every item of the offer for the acceptance to be complete. If the original terms are changed in any way in the acceptance, the offer becomes a **Counteroffer**, and the first offer is terminated. The person making the original offer is no longer bound by that offer, and may accept the counteroffer or not. The counteroffer becomes a new offer, made by the original offeree.

Acceptance of an offer must be communicated to the offeror, in the manner specified, before a contract becomes binding between the parties. Silence is not considered to be acceptance.

Termination

An offeror is hopeful that his offer will be accepted in a **Timely Manner** and a contract will be formed. An offer is specific, however, and an offeror does not have to wait indefinitely for an answer. An offer may be terminated by the following acts.

<u>Termination of an Offer</u>

- Lapse of time: an offer is revoked if the offeree fails to accept it within a prescribed period

- Communication of notice of revocation: this can be done by the offeror anytime before the other party has communicated acceptance

- Failure of offeree to fulfill a condition of acceptance prescribed by the offeror

- A qualified acceptance, or counteroffer by the offeree

- Rejection by the offeree

- Death or insanity of the offeror or offeree

- Unlawful object of the proposed contract

Genuine Assent

A final requirement for mutual consent is that the offer and acceptance be genuine and freely made by all parties. Genuine assent does not exist if there is *Fraud, Misrepresentation, Mistake, Duress, Menace or Undue Influence* involved in reaching an agreement.

Fraud is an act meant to deceive in order to get someone to part with something of value. An outright lie, or making a promise with no intention of carrying it out, can be fraud. Lack of disclosure—causing someone to make or accept an offer—is also fraud. For example, failure to tell a prospective buyer who makes an offer to purchase on a sunny day that the roof leaks is fraud. It can make the contract voidable.

Innocent **Misrepresentation** occurs when the person providing the wrong information is not doing it to deceive, but for the purpose of reaching an agreement. Even though no dishonesty is involved, a contract may be rescinded or revoked by the party who feels misled.

Mistake, in contract law, means negotiations were clouded or there was a misunderstanding in the material facts. It does not include ignorance, inability or poor judgment. For example, if you accepted an offer to purchase your home based on what you thought was an all cash offer, and later found that you had agreed to carry a second trust deed, you would be expected to carry through with the agreement. Even though you made a "mistake" in reading the sales contract, you now have a binding agreement.

There are times when you could be credited with a misunderstanding, and ultimately get out of the contract. For instance, what if you were given directions to a friend's beach house, went there on your own and fell in love with it. You immediately made an offer, which was accepted, only to discover you had gone to the wrong house. Because you thought you were purchasing a different property than the one the seller was selling, this could be considered a "major misunderstanding of a material fact," and there would be no mutual agreement, voiding any contract that was signed.

Use of force, known as **Duress**, or **Menace**, which is the threat of violence, may not be used to get agreement. **Undue Influence** or using unfair advantage is also unacceptable. All can cause a contract to be voidable by the injured party.

Remember

No Genuine Assent If:

- Fraud

- Misrepresentation

- Mistake

- Duress

- Menace

- Undue Influence

Lawful Objective

Even though the parties are capable, and mutually agreeable, the object of the contract must be lawful. A contract requiring the performance of an illegal act would not be valid, nor would one where the consideration was stolen.

The contract also must be legal in its formation and operation. For example, a note bearing an interest rate in excess of that allowed by law would be void. Contracts contrary to good morals and general public policy are also unenforceable.

Sufficient Consideration

All contracts require consideration. There are several types of **Consideration** in a contract. Generally, it is something of value such as a promise of future payment, money, property or personal services. For example, there can be an exchange of a promise for a promise, money for a promise, money for property, or goods for services.

Forbearance, or forgiving a debt or obligation, also qualifies as consideration. As a group, the above qualify as **Valuable Consideration**. Gifts such as real property based solely on love and affection are considered to be **Good Consideration**. They meet the legal requirement that consideration be present in a contract.

In an option, the promise of the offeror is the consideration for the forbearance desired from the offeree. In other words, the person wanting the option promises to give something of value in return for being able to exercise the option to purchase at some specifically named time in the future.

In a bilateral contract, a promise of one party is consideration for the promise of another. For example, in the sale of real property, the buyer promises to pay a certain amount and the seller promises to transfer title.

It should be noted that the earnest money given at the time of an offer is *not* the consideration for the sale. It is simply an indication of the buyer's intent to perform the contract, and may be used for damages, even if the buyer backs out of the sale.

Contract In Writing

In California, the Statute of Frauds requires that certain contracts be **In Writing** to prevent fraud in the sale of land or an interest in land. Included in this are offers, acceptances, loan assumptions, land contracts, deeds, escrows and options to purchase. Trust deeds, promissory notes and leases for more than one year also must be in writing to be enforceable.

Statute of Frauds

Most contracts required by law to be in writing are found under the **Statute of Frauds**. The statute was first adopted in England in 1677 and became part of English common law. Later it was introduced to this country and is now part of California's law.

The statute's primary purpose is to prevent forgery, perjury and dishonest conduct on the part of scoundrels and crooks against citizens. Thus, it improves the existence and terms of certain important types of contracts.

The law provides that certain contracts are invalid unless they are in writing and signed by either the parties involved or their agents. Under California's Civil Code, the following contracts must be in writing:

- Any agreement where the terms are not to be performed within a year from making the contract

- A special promise to answer for the debt, default or non-performance of another, except in cases covered by the Civil Code

- An agreement made upon the consideration of marriage, other than a mutual promise to marry

- An agreement to lease real property for a period longer than one year, or to sell real property or an interest therein; also, any agreement authorizing an agent to perform the above acts

- An agreement employing an agent, broker or any other person to purchase, sell or lease real estate for one year; or find a buyer, seller, lessee or lessor for more than one year in return for compensation

- An agreement, which by its terms is not to be performed during the lifetime of the promisor, or an agreement that devises or bequeaths any property, or makes provisions for any reason by will

- An agreement by a purchaser of real estate to pay a debt secured by a trust deed or mortgage on the property purchased, unless assumption of that debt by the purchaser is specifically designated in the conveyance of such property

Personal property is also affected by the Statute of Frauds. The sale of personal property with a value of more than $500 must be accompanied by a bill of sale in writing.

Parol Evidence Rule

When two parties make oral promises to each other, and then write and sign a contract promising something different, the written contract will be considered the valid one.

The **Parol Evidence Rule** prohibits introducing outside evidence to vary or add to the terms of deeds, contracts or other writings once they have been executed. Under the parol evidence rule, when a contract is intended to be the parties' complete and final agreement, no further oral promises are allowed. Occasionally a contract is ambiguous or vague. Then the courts will allow use of prior agreements to clarify an existing disputed contract.

One of a real estate agent's major duties is to make sure all contract language conveys the parties' wishes and agreements. Oral agreements have caused much confusion and bad feelings over the years, particularly in real estate. Even a lease for less than one year should be in writing, though it is not required by the Statute of Frauds. It is easy to forget verbal agreements. A written contract is the most reasonable way to ensure mutual assent.

What about using and changing preprinted real estate forms? If the parties involved want to make handwritten changes and initial them, those changes control the document.

Performance of Contracts

A principal has several choices when considering the performance of a contract. One is by the **Assignment** of the contract to an **Assignee**. The effect of assignment is to transfer to the assignee all the interests of the **Assignor**, with the assignee taking over the assignor's rights, remedies, benefits and duties.

For example, the original renter assigns rental interest to a new tenant, who is then responsible for the lease. The assignor is still liable in case the assignee does not perform, but the assignee is now primarily responsible for the contract.

If the assignor wants to be released entirely from any obligation for the contract, it may be done by **Novation**. That is the substitution, by agreement, of a new obligation for an existing one, with the intent to extinguish the original contract. For example, novation occurs when a buyer assumes a seller's loan, and the lender releases the seller from the loan contract by substituting the buyer's name on the loan.

Time is often significant in a contract; indeed, its performance may be measured by the passage of time. By law, if no time is required by the contract, a reasonable time is allowed. If the act can be done instantly— as in the payment of money— it must be done at once.

Discharge of Contracts

http://www.dre.ca.gov
Reference Book, Ch. 6

Commonly the discharge of a contract occurs when the contract has been fully performed. Occasionally, the end result is a breach of contract, where someone does not fulfill the agreement. The following are the ways a contract may be discharged.

Discharge of Contracts

- Full performance
- Breach of contract
- Part performance
- Substantial performance
- Impossibility of performance
- Release of one or all of the parties
- Operation of law
- Acceptance of breach of contract

Statute of Limitations

Under California law, any person seeking relief for a breach of contract must do so within the guidelines of the **Statute of Limitations**. This set of laws determines that civil **Actions** can be started only within the time periods prescribed by law. Lawsuits must be brought within the allowed time or the right to do so will expire. Here are some actions of special interest to real estate agents, with the timeframes required.

Actions Which Must Be Brought Within 90 Days: Civil actions to recover personal property such as suitcases, clothing or jewelry alleged to have been left at a hotel or in an apartment; must begin within 90 days after the owners depart from the personal property.

Actions Which Must Be Brought Within Six Months: An action against an officer to recover property seized in an official capacity—such as by a tax collector.

Actions Which Must Be Brought Within One Year: Libel or slander, injury or death caused by wrongful act, or loss to depositor against a bank for the payment of a forged check.

Actions Which Must Be Brought Within Two Years: Action on a contract, not in writing; action based on a policy of title insurance.

Actions Which Must Be Brought Within Three Years: Action on a liability created by statute; action for trespass on or injury to real property, such as encroachment; action for relief on the grounds of fraud or mistake; attachment.

Actions Which Must Be Brought Within Four Years: An action on any written contract; includes most real estate contracts.

Actions Which Must Be Brought Within 10 Years: Action on a judgment or decree of any court in the United States.

Remedies for Breach of Contract

A **Breach of Contract** is a failure to perform on part or all of the terms and conditions of a contract. A person harmed by non-performance can accept the failure to perform or has a choice of three remedies.

Unilateral Rescission is available to a person who enters a contract without genuine assent because of fraud, mistake, duress, menace, undue influence or faulty consideration. Rescission may be used as a means of discharging a contract by agreement, as we have mentioned.

If one of the parties has been wronged by a breach of contract, however, that innocent party can stop performing all obligations as well, therefore unilaterally rescinding the contract. It must be done promptly, restoring to the other party everything of value received as a result of the breached contract, on condition that the other party shall do the same.

When a party is a breach-of-contract victim, a second remedy is a **Lawsuit for Money Damages**. If damages to an injured party can be reasonably expressed in a dollar amount, the innocent party could sue for money damages to include: the price paid by the buyer, the difference between the contract price and the value of the property, title and document expenses, consequential damages and interest.

A third remedy for breach of contract is a **Lawsuit for Specific Performance**. This is an action in court by the injured party to force the breaching party to carry out the remainder of the contract according to the precise terms, price and conditions agreed upon. Generally, this remedy is used when money cannot restore an injured party's position. This is often the case in real estate because of the difficulty in finding a similar property.

Remember

Three Remedies for Breach of Contract

- Rescission
- Lawsuit for money damages
- Lawsuit for specific performance

Real Estate Contracts

Real estate contracts include:

- Contracts for the sale of real property, or of an interest therein
- Agreements authorizing or employing an agent or broker to buy or sell real estate for compensation or commission
- Agreements for leasing realty for more than a year

Of course, most real estate contracts must be in writing, according to the Statute of Frauds, and must be signed by the parties.

The two most important sales contracts that an agent must know well are the **Listing Agreement**, as it is known, and the **Deposit Receipt**. Leasing agreements will be discussed in another chapter.

Listing Agreement

http://www.dre.ca.gov
Reference Book, Ch. 22

A **Listing** is a contract by which a principal, or seller, employs a broker to sell real estate. The listing broker—as well as the seller—is bound by the law of agency, and both have certain obligations. If an agent does not comply with the two following obligations, the punishment may be suspension or revocation of the real estate license.

Remember

Listing Violations

- Failure to specify a definite termination date in exclusive listings

- Failure to give a copy of the listing to the seller at the time the seller signs it

Primarily, a listing agreement is an employment contract between a seller and broker. It is a bilateral agreement where the seller agrees to pay a commission if the broker finds a buyer, and the broker promises to use due diligence to procure a buyer.

There are a few misconceptions about a listing contract. The seller is *not* promising to sell the house, but *is* promising to pay a commission if the broker brings a ready, willing and able buyer. Also, the broker is *not* the one who makes the decision about selling. The owner is the only one who can do that.

A seller cannot be forced to sell, even after signing a listing agreement, but can be compelled to pay a commission if the broker finds a buyer, even if the seller refuses to sell to that buyer.

Here are the four most common types of listing agreements.

http://www.dre.ca.gov
Reference Book, Ch. 6

Net Listing

A listing where the commission is not definitely set, but is determined by whatever money is received in excess of the selling price set by the seller. The agent, within 30 days after closing the transaction, must disclose the selling price to both buyer and seller.

Open Listing

Permission given by a seller authorizing an agent to represent the seller in the sale of a certain property. It is not exclusive and may be given to any number of agents at the same time. The agent finding a buyer who meets the terms of the listing, and whose offer is accepted by the seller, earns the commission. That agent is known as the procuring cause of the sale. The owner may sell the property without an agent, owing no commission.

Exclusive Agency Listing

An exclusive contract where the seller must pay the listing broker a commission if any broker sells the property. However, the seller has the right to sell the property without a broker, and pay no commission. Must specify a definite termination date.

Exclusive Right to Sell Listing

An exclusive contract where the seller must pay the listing broker a commission if the property is sold within the time limit by the listing broker or any other broker, or even by the owner. If the broker brings the seller a "mirror offer," or an offer that matches exactly all terms in the listing, the seller does not have to accept the offer. However, under the terms of the listing, the seller must pay the broker a commission. Must specify a definite termination date.

Safety Clause

The **Safety Clause** is found in the CAR Exclusive Authorization and Right to Sell listing form (section 5. A, 2).

> If within _____ calendar days after expiration of the Listing Period or any extension, the Property is sold, conveyed, leased or otherwise transferred to anyone with whom the broker or a cooperating broker has had negotiations, provided that Broker gives Seller prior to or within 5 calendar days after expiration of the Listing Period or any extension, a written notice with the name(s) of the prospective buyers.

It allows a certain time period, after a listing has expired, during which the listing broker's commission is protected if the owner personally sells to someone who was shown the property or made an offer during the term of listing. The broker must have supplied the seller with a list of prospective buyers who were shown the property during the listed period for the clause to be enforceable.

Exclusive Authorization and Right to Sell (1 of 3)

CALIFORNIA ASSOCIATION OF REALTORS®

RESIDENTIAL LISTING AGREEMENT
(Exclusive Authorization and Right to Sell)

1. **EXCLUSIVE RIGHT TO SELL:** _____ ("Seller") hereby employs and grants _____ ("Broker") the exclusive and irrevocable right to sell or exchange the real property in the City of _____, County of _____ ("Property"), California, described as: _____ beginning (date) _____ and ending at 11:59 P.M. on (date) _____ ("Listing Period").

2. **TERMS OF SALE:**
   A. **LIST PRICE:** The listing price shall be _____ ($_____).
   B. **ITEMS INCLUDED IN SALE:** All fixtures and fittings which are attached to the Property and the following items of personal property: _____
   C. **ITEMS EXCLUDED FROM SALE:** _____
   D. **ADDITIONAL TERMS:** _____

3. **COMPENSATION TO BROKER:**
   Notice: The amount or rate of real estate commissions is not fixed by law. They are set by each Broker individually and may be negotiable between Seller and Broker.
   A. Seller agrees to pay to Broker as compensation for services irrespective of agency relationship(s), either ☐ _____ percent of the listing price (or if a sale contract is entered into, of the sale price), or ☐ $_____, AND (if checked) ☐ an administrative/ transaction fee of $_____, as follows:
      (1) If Broker, Seller, cooperating broker, or any other person produces a buyer(s) who offers to purchase the Property on the above price and terms, or on any price and terms acceptable to Seller during the Listing Period, or any extension;

Safety Clause →

      (2) If Seller, within _____ calendar days after the end of the Listing Period or any extension, enters into a contract to sell, convey, lease or otherwise transfer the Property to anyone ("Prospective Transferee") or that person's related entity (i) who physically entered and was shown the Property during the Listing Period or any extension by Broker or a cooperating broker, or (ii) for whom Broker or any cooperating broker submitted to Seller a signed, written offer to acquire, lease, exchange or obtain an option on the Property. Seller, however, shall have no obligation to Broker under this sub-paragraph (3A(2)) unless, not later than **5 calendar days** after the end of the Listing Period or any extension, Broker has given Seller a written notice of the names of such Prospective Transferees.
      (3) If, without Broker's prior written consent, the Property is withdrawn from sale, conveyed, leased, rented, otherwise transferred, or made unmarketable by a voluntary act of Seller during the Listing Period, or any extension.
   B. If completion of the sale is prevented by a party to the transaction other than Seller, then compensation due under paragraph 3A shall be payable only if and when Seller collects damages by suit, arbitration, settlement, or otherwise, and then in an amount equal to the lesser of one-half of the damages recovered or the above compensation, after first deducting title and escrow expenses and the expenses of collection, if any.
   C. In addition, Seller agrees to pay: _____
   D. Broker is authorized to cooperate and compensate other brokers in any manner unless otherwise specified in paragraph 4.
   E. Seller hereby irrevocably assigns to Broker the above compensation from Seller's funds and proceeds in escrow.
   F. Seller warrants that Seller has no obligation to pay compensation to any other broker regarding the transfer of the Property except: _____
      If the Property is sold to anyone listed above during the time Seller is obligated to compensate another broker: (a) Broker is not entitled to compensation under this Agreement and (b) Broker is not obligated to represent Seller in such transaction.

4. **MULTIPLE LISTING SERVICE:** Information about this listing will, (or ☐ will not), be provided to a multiple listing service(s) ("MLS") of Broker's selection. All terms of the transaction, including financing, if applicable, will be provided to the selected MLS for publication, dissemination and use by persons and entities on terms approved by the MLS. Seller authorizes Broker to comply with all applicable MLS rules. MLS rules allow MLS data to be made available by the MLS to additional Internet sites unless Broker gives the MLS instructions to the contrary. Broker shall offer to compensate brokers participating through the MLS and subject to such MLS rules in any manner or, (if checked) as follows: either ☐ _____ percent of the sales price, or ☐ $_____.

5. **OWNERSHIP, TITLE AND AUTHORITY:** Seller warrants that (i) Seller is the owner of the Property, (ii) no other persons or entities have title to the Property, and (iii) Seller has the authority to both execute this contract and sell the Property. Exceptions to ownership, title and authority: _____

Seller acknowledges receipt of copy of this page.
Seller's Initials (_____)(_____)

EQUAL HOUSING OPPORTUNITY

REVISION DATE 4/2000   Print Date BDC May 01

Reviewed by
Broker or Designee _____ Date _____

BROKER'S COPY

RESIDENTIAL LISTING AGREEMENT-EXCLUSIVE (LA-11 PAGE 1 OF 3)

Exclusive Authorization and Right to Sell (2 of 3)

Property Address: _____ Date: _____

6. **SELLER REPRESENTATIONS:** Seller represents that Seller is unaware of (i) any Notice of Default recorded against the Property, (ii) any delinquent amounts due under any loan secured by, or other obligation affecting, the Property, (iii) any bankruptcy, insolvency or similar proceeding affecting the Property, (iv) any litigation, arbitration, administrative action, government investigation, or other pending or threatened action which does or may affect the Property or Seller's ability to transfer it, and (v) any current, pending or proposed special assessments affecting the Property. Exceptions: _____
_____.

7. **BROKER'S AND SELLER'S DUTIES:** Broker agrees to exercise reasonable effort and due diligence to achieve the purposes of this Agreement. Unless Seller gives Broker written instructions to the contrary, Broker is authorized to advertise and market the Property in any medium including the Internet (e-commerce) selected by Broker, and, to the extent permitted by these media, including MLS, control the dissemination of the information submitted to any medium. Seller agrees to consider offers presented by Broker, and to act in good faith to accomplish the sale of the Property by, among others things, making the Property available for showing at reasonable times and referring to Broker all inquiries of any party interested in the Property. Seller is responsible for determining at what price to list and sell the Property. **Seller further agrees, regardless of responsibility, to indemnify, defend and hold Broker harmless from all claims, disputes, litigation, judgments and attorney's fees arising from any incorrect information supplied by Seller, whether contained in any document, omitted therefrom, or otherwise, or from any material facts which Seller knows but fails to disclose.**

8. **DEPOSIT:** Broker is authorized to accept and hold on Seller's behalf any deposits to be applied toward the sales price.

9. **AGENCY RELATIONSHIPS:**
   A. **Disclosure:** If the Property includes residential property with one-to-four dwelling units, Seller acknowledges receipt of the "Disclosure Regarding Agency Relationships" form.
   B. **Seller Representation:** Broker shall represent Seller in any resulting transaction, except as specified in paragraph 3F.
   C. **Possible Dual Agency With Buyer:** Depending upon the circumstances, it may be necessary or appropriate for Broker to act as an agent for both Seller and buyer, exchange party, or one or more additional parties ("Buyer"). Broker shall, as soon as practicable, disclose to Seller any election to act as a dual agent representing both Seller and Buyer. If a Buyer is procured directly by Broker or an associate licensee in Broker's firm, Seller hereby consents to Broker acting as a dual agent for Seller and such Buyer. In the event of an exchange, Seller hereby consents to Broker collecting compensation from additional parties for services rendered, provided there is disclosure to all parties of such agency and compensation. Seller understands and agrees that: (i) Broker, without the prior written consent of Seller, will not disclose to Buyer that Seller is willing to sell Property at a price less than the listing price; (ii) Broker, without the prior written consent of Buyer, will not disclose to Seller that Buyer is willing to pay a price greater than the offered price; and (iii) except for (i) and (ii) above, a dual agent is obligated to disclose known facts materially affecting the value or desirability of the Property to both parties.
   D. **Other Sellers:** Seller understands that Broker may have or obtain listings on other properties, and that potential buyers may consider, make offers on, or purchase through Broker, property the same as or similar to Seller's Property. Seller consents to Broker's representation of sellers and buyers of other properties before, during, and after the end of this Agreement.
   E. **Confirmation:** If the Property includes residential property with one-to-four dwelling units, Broker shall confirm the agency relationship described above, or as modified, in writing, prior to or coincident with Seller's execution of a purchase contract.

10. **KEYSAFE/LOCKBOX:** (a) A keysafe/lockbox is designed to hold a key to the Property to permit access to the Property by Broker, cooperating brokers, MLS participants, their authorized licensees and representatives, authorized inspectors, and accompanied prospective buyers. (b) Broker, cooperating brokers, MLS and Associations/Boards of REALTORS® are **not** insurers against theft, loss, vandalism, or damage attributed to the use of a keysafe/lockbox. (c) Seller authorizes Broker to install a keysafe/lockbox unless otherwise indicated in writing. If Seller does not occupy the Property, Seller shall be responsible for obtaining occupant(s)' written permission for use of a keysafe/lockbox.

11. **SECURITY AND INSURANCE:** Seller agrees: (i) that Broker is not responsible for loss of or damage to personal or real property or person, whether attributable to use of a keysafe/lockbox or a showing of the Property; (ii) to take reasonable precautions to safeguard, protect, or insure valuables that might be accessible during showings of the Property; and (iii) to obtain insurance to protect against these risks. Broker does not maintain insurance to protect Seller.

12. **SIGN:** Seller authorizes Broker to install a FOR SALE/SOLD sign on the Property unless otherwise indicated in writing.

13. **EQUAL HOUSING OPPORTUNITY:** The Property is offered in compliance with federal, state, and local anti-discrimination laws.

14. **ATTORNEY'S FEES:** In any action, proceeding, or arbitration between Seller and Broker regarding the obligation to pay compensation under this Agreement, the prevailing Seller or Broker shall be entitled to reasonable attorney's fees and costs, except as provided in paragraph 18A.

15. **ADDITIONAL TERMS:** _____
_____
_____
_____
_____

16. **MANAGEMENT APPROVAL:** If a salesperson or broker-associate enters this agreement on Broker's behalf, and broker/manager does not approve of its terms, broker/manager has the right to cancel this agreement, in writing, within 5 days after its execution.

17. **SUCCESSORS AND ASSIGNS:** This agreement shall be binding upon Seller, and Seller's successors and assigns.

REVISION DATE 4/2000

Seller acknowledges receipt of copy of this page.

Seller's Initials (_____)(_____)

EQUAL HOUSING OPPORTUNITY

Reviewed by
Broker or Designee _____ Date _____

BROKER'S COPY

RESIDENTIAL LISTING AGREEMENT-EXCLUSIVE (LA-11 PAGE 2 OF 3)

(Additional forms are located in the back of the book.)

Deposit Receipt

http://www.dre.ca.gov
Reference Book, Ch. 22
p. 450

In California, most real estate agents use an Offer to Purchase, commonly known as a *deposit receipt*, when writing an offer on real property. The *deposit receipt* acts as the receipt for earnest money given by the buyer to secure an offer, as well as being the basic contract, or agreement, between the buyer and seller.

Upon writing an offer to purchase real property, a buyer may give some consideration such as a personal check, commonly in the amount of 1% of the purchase price as a sign that he or she is serious about making the offer. The real estate agent holds on to the check, which is made out to an escrow company or the listing broker, until either the seller refuses the offer, in which case the check is returned to the buyer, or the seller accepts the offer and the buyer's agent deposits the check into either an escrow account or the broker's own trust account within three business days after receiving it. Once the seller agrees to the offer and the buyer is informed of the seller's acceptance, the *deposit receipt* is a legal binding contract. All parties then must execute, or sign the *deposit receipt*.

The *deposit receipt* includes all terms of the sale, including agreements about financing. The buyer and seller are bound by the contract when the buyer receives notification of the seller's acceptance of the offer, without any changes. The *deposit receipt*, as the original agreement between the buyer and seller, may become the actual escrow instructions or simply the basic agreement for escrow instructions which will follow when escrow is opened.

In most cases, a standard California of Realtors Offer to Purchase (RPA-11) contract is used by real estate agents when a buyer makes an offer anywhere in California. The Department of Real Estate does not officially recommend this form nor is any type of specific form required by law. Real estate agents do have an alternative, however, among the standard CAR forms, depending on the custom in their area of the state. Real estate practices differ significantly in different parts of California and some of those differences are not reflected in the commonly used deposit receipt. An alternate form, Area Edition Residential Purchase Agreement (AEPA-11) is available to real estate agents who desire features not included in the other form.

A **Tender** in a real estate transaction is an offer by one of the parties to carry out his or her part of the contract. A tender of performance by the buyer, for example, by depositing the purchase money into escrow, places the seller in default, if the seller refuses to accept it and deliver a deed.

> ## The deposit receipt includes:
>
> - Date of the agreement
> - Names and addresses of the parties to the contract
> - Description of the property
> - The consideration or price
> - Financing and terms
> - Date and place of closing
> - Signatures of buyer and seller

Any earnest money or deposit received by an agent must be considered trust funds and handled as prescribed by the Real Estate Law and Regulations.

If a sales contract is executed by both parties, and the seller dies before the buyer takes title, the seller's heirs must complete the sale.

Remember, the deposit receipt is probably the most important real estate document you—as an agent—will have to understand. The consumer relies on your knowledge, and your commission depends on your ability to explain a sometimes difficult transaction to them. Also, the state exam contains a section on completing a deposit receipt.

California Residential Purchase Agreement (1 of 8)

FORM RPA-CA

CALIFORNIA ASSOCIATION OF REALTORS®

CALIFORNIA
RESIDENTIAL PURCHASE AGREEMENT
AND JOINT ESCROW INSTRUCTIONS
For Use With Single Family Residential Property — Attached or Detached
(C.A.R. Form RPA-CA, Revised 10/02)

Date _____, at _____, California.
1. **OFFER:**
   A. **THIS IS AN OFFER FROM** _____ ("Buyer").
   B. **THE REAL PROPERTY TO BE ACQUIRED** is described as _____
   _____, Assessor's Parcel No. _____, situated in
   _____, County of _____, California, ("Property").
   C. **THE PURCHASE PRICE** offered is _____
   _____ Dollars $ _____.
   D. **CLOSE OF ESCROW** shall occur on _____ (date)(or ☐ _____ **Days** After Acceptance).
2. **FINANCE TERMS:** Obtaining the loans below **is a contingency** of this Agreement unless: **(i)** either 2K or 2L is checked below; or **(ii)** otherwise agreed in writing. Buyer shall act diligently and in good faith to obtain the designated loans. Obtaining deposit, down payment and closing costs **is not a contingency.** Buyer represents that funds will be good when deposited with Escrow Holder.
   A. **INITIAL DEPOSIT:** Buyer has given a deposit in the amount of ....$ _____
   to the agent submitting the offer (or to ☐ _____), by personal check
   (or ☐ _____), made payable to _____
   which shall be held uncashed until Acceptance and then deposited within **3** business days after
   Acceptance (or ☐ _____), with
   Escrow Holder, (or ☐ into Broker's trust account).
   B. **INCREASED DEPOSIT:** Buyer shall deposit with Escrow Holder an increased deposit in the amount of ...$ _____
   within _____ **Days** After Acceptance, or ☐ _____.
   C. **FIRST LOAN IN THE AMOUNT OF** ....$ _____
   (1) NEW First Deed of Trust in favor of lender, encumbering the Property, securing a note payable at
   maximum interest of _____% fixed rate, or _____% initial adjustable rate with a maximum
   interest rate of _____%, balance due in _____ years, amortized over _____ years. Buyer
   shall pay loan fees/points not to exceed _____. (These terms apply whether the designated loan
   is conventional, FHA or VA.)
   (2) ☐ FHA ☐ VA: (The following terms only apply to the FHA or VA loan that is checked.)
   Seller shall pay _____% discount points. Seller shall pay other fees not allowed to be paid by
   Buyer, ☐ not to exceed $_____. Seller shall pay the cost of lender required Repairs
   (including those for wood destroying pest) not otherwise provided for in this Agreement, ☐ not to
   exceed $ _____. (Actual loan amount may increase if mortgage insurance premiums,
   funding fees or closing costs are financed.)
   D. **ADDITIONAL FINANCING TERMS:** ☐ Seller financing, (C.A.R. Form SFA); ☐ secondary financing, ...$ _____
   (C.A.R. Form PAA, paragraph 4A); ☐ assumed financing (C.A.R. Form PAA, paragraph 4B)
   _____
   _____
   E. **BALANCE OF PURCHASE PRICE** (not including costs of obtaining loans and other closing costs) in the amount of ...$ _____
   to be deposited with Escrow Holder within sufficient time to close escrow.
   F. **PURCHASE PRICE (TOTAL):** ....$ _____
   G. **LOAN APPLICATIONS:** Within **7 (or ☐ _____) Days** After Acceptance, Buyer shall provide Seller a letter from lender or
   mortgage loan broker stating that, based on a review of Buyer's written application and credit report, Buyer is prequalified or
   preapproved for the NEW loan specified in 2C above.
   H. **VERIFICATION OF DOWN PAYMENT AND CLOSING COSTS:** Buyer (or Buyer's lender or loan broker pursuant to 2G) shall, within
   7 (or ☐ _____) Days After Acceptance, provide Seller written verification of Buyer's down payment and closing costs.
   I. **LOAN CONTINGENCY REMOVAL: (i)** Within **17 (or ☐ _____) Days** After Acceptance, Buyer shall, as specified in paragraph
   14, remove the loan contingency or cancel this Agreement; **OR (ii)** (if checked) ☐ the loan contingency shall remain in effect
   until the designated loans are funded.
   J. **APPRAISAL CONTINGENCY AND REMOVAL:** This Agreement is (**OR,** if checked, ☐ is NOT) contingent upon the Property
   appraising at no less than the specified purchase price. Buyer shall, as specified in paragraph 14, remove the appraisal
   contingency or cancel this Agreement when the loan contingency is removed (or, if checked, ☐ within **17 (or ☐ _____) Days**
   After Acceptance).
   K. ☐ **NO LOAN CONTINGENCY** (If checked): Obtaining any loan in paragraphs 2C, 2D or elsewhere in this Agreement is NOT
   a contingency of this Agreement. If Buyer does not obtain the loan and as a result Buyer does not purchase the Property, Seller
   may be entitled to Buyer's deposit or other legal remedies.
   L. ☐ **ALL CASH OFFER** (If checked): No loan is needed to purchase the Property. Buyer shall, within **7 (or ☐ _____) Days** After Acceptance,
   provide Seller written verification of sufficient funds to close this transaction.
3. **CLOSING AND OCCUPANCY:**
   A. Buyer intends (or ☐ does not intend) to occupy the Property as Buyer's primary residence.
   B. **Seller-occupied or vacant property:** Occupancy shall be delivered to Buyer at _____ AM/PM, ☐ on the date of Close Of
   Escrow; ☐ on _____; or ☐ no later than _____ **Days** After Close Of Escrow. (C.A.R. Form PAA, paragraph 2.) If
   transfer of title and occupancy do not occur at the same time, Buyer and Seller are advised to: **(i)** enter into a written occupancy
   agreement; and **(ii)** consult with their insurance and legal advisors.

Buyer's Initials (_____)(_____)
Seller's Initials (_____)(_____)

Reviewed by _____ Date _____

EQUAL HOUSING OPPORTUNITY

RPA-CA REVISED 10/02 (PAGE 1 OF 8) Print Date BDC Oct 02

MASTER COPY
CALIFORNIA RESIDENTIAL PURCHASE AGREEMENT (RPA-CA PAGE 1 OF 8)

California Residential Purchase Agreement (2 of 8)

Property Address: _____ Date: _____

C. Tenant-occupied property: (i) Property shall be vacant at least **5 (or ☐ _____) Days** Prior to Close Of Escrow, unless otherwise agreed in writing. **Note to Seller: If you are unable to deliver Property vacant in accordance with rent control and other applicable Law, you may be in breach of this Agreement.**

OR (ii) (if checked) ☐ **Tenant to remain in possession.** The attached addendum is incorporated into this Agreement (C.A.R. Form PAA, paragraph 3.);

OR (iii) (if checked) ☐ **This Agreement is contingent** upon Buyer and Seller entering into a written agreement regarding occupancy of the Property within the time specified in paragraph 14. If no written agreement is reached within this time, either Buyer or Seller may cancel this Agreement in writing.

D. At Close Of Escrow, Seller assigns to Buyer any assignable warranty rights for items included in the sale and shall provide any available Copies of such warranties. Brokers cannot and will not determine the assignability of any warranties.

E. At Close Of Escrow, unless otherwise agreed in writing, Seller shall provide keys and/or means to operate all locks, mailboxes, security systems, alarms and garage door openers. If Property is a condominium or located in a common interest subdivision, Buyer may be required to pay a deposit to the Homeowners' Association ("HOA") to obtain keys to accessible HOA facilities.

4. ALLOCATION OF COSTS (If checked): Unless otherwise specified here, this paragraph only determines who is to pay for the report, inspection, test or service mentioned. If not specified here or elsewhere in this Agreement, the determination of who is to pay for any work recommended or identified by any such report, inspection, test or service shall be by the method specified in paragraph 14.

A. WOOD DESTROYING PEST INSPECTION:

(1) ☐ Buyer ☐ Seller shall pay for an inspection and report for wood destroying pests and organisms ("Report") which shall be prepared by _____, a registered structural pest control company. The Report shall cover the accessible areas of the main building and attached structures and, if checked: ☐ detached garages and carports, ☐ detached decks, ☐ the following other structures or areas _____. The Report shall not include roof coverings. If Property is a condominium or located in a common interest subdivision, the Report shall include only the separate interest and any exclusive-use areas being transferred and shall not include common areas, unless otherwise agreed. Water tests of shower pans on upper level units may not be performed without consent of the owners of property below the shower.

OR (2) ☐ (If checked) The attached addendum (C.A.R. Form WPA) regarding wood destroying pest inspection and allocation of cost is incorporated into this Agreement.

B. OTHER INSPECTIONS AND REPORTS:

(1) ☐ Buyer ☐ Seller shall pay to have septic or private sewage disposal systems inspected _____.

(2) ☐ Buyer ☐ Seller shall pay to have domestic wells tested for water potability and productivity _____.

(3) ☐ Buyer ☐ Seller shall pay for a natural hazard zone disclosure report prepared by _____.

(4) ☐ Buyer ☐ Seller shall pay for the following inspection or report _____.

(5) ☐ Buyer ☐ Seller shall pay for the following inspection or report _____.

C. GOVERNMENT REQUIREMENTS AND RETROFIT:

(1) ☐ Buyer ☐ Seller shall pay for smoke detector installation and/or water heater bracing, if required by Law. Prior to Close Of Escrow, Seller shall provide Buyer a written statement of compliance in accordance with state and local Law, unless exempt.

(2) ☐ Buyer ☐ Seller shall pay the cost of compliance with any other minimum mandatory government retrofit standards, inspections and reports if required as a condition of closing escrow under any Law. _____.

D. ESCROW AND TITLE:

(1) ☐ Buyer ☐ Seller shall pay escrow fee _____.
Escrow Holder shall be _____.

(2) ☐ Buyer ☐ Seller shall pay for **owner's** title insurance policy specified in paragraph 12 _____.
Owner's title policy to be issued by _____.
(Buyer shall pay for any title insurance policy insuring Buyer's **lender**, unless otherwise agreed in writing.)

E. OTHER COSTS:

(1) ☐ Buyer ☐ Seller shall pay County transfer tax or transfer fee _____.

(2) ☐ Buyer ☐ Seller shall pay City transfer tax or transfer fee _____.

(3) ☐ Buyer ☐ Seller shall pay HOA transfer fee _____.

(4) ☐ Buyer ☐ Seller shall pay HOA document preparation fees _____.

(5) ☐ Buyer ☐ Seller shall pay the cost, not to exceed $ _____, of a one-year home warranty plan, issued by _____ with the following optional coverage: _____.

(6) ☐ Buyer ☐ Seller shall pay for _____.

(7) ☐ Buyer ☐ Seller shall pay for _____.

5. STATUTORY DISCLOSURES (INCLUDING LEAD-BASED PAINT HAZARD DISCLOSURES) AND CANCELLATION RIGHTS:

A. (1) Seller shall, within the time specified in paragraph 14, deliver to Buyer, if required by Law: **(i)** Federal Lead-Based Paint Disclosures and pamphlet ("Lead Disclosures"); and **(ii)** disclosures or notices required by sections 1102 et. seq. and 1103 et. seq. of the California Civil Code ("Statutory Disclosures"). Statutory Disclosures include, but are not limited to, a Real Estate Transfer Disclosure Statement ("TDS"), Natural Hazard Disclosure Statement ("NHD"), notice or actual knowledge of release of illegal controlled substance, notice of special tax and/or assessments (or, if allowed, substantially equivalent notice regarding the Mello-Roos Community Facilities Act and Improvement Bond Act of 1915) and, if Seller has actual knowledge, an industrial use and military ordnance location disclosure (C.A.R. Form SSD).

(2) Buyer shall, within the time specified in paragraph 14, return Signed Copies of the Statutory and Lead Disclosures to Seller.

(3) In the event Seller, prior to Close Of Escrow, becomes aware of adverse conditions materially affecting the Property, or any material inaccuracy in disclosures, information or representations previously provided to Buyer of which Buyer is otherwise unaware, Seller shall promptly provide a subsequent or amended disclosure or notice, in writing, covering those items. **However, a subsequent or amended disclosure shall not be required for conditions and material inaccuracies disclosed in reports ordered and paid for by Buyer.**

Buyer's Initials (_____)(_____)
Seller's Initials (_____)(_____)

RPA-CA REVISED 10/02 (PAGE 2 OF 8)

MASTER COPY

Reviewed by _____ Date _____

EQUAL HOUSING OPPORTUNITY

CALIFORNIA RESIDENTIAL PURCHASE AGREEMENT (RPA-CA PAGE 2 OF 8)

California Residential Purchase Agreement (3 of 8)

Property Address: _____   Date: _____

    (4) If any disclosure or notice specified in 5A(1), or subsequent or amended disclosure or notice is delivered to Buyer after the offer is Signed, Buyer shall have the right to cancel this Agreement within **3 Days** After delivery in person, or **5 Days** After delivery by deposit in the mail, by giving written notice of cancellation to Seller or Seller's agent. (Lead Disclosures sent by mail must be sent certified mail or better.)

    (5) Note to Buyer and Seller: Waiver of Statutory and Lead Disclosures is prohibited by Law.

  B. **NATURAL AND ENVIRONMENTAL HAZARDS:** Within the time specified in paragraph 14, Seller shall, if required by Law: **(i)** deliver to Buyer earthquake guides (and questionnaire) and environmental hazards booklet; **(ii)** even if exempt from the obligation to provide a NHD, disclose if the Property is located in a Special Flood Hazard Area; Potential Flooding (Inundation) Area; Very High Fire Hazard Zone; State Fire Responsibility Area; Earthquake Fault Zone; Seismic Hazard Zone; and **(iii)** disclose any other zone as required by Law and provide any other information required for those zones.

  C. **DATA BASE DISCLOSURE:** NOTICE: The California Department of Justice, sheriff's departments, police departments serving jurisdictions of 200,000 or more and many other local law enforcement authorities maintain for public access a data base of the locations of persons required to register pursuant to paragraph (1) of subdivision (a) of Section 290.4 of the Penal Code. The data base is updated on a quarterly basis and a source of information about the presence of these individuals in any neighborhood. The Department of Justice also maintains a Sex Offender Identification Line through which inquiries about individuals may be made. This is a "900" telephone service. Callers must have specific information about individuals they are checking. Information regarding neighborhoods is not available through the "900" telephone service.

6. **CONDOMINIUM/PLANNED UNIT DEVELOPMENT DISCLOSURES:**

  A. **SELLER HAS: 7 (or ☐ _____) Days** After Acceptance to disclose to Buyer whether the Property is a condominium, or is located in a planned unit development or other common interest subdivision.

  B. If the Property is a condominium or is located in a planned unit development or other common interest subdivision, Seller has **3 (or ☐ _____) Days** After Acceptance to request from the HOA (C.A.R. Form HOA): **(i)** Copies of any documents required by Law; **(ii)** disclosure of any pending or anticipated claim or litigation by or against the HOA; **(iii)** a statement containing the location and number of designated parking and storage spaces; **(iv)** Copies of the most recent 12 months of HOA minutes for regular and special meetings; and **(v)** the names and contact information of all HOAs governing the Property (collectively, "CI Disclosures"). Seller shall itemize and deliver to Buyer all CI Disclosures received from the HOA and any CI Disclosures in Seller's possession. Buyer's approval of CI Disclosures is a contingency of this Agreement as specified in paragraph 14.

7. **CONDITIONS AFFECTING PROPERTY:**

  A. Unless otherwise agreed: **(i) the Property is sold (a) in its PRESENT physical condition as of the date of Acceptance and (b) subject to Buyer's Investigation rights; (ii)** the Property, including pool, spa, landscaping and grounds, is to be maintained in substantially the same condition as on the date of Acceptance; and **(iii)** all debris and personal property not included in the sale shall be removed by Close Of Escrow.

  B. **SELLER SHALL, within the time specified in paragraph 14, DISCLOSE KNOWN MATERIAL FACTS AND DEFECTS AFFECTING THE PROPERTY, including known insurance claims within the past five years, AND MAKE OTHER DISCLOSURES REQUIRED BY LAW.**

  C. **NOTE TO BUYER: You are strongly advised to conduct investigations of the entire Property in order to determine its present condition since Seller may not be aware of all defects affecting the Property or other factors that you consider important. Property improvements may not be built according to code, in compliance with current Law, or have had permits issued.**

  D. **NOTE TO SELLER: Buyer has the right to inspect the Property and, as specified in paragraph 14, based upon information discovered in those inspections: (i) cancel this Agreement; or (ii) request that you make Repairs or take other action.**

8. **ITEMS INCLUDED AND EXCLUDED:**

  A. **NOTE TO BUYER AND SELLER**: Items listed as included or excluded in the MLS, flyers or marketing materials are **not** included in the purchase price or excluded from the sale unless specified in 8B or C.

  B. **ITEMS INCLUDED IN SALE:**

    (1) All EXISTING fixtures and fittings that are attached to the Property;

    (2) Existing electrical, mechanical, lighting, plumbing and heating fixtures, ceiling fans, fireplace inserts, gas logs and grates, solar systems, built-in appliances, window and door screens, awnings, shutters, window coverings, attached floor coverings, television antennas, satellite dishes, private integrated telephone systems, air coolers/conditioners, pool/spa equipment, garage door openers/remote controls, mailbox, in-ground landscaping, trees/shrubs, water softeners, water purifiers, security systems/alarms;

    (3) The following items: _____
_____.

    (4) Seller represents that all items included in the purchase price, unless otherwise specified, are owned by Seller.

    (5) All items included shall be transferred free of liens and without Seller warranty.

  C. **ITEMS EXCLUDED FROM SALE:** _____
_____.

9. **BUYER'S INVESTIGATION OF PROPERTY AND MATTERS AFFECTING PROPERTY:**

  A. Buyer's acceptance of the condition of, and any other matter affecting the Property, is a contingency of this Agreement as specified in this paragraph and paragraph 14. Within the time specified in paragraph 14, Buyer shall have the right, at Buyer's expense unless otherwise agreed, to conduct inspections, investigations, tests, surveys and other studies ("Buyer Investigations"), including, but not limited to, the right to: **(i)** inspect for lead-based paint and other lead-based paint hazards; **(ii)** inspect for wood destroying pests and organisms; **(iii)** review the registered sex offender database; **(iv)** confirm the insurability of Buyer and the Property; and **(v)** satisfy Buyer as to any matter specified in the attached Buyer's Inspection Advisory (C.A.R. Form BIA). Without Seller's prior written consent, Buyer shall neither make nor cause to be made: **(i)** invasive or destructive Buyer Investigations; or **(ii)** inspections by any governmental building or zoning inspector or government employee, unless required by Law.

  B. Buyer shall complete Buyer Investigations and, as specified in paragraph 14, remove the contingency or cancel this Agreement. Buyer shall give Seller, at no cost, complete Copies of all Buyer Investigation reports obtained by Buyer. Seller shall make the Property available for all Buyer Investigations. Seller shall have water, gas, electricity and all operable pilot lights on for Buyer's Investigations and through the date possession is made available to Buyer.

Buyer's Initials (_____)(_____)
Seller's Initials (_____)(_____)

RPA-CA REVISED 10/02 (PAGE 3 OF 8)

Reviewed by _____ Date _____

EQUAL HOUSING OPPORTUNITY

MASTER COPY
CALIFORNIA RESIDENTIAL PURCHASE AGREEMENT (RPA-CA PAGE 3 OF 8)

California Residential Purchase Agreement (4 of 8)

Property Address: _____ Date: _____

10. REPAIRS: Repairs shall be completed prior to final verification of condition unless otherwise agreed in writing. Repairs to be performed at Seller's expense may be performed by Seller or through others, provided that the work complies with applicable Law, including governmental permit, inspection and approval requirements. Repairs shall be performed in a good, skillful manner with materials of quality and appearance comparable to existing materials. It is understood that exact restoration of appearance or cosmetic items following all Repairs may not be possible. Seller shall: **(i)** obtain receipts for Repairs performed by others; **(ii)** prepare a written statement indicating the Repairs performed by Seller and the date of such Repairs; and **(iii)** provide Copies of receipts and statements to Buyer prior to final verification of condition.

11. BUYER INDEMNITY AND SELLER PROTECTION FOR ENTRY UPON PROPERTY: Buyer shall: **(i)** keep the Property free and clear of liens; **(ii)** Repair all damage arising from Buyer Investigations; and **(iii)** indemnify and hold Seller harmless from all resulting liability, claims, demands, damages and costs. Buyer shall carry, or Buyer shall require anyone acting on Buyer's behalf to carry, policies of liability, workers' compensation and other applicable insurance, defending and protecting Seller from liability for any injuries to persons or property occurring during any Buyer Investigations or work done on the Property at Buyer's direction prior to Close Of Escrow. Seller is advised that certain protections may be afforded Seller by recording a "Notice of Non-responsibility" (C.A.R. Form NNR) for Buyer Investigations and work done on the Property at Buyer's direction. Buyer's obligations under this paragraph shall survive the termination of this Agreement.

12. TITLE AND VESTING:
A. Within the time specified in paragraph 14, Buyer shall be provided a current preliminary (title) report, which is only an offer by the title insurer to issue a policy of title insurance and may not contain every item affecting title. Buyer's review of the preliminary report and any other matters which may affect title are a contingency of this Agreement as specified in paragraph 14.
B. Title is taken in its present condition subject to all encumbrances, easements, covenants, conditions, restrictions, rights and other matters, whether of record or not, as of the date of Acceptance except: **(i)** monetary liens of record unless Buyer is assuming those obligations or taking the Property subject to those obligations; and **(ii)** those matters which Seller has agreed to remove in writing.
C. Within the time specified in paragraph 14, Seller has a duty to disclose to Buyer all matters known to Seller affecting title, whether of record or not.
D. At Close Of Escrow, Buyer shall receive a grant deed conveying title (or, for stock cooperative or long-term lease, an assignment of stock certificate or of Seller's leasehold interest), including oil, mineral and water rights if currently owned by Seller. Title shall vest as designated in Buyer's supplemental escrow instructions. THE MANNER OF TAKING TITLE MAY HAVE SIGNIFICANT LEGAL AND TAX CONSEQUENCES. CONSULT AN APPROPRIATE PROFESSIONAL.
E. Buyer shall receive a CLTA/ALTA Homeowner's Policy of Title Insurance. A title company, at Buyer's request, can provide information about the availability, desirability, coverage, and cost of various title insurance coverages and endorsements. If Buyer desires title coverage other than that required by this paragraph, Buyer shall instruct Escrow Holder in writing and pay any increase in cost.

13. SALE OF BUYER'S PROPERTY:
A. This Agreement is NOT contingent upon the sale of any property owned by Buyer.
OR B. ☐ (If checked): The attached addendum (C.A.R. Form COP) regarding the contingency for the sale of property owned by Buyer is incorporated into this Agreement.

14. TIME PERIODS; REMOVAL OF CONTINGENCIES; CANCELLATION RIGHTS: The following time periods may only be extended, altered, modified or changed by mutual written agreement. Any removal of contingencies or cancellation under this paragraph must be in writing (C.A.R. Form RRCR).
A. SELLER HAS: 7 (or ☐ _____) Days After Acceptance to deliver to Buyer all reports, disclosures and information for which Seller is responsible under paragraphs 4, 5A and B, 6A, 7B and 12.
B. (1) BUYER HAS: 17 (or ☐ _____) Days After Acceptance, unless otherwise agreed in writing, to:
  (i) complete all Buyer Investigations; approve all disclosures, reports and other applicable information, which Buyer receives from Seller; and approve all matters affecting the Property (including lead-based paint and lead-based paint hazards as well as other information specified in paragraph 5 and insurability of Buyer and the Property); and
  (ii) return to Seller Signed Copies of Statutory and Lead Disclosures delivered by Seller in accordance with paragraph 5A.
  (2) Within the time specified in 14B(1), Buyer may request that Seller make repairs or take any other action regarding the Property (C.A.R. Form RR). Seller has no obligation to agree to or respond to Buyer's requests.
  (3) By the end of the time specified in 14B(1) (or 2I for loan contingency or 2J for appraisal contingency), Buyer shall, in writing, remove the applicable contingency (C.A.R. Form RRCR) or cancel this Agreement. However, if the following inspections, reports or disclosures are not made within the time specified in 14A, then Buyer has **5 (or ☐ _____) Days** after receipt of any such items, or the time specified in 14B(1), whichever is later, to remove the applicable contingency or cancel this Agreement in writing: **(i)** government-mandated inspections or reports required as a condition of closing; or **(ii)** Common Interest Disclosures pursuant to paragraph 6B.
C. CONTINUATION OF CONTINGENCY OR CONTRACTUAL OBLIGATION; SELLER RIGHT TO CANCEL:
  (1) Seller right to Cancel; Buyer Contingencies: Seller, after first giving Buyer a Notice to Buyer to Perform (as specified below), may cancel this Agreement in writing and authorize return of Buyer's deposit if, by the time specified in this Agreement, Buyer does not remove in writing the applicable contingency or cancel this Agreement. Once all contingencies have been removed, failure of either Buyer or Seller to close escrow on time may be a breach of this Agreement.
  (2) Continuation of Contingency: Even after the expiration of the time specified in 14B(1), Buyer retains the right to make requests to Seller, remove in writing the applicable contingency or cancel this Agreement until Seller cancels this Agreement pursuant to 14C(1). Once Seller receives Buyer's written removal of all contingencies, Seller may not cancel this Agreement pursuant to 14C(1).
  (3) Seller right to Cancel; Buyer Contract Obligations: Seller, after first giving Buyer a Notice to Buyer to Perform (as specified below), may cancel this Agreement in writing and authorize return of Buyer's deposit for any of the following reasons: **(i)** if Buyer fails to deposit funds as required by 2A or 2B; **(ii)** if the funds deposited pursuant to 2A or 2B are not good when deposited; **(iii)** if Buyer fails to provide a letter as required by 2G; **(iv)** if Buyer fails to provide verification as required by 2H or 2L; **(v)** if Seller reasonably disapproves of the verification provided by 2H or 2L; **(vi)** if Buyer fails to return Statutory and Lead Disclosures as required by paragraph 5A(2); or **(vii)** if Buyer fails to sign or initial a separate liquidated damage form for an increased deposit as required by paragraph 16. **Seller is not required to give Buyer a Notice to Perform regarding Close of Escrow.**
  (4) Notice To Buyer To Perform: The Notice to Buyer to Perform (C.A.R. Form NBP) shall: **(i)** be in writing; **(ii)** be signed by Seller; and **(iii)** give Buyer at least **24 (or ☐ _____)** hours (or until the time specified in the applicable paragraph, whichever occurs last) to take the applicable action. A Notice to Buyer to Perform may not be given any earlier than **2 Days** Prior to the expiration of the applicable time for Buyer to remove a contingency or cancel this Agreement or meet a 14C(3) obligation.

RPA-CA REVISED 10/02 (PAGE 4 OF 8)

Buyer's Initials (_____)(_____)
Seller's Initials (_____)(_____)

Reviewed by _____ Date _____

EQUAL HOUSING OPPORTUNITY

California Residential Purchase Agreement (5 of 8)

Property Address: _____ Date: _____

D. EFFECT OF BUYER'S REMOVAL OF CONTINGENCIES : If Buyer removes, in writing, any contingency or cancellation rights, unless otherwise specified in a separate written agreement between Buyer and Seller, Buyer shall conclusively be deemed to have: **(i)** completed all Buyer Investigations, and review of reports and other applicable information and disclosures pertaining to that contingency or cancellation right; **(ii)** elected to proceed with the transaction; and **(iii)** assumed all liability, responsibility and expense for Repairs or corrections pertaining to that contingency or cancellation right, or for inability to obtain financing.

E. EFFECT OF CANCELLATION ON DEPOSITS: If Buyer or Seller gives written notice of cancellation pursuant to rights duly exercised under the terms of this Agreement, Buyer and Seller agree to Sign mutual instructions to cancel the sale and escrow and release deposits, less fees and costs, to the party entitled to the funds. Fees and costs may be payable to service providers and vendors for services and products provided during escrow. **Release of funds will require mutual Signed release instructions from Buyer and Seller, judicial decision or arbitration award. A party may be subject to a civil penalty of up to $1,000 for refusal to sign such instructions if no good faith dispute exists as to who is entitled to the deposited funds (Civil Code §1057.3).**

15. FINAL VERIFICATION OF CONDITION: Buyer shall have the right to make a final inspection of the Property within **5 (or _____) Days** Prior to Close Of Escrow, NOT AS A CONTINGENCY OF THE SALE, but solely to confirm: **(i)** the Property is maintained pursuant to paragraph 7A; **(ii)** Repairs have been completed as agreed; and **(iii)** Seller has complied with Seller's other obligations under this Agreement.

16. LIQUIDATED DAMAGES: If Buyer fails to complete this purchase because of Buyer's default, Seller shall retain, as liquidated damages, the deposit actually paid. If the Property is a dwelling with no more than four units, one of which Buyer intends to occupy, then the amount retained shall be no more than 3% of the purchase price. Any excess shall be returned to Buyer. Release of funds will require mutual, Signed release instructions from both Buyer and Seller, judicial decision or arbitration award.
BUYER AND SELLER SHALL SIGN A SEPARATE LIQUIDATED DAMAGES PROVISION FOR ANY INCREASED DEPOSIT. (C.A.R. FORM RID)

Buyer's Initials _____/_____	Seller's Initials _____/_____

17. DISPUTE RESOLUTION:

A. MEDIATION: Buyer and Seller agree to mediate any dispute or claim arising between them out of this Agreement, or any resulting transaction, before resorting to arbitration or court action. Paragraphs 17B(2) and (3) below apply whether or not the Arbitration provision is initialed. Mediation fees, if any, shall be divided equally among the parties involved. If, for any dispute or claim to which this paragraph applies, any party commences an action without first attempting to resolve the matter through mediation, or refuses to mediate after a request has been made, then that party shall not be entitled to recover attorney fees, even if they would otherwise be available to that party in any such action. THIS MEDIATION PROVISION APPLIES WHETHER OR NOT THE ARBITRATION PROVISION IS INITIALED.

B. ARBITRATION OF DISPUTES: (1) Buyer and Seller agree that any dispute or claim in Law or equity arising between them out of this Agreement or any resulting transaction, which is not settled through mediation, shall be decided by neutral, binding arbitration, including and subject to paragraphs 17B(2) and (3) below. The arbitrator shall be a retired judge or justice, or an attorney with at least 5 years of residential real estate Law experience, unless the parties mutually agree to a different arbitrator, who shall render an award in accordance with substantive California Law. The parties shall have the right to discovery in accordance with California Code of Civil Procedure §1283.05. In all other respects, the arbitration shall be conducted in accordance with Title 9 of Part III of the California Code of Civil Procedure. Judgment upon the award of the arbitrator(s) may be entered into any court having jurisdiction. Interpretation of this agreement to arbitrate shall be governed by the Federal Arbitration Act.
(2) EXCLUSIONS FROM MEDIATION AND ARBITRATION: The following matters are excluded from mediation and arbitration: **(i)** a judicial or non-judicial foreclosure or other action or proceeding to enforce a deed of trust, mortgage or installment land sale contract as defined in California Civil Code §2985; **(ii)** an unlawful detainer action; **(iii)** the filing or enforcement of a mechanic's lien; and **(iv)** any matter that is within the jurisdiction of a probate, small claims or bankruptcy court. The filing of a court action to enable the recording of a notice of pending action, for order of attachment, receivership, injunction, or other provisional remedies, shall not constitute a waiver of the mediation and arbitration provisions.
(3) BROKERS: Buyer and Seller agree to mediate and arbitrate disputes or claims involving either or both Brokers, consistent with 17 A and B, provided either or both Brokers shall have agreed to such mediation or arbitration prior to, or within a reasonable time after, the dispute or claim is presented to Brokers. Any election by either or both Brokers to participate in mediation or arbitration shall not result in Brokers being deemed parties to the Agreement.

"NOTICE: BY INITIALING IN THE SPACE BELOW YOU ARE AGREEING TO HAVE ANY DISPUTE ARISING OUT OF THE MATTERS INCLUDED IN THE 'ARBITRATION OF DISPUTES' PROVISION DECIDED BY NEUTRAL ARBITRATION AS PROVIDED BY CALIFORNIA LAW AND YOU ARE GIVING UP ANY RIGHTS YOU MIGHT POSSESS TO HAVE THE DISPUTE LITIGATED IN A COURT OR JURY TRIAL. BY INITIALING IN THE SPACE BELOW YOU ARE GIVING UP YOUR JUDICIAL RIGHTS TO DISCOVERY AND APPEAL, UNLESS THOSE RIGHTS ARE SPECIFICALLY INCLUDED IN THE 'ARBITRATION OF DISPUTES' PROVISION. IF YOU REFUSE TO SUBMIT TO ARBITRATION AFTER AGREEING TO THIS PROVISION, YOU MAY BE COMPELLED TO ARBITRATE UNDER THE AUTHORITY OF THE CALIFORNIA CODE OF CIVIL PROCEDURE. YOUR AGREEMENT TO THIS ARBITRATION PROVISION IS VOLUNTARY."

"WE HAVE READ AND UNDERSTAND THE FOREGOING AND AGREE TO SUBMIT DISPUTES ARISING OUT OF THE MATTERS INCLUDED IN THE 'ARBITRATION OF DISPUTES' PROVISION TO NEUTRAL ARBITRATION."

Buyer's Initials _____/_____	Seller's Initials _____/_____

RPA-CA REVISED 10/02 (PAGE 5 OF 8)

Buyer's Initials (_____)(_____)
Seller's Initials (_____)(_____)

Reviewed by _____ Date _____

MASTER COPY

CALIFORNIA RESIDENTIAL PURCHASE AGREEMENT (RPA-CA PAGE 5 OF 8)

Liquidated Damages

http://www.dre.ca.gov
Reference Book, Ch. 22
p. 455

Parties to a contract may decide in advance the amount of damages to be paid, should either party breach the contract. In fact, the offer to purchase, or sales contract, usually contains a printed clause that says the seller may keep the deposit as **Liquidated Damages** if the buyer backs out without good reason.

Option

http://www.dre.ca.gov
Reference Book, Ch. 6
p. 129

An **Option** is a right, given for consideration, to a party (optionee) by a property owner (optionor), to purchase or lease property within a specified time at a specified price and terms. It is a written, unilateral contract between the owner of real property and a prospective buyer, stating the right to purchase, a fixed price and timeframe. The price and all other terms should be stated clearly, as the option will become the sales agreement when the optionee exercises the right to purchase.

The optionee is the only one who has a choice, once the contract is signed and the consideration given. The option does not bind the optionee to any performance. It merely provides the right to demand performance from the optionor, who must sell if the optionee decides to buy the property during the course of the option. If the optionee decides not to buy the property during the term of the option, the consideration remains with the optionor.

The option may be assigned or sold without permission of the optionor during the course of the term, or the optionee may find another buyer for the property to exercise the option.

A real estate agent earns commission on an option when it is exercised.

Post Test

The following self test repeats the one you took at the beginning of this chapter. Now take the exam again—since you have read all the material— and check your knowledge of contracts.

1. Which of the following is an example of a unilateral contract?
   a. listing
   b. option
   c. offer to purchase
   d. rental agreement

2. Escrow instructions were signed by a buyer and seller, stating the selling price for a property, along with several other agreements. As part of the contract, the buyer could cancel the sale if the house did not sell within 45 days. The contract between the buyer and seller is:
   a. voidable
   b. invalid
   c. executory
   d. void

3. Adam, age 17, inherited a farm from his uncle. He sold it immediately, but later changed his mind and decided to cancel the sale. On what grounds could he do that?
   a. as a minor, the contract is void
   b. as a minor, the contract is voidable
   c. as a minor, the contract is unenforceable
   d. he cannot cancel the sale

4. A contract is only valid if:
   a. it is executory
   b. it is unilateral
   c. it is for a legal purpose
   d. it is bilateral

5. A written contract takes precedence over oral agreements. This principle is expressed by:
   a. the parol evidence rule
   b. the Statute of Limitations
   c. the Statute of Frauds
   d. the rule of previous evidence

6. An agreement to do or not to do a certain thing is called:
   a. negotiation
   b. a contract
   c. mutual consent
   d. forbearance

7. When a promise is given by one party with the expectation of performance by the other party, it is known as:
   a. a bilateral contract
   b. a unilateral contract
   c. implied contract
   d. express contract

8. Which of the following is no contract at all?
   a. void contract
   b. voidable contract
   c. unenforceable contract
   d. contract under duress

9. A contract that has been approved is said to be:
   a. rescinded
   b. revoked
   c. ratified
   d. executory

10. Another name for mutual consent is:
    a. implied agreement
    b. executory agreement
    c. unilateral agreement
    d. meeting of the minds

Vocabulary

Read the definition, find the matching term and write the corresponding term number on the line provided.

Terms

1. Action
2. Assignee
3. Assignor
4. Consideration
5. Execute
6. Executory Contract
7. Express Contract
8. Forbearance
9. Novation
10. Offer
11. Offeree
12. Offeror
13. Ratified
14. Rescission
15. Revocation
16. Specific Performance
17. Tender
18. Timely Manner
19. Void
20. Voidable

Definitions

1. ___ Refraining from action by a creditor against the debt owed by a borrower after the debt has become due

2. ___ Something of value—such as money, a promise, property or personal services

3. ___ A presentation or proposal for acceptance to form a contract

4. ___ An action brought in a court to compel a party to carry out the terms of a contract

5. ___ An agreement in which one or more parties may choose to accept the legal obligations created by a contract

6. ___ An act must be performed within certain time limits described in a contract

7. ___ A lawsuit brought to court

8. ___ The party making an offer

9. ___ A contract in which obligation to perform exists on one or both sides of the contract

10. ___ The substitution by agreement of a new obligation for an existing one

11. ___ The person transferring a claim, benefit or right in property to another

12. ___ The parties declare the terms and put their intentions in words, either oral or written

13. ___ An offer by one of the parties to a contract to carry out his or her part of the contract

14. ___ The person to whom a claim, benefit or gift in property is made

15. ___ An agreement which is totally absent of legal effect

16. ___ The cancelling of an offer to contract by the person making the original offer

115

17. ___ To perform or complete; to sign

18. ___ Approved

19. ___ The party receiving an offer

20. ___ Legal action taken to repeal a contract either by mutual consent of the parties or by one party when the other party has breached a contract

Answers

Pre-Test/Post Test

1. b
2. c
3. b
4. c
5. a
6. b
7. b
8. a
9. c
10. d

Vocabulary

1. 8
2. 4
3. 10
4. 16
5. 20
6. 18
7. 1
8. 12
9. 6
10. 9
11. 3
12. 7
13. 17
14. 2
15. 19
16. 15
17. 5
18. 13
19. 11
20. 14

CHAPTER

5

TRANSFER OF OWNERSHIP AND ESCROW

Focus

- **How real estate is acquired or conveyed**

- **Escrow**

- **General escrow principles and rules**

- **Escrow procedures**

- **Termination of an escrow**

- **Rights and obligations of parties to an escrow**

- **Relationship of the escrow holder and real estate agent**

- **Designating the escrow holder**

- **Real Estate Settlement Procedures Act (RESPA)**

- **Title insurance**

Pre-Test

The following is a self test to determine how much you know about transfer of ownership in real property and escrow before reading this chapter. Take it without studying, then read the material presented in the text. At the end of the chapter you will find a repeat of this exam. Test your knowledge by answering the questions again, then check your improvement. (The answers are found at the end of this chapter.) Good luck!

1. All of the following are common uses for a quitclaim deed except:
   - a. family transfers
   - b. divorce settlements
   - c. to clear a cloudy title
   - d. to guarantee clear title to a property

2. A quiet title action is:
   - a. a landlord's action to stop tenants from being noisy
   - b. a court proceeding to clear a cloud on the title to real property
   - c. a court proceeding to settle disputes between co-owners
   - d. a forced sale to satisfy a judgment

3. If a person dies and does not leave a will, that person is known to have died:
   - a. by eminent domain
   - b. intestate
   - c. testate
   - d. in probate

4. Which one of the following instruments transfers title to real property?
   - a. lien
   - b. security instrument
   - c. bill of sale
   - d. grant deed

5. Property may be acquired in all of the following ways except:
   - a. succession
   - b. assessment
   - c. occupancy
   - d. accession

6. In an escrow, who is the neutral party?
   - a. escrow holder
   - b. principal
   - c. real estate broker
   - d. Corporations Commissioner

7. To have a valid escrow, which of the following is not required?
   - a. instructions signed by buyer and seller
   - b. termite clearance
   - c. neutral third party
   - d. conditional delivery of documents to escrow

8. Which of the following may not be a neutral third party to an escrow?
   - a. real estate broker
   - b. principal
   - c. title company
   - d. attorney

9. The term vesting means:
   - a. an outer garment
   - b. how the seller will convey title
   - c. how the buyer will take title
   - d. how pests will be exterminated

10. At the close of escrow, the division of expenses between buyer and seller is known as:
    - a. conciliation
    - b. correlating
    - c. proration
    - d. disbursement

Terms

The following terms are the keys to your success in learning about real estate. Refer to them as you study this chapter for greater understanding of subjects presented here.

Abstract of Title

A summary of all relevant documents discovered in a title search

Accession

The acquisition of title to additional land or to improvements as a result of annexing fixtures or as a result of natural causes such as alluvial deposits along the banks of streams by accretion

Accretion

A buildup of soil by natural causes on property bordering a river, lake or ocean

Acknowledgment

A signed statement, made before a notary public, by a named person confirming the signature on a document and that it was made of free will

Administrator/Administratrix

A person appointed by the court to handle the affairs of a deceased person when there is no one mentioned in a will to do so

Adverse Possession

Acquiring title to property by continued possession and payment of taxes

After Acquired Title

Any benefits that come to a property after a sale must follow the sale and accrue to the new owner

Alienate

Transfer ownership or sell

Alluvial Deposit

Sand or mud, carried by water and deposited on land

Alluvium

Soil that builds up as a result of accretion

A.L.T.A.

American Land Title Association

Avulsion

The sudden washing or tearing away of land by the action of water

Beneficiary Statement

A statement of the unpaid balance of a loan and the condition of the debt, as it relates to a deed of trust

Bequest

A gift of personal property by will; see legacy

Chain of Title

A chronological history of property's ownership

C.L.T.A.

California Land Title Association

Codicil

A change in a will before the maker's death

Convey

To transfer ownership or title

Devise

A gift of real property by will

Erosion

The gradual wearing away of land by natural processes

Escrow

The deposit of funds or documents with a neutral third party who is instructed to carry out the provisions of an agreement

Escrow Holder

An independent third party legally bound to carry out the written provisions of an escrow agreement; a neutral, bonded third party who is a dual agent for the principals; sometimes called an escrow agent

Escrow Instructions

Written directions, signed by a buyer and seller, detailing the procedures necessary to close a transaction and directing the escrow agent how to proceed

Execution

Completion of an act or process, such as an escrow

Executor/Executrix

A person named in a will to handle the affairs of a deceased person

Gift Deed

Used to make a gift of property to a grantee, usually a close friend or relative

Grant Deed

A written instrument that transfers title to real property. Must contain a "granting clause".

Grantee

The person receiving the property, or the one to whom it is being conveyed

Grantor

The person conveying, or transferring, the property

Holographic Will

Written in the maker's own handwriting, dated and signed by the maker

Impound Account

A bank account established by a lender, in the name of a borrower, for the purpose of paying periodic expenses such as property taxes and property insurance. The borrower then makes pre-calculated monthly payments into the account. When the taxes or property insurance are due, the amount is paid from the impound account, usually by the lender.

Instrument

A document in real estate

Intestate

Dying without leaving a will

Legacy

A gift of personal property by will

Love and Affection

Consideration used in a gift deed

Patent Deed

A deed given by the government to a private individual as evidence of title transfer from the government to the private person

Preliminary Title Report

An examination of the public land records to determine the extent to which someone has legal interest in a parcel; a report on the quality of the title that searches for encumbrances and liens or any other items of record that might effect ownership; used as a basis for title insurance

Principal

Someone who directs or authorizes another to act in his or her place regarding relations with third persons; buyer or seller

Private Grant

The granting of private property to other private persons

Proration

The division and distribution of expenses and/or income between the buyer and seller of property as of the date of closing or settlement

Public Dedication

When private property is intended for public use, it may be acquired in this manner

Public Grant

The transfer of title by the government to a private individual

Quitclaim Deed

Transfers any interest the grantor may have at the time the deed is signed with no warranties of clear title

Reconveyance Deed

Conveys title to property from a trustee back to the borrower (trustor) upon payment in full of the debt secured by the trust deed

Reliction

Occurs when land that has been covered by water is exposed by receding water

Sheriff's Deed

A deed given to a buyer when property is sold through court action in order to satisfy a judgment for money or foreclosure of a mortgage

Succession

The legal transfer of a person's interest in real and personal property under the laws of descent

Testator/Testatrix

A person who has made a will

Title Insurance

An insurance policy that protects the named insured against loss or damage due to defect in the property's title

Trust Deed

A security instrument that conveys title to land as security for the payment of a debt

Warranty Deed

No longer used in California; a deed used to transfer title to property, guaranteeing that the title is clear and the grantor has the right to transfer it

Will

A written instrument whereby a person makes a disposition of his property to take effect after his death

Witnessed Will

Will usually prepared by an attorney and signed by the maker and two witnesses

Introduction

Clearly, we need an organized system for keeping track of property ownership: who owns what, and how ownership can be transferred. Of course, the system—which serves you as a real estate agent *and* a consumer—must be totally reliable.

In the preceding chapter, you learned how contracts are used to indicate agreements about real property. Those agreements usually lead to a transfer of interest, which is the subject of this chapter.

In the first part, this chapter covers the ways real property can be transferred and what deeds are used to transfer ownership from one person to another. In the second part, the subject changes to escrow to complete the discussion of how property is transferred.

In California, when ownership transfers from one person to another, there is usually a neutral third party, called an escrow agent, involved in handling the details of the sale. After the principals of a sale make an agreement, an agent normally opens escrow, during which time the agreement between the buyer and the seller is executed. We will study here how that is accomplished.

How Real Estate is Acquired or Conveyed

http://www.dre.ca.gov
Reference Book, Ch. 6
p. 132

Acquisition and conveyance is also defined as "buying and selling." If one person is buying, someone must be selling, so this section studies the two functions together.

Real property may be acquired or conveyed in the following ways: will, accession, succession, transfer and occupancy.

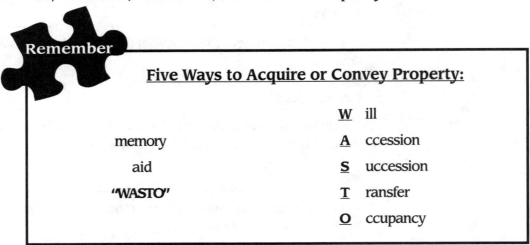

Remember

Five Ways to Acquire or Convey Property:

	W ill
memory	**A** ccession
aid	**S** uccession
"WASTO"	**T** ransfer
	O ccupancy

Will

A **Will** disposes of property after death. One type is a **Witnessed Will**, usually prepared by an attorney and signed by the maker and two witnesses. A **Holographic Will** is written in the maker's own handwriting, dated and signed by the maker.

Probate proceedings are held in the superior court to determine creditors' claims and beneficiaries' interests in an estate upon the death of the owner. A hearing is held and a representative to handle the estate of the deceased is appointed.

If that person is named in a will, he or she is referred to as an **Executor/Executrix**. If there is no will nor anyone named in a will to administer the estate, the court will appoint an **Administrator/Administratrix**. A person who has made a will is known as a **Testator/Testatrix**. A person who dies without making a will is known as having died **Intestate**.

A gift of real property by will is known as a **Devise**, while a gift of personal property by will is known as a **Bequest** or **Legacy**. The maker may, before death, change a will by a **Codicil**.

Estate property may be sold during the probate period. A public auction may be held or the property may be sold privately. An administrator or executor may list the property for up to 90 days with court permission, and the court confirms the final sale and sets the broker's commission. The first offer must be for at least 90% of the appraised value, and a subsequent offer at least 10% of the first $10,000 originally bid, plus 5% of the remainder.

<u>**Sample Probate Bid**</u>

- Appraised value: $100,000
- First bid: at least 90% of appraised value $90,000
- Second bid: at least 10% of first $10,000 $1,000
- plus 5% of the remainder ($80,000) <u>$4,000</u>
- Total minimum second bid required: $95,000

Accession

A process by which there is an addition to property by the efforts of man or nature is called **Accession**. Ownership is extended to include the property that has been gained. The gradual build-up of soil, or **Alluvium**, by natural causes on property bordering a river, lake or ocean is called **Accretion**. **Erosion** is the gradual wearing away of land by natural processes. The sudden washing or tearing away of land by water action is known as **Avulsion**. Accession can occur by **Reliction** when land that has been covered by water is exposed by the water receding, or as a result of alluvial deposits along the banks of streams.

Accession also can occur by the addition of personal property to land so that it becomes a fixture, or by improvements to land made in error. If an improvement was made innocently, the person responsible may remove it, provided he or she pays for any damage to the property.

Succession

When a person inherits property as a result of someone dying without a will, it is called Intestate Succession. An intestate decedent's property passes to his or her heirs according to the laws of descent in the state where such real property is located. The law provides for disposition of the deceased's property by statute.

If the deceased was married, and died intestate—or without a will, the surviving spouse receives all community property. Separate property is divided between a surviving spouse and any children. If there is only one child, the separate property is split equally. If there is more than one child, the surviving spouse receives one-third and the children, two-thirds.

Transfer

Property is acquired by transfer when, by an act of the parties or law, title is **Conveyed**, or passed, from one person to another. The transfer may be voluntary, such as the sale of a home, or involuntary by act of law, such as a foreclosure sale. Real property may be transferred, or **Alienated**—as it is called, by private grant, public grant, public dedication or operation of law (court action).

Private Grant

http://www.dre.ca.gov
Reference Book, Ch. 7
p. 139

Grant Deed: When property is transferred by **Private Grant** the **Instrument** usually used is a **Grant Deed**. The parties involved are the **Grantor**, or the person conveying the property, and the **Grantee**, the person receiving the property or to whom it is being conveyed.

Grant Deed:

- A written document that transfers title to real property.
- Must contain a "granting clause".

A grant deed contains two implied warranties by the grantor. One is that the grantor has not already conveyed title to any other person, and the other is that the estate is free from encumbrances other than those disclosed by the grantor.

The grantor also promises to deed any rights he or she might acquire to the property after conveying it to the grantee. For example, oil or mineral rights might revert to the property at some time in the future, after the present owner has sold the property. **After Acquired Title** means any benefits that come to the property after a sale must follow the sale and accrue to the new owner.

A grant deed must contain certain basics in order to be legally binding.

Requirements for a Valid Grant Deed:

- In writing—according to the Statute of Frauds
- Parties identified: the parties to the transfer (grantor and grantee) sufficiently described
- Competent to convey: the grantor must be competent to convey the property (not a minor or incompetent)
- Capable of holding title: the grantee must be capable of holding title (must be a real living person, not fictitious)
- Adequately described: the property being conveyed must be adequately described
- Words of granting: words to indicate the act of granting (grant, convey) must be included
- Signed: the deed must be signed by the grantor
- Delivered to and accepted by the grantee

A grant deed is not effective until it is delivered. It must be the intention of the grantor that the deed be delivered and title be transferred during his or her lifetime. For example, a deed would not be valid if signed and put in a safe place until the death of the grantor, and then recorded. **Recording** a deed is considered the same as delivery. After a deed has been acknowledged, by the grantor, it may be filed with the county recorder, giving **Constructive Notice** of the sale. An **Acknowledgment** is a signed statement, made before a notary public, by a named person confirming that the signature on a document is genuine and that it was made of free will. A deed does not have to be acknowledged to be valid, but must be acknowledged to be recorded.

The purpose of recording a deed is to protect the **Chain of Title**, which is a sequential record of changes in ownership showing the connection from one owner to the next. A complete chain of title is desirable whenever property is transferred and required by title insurance companies if they are writing a policy on a property.

Jane Borden, a single woman, owned the house in which she lived, as her sole and separate property. After marrying Sam Jones, she decided to sell the house. However, because the chain of the title showed that Jane Borden owned it, reference had to be made, in the grant deed to the buyer, that Jane Jones, a married woman, previously known as Jane Borden, was conveying her interest in the property. In that way the chain of title remained unbroken.

The priority of a deed is determined by the date it is recorded. In other words, recording establishes a claim of ownership which has priority over any deeds recorded after it. The first to record a deed is the first in right.

Cal sells his house to Margaret, and, without telling Margaret, also sells it to Anita. Anita records her deed before Margaret has a chance to record hers. Anita is the owner of record and gets the house. Margaret has a definite cause for a lawsuit against Cal.

However, there are some exceptions to the "first to record is first in right" rule. If the same property is sold to two parties, where the second party knows of the first sale and is aware of the fraud intended by the seller, the original sale is valid, even if it was not recorded first.

Also, as you recall, possession is considered constructive notice, just like recording. So, if a deed is not recorded, but the buyer moves in, that sale has priority over later recorded deeds.

Greta sells her house to Victor, who moves in without recording the deed. Greta also sells the house to Alex, telling him to record the deed quickly, making him aware that she had previously sold it to Victor. In this case, Victor gets the house because of Alex's knowledge of the prior sale and also because of Victor's possession of the property (he had moved in), which established his right of ownership.

A grantee must accept a deed before it is considered effective. Acceptance is automatic if the grantee is an infant or incompetent person. Acceptance may be shown by the acts of the grantee, such as moving onto the property.

The grant deed need not be signed by the grantee. An undated, unrecorded and unacknowledged grant deed may be valid as long as it contains the essential items noted in the requirements box on page 126.

Grant Deed

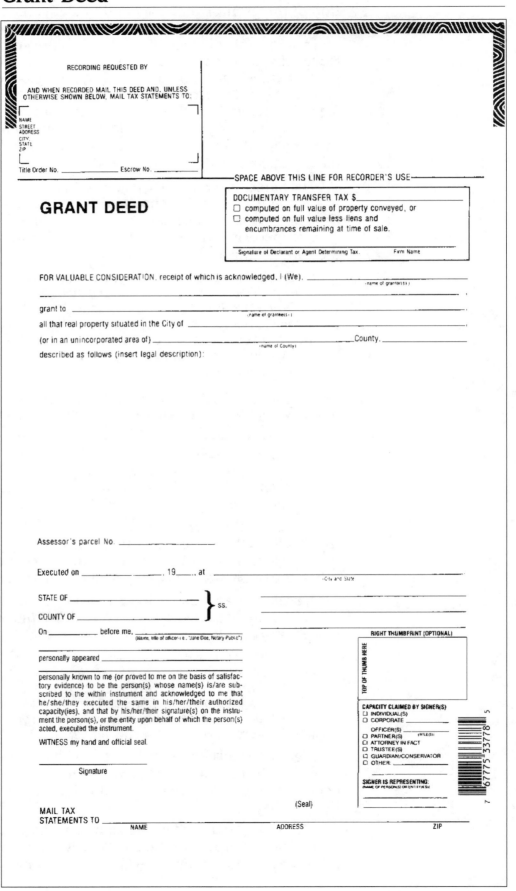

Here is a list of non-essentials for a grant deed to be valid.

Not Necessary for Valid Grant Deed:

- Acknowledgment
- Competent grantee; may be a minor, felon or incompetent
- Date
- Legal description
- Mention of the consideration
- Recording
- Signature of grantee

Quitclaim Deed

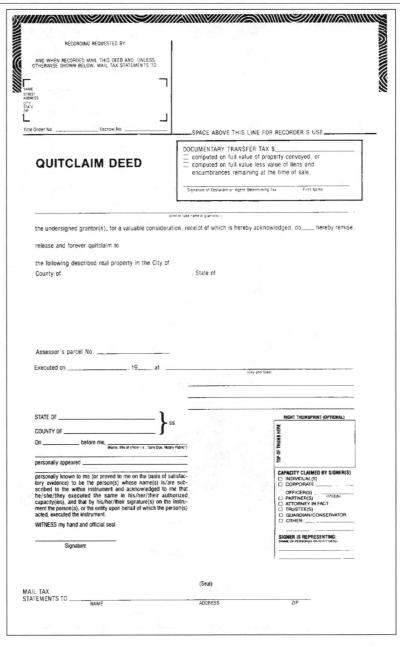

Quitclaim Deed: Another type of deed used to transfer property is a **Quitclaim Deed**. This type of deed is commonly used to transfer interests between husband and wife or to terminate an easement. A quitclaim deed transfers any interest the grantor may have at the time the deed is signed with no warranties of clear title. A quitclaim deed is often used to clear a cloud on the title; there might be a minor defect in the chain of title which needs to be removed.

Warranty Deed: A **Warranty Deed** is one which contains express covenants of title. In other words, the seller who uses a warranty deed to transfer the property title to a buyer is guaranteeing clear title as well as the right to transfer it. Rarely is it used in California because title companies have taken over the role of insuring title to property.

Trust Deed: A **Trust Deed** (or Deed of Trust) is a security instrument that conveys title to a trustee to hold as security for the payment of a debt. There are three parties to a trust deed: the borrower (trustor), lender (beneficiary) and a neutral third party called a trustee. The only interest conveyed to the trustee is bare legal title, and the only obligation is to foreclose if there is a default on the loan, or reconvey the title to the borrower when the debt is paid in full. Trust deeds are discussed at length in Chapter 8.

Reconveyance Deed: A **Reconveyance Deed** conveys title to property from a trustee back to the borrower (trustor) upon payment in full of the debt secured by the trust deed.

Sheriff's Deed: A **Sheriff's Deed** is given to a buyer when property is sold through court action in order to satisfy a judgment for money or foreclosure of a mortgage.

Gift Deed: A **Gift Deed** is used to make a gift of property to a grantee, usually a close friend or relative. The consideration in a gift deed is called **Love and Affection**.

Remember

The Seven Kinds of Deeds for Private Grants

- Grant Deed
- Quitclaim Deed
- Warranty Deed
- Trust Deed
- Reconveyance Deed
- Sheriff's Deed
- Gift Deed

Public Grant

Real property can be transferred by **Public Grant**. An example of a public grant is the transfer of title by the government to a private individual. In the last century many people moved west and improved land by building and planting. As they qualified for ownership under the homestead laws, they received a **Patent Deed** from the government as proof of ownership.

Public Dedication

When real property is intended for public use, it may be acquired as a **Public Dedication**. Dedication may be by common law dedication, statutory dedication or deed.

Three Means of Public Dedication

Common Law Dedication

- An owner implies through conduct the intention that the public use the land

Statutory Dedication

- This is a dedication by a private individual to the public. An owner follows procedures outlined in the Subdivision Map Act— commonly used by developers to dedicate streets and common areas to the public.

Deed

- This is a formal transfer by a party as in a gift deed where there is no consideration.

Operation of Law

Sometimes property is transferred by the operation of law. It is usually an involuntary transfer involving foreclosure or is the result of a judgment or some other lien against the title.

When transfer of title occurs involuntarily, the courts may get involved for the following reasons:

1. *Quiet Title Action:* A court proceeding to clear a cloud on the title of real property

2. *Partition Action:* A court proceeding to settle a dispute between co-owners about dividing their interests in real property

3. *Foreclosure Action:* Public sale after default on a loan occurs and the statutory time requirements have been met

4. *Execution Sale:* Forced sale to satisfy a judgment

5. *Bankruptcy Sale:* Sale of property to satisfy creditors

6. *Escheat:* Reverting of property to the state after five years when there are no heirs of a deceased person

7. *Eminent Domain:* Power of the government to take over private property for the public good after paying just compensation to the owner; sometimes known as **Condemnation**

Occupancy

A final way to acquire property is through **Occupancy**.

Abandonment is one way to effect the transfer of property. For example, a tenant may abandon the lease voluntarily and the landlord reacquires possession.

Adverse Possession also can effect a transfer. It is accomplished by acquiring title to property through continued possession and payment of taxes. There are five requirements:

1. The possession must be by actual occupation, and be open and notorious.

2. It must be hostile to the present owner's title and wishes.

3. It must be under a claim of right or color of title. In other words, there has to be some reasonable right to a claim of adverse possession.

4. Possession must be continuous and uninterrupted for five years.

5. Claimant must have paid all real property taxes for five continuous years.

In our study of easements in the previous chapter, we considered their creation by prescription. If you recall, prescription is the process of acquiring an interest, not ownership, in a certain property. The method used for acquiring property rights through prescription is much like that used for adverse possession.

The main difference is the payment of taxes. Adverse possession requires the payment of taxes for five continuous years, while prescription does not. Also remember, one acquires title to property through adverse possession, but only a specified interest in property through prescription.

Escrow

http://www.dre.ca.gov
Reference Book, Ch. 8
p. 147

For a large number of people, escrow is a mysterious, obscure process. They don't know what "going to escrow" means, nor how you "open an escrow." There is no real mystery about it, however. An **Escrow** is a time period during which the paperwork required for the sale of real property is processed. An **Escrow Holder**, otherwise known as an escrow company, or some other eligible person, acts as a neutral agent of both buyer and seller. The escrow holder follows the directions of the principals and collects and distributes documents and money as agreed upon in the purchase agreement.

If escrow instructions are drawn, they must reflect the understanding and agreement of the **Principals**, who may not always be a buyer and seller, since transactions involving the sale of real estate are not the only kind that require the use of an escrow. Any time a neutral third party is needed to handle documents or money, such as leases, sales of personal property, sales of securities, loans, or mobile home sales, an escrow might be required. For the purpose of this chapter, we will discuss escrow as it relates to the sale of real estate.

No one is required by law to use an escrow for any of the above transactions, including the sale of real property. However, when a buyer and seller reach an agreement about the sale of property, including terms and price, it is usually advisable to invite a neutral third party to handle the details of completing the agreement.

Misunderstanding, or even criminal or innocent negligence, on the part of the principals could be the cause of loss to one or both parties if the contract is not handled by an outside professional whose business it is to conduct escrows.

After escrow is opened, it is the escrow holder's job to follow the buyer's and seller's instructions and request all parties involved to observe the terms and conditions of the contract. The escrow holder coordinates communication between the principals, the agents involved and any other professionals —such as the lender, title company or pest control company, whose services are called for in the instructions.

So an escrow is a small and short-lived trust arrangement. The principals trust that the escrow holder will carry out their wishes, and the escrow holder has a duty to be trustworthy, as the agent of both parties. As a neutral third party, the escrow holder may only operate at the direction of all parties to a transaction. We shall see in this chapter how that is accomplished.

Basic Requirements For a Valid Binding Contract

An escrow must include the following to be valid: a binding contract between the buyer and seller, and conditional delivery of transfer documents to a third party. The binding contract can be an offer to purchase (deposit receipt), agreement of sale, exchange agreement, option or mutual escrow instructions of the buyer and seller.

Purchase Agreement as Escrow Instructions

A new approach to conducting escrow is to use the purchase agreement as escrow instructions. The California Association of Realtors (CAR) created a new form in 2000 (Form RPA-11, known as the Residential Purchase Agreement and Joint Escrow Instructions) that seems to offer the best of all approaches to the escrow process.

In an effort to make escrow all over the state more conforming and less redundant and repetitive, the form combines the strength of the offer to purchase and escrow instructions into one contract.

Because the purchase agreement *is* the original agreement between the buyer and seller, it will reflect the mutual and agreed upon desires of the parties when it becomes the actual escrow instructions. Any mutual changes are made using an addendum to the original contract rather than amendments to escrow instructions.

An escrow is opened when a real estate agent brings the signed purchase agreement to the escrow holder, who makes a copy and accepts it by signing off in the required box in the document (RPA-11, page 8). The escrow holder should be concerned with whether or not the contract is complete, fully signed and initialed before accepting it. It must be a valid contract before becoming instructions for the escrow.

In addition to the purchase agreement as escrow instructions, an escrow holder will submit acceptance or additional escrow instructions for buyer and seller signature. These instructions will include any other terms that need to be agreed upon by buyer and seller to complete the escrow.

Conditional Delivery

A conditional delivery of transfer documents and funds, the second requirement for a valid escrow, means the seller will deliver a signed grant deed which conveys the title to the buyer, and the buyer and/or the lender will deliver to escrow whatever funds are required for the sale.

Also, the escrow agent will hold the security for any loan (trust deed) conditionally until directed by the terms of the escrow. The escrow agent will keep documents and funds until all other terms of the escrow have been completed, and then distribute them according to the expressed conditions of the escrow.

Sometime before the escrow closes, the seller will be asked to sign a grant deed conveying title to the buyer. Because the seller will sign over the ownership to the buyer before getting the money, the escrow holder is instructed to hold the signed deed until funds from the buyer are deposited in escrow and all the other terms of the escrow have been met. Conditional delivery of the grant deed has been made.

Toward the end of the escrow period, the buyer will be asked to sign a note and trust deed for the loan. The buyer is promising to pay back the money, using the property as security for the loan. Escrow has not closed, and the buyer doesn't own the house yet. Nor has the seller been given the promised money, but the note and trust deed are signed and deposited into escrow, conditionally, until all other terms have been met. At that time the money will be released by the lender to escrow.

After the escrow has been completed, the buyer gets a grant deed, after it has been recorded, and the seller gets the money. The escrow closes shortly thereafter.

General Escrow Principles and Rules

Once escrow instructions or the purchase agreement as escrow instructions have been signed by the buyer and seller and returned to the escrow holder, neither party may unilaterally change the escrow instructions. Any changes must be made by mutual agreement between the buyer and seller. The escrow agent does not have the authority to make changes in the contract upon the direction of either the buyer or seller, unless both agree to the change in the form of an amendment or addendum to the purchase agreement.

Also, it should be noted, the broker has no authority whatsoever to amend or change any part of the escrow instructions without the knowledge of the principals. The written consent of both buyer and seller, in the form of an amendment to the original instructions or an addendum to the purchase agreement, must be given before any change may be made.

The Clarks and the Marshalls signed escrow instructions on June 9. The agreement reflected a sales price of $450,000, with $90,000 as a down payment. After signing the instructions, however, the buyers decided they only wanted to put $80,000 down, and told the escrow officer to change the instructions. An amendment was written for them to sign, and a copy sent to the sellers to sign.

The buyers were disappointed when the Clarks did not want to change the contract and refused to sign the amendment. When the Marshalls wanted to back out, the escrow officer reminded them that they had a mutually binding legal agreement with the sellers. Neither side could change any part of the agreement, including terminating it, without the written agreement of the other.

As agent for both parties to an escrow, the escrow agent is placed in a position of trust. By operating as a dual agent, the escrow holder sits between the buyer and seller as a stakeholder with an obligation to both sides. As a neutral third party, the escrow officer must observe the following rules:

1. Escrow instructions must be understood by the principals to the escrow and must be mutually binding. Carefully written instructions, or the offer to purchase are very clear about the agreement between the buyer and seller. Each party must understand his or her obligation to carry out the terms of the contract without assuming the escrow holder has any power to force compliance. The escrow holder may not act unless directed by the principals.

2. The escrow holder does not get personally involved in disagreements between the buyer and seller, nor act as a negotiator for the principals. Escrow instructions make each party's obligations and agreements clear, and it is up to the buyer and seller to keep the promises they each made in their agreement with the other.

3. An escrow agent usually is not an attorney, and must advise anyone seeking legal advice to get counsel from a professional.

4. An escrow agent has a limited capacity as agent for buyer and seller, and may only perform acts described in the contents of escrow instructions. While acting as a dual agent, the escrow officer must operate in the best interests of both parties, without special preference to either. The escrow agent may serve each principal after escrow closes, in dealing with their separate interests.

5. All parties must sign escrow instructions or the offer to purchase as escrow instructions for the contract to be binding. An escrow is officially open when both buyer and seller have signed the instructions and delivered them to escrow.

6. If separate escrow instructions are written, they must be clear and certain in their language. When there is a conflict between the signed instructions and the original agreement of the principals, the signed instructions will prevail as long as they reflect the intent of the parties.

7. All documents to be recorded must be sent to the title company in a timely manner (as quickly as possible), and all interested parties should receive copies of recorded documents.

8. Escrow instructions should specify which documents or funds the escrow holder may accept.

9. Overdrawn escrow trust accounts (debit balances) are prohibited by law.

10. Information regarding any transaction is held in trust by the escrow officer and may not be released to anyone without written permission of the principals.

11. An escrow holder has a duty to disclose to the principals any previously undisclosed information that might affect them. An amendment would be drawn at the direction of the buyer and seller to reflect any change as a result of new disclosures.

12. A high degree of trust, good customer service and relations must be provided by an escrow holder.

13. An escrow holder must remain strictly neutral regarding the buyer's and the seller's interests.

14. Escrow records and files must be maintained daily. A systematic review of open escrow files will make sure no procedure has been overlooked, or time limit ignored.

15. Before closing an escrow, all files must be audited carefully.

16. All checks or drafts must have cleared before any funds may be released to the seller.

17. Escrow must close in a timely manner, according to the agreement between buyer and seller. A prompt settlement must be made to all principals.

Escrow Procedures

Escrow procedures may vary according to local custom. In some areas of California, escrow companies or banks conduct escrows. In other areas, title companies do the job. However, there are certain procedures that are followed during the regular course of all escrows.

Open Escrow

The person who usually opens escrow, if there is a real estate agent involved, is the selling agent. That person usually has an earnest money check that must be deposited into escrow or some other trust account no more than three business days after buyer and seller have signed the deposit receipt.

So, at the first opportunity, the real estate agent must take the buyer's check to the escrow officer to put in a trust account. The agent then gives the escrow officer all the information needed to draw escrow instructions, or may give the escrow holder the original signed purchase agreement which then becomes the escrow instructions. If instructions are being drawn, usually within a day or two, computer-generated instructions will be ready for the buyer and seller to sign. The instructions, as you recall, reflect the agreement between the buyer and seller as seen in the offer to purchase.

The principals may go to the escrow office if there is no real estate agent involved, and tell the escrow officer to prepare instructions according to their agreement.

Prepare Escrow Instructions

When escrow instructions are drawn, the escrow holder prepares them on a computer-generated form, with details of the particular transaction completed in the blank spaces on the form. All parties sign identical instructions, with the exception of the commission agreement that is prepared for the seller to sign—if the seller in fact is paying the commission. Buyer and seller sign the instructions, which are then returned to the escrow holder who follows the directions in the agreement to complete the escrow.

Imagine you are involved in the sale of your home. The following would probably be included in your escrow instructions or purchase agreement.

In California, the purchase agreement becomes the escrow instructions. The escrow is officially opened when the escrow holder accepts the purchase agreement that has been signed by all parties to the escrow.

1. *Purchase Price:* This is the amount of money the buyer and seller have agreed upon for the sale of the property.

2. *Terms:* This is where the buyer and seller agree on how the buyer will purchase the property; cash, new loan, loan assumption, V.A. or FHA loan, seller to carry a trust deed, trade, or any other special agreements provided in the contract between buyer and seller. This is the section that describes the amount of the down payment and the terms of any loans for which the buyer will apply.

3. *Vesting:* The buyer will take title in one of the following ways: sole ownership, joint tenancy, tenants in common, or tenancy in partnership. How the buyer will take title may be important for tax or inheritance purposes and the escrow holder must be directed how to draw the deed to reflect the wishes of the buyer.

4. *Matters of Record:* Buyer and seller may agree on some matter of record or, in other words, some matter that is recorded, affecting the property. It may be an easement, an existing street bond or a trust deed. An agreement may be made about who will be respon-

sible for whatever exists as a recorded encumbrance on the title at the time of the sale.

5. *Closing*: Buyer and seller will agree on how long they want the escrow to last. They will mention a specific length of time for the escrow and instruct the escrow holder accordingly.

6. *Inspections*: Buyer and seller will agree on whether or not to have certain inspections of the property before the close of escrow, such as a pest control inspection, property inspection to identify any plumbing, electrical or structural problems, a soil inspection to check for slippage or unstable compaction. The buyer's approval of the reports will be a contingency of the sale and must be mentioned in the escrow instructions.

7. *Prorations*: The division of expenses and income between the buyer and seller as of the date of closing is known as **Proration**. Some items that are prorated are: taxes, rental deposits or income, insurance premiums. The reason for prorations is that some payments may have been made by the seller for a time period beyond the agreed upon date of closing of escrow. Or the seller may be in arrears on taxes or insurance. The escrow holder debits or credits the seller or buyer, depending on the escrow closing date. Normally, prorations are based on a 30 day month and a 360 day year.

8. *Possession*: The buyer and seller will have agreed on when the buyer can move into the house, and the escrow instructions must reflect their agreement on the date the buyer will take possession of the property. The close of escrow could be the date of possession, or sometimes the seller will rent the property back from the buyer after the close of escrow. In that case, a lease agreement should be signed and deposited in escrow.

9. *Documents*: The escrow holder will need to know which documents to prepare, have signed by the proper party, and record at the close of escrow. Usually, these will be a grant deed and a trust deed.

10. *Disbursements*: The escrow holder must settle the accounts of the buyer and seller according to the escrow instructions. A closing statement of costs and charges to each party and a final distribution of funds also is done by the escrow holder at the close of escrow.

Order Title Search

At the time the buyer and seller reached an agreement about the sale of the property, they also selected a title company. One of the jobs of the escrow officer, after escrow has been opened, is to order a search of the title of the subject property.

In the preliminary title search, the title company searches the records for any encumbrances or liens against the property, checks to make sure the seller is the owner of record, and inspects the history of ownership, or chain of title. After completing this search, the title company prepares a Preliminary Title Report. The purpose is to ensure all transfers of ownership have been recorded correctly, that there are no unexplained gaps and that there are no liens or encumbrances which will not be released.

The buyer is allowed a certain number of days to approve this preliminary title report. Buyer approval is important to eliminate surprises regarding the title as the escrow progresses. The escrow holder should notify the buyer and seller if there is any difference in the preliminary report and the escrow instructions, by way of an addendum "for information only."

As you recall, the escrow agent is a neutral party and only has the authority to do what is described in the escrow instructions. The escrow officer must wait for instructions about what to do next. The preliminary title report is the foundation for the title insurance policy insuring the buyer's title as instructed by the buyer and seller in the escrow instructions.

The Clarks and the Marshalls had instructed their escrow officer to order a preliminary title search. The Marshalls had three days to approve the report, as a contingency of the sale. When they examined it, however, they found there was a bond against the property for street repairs. They had not been aware of it.

The bond was a lien in the amount of $3,500. The buyers could not approve the preliminary title report until the issue was cleared up. An agreement about who would pay the bond had to be reached by the buyers and sellers, then new instructions given to the escrow officer, who would prepare an amendment for both parties' signatures, to indicate their agreement.

Request Demands and/or Beneficiary Statements

The escrow officer must also see that existing loans are paid off, or assumed, depending on the agreement of the buyer and seller.

If the existing loan, or the seller's debt, is going to be paid off with proceeds from the sale, a demand from the lender holding the note and trust deed is needed, along with the unpaid principal balance and any other amounts that are due. The escrow officer requests a demand for pay-off of a loan from the lender who holds a loan against the subject property. The exact amount of loans that are to be paid off must be known so the escrow officer's accounting will be correct at the close of escrow.

If an existing loan is going to be assumed, or taken "subject to," a **Beneficiary Statement** is requested by the escrow holder from the lender. A statement of the unpaid balance of a loan, the beneficiary statement also describes the condition of the debt.

The escrow agent follows instructions about financing the property, and prepares any documents necessary for completing the escrow at the close. These might be a note and trust deed, or assumption papers.

The buyers are obtaining an adjustable loan in the amount of $360,000. The down payment will be $90,000, to make the purchase price of $450,000. The existing $250,000 loan on the property is held by Union Bank. The existing loan will be paid off when the buyer's new loan is funded, and the seller will get the remainder of $110,000 along with the down payment.

Union Bank is notified of the expected pay-off and asked by the escrow officer to send a statement of the unpaid balance and condition of the existing loan. This is known as a request for demand for pay-off.

Other Reports

The parties to an escrow may request any number of reports about the condition of the property. The escrow holder is asked in the instructions to accept any reports submitted into escrow. These may include a structural pest control report (termite report), property inspection report, soil condition report or environmental report. Any approval from the buyer or seller about a report is held in escrow until needed, or given to the appropriate party at the close of escrow.

New Loan Instructions and Documents

Escrow accepts loan documents or instructions about financing the subject property and completes them as directed. The escrow agent gets the buyer's approval of and signature on loan documents and receives and disburses loan funds as instructed.

Fire Insurance Policies

The parties to an escrow will have agreed on fire insurance policies and will instruct the escrow officer accordingly. The escrow holder will accept, hold and deliver any policies and will follow instructions about transferring them. A lender will require fire insurance, and will expect the escrow holder and the buyer to be accountable for either a new policy or the transfer of an existing one.

Settlement

The escrow holder will be instructed by the buyer and seller about prorations and other accounting to be done at the close of escrow.

> ### Prorations Normally Include:
>
> - Interest
> - Premiums on fire insurance
> - Security deposits and rents (if the property is a rental)
> - Seller's current property taxes

The buyer and seller will have agreed on impound accounts, and the escrow holder will be guided on how to handle the credit and debit. After the escrow agent completes the accounting, the agent tells the buyer to deliver the down payment (usually a cashier's check is required), plus other escrow costs, to the escrow office.

At this time, the buyers sign the loan documents, and any other paperwork required for the financing is completed. If all is in order, the loan will be funded and the money sent to the escrow office along with the buyer's funds. Then the escrow may close.

Audit File

At the close of escrow, the escrow officer must examine each file to make sure all accounting has been accurate, and that escrow instructions have been followed. A cash reconciliation statement is completed by the escrow holder and closing statements are prepared for all principals.

Recording

The escrow holder records all transaction documents as instructed by the buyer and seller after a final check of the title company records to be sure nothing has changed since the preliminary title search was done. Then the title company will issue a policy of title insurance to insure the buyer's title. Documents that might require recording are the grant deed, trust deed, contract of sale or option.

Close Escrow

The last job of the escrow holder is to close the escrow. The escrow officer gives closing statements to buyer and seller, disburses all money and delivers all documents to the proper parties after making sure all documents have been recorded by the title company. The seller gets a check for the proceeds of the sale minus escrow fees, real estate commissions, loan payoffs and all other costs of selling, and any pertinent documents; and the buyer gets a grant deed.

Termination of an Escrow

Full performance, by completion of the escrow, terminates the escrow. The authority to conduct an escrow is mutually given by the buyer and seller in the escrow instructions and may be terminated by mutual agreement. Neither party may end the escrow without the agreement of the other, in writing. Also, the escrow officer may not return any funds or documents to either party without agreement from all parties.

During the escrow, the escrow officer is an agent for both buyer and seller, as you recall, and must operate from the original escrow instructions. When they instruct the escrow agent to prepare an amendment cancelling the escrow, a buyer and seller mutually end their agreement after they have both signed the amendment.

Rights and Obligations of the Parties to an Escrow

A buyer and a seller are known as principals in an escrow. The escrow holder is a neutral third party who is a dual agent for buyer and seller. A real estate agent is not a party to an escrow unless he or she is the buyer or the seller.

A buyer is the party purchasing the property and who will receive a deed conveying the title.

A seller is the owner of record who must deliver the title agreed upon in the contract.

An escrow agent is an impartial third party who collects all documents and money, through the escrow, and transfers them to the proper parties at the close of escrow.

An escrow agent may be a bank, savings and loan, title insurance company, attorney, real estate broker or an escrow company. A real estate broker may act as an escrow agent in the course of a regular transaction for which a real estate license is necessary. The broker may conduct the escrow as a service only if he or she is the listing or selling broker to the subject sale.

Escrow Companies Must be Incorporated

The Commissioner of Corporations licenses escrow companies, but does not allow individuals to apply. Only a corporation is qualified and must make an application. A bond based upon predicted yearly average transactions and trust fund use must be furnished by an applicant for an escrow office license. A bond must be posted by all parties (officers, directors, trustees and employees) having access to money or securities being held by the escrow company as safety against loss. Exempt from Commissioner of Corporation licensing are banks, savings and loans, title insurance companies, attorneys and real estate brokers.

Audit

An escrow company must keep accounts and records which can be examined by the Commissioner of Corporations. A yearly inspection prepared by an independent certified public accountant, describing operations, must be delivered to the Commissioner.

Prohibitions

- Referral fees may not be paid by an escrow company to anyone as a reward for sending business to them.
- Commissions may not be paid to a real estate broker until the closing of an escrow.
- Blank escrow instructions to be filled in after signing are not acceptable. Initials must be placed wherever there is a change or deletion.
- Information regarding an escrow may only be provided to parties to the escrow.
- Copies of escrow instructions must be provided to anyone signing them.

Agency

An escrow agent holds a limited agency, or authority. Any duties to be conducted must be mentioned specifically in escrow instructions or they are not authorized by the buyer and seller. The escrow holder must remain neutral, as the agent of both the buyer and seller, during the course of the escrow. After all conditions of the escrow have been met, the escrow officer is the agent of each of the parties in dealing with their individual needs.

Relationship of the Escrow Holder and the Real Estate Agent

No transaction can be completed without a good relationship between a broker and an escrow agent. The goodwill, positive guidance and technical knowledge of an escrow officer has helped many brokers to get through an escrow, especially those new to the business.

After the real estate broker negotiates the sale, it is the job of the escrow agent to see that the agreements made by the parties are carried out. The broker and the escrow agent must check with each other regularly to make sure information is correct and to inform each other of how the escrow is progressing.

Designating the Escrow Holder

The choice of an escrow agent is always that of the buyer and seller. However, they probably do not have a relationship with an escrow agent, and may rely on the advice of their real estate broker.

Real Estate Settlement Procedures Act (RESPA)

http://www.hsh.com/
pamphlets/s

The Real Estate Settlement Procedures Act (RESPA) is a federal loan disclosure law applicable to first mortgage loans on residential property. It requires certain disclosures to borrowers and provides the consumer with information on settlement costs. A special information booklet and good-faith estimate of costs must be given to a borrower when he or she applies for a loan.

Almost all lenders fall under RESPA, except for loans made by private parties. Violators of this law can be penalized by up to one year in jail and/or a $10,000 fine.

Title Insurance

The job of title insurance companies is to ensure the clear title of property. They search existing public records to make sure the chain of title is correct. If there is a missing connection in a property's history or ownership, or if a deed was recorded in error or is incomplete, the title company will notify escrow.

Any problems that arise may be corrected during the escrow period. Then the new owner gets a clear title. A summary of all useful documents discovered in a title search is known as an Abstract of Title.

http://www.alta.org

A marketable title is guaranteed because of title insurance, and a new owner is protected against recorded and unrecorded matters. There are two types of title insurance that are normally used:

1. *Standard Policy of Title Insurance,* California Land Title Association (C.L.T.A.). This is the type of policy usually issued to home buyers. No physical inspection of the property is required and the buyer is protected against all recorded matters, and certain risks such as forgery and incompetence.

http://yosemitetitle.com/
cgi-bin/h-lib.pl

2. *Extended Coverage Policy,* American Land Title Association (A.L.T.A.). All risks covered by a standard policy are covered by this policy, plus other unrecorded hazards, such as outstanding mechanic's liens, unrecorded physical easements, facts a correct survey would show, certain water claims, and rights of parties in possession—including tenants and owners under unrecorded deeds. The Extended Coverage Policy is used to protect lenders, and most title insurance companies now offer an owner's extended coverage policy.

Post Test

The following self test repeats the one you took at the beginning of this chapter. Now take the exam again—since you have read all the material—and check your knowledge of transferring ownership in real property and escrow:

1. All of the following are common uses for a quitclaim deed except:
   a. family transfers
   b. divorce settlements
   c. to clear a cloudy title
   d. to guarantee clear title to a property

2. A quiet title action is:
   a. a landlord's action to stop tenants from being noisy
   b. a court proceeding to clear a cloud on the title to real property
   c. a court proceeding to settle disputes between co-owners
   d. a forced sale to satisfy a judgment

3. If a person dies, and does not leave a will, that person is known to have died:
   a. by eminent domain
   b. intestate
   c. testate
   d. in probate

4. Which one of the following instruments transfers title to real property?
   a. lien
   b. security instrument
   c. bill of sale
   d. grant deed

5. Property may be acquired in all of the following ways except:
   a. succession
   b. assessment
   c. occupancy
   d. accession

6. In an escrow, who is the neutral party?
   a. escrow holder
   b. principal
   c. real estate broker
   d. Corporations Commissioner

7. To have a valid escrow, which of the following is not required?
   a. instructions signed by buyer and seller
   b. termite clearance
   c. neutral third party
   d. conditional delivery of documents to escrow

8. Which of the following may not be a neutral third party to an escrow?
   a. real estate broker
   b. principal
   c. title company
   d. attorney

9. The term vesting means:
   a. an outer garment
   b. how the seller will convey title
   c. how the buyer will take title
   d. how pests will be exterminated

10. At the close of escrow, the division of expenses between buyer and seller is known as:
    a. conciliation
    b. correlating
    c. proration
    d. disbursement

Vocabulary

Read the definition, find the matching term and write the corresponding term number on the line provided.

Terms

1. Accession
2. Accretion
3. Acknowledgment
4. Administrator/Administratrix
5. Alienate
6. Alluvium
7. Avulsion
8. Bequest
9. Codicil
10. Convey
11. Devise
12. Executor/Executrix
13. Grantee
14. Grantor
15. Instrument
16. Intestate
17. Principal
18. Proration
19. Reliction
20. Succession

Definitions

1. ___ A person named in a will to handle the affairs of a deceased person

2. ___ A person appointed by the court to handle the affairs of a deceased person when there is no one mentioned in a will to do so

3. ___ Dying without leaving a will

4. ___ A gift of real property by will

5. ___ A gift of personal property by will

6. ___ Soil that builds up as a result of accretion

7. ___ A change in a will before the maker's death

8. ___ A buildup of soil by natural causes on property bordering a river, lake or ocean

9. ___ The sudden washing or tearing away of land by water action

10. ___ Occurs when land that has been covered by water is exposed by receding of the water

11. ___ The acquisition of title to additional land or to improvements as a result of annexing fixtures, or as a result of natural causes such as alluvial deposits along the banks of streams by accretion

12. ___ The legal transfer of a person's interest in real and personal property under the laws of descent and distribution

13. ___ To transfer ownership or title

14. ___ Transfer ownership or sell

15. ___ A document in real estate

16. ___ The person conveying, or transferring, the property

17. ___ The person receiving the property, or to whom it is being conveyed

18. ___ A signed statement, made before a notary public, by a named person confirming the signature on a document, made of free will

19. ___ Someone who directs or authorizes another to act in his or her place regarding relations with third persons; buyer or seller

20. ___ The division and distribution of expenses and/or income between the buyer and seller of property as of the date of closing or settlement

Answers

Pre-Test/Post Test

1. d
2. b
3. b
4. d
5. b
6. a
7. b
8. b
9. c
10. c

Vocabulary

1. 12
2. 4
3. 16
4. 11
5. 8
6. 6
7. 9
8. 2
9. 7
10. 19
11. 1
12. 20
13. 5 or 10
14. 5 or 10
15. 15
16. 14
17. 13
18. 3
19. 17
20. 18

CHAPTER

LANDLORD AND TENANT

Focus

- **Types of leasehold estates**
- **Payment of rent**
- **Creation of a lease**
- **Responsibilities of a landlord**
- **Responsibilities and rights of a tenant**
- **Transfer of a lease**
- **Termination of a lease**
- **Discrimination**

Pre-Test

The following is a self test to determine how much you know about landlords and tenants before reading this chapter. Take it without studying, then read the material presented in the text. At the end of the chapter you will find a repeat of this exam. Test your knowledge by answering the questions again, then check your improvement. (The answers are found at the end of this chapter.) Good luck!

1. Which of the following is an estate for years?
   a. a lease for an uncertain length of time
   b. a month to month rental
   c. a lease that must be renegotiated
   d. a lease at sufferance

2. A lessor is described as:
   a. tenant
   b. landlord
   c. having a less-than-freehold estate
   d. having an estate at will

3. A month to month tenancy also can be called:
   a. an estate from period to period
   b. an estate at severance
   c. an estate for months
   d. an estate at sufferance

4. What is the meaning of demise?
   a. to list
   b. to rent
   c. to will
   d. to convey

5. What is the longest period that property within a city can be leased:
   a. 99 years
   b. 51 years
   c. one year
   d. there is no time limit

6. Income from apartments, as stated in a rental agreement, is known as:
   a. economic rent
   b. gross rent
   c. contract rent
   d. implied rent

7. Ruby wanted to transfer her entire leasehold interest in a lease to her friend, Estella. What should she use to show that she no longer has any interest in the property?
   a. sublease
   b. new lease contract
   c. demise
   d. assignment

8. How long after a tenant moves out can a lessor keep a security deposit?
   a. two months
   b. there is no maximum time set by law
   c. one week
   d. three weeks

9. Waylon wanted to evict his tenant, Jason, because he was behind in his rent. What should Waylon do first?:
   a. file an unlawful detainer
   b. file a writ of execution
   c. file a notice of nonresponsibility
   d. serve a notice to pay or quit

10. A tenant must answer a notice to pay or quit in how many days?
    a. two
    b. three
    c. seven
    d. there is no time limit set by law

Terms

The following terms are the keys to your success in learning about real estate. Refer to them as you study this chapter for greater understanding of subjects presented here.

Assignee

Party to whom a lease is assigned or transferred

Assignment

Transfer of the entire leasehold interest for a lease from the original lessee to the assignee

Chattel Real

A lease; personal property

Contract Rent

The amount of rental income due from the tenant as agreed in the lease agreement

Demise

A conveyance of an estate in real property to someone for a certain length of time, as in a lease; to let

Economic Rent

What a leased property would be expected to rent for under current market conditions if the property were vacant and available for rent

Estate at Sufferance

A tenancy created when one is in wrongful possession of real estate even though the original possession may have been legal

Estate at Will

The tenancy may be ended by the unilateral decision of either party; no agreed upon termination date, however, and either party must give 30 days notice before ending the tenancy

Estate for Years

A leasehold estate with a definite end date; must be renegotiated; a lease for some fixed period

Estate from Period to Period

A leasehold estate that is automatically renewed for the same term; a conveyance for an indefinite period of time; does not need to be renegotiated upon each renewal; commonly a month to month rental

Eviction

The legal process of removing a tenant from the premises for some breach of the lease

Graduated Payment Lease

A lease calling for periodic increases in the rental payments; sometimes called a stair-step lease

Gross Lease

Landlord pays for most of the operating expenses, including property taxes, maintenance and repairs

Landlord

Lessor; property owner

Leasehold or Lease

An agreement, written or unwritten, transferring the right to exclusive possession and use of real estate for a definite period of time

Lessee

Tenant; renter

Lessor

Landlord; property owner

Less-than-Freehold

An estate of a tenant or renter; a leasehold

Net Lease

A lease where the tenant pays such costs as taxes, insurance and repairs, as well as a set amount for rent; a triple net lease is one where the tenant pays all expenses of operating the property as well as a set amount of rent

Percentage Lease

A lease where the landlord receives a percentage of the gross sales as part or all of the rental payment

Rent

Consideration paid for the use of a property

Residential Rental Property

Property from which 80% or more of the gross rental income is from dwelling units

Retaliatory Eviction

An act whereby a landlord evicts a tenant in response to some complaint made by the tenant

Reversionary Right

The lessor (landlord) grants the right of possession to the lessee (tenant), but retains the right to retake possession after the lease's term has expired

Sandwich Lease

A lease agreement created when a tenant sublets the property to another person, thus creating a sublessor-sublessee relationship. The person in the "sandwich" is a lessee to the owner and a lessor to the sub-lessee

Sublease

Transfers less than the entire leasehold, with the original lessee being primarily liable for the rental agreement

Surrender

The giving up of a lease, voluntarily

Tenant

A renter

Unlawful Detainer Action

A lawsuit filed with the court against a tenant who remains in unlawful possession of rental property after breaching the terms of a lawful lease

Writ of Possession

A court order directing the sheriff to remove the tenant and his or her possessions within five days

Introduction

In a previous chapter, you learned about the difference between free hold and less-than freehold estates. As you recall, a freehold estate is one held by a real property owner. The holder of a freehold estate enjoys all the benefits of the bundle of rights that accompany ownership. A **Less-than-Freehold** estate is one of a **Tenant** or renter. It is commonly called a **Leasehold** or **Lease**. The main feature of a leasehold interest is the right to exclusive possession and use of real property for a fixed period of time. The lease holder has the right to the use and quiet possession of the premises during the term of the lease.

Leasehold estates are known as **Chattel Real**. Even though they give the renter an estate in real property (a less-than-freehold estate), a lease is personal property. Remember, anything movable becomes personal property. The lease is a movable document describing the temporary possession and use of the property, and thus is personal property.

The law describes certain types of leasehold estates and regulates the requirements for leasing. There are many varieties of lease contracts, however, and if a lessee and lessor agree on terms that differ from the law, both will be required to meet the terms of their written agreement. For example, a new two-page lease agreement, adopted by the California Association of Realtors, only requires a four-hour notice for a landlord to inspect a leased property. The law states that 24 hours is necessary, unless landlord and tenant have a different written agreement.

Types of Leasehold Estates

The duration of a leasehold is known as a tenancy. Each of the four types of leases is distinctive because of its duration.

> ### Types of Lease
> - Estate for years
> - Estate from period to period (periodic tenancy)
> - Estate at will
> - Estate at sufferance

Estate for Years

http://cses.com/rental/
tenancy.htm

The first kind of lease is an **Estate for Years**. It is a lease for a definite duration. It does not have to be for only a year, but if a definite time is mentioned for the end date of the lease, it nevertheless is known as an estate for years. The lease of office space or a commercial center is commonly an estate for years. It is not automatically renewable and does not require notice to quit at the end of the lease. (Must be renegotiated.) It is a less-than freehold estate.

When an apartment rental agreement mentions an end date, it is considered an estate for years. Increasingly, owners of residential income property (apartment buildings) are using this type of an agreement to guarantee that a tenant will stay, at least until the lease expires.

The benefit of an estate for years to the **Landlord** is that a desirable, long term tenant may be attracted to the apartment or house. The benefit to the renter is assurance that the rent will remain the same over the period of the lease. At the expiration of the lease, terms must be mutually renegotiated.

Estate from Period to Period

Another kind of lease or rental agreement, probably the most common for residential use, is the **Estate from Period to Period**, also known as periodic tenancy. This is the typical month to month tenancy that requires 30 days notice to quit. It automatically renews itself unless terminated by landlord or tenant.

Estate at Will

When there is no written agreement between the landlord and tenant, the tenancy is known as an **Estate at Will**. The tenancy may be ended by the unilateral decision of either party. There is no agreed upon termination date, however, and either party must give 30 days notice before ending the tenancy.

Estate at Sufferance

An **Estate at Sufferance** occurs when a tenant occupies the property without paying rent and without the permission of the landlord.

Payment of Rent

There are various types of agreements for payment of rent between **Lessor** (landlord) and **Lessee** (tenant). One type is where the tenant pays an agreed upon sum as **Rent** and the landlord pays any other expenses such as taxes, maintenance or insurance.

This type of lease is known as a **Gross Lease** or a fixed lease. A **Net Lease** is one where the tenant pays an agreed upon sum as rent, plus the landlord's expenses. A varying rental rate is provided by a **Graduated Lease**. A commercial lease might be based on a percentage of the tenant's gross sales and is known as a **Percentage Lease**.

<u>Types of rental payments</u>
• Gross lease
• Net lease
• Graduated lease
• Percentage lease

Contract Rent, or the amount actually paid by a renter for use of the premises, may or may not be the same as **Economic Rent**, or the amount the rental could bring in an open market. An appraiser valuating a property looks at the economic rent, rather than the contract rent, in order to discover the fair income of the property.

Creation of a Lease

A *Lease* is a contract between an owner, called a lessor or landlord, and a lessee or tenant, in which a tenant is given possession and use of a property in return for rent payment.

Another name for a lease is a rental agreement. A lease can be described in any number of ways, as long as the names of the parties, description of the property, rent amount, and duration of lease are included in the rental agreement. Sometimes the words "to let" or to **Demise** will be found in a rental agreement, but those words are optional.

Leases for longer than one year must be in writing, according to the Statute of Frauds. However, it is common practice, and makes common sense to produce all lease agreements in writing. It must be signed by the lessor or landlord, but not necessarily by the lessee, or tenant. Again, it is common practice for the tenant to sign the lease, but the law requires only that the lease be delivered to the lessee for it to be binding.

The tenant's acceptance of the lease signed by the landlord, or the tenants paying rent and taking possession of the property binds both parties to the terms of the agreement. The right of the landlord to reclaim the property after the lease has expired is known as the **Reversionary Right**.

All Leases Should Include:

- Names of parties
- Description of the property
- Amount of rental payments
- Duration of lease
- If *more* than 1 year, must be in writing
- Signed by lessor (landlord)

Remember

Facts About Leases

- Lessee does *not* have to sign lease
- Reversionary right belongs to the lessor
- Possessory right belongs to the lessee
- A rental is presumed to be month to month unless specified otherwise
- Agricultural lease limited to maximum of 51 years
- Urban lease limited to maximum of 99 years

Responsibilities of a Landlord

http://home.navisoft.com/
johng/conflictarticle.html

In every lease the law implies a promise on the part of the lessor to the quiet enjoyment and possession of the property by the lessee during the term of the lease. In exchange for rent, a landlord gives up the use and possession of the property to a tenant. The landlord also has certain duties and responsibilities:

1. A landlord guarantees that health and safety codes are being met. With residential property, a landlord usually is liable for injuries occurring as a result of unsafe conditions in common areas such as hallways, stairwells or surrounding grounds.

2. Periodic inspection of the property is allowed by a landlord, who must give reasonable notice of intent to enter, and then only during normal business hours. Twenty-four hours is considered reasonable notice. Some rental agreements only require a four-hour notice of entry to be given by the landlord. Terms of a lease should be negotiated at the time of the signing, however, if the tenant wants any changes made. All leases are not the same, and should be read carefully by both landlord and tenant before signing.

3. California and federal laws state that a landlord may not refuse to rent to anyone based on race, color, national origin, religion or creed, sex, marital status or physical handicap. Also, a landlord may not refuse to rent to families with children.

4. A month-to-month rental agreement may be terminated by the landlord, provided the renter is given 30 days notice to vacate the property. The tenant does have recourse, however, if eviction is unfair, based on fair housing laws, or if the eviction is **Retaliatory**.

   If the lease or rental agreement is for a specific period, a landlord may not force the tenant to move out before the period has expired. Sale of the property or death of the landlord does not break a lease.

5. A security deposit must be refundable. The landlord has 21 days after the tenant has moved to return all unused portions of the security deposit, with a written statement showing how the remainder was used (to repair damage, replace windows, etc.). A landlord who keeps deposits without reason for more than three weeks after the tenant has moved may be subject to damages up to $600.

6. On **Residential Rental Property** the maximum deposit allowed on an *unfurnished property* is not more than the amount of two months rent.

7. On residential rental property, the maximum deposit allowed on a *furnished property* is not more than the amount of three months rent.

Remember

Landlords Must:

- Protect health and safety of tenants

- Give 24 hours notice before entering

- Obey fair housing laws

- Give 30 days notice before ending month-to-month tenancy

- Return deposit within three weeks after tenant leaves

Responsibilities and Rights of a Tenant

In return for the payment of rent, a tenant has certain obligations and rights by law:

- A tenant must pay the rent when it is due.

- A tenant must give 30 days notice before moving out, unless there is an agreement otherwise.

- A tenant may not interfere with the rights of other tenants.

- If there is a problem involving the tenant's health, welfare or safety, the landlord has a duty to make needed repairs. If the landlord refuses, under the law, a tenant may spend up to one month's rent to make repairs, and subtract the amount from the rent. The tenant may do this only two times in any 12-month period. A landlord may not retaliate by eviction or raising the rent for 180 days after this rent offset is used by the tenant to make lawful repairs.

- Rent is due at the end of each month unless otherwise agreed upon in the lease.

Remember

A Tenant Must:

- Pay rent when due

- Give 30 days notice before ending month-to-month tenancy

A Tenant May:

- Make needed repairs twice yearly and deduct from rent

Transfer of a Lease

A tenant or lessee may transfer interest in a lease in two ways: by assigning or by subleasing the property.

An **Assignment** is the transfer of the entire leasehold estate to the **Assignee**. The original lessee steps out of primary responsibility for the lease and a new lessee (assignee) becomes responsible to the landlord for all the terms of the original rental agreement.

Brad leases a two bedroom apartment from Al and lives there for six months until he is transferred to another part of the country. The term of the lease is one year and he has six months left before it expires. Melissa accepts Brad's offer of assignment of his lease and moves into the apartment when Brad moves out. Melissa is responsible directly to the landlord (Al) who also collects the rent. Brad no longer has any interest in the lease.

ASSIGNMENT:

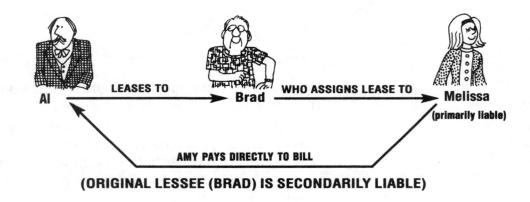

AL — **LEASES TO** → **Brad** — **WHO ASSIGNS LEASE TO** → **Melissa** **(primarily liable)**

AMY PAYS DIRECTLY TO BILL

(ORIGINAL LESSEE (BRAD) IS SECONDARILY LIABLE)

A **Sublease** transfers less than the entire leasehold, with the original lessee being primarily liable. The sublessee is liable only to the sublessor.

Bruce leases a two bedroom apartment from Al in a good area and lives there for six months until he is transferred to another part of the country. The term of the lease is one year and he has six months left before it expires. Bruce knows the transfer is temporary and wants to return to his apartment at some time in the future.

Shawn accepts Bruce's offer to sublease and moves into the apartment when he moves out. Shawn is responsible to Bruce, not the landlord, and sends his rent check to Bruce each month, who then sends it to the landlord.

*Bruce is still responsible for his original agreement with the lessor and keeps his interest as lessee in the property. Bruce holds what is known as a **Sandwich Lease**, or a position in between the original lessor (Al) and the sublessee.*

SUBLEASE:

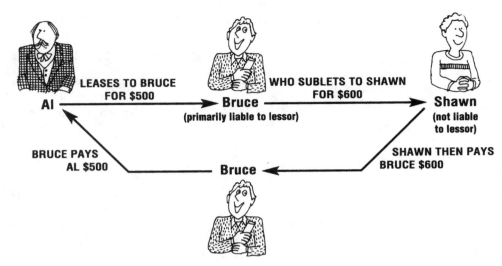

Termination of a Lease

The majority of leases end either by expiration of the agreed upon term or by mutual consent. Breach of conditions by either lessor or lessee, destruction of the premises or **Eviction** are other causes of termination.

When a tenant gives up a lease voluntarily, it is known as **Surrender**. By abandoning the premises, a tenant gives up any rights of possession, and has surrendered the property back to the landlord. If the tenant refuses to give up the lease, the landlord may have to resort to the operation of law for removal.

The law is very specific about remedies available to a landlord when a tenant defaults on the rent. The landlord can sue for each installment of rent when it is due, re-let the premises and sue for damages, or serve a Three-Day Notice to Pay or Quit to the tenant.

What a landlord may *not* do is give in to frustration about the delinquent or remiss tenant by committing unlawful acts, such as removing the tenant's belongings, changing the locks, shutting off the utilities or bullying the tenant with threats of bodily harm.

Unlawful Acts by a Landlord (Lessor)

- Tenant Lockout

- Taking Tenant Property

- Removing Doors and Windows

- Shutting Off Utilities

- Trespassing

If a tenant fails to meet the terms of the rental agreement, or has not paid the rent, the landlord only has to give a three-day notice in writing, asking the tenant to conform. The tenant then must move out within three days or meet the landlord's requirements. This Notice to Pay Rent or Quit is commonly known as an eviction notice.

CALIFORNIA
ASSOCIATION
OF REALTORS®

THREE-DAY NOTICE TO PAY RENT OR QUIT
(C.A.R. Form PRQ, Revised 10/01)

To: _____

and all subtenants and any other occupants in possession of the premises located at (Street Address) _____

_____ (Unit/Apartment #) _____

(City) _____ (State) _____ (Zip Code) _____, ("Premises").

WITHIN THREE DAYS from service of this Notice you are required to either: (i) pay rent for the Premises in the following

amount, which is past due, to (Name) _____

(Phone) _____ at (Address) _____

_____

between the hours of _____ on the following days: _____.

Past Due Rent: $ _____ for the period _____ to _____

$ _____ for the period _____ to _____

$ _____ for the period _____ to _____

Total Due: $ _____.

OR (ii) vacate the Premises and surrender possession.

If you do not pay the past due amount or give up possession, a legal action will be filed seeking not only damages and possession, but also a statutory damage penalty for an additional $600.00. Landlord declares a forfeiture of the lease if past due rent is not paid and you continue to occupy the Premises. As required by law, you are hereby notified that a negative credit report reflecting on your credit record may be submitted to a credit reporting agency if you fail to pay your rent.

Landlord (Owner or Agent) _____ Date _____

(Keep a copy for your records.)

Published and Distributed by:
REAL ESTATE BUSINESS SERVICES, INC.
a subsidiary of the CALIFORNIA ASSOCIATION OF REALTORS®
525 South Virgil Avenue, Los Angeles, California 90020

OFFICE USE ONLY
Reviewed by Broker
or Designee _____
Date _____

EQUAL HOUSING OPPORTUNITY

PRQ-11 REVISED 10/01 (PAGE 1 OF 1) Print Date BDC OCT 01

THREE-DAY NOTICE TO PAY RENT OR QUIT (PRQ-11 PAGE 1 OF 1)

The landlord may file an **Unlawful Detainer Action** in the municipal court if a tenant ignores or fails to respond to the notification to pay or quit. This document lists the charges against the tenant, who then has five days to respond after being served, otherwise, a default hearing is set.

A **Writ of Possession** is granted by the court to the landlord if the tenant does not move out or answer the lawsuit. This authorizes the sheriff to send an eviction notice to the tenant, and then after five days, physically remove the tenant from the premises.

http://ca-apartment.org

The landlord must store any belongings left behind by the tenant after the eviction for 30 days, charging the tenant a reasonable storage fee. After that time, a public sale may be held and the proceeds used by the owner to pay costs of storage and sale. Any balance remaining after payment of these costs must be returned to the tenant.

Steps of the Eviction Process

- Notice to Pay or Quit served
  Tenant has three days to respond

- Unlawful Detainer filed
  Tenant has five days to respond after being served

- Writ of Possession granted
  Sheriff sends eviction notice and physically removes tenant if no response within five days

---

Remember

Termination of a Lease

- Expiration of the Term

- Mutual Agreement

- Violations of Terms and Conditions

- Destruction of the Premises

- Eviction
  Notice
  Unlawful Detainer Action
  Sheriff Serves the Eviction

Discrimination

Discrimination on the basis of sex, race, religion, marital status, age or physical disability is not permitted under Fair Housing Laws. Any landlord or property manager should be aware of these laws, as should tenants.

Victims of discrimination in rental housing should contact the nearest office of the California State Department of Fair Employment and Housing. The U.S. Department of Housing and Urban Development (HUD) handles complaints about racial or religious discrimination. Also, those injured by discrimination may seek justice in a court of law. You will learn more about fair housing laws in a later chapter.

The California Fair Employment and Housing Act (formerly Rumford Fair Housing Act)

Prohibits Housing Discrimination Based On:

- Race
- Religion
- National Ancestry
- Sex
- Marital Status

This chapter presented an overview of landlord and tenant interaction. There is much more material on the subject at the public library and local public agencies with authority over such matters.

Post Test

The following self test repeats the one you took at the beginning of this chapter. Now take the exam again—since you have read all the material— and check your knowledge of landlords and tenants.

1. Which of the following is an estate for years?
   a. a lease for an uncertain length of time
   b. a month to month rental
   c. a lease that must be renegotiated
   d. a lease at sufferance

2. A lessor is described as:
   a. tenant
   b. landlord
   c. having a less-than-freehold estate
   d. having an estate at will

3. A month to month tenancy also can be called:
   a. an estate from period to period
   b. an estate at severance
   c. an estate for months
   d. an estate at sufferance

4. What is the meaning of demise?
   a. to list
   b. to rent
   c. to will
   d. to convey

5. What is the longest period that property within a city can be leased:
   a. 99 years
   b. 51 years
   c. one year
   d. there is no time limit

6. Income from apartments, as stated in a rental agreement, is known as:
   a. economic rent
   b. gross rent
   c. contract rent
   d. implied rent

7. Ruby wanted to transfer her entire leasehold interest in a lease to her friend, Estella. What should she use to show that she no longer has any interest in the property?
   a. sublease
   b. new lease contract
   c. demise
   d. assignment

8. How long after a tenant moves out can a lessor keep a security deposit?
   a. two months
   b. there is no maximum time set by law
   c. one week
   d. three weeks

9. Waylon wanted to evict his tenant, Jason, because he was behind in his rent. What should Waylon do first?:
   a. file an unlawful detainer
   b. file a writ of execution
   c. file a notice of nonresponsibility
   d. serve a notice to pay or quit

10. A tenant must answer a notice to pay or quit in how many days?
    a. two
    b. three
    c. seven
    d. there is no time limit set by law

Vocabulary

Read the definition, find the matching term and write the corresponding term number on the line provided.

Terms

1. Assignee
2. Assignment
3. Chattel Real
4. Contract Rent
5. Demise
6. Economic Rent
7. Estate at Sufferance
8. Estate at Will
9. Estate for Years
10. Estate from Period to Period
11. Eviction
12. Graduated Lease
13. Gross Lease
14. Landlord
15. Leasehold or Lease
16. Less-than-Freehold
17. Lessee
18. Lessor
19. Net Lease
20. Percentage Lease

Definitions

1. ___ An estate of a tenant or renter, a leasehold

2. ___ An agreement, written or unwritten, transferring the right to exclusive possession and use of real estate for a definite period of time

3. ___ A lease; personal property

4. ___ A leasehold estate with a definite end date; must be renegotiated

5. ___ A leasehold estate that is automatically renewed for the same term; a conveyance for an indefinite period of time; does not need to be renegotiated upon each renewal; commonly a month to month rental

6. ___ Lessor; property owner

7. ___ The tenancy may be ended by the unilateral decision of either party; no agreed upon termination date, however, and either party must give 30 days notice before ending the tenancy

8. ___ A tenancy created when one is in wrongful possession of real estate even though the original possession may have been legal

9. ___ Landlord, property owner

10. ___ Tenant, renter

11. ___ A conveyance of an estate in real property to someone for a certain length of time, as in a lease; to let

12. ___ A lease in which the landlord pays for most of the operating expenses, including property taxes, maintenance and repairs

13. ___ A lease where the tenant pays such costs as taxes, insurance, repairs as well as a set amount for rent; a triple net lease is one where the tenant pays all expenses of operating the property as well as a set amount of rent

14. ___ A lease calling for periodic increases in the rental payments; sometimes called a stair-step lease

15. ___ A lease where the landlord receives a percentage of the gross sales as part or all of the rental payment

16. ___ Transfer of the entire leasehold interest for a lease from the original lessee to the assignee

17. ___ Party to whom a lease is assigned or transferred

18. ___ The legal process of removing a tenant from the premises for some breach of the lease

19. ___ The amount of rental income due from the tenant as agreed in the lease agreement

20. ___ What a leased property would be expected to rent for under current market conditions if the property were vacant and available for rent

Answers

Pre-Test/Post Test

1. c
2. b
3. a
4. b
5. a
6. c
7. d
8. d
9. d
10. b

Vocabulary

1. 16
2. 15
3. 3
4. 9
5. 10
6. 14
7. 8
8. 7
9. 18
10. 17
11. 5
12. 13
13. 19
14. 12
15. 20
16. 2
17. 1
18. 11
19. 4
20. 6

AGENCY

Focus

- **What is agency?**
- **Special distinctions of a general agency**
- **Creation of an agency relationship**
- **Disclosure and confirmation of agency**
- **Ostensible agency**
- **Dual agency**
- **Cooperating agent and subagent**
- **Agent's authority**
- **Duties of an agent toward a principal**
- **Real estate transfer disclosure**
- **Duties and liabilities of an agent**
- **Rights of an agent**
- **Termination of agency**
- **Multiple listing service**

Pre-Test

The following is a self test to determine how much you know about agency before reading this chapter. Take it without studying, then read the material presented in the text. At the end of the chapter you will find a repeat of this exam. Test your knowledge by answering the questions again, then check your improvement. (The answers are found at the end of this chapter.) Good luck!

1. By authorizing an agent to perform particular acts in a listing, the seller is establishing a:
   - a. third party agency
   - b. special agency
   - c. ordinary agency
   - d. general agency

2. With whom do a principal and agent negotiate during the sale of a property?
   - a. broker
   - b. seller
   - c. third party
   - d. buyer

3. Ben put an ad in the local newspaper to sell his home. He only wanted legitimate buyers, and no agents, to respond to his advertisement. The phrase he would probably use is:
   - a. third parties only
   - b. buyers only
   - c. no general agents
   - d. principals only

4. Barbara, a broker, wrote an offer on a house that was not currently listed. The seller had not authorized her to act in his behalf, but said she could present her offer. The seller accepted the offer and agreed to pay the broker a commission as his agent. This is an example of:
   - a. ratification
   - b. specific agency
   - c. ostensible agency
   - d. estoppel

5. An agency is normally established between a broker and a principal by:
   - a. ostensible agreement
   - b. ratification
   - c. express contract
   - d. implied contract

6. Lonnie, an agent, has an exclusive agency listing with Keith and Sarah to sell their house. Her fiduciary duty is to:
   - a. the buyer and seller
   - b. the buyer
   - c. no one
   - d. the seller

7. Calvin, a homeowner, through carelessness led a third party to believe a broker named Harry was his agent, when in fact he was not. This is an example of:
   - a. ostensible agency
   - b. ratification
   - c. bilateral agency
   - d. express agency

8. Lori and Bryan listed their house with broker Jenny. The listing was an exclusive right to sell, and Jenny put it on the multiple listing service immediately. At an open house one weekend, a couple came in and made an offer on the house, and Jenny wrote up the offer. To whom does Jenny owe a fiduciary duty?
   - a. the seller and buyer
   - b. Lori and Bryan
   - c. primarily to the seller, secondarily to the buyer
   - d. the buyer

9. A listing is terminated by all of the following except:
   - a. death of the seller
   - b. destruction of the property
   - c. death of the listing salesperson
   - d. bankruptcy of the seller

10. The disclosure statement that must be signed by the seller and given to the buyer is known as a:
    - a. listing
    - b. deposit receipt
    - c. seller's disclosure of liens
    - d. real estate transfer disclosure statement

Terms

The following terms are the keys to your success in learning about real estate. Refer to them as you study this chapter for greater understanding of subjects presented here.

Agency

A relationship in which one party (principal) authorizes another party (agent) to act as the principal's representative in dealing with third parties

Agent

A person who acts for and in the place of another, called a principal, for the purpose of effecting the principal's legal relationship with third persons

Arm's Length Transaction

A transaction, such as a sale of property, in which all parties involved are acting in their own self-interest and are under no undue influence or pressure from the other parties

Attorney in Fact

A competent and disinterested person who is authorized by another person to act in his or her place

Client

The person who employs an agent to perform a service for a fee

Commingling

To deposit client funds in the broker's personal account

Cooperating Agent

A selling agent who is not the listing agent

Conversion

The appropriation of property belonging to another

Customer

A prospective buyer of real estate

Dual Agent

An agent who represents both parties in a transaction

Estoppel

A legal doctrine which prevents a person from denying something to be true or a fact which is contrary to previous statements made by that same person

Fiduciary

A relationship that implies a position of trust or confidence

Principal

A person who authorizes another to act in his or her place in regard to relations with third persons

Procuring Cause

The real estate agent who actually wrote the offer and presented it to the seller for acceptance.

Puffing

Exaggerated comments or opinions not made as representations of fact, thus not grounds for misrepresentation

Ratification

The approval of a previously authorized act, performed on behalf of a person, which makes the act valid and legally binding

Red Flag

Something that would warn a reasonably observant person of a potential problem, thus requiring further investigation

Subagent

An agent of a person who is already acting as an agent for a principal

Third Party

A person who may be affected by the terms of an agreement but who is not a party to the agreement

Tort

A negligent or intentional wrongful act arising from breach of duty created by law and not contract

Introduction

As a real estate agent, your main job will be to represent someone else in a real estate transaction. The law wants to make sure you know who you are representing and what your obligations are when you act for another person. This chapter will explain the law, called Agency, and how it affects all of your dealings as a licensee. To give you an idea how important the subject of agency is, you will be required, every four years when you renew your license, to complete a continuing education course on agency.

Your success as a real estate agent will depend on your knowledge of the law of agency and how well you understand it. The consumer relies on you to explain the law as well as make sure it is carried out. All the consumer wants is to be assured that you are representing his or her best interests. Because of real estate agents' careful handling of the rules of agency, the public is slowly gaining confidence in an industry that sometimes has had a tarnished image.

There is no subject that affects you and the consumer more than that which we will examine here.

What is Agency?

http://www.leginfo.ca.gov

(click on California Law, check Civil Code and type in Agency at the bottom)

The relationship between an agent and principal is called **Agency**. The person who gives authority to an **Agent** to represent his or her interests in dealing with a **Third Party** is the **Principal**, sometimes called the **Client**. A third party may be referred to as the broker's **Customer**, and is the person or firm with whom the principal and agent negotiate.

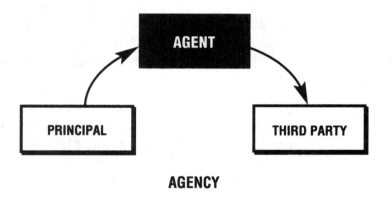

AGENCY

The agent is bound by the laws of agency, which we are about to examine, to act in the best interests of the principal in dealing with third parties. The agent owes loyalty and has a fiduciary duty to the principal, with an obligation always to act fairly and honestly with the third party. This means in real life that the buyer, seller and agent are bound together in a legal relationship, with all the duties and rights that go with that connection.

A real estate broker is an agent who is allowed by the principal to act on the principal's behalf for a specified purpose. A listing authorizes an agent to perform particular acts, establishing a special agency. The real estate salesperson, as an independent contractor in the employ of the broker, operates as an agent for the broker, who bears the final responsibility for any agency relationships created by a salesperson in the broker's employ.

Rose, an agent in the employ of broker Dan, listed a property owned by the Miranda family. Under the law, the agency has been created between the Mirandas and Dan, as broker. Rose is bound by the agency because she represents Dan.

Special Distinctions of a General Agency

In understanding agency, let's look at some other types of relationships where the real estate broker acts on his or her own account as a principal, there is an ordinary employer-employee relationship, or services are carried out by an independent contractor.

Broker Acting on Own Account

Many times in your career as a licensed real estate agent you will have the opportunity to buy or sell for yourself. The utmost care must be taken to observe all ethical and legal obligations in your role as principal. You must make sure all profits are a result of lawful dealings, and not an exploitation of an opportunity because you are licensed.

You may have a chance from time to time to participate, as a principal, in dealing with clients. In other words, you may become the buyer or seller. You may do that, legally, as long as you disclose your position as a principal. You may take an option to buy on one of your listings, take a net listing, or in some other way become involved personally with a sale.

As long as there is a full disclosure of your involvement in the transaction, and the legal effect of the contract is made known to the persons with whom you are dealing, you are within the law. The other party to the prospective transaction must be told and must understand that you are acting as a principal rather than as an agent so that the transaction may be conducted at **Arm's Length**.

The danger of an agent becoming involved with a client as a principal is that the client may not realize the agent is no longer representing the client, and that each must look out for their own interests. At this point, the agent must inform all parties in writing that there is no agency relationship between them, and that the agent is operating on his or her own behalf, not theirs.

Merry, a real estate salesperson, listed a home for sale for George, and after three weeks decided that she was interested in buying it. Her offer to purchase included the disclosure that she was operating as a buyer for her own account, and not as an agent for the seller. Through this, the seller was informed that he should seek his own counsel, or represent himself in the transaction.

Another type of situation may occur if a broker employed to sell property is also given an option to purchase the property. The broker then occupies the dual status of agent and possible purchaser, and may not exercise an option except by making a full disclosure of all information regarding the prospect of making a sale to someone else. As you can see, this is an awkward position for an agent, and must be handled in the most straightforward manner to disclose all facts, including revealing any profit made on an option sale.

Full disclosure includes the obligation to tell all material facts fully and completely. That means any fact that would seem likely to affect the judgment of the principal in giving consent to the agent to enter into the particular transaction on the specified terms. So the agent must divulge all self interest, and disclose any facts that might have a bearing on the transaction's desirability from the principal's viewpoint.

Employer-employee relationship

Basically, an agent is employed by a principal for representation. An ordinary employee is defined as someone who is under the control and direction of an employer. As an independent contractor, an agent does this and also speaks for the principal when negotiating agreements. An example of this is a listing contract, which we examined in another chapter.

Independent Contractor

Independent contractors are responsible for the results of their labor, unlike employees who must follow employers' directions in completing the work. The independent contractor decides on the method to use in accomplishing the work under contract, and is held accountable for the results—not how they are accomplished, as long as all is within the law. As we discussed earlier, the salesperson is employed as an independent contractor, thus carries on the business of real estate within the framework of that job description.

Remember

A salesperson is usually:

- An independent contractor

- A representative of the broker

The principal employs the broker and the sales agent represents the broker.

A real estate broker is almost always an independent contractor. Under the law of agency, the broker is a special agent who deals in the name of the principal to negotiate the sale of property. The broker does not have control over the property itself, while acting within the course of a special agency, but only has the right to represent that principal.

A listing contract does not give a broker the right to convey any property belonging to the principal unless the agent has a power of attorney to do so. As we will see in the next section, a listing contract is the most common way an agency is created, and only gives the agent the right to be paid after doing the job, or producing results. Think of it as simply an employment contract between the seller and the agent.

A real estate agent holds:

- A special agency with the duty to represent the principal in negotiating the sale of a certain property

The Real Estate License Law considers a licensed salesperson to be an employee of the broker, however, and not an independent contractor for purposes of supervision. The broker-salesperson relationship is viewed in this manner *only* by the License Law, not by other agencies. A salesperson's status under one law does not establish what that status is under different circumstances, such as federal and state income tax, workers' compensation, unemployment insurance or other matters not covered by the Real Estate Law.

Regarding legal status of an agent:

- License Law considers salesperson an employee for purposes of supervision
- For all other purposes he or she is an independent contractor

Creation of an Agency Relationship

An agency relationship can be created between an agent and a principal in one of these ways:

Agency Relationship Created Through:
- Agreement
- Ratification
- Estoppel

Agreement

An express agreement may be made between a principal and agent. It must be in writing and usually is in the form of a listing contract which authorizes the agent to represent the seller in finding a buyer and negotiating the sale. The listing contract is where the seller promises to pay a commission upon presentation of a ready, willing and able buyer who meets all the terms of the listing. This is the most common way to create an agency.

When the principal (seller) signs a listing agreement promising payment for service by a listing broker and the broker promises to provide the service, the agreement is described as being bilateral—in that a promise is given in exchange for a promise. When the broker makes a counterpromise in the listing agreement to "use due diligence" in finding a buyer, it is a bilateral contract— in that the payment is a promise for a promise.

Ellen worked hard as an agent in her farm area, making sure she spoke to everyone in her territory of 500 homes at least once a month. She was well known in the area, and when owners wanted to sell their homes, they called Ellen to list the property. She would then set a time to go to the designated home and complete the listing. An agency by express agreement had been created.

Ratification

A principal can accept an offer presented by a licensee and agree to pay a commission, even though no agency has been approved. The seller is creating an agency by **Ratification** by accepting the actions of the agent, after the fact.

As Ellen walked through the neighborhoods, knocking on doors, talking to people, she became familiar with most of the homes in the area. One day, she answered the office phone and talked to a caller who described the type of home he was looking for. She knew of one just like his description, but it was not listed for sale. After calling the owner of the house, who told her she could show it to the prospective buyer, she presented an offer from the buyer, which the owner accepted, agreeing to pay Ellen a commission. Thus an agency by ratification was created.

Estoppel

Finally, an agency relationship can be created by **Estoppel**. This is also called an ostensible or implied agency (see page 181). Agency is created when the principal causes a third party to believe another person is the agent of the principal. Authority is given when a principal allows a third party to believe that another person is the agent, even though that person is unaware of the appointment. If a seller allows a buyer to believe an agent represents the seller, and the buyer believes that to be so, the existence of an agency cannot be denied by the seller, who will be bound by the actions of the agent. This is known as the doctrine of estoppel.

Disclosure and Confirmation of Agency

Traditionally, the principal in a real estate transaction was a seller, represented by the listing agent. The selling agent might have represented the principal, too, as subagent of the listing agent under the law, and therefore was legally bound by a **Fiduciary Duty** to the seller. So who represented the buyer when the listing agent wrote up the offer? Who represented the buyer when a selling agent wrote up the offer and presented it to the seller?

The answer is—no one. Legally, the buyer had no representation, even though it appeared to be the licensed agent showing the property and writing up the offer.

The terms clients and customer are used loosely in the real estate industry, without a precise legal definition, but are useful in helping a real estate agent determine what his or her role is in dealing with buyers and sellers. A client is commonly thought of as a principal who uses the professional services of an agent and whose interests are protected by the specific duties and loyalties of a fiduciary relationship. Someone who seeks to buy property or the services of a real estate agent without the protection of a fiduciary relationship is a customer. He or she receives services provided for the benefit of someone else (the client). A client is represented by an agent; customers represent themselves.

Commonly, a third party is referred to as the agent's customer, and is the person with whom the principal and listing agent negotiate. Traditionally, the seller has been the principal. The buyer has been the third party. So traditionally, the listing agent represents the seller (principal) in dealing with the buyer (third party).

So as of January 1, 1988, for every residential property transaction of one to four units, the law requires that an agent supply a written document, called an Agency Disclosure, explaining the nature of agency to a seller before listing a property, or to a buyer before writing an offer.

Also, a selling agent (representing the buyer) must provide the form to the seller prior to presenting an offer. This document describes the obligations of an agent as "seller's agent," "buyer's agent" or "dual agent." At this point, all parties are made aware that they do have a choice of who is to represent them as their own agent. A copy of the disclosure must be given to all parties at the time of signing.

**DISCLOSURE REGARDING
REAL ESTATE AGENCY RELATIONSHIPS**
(As required by the Civil Code)
CALIFORNIA ASSOCIATION OF REALTORS® (CAR) STANDARD FORM

When you enter into a discussion with a real estate agent regarding a real estate transaction, you should from the outset understand what type of agency relationship or representation you wish to have with the agent in the transaction.

SELLER'S AGENT

A Seller's agent under a listing agreement with Seller acts as the agent for the Seller only. A Seller's agent or a subagent of that agent has the following affirmative obligations:
To the Seller:
   (a) A Fiduciary duty of utmost care, integrity, honesty, and loyalty in dealings with the Seller.
To the Buyer & the Seller:
   (a) Diligent exercise of reasonable skill and care in performance of the agent's duties.
   (b) A duty of honest and fair dealing and good faith.
   (c) A duty to disclose all facts known to the agent materially affecting the value or desirability of property that are not known to, or within the diligent attention and observation of, the parties.

An agent is not obligated to reveal to either party any confidential information obtained from the other party which does not involve the affirmative duties set forth above.

BUYER'S AGENT

A selling agent can, with a Buyer's consent, agree to act as agent for the Buyer only. In these situations, the agent is not the Seller's agent, even if by agreement the agent may receive compensation for services rendered, either in full or in part from the Seller. An agent acting only for a Buyer has the following affirmative obligations:
To the Buyer:
   (a) A fiduciary duty of utmost care, integrity, honesty, and loyalty in dealings with the Buyer.
To the Buyer & Seller:
   (a) Diligent exercise of reasonable skill and care in performance of the agent's duties.
   (b) A duty of honest and fair dealing and good faith.
   (c) A duty to disclose all facts known to the agent materially affecting the value or desirability of the property that are not known to, or within the diligent attention and observation of, the parties.

An agent is not obligated to reveal to either party any confidential information obtained from the other party which does not involve the affirmative duties set forth above.

AGENT REPRESENTING BOTH SELLER & BUYER

A real estate agent, either acting directly or through one or more associate licensees, can legally be the agent of both the Seller and the Buyer in a transaction, but only with the knowledge and consent of both the Seller and the Buyer.

In a dual agency situation, the agent has the following affirmative obligations to both the Seller and the Buyer:
   (a) A fiduciary duty of utmost care, integrity, honesty and loyalty in the dealings with either Seller or the Buyer.
   (b) Other duties to the Seller and the Buyer as stated above in their respective sections.

In representing both Seller and Buyer, the agent may not, without the express permission of the respective party, disclose to the other party that the Seller will accept a price less than the listing price or that the Buyer will pay a price greater than the price offered.

The above duties of the agent in a real estate transaction do not relieve a Seller or a Buyer from the responsibility to protect their own interests. You should carefully read all agreements to assure that they adequately express your understanding of the transaction. A real estate agent is a person qualified to advise about real estate. If legal or tax advice is desired, consult a competent professional.

Throughout your real property transaction you may receive more than one disclosure form, depending upon the number of agents assisting in the transaction. The law requires each agent with whom you have more than a casual relationship to present you with this disclosure form. You should read its contents each time it is presented to you, considering the relationship between you and the real estate agent in your specific transaction.

This disclosure form includes the provisions of article 2.5 (commencing with Section 2373) of Chapter 2 of Title 9 of Part 4 of Division 3 of the Civil Code set forth on the reverse hereof. Read it carefully.

I/WE ACKNOWLEDGE RECEIPT OF A COPY OF THIS DISCLOSURE.

BUYER/SELLER_____ Date_____ TIME_____ AM/PM

BUYER/SELLER_____ Date_____ TIME_____ AM/PM

AGENT _____ By _____ Date_____
(Please Print)   (Associate Licensee or Broker-Signature)

The Basic Requirements of the Disclosure of Agency Are:

1. A duty of utmost care, integrity, honesty and loyalty in dealings with the agent's principal and duties of skill and care in performance of duties

2. Honest and fair dealing and good faith

3. Disclosure of all facts known to the agent materially affecting the value or desirability of the property not known to the other parties

The second part of the agency disclosure form requires all parties involved to confirm that they understand the agent's role. In other words, the first part of the disclosure reveals that the agent may represent only the buyer, only the seller, or both. All parties acknowledge their understanding at this point. Then, at the appropriate time for each party, everyone is required to acknowledge that they understand who is representing whom, and sign the second part of the disclosure. A copy of both parts of the agency disclosure is included here.

CONFIRMATION
REAL ESTATE AGENCY RELATIONSHIPS

Subject Property Address_____

The following agency relationship(s) is/are hereby confirmed for this transaction:

LISTING AGENT: _____ **SELLING AGENT:** _____
                                                 (if not the same as Listing Agent)
is the agent of (check one):   is the agent of (check one):
☐ the Seller exclusively; or   ☐ the Buyer exclusively; or
☐ both the Buyer and Seller   ☐ the Seller exclusively; or
                                                 ☐ both the Buyer and Seller

I/WE ACKNOWLEDGE RECEIPT OF A COPY OF THIS CONFIRMATION.

Seller_____ Date_____ Buyer _____ Date_____

Seller_____ Date_____ Buyer _____ Date_____

Listing Agent _____ By _____ Date_____
              (Please Print)   (Associate Licensee or Broker-Signature)

Selling Agent _____ By _____ Date_____
              (Please Print)   (Associate Licensee or Broker-Signature)

A REAL ESTATE BROKER IS QUALIFIED TO ADVISE ON REAL ESTATE. IF YOU DESIRE LEGAL ADVICE, CONSULT YOUR ATTORNEY.

This form is available for use by the entire real estate industry. The use of this form is not intended to identify the user as a REALTOR®. REALTOR® is a registered collective membership mark which may be used only by real estate licensees who are members of the NATIONAL ASSOCIATION OF REALTORS® and who subscribe to its Code of Ethics.

Copyright© 1987, CALIFORNIA ASSOCIATION OF REALTORS®   FORM AD-11/AC-6   OFFICE USE ONLY
525 South Virgil Avenue, Los Angeles, California 90020   (combined)   Reviewed by Broker or Designee _____
                                                                                Date _____
                                                                                M-SC-MAY-93

One more time, the relationship will be confirmed in the sales contract, which is signed by all parties.

In case you are wondering why all this repetition and paperwork, the agency disclosure is probably one of the most important documents available to the consumer. After years of ambiguity, the law is clear about who is legally representing whom. Buyers or sellers can be confident that their best interests are being represented by an agent on their side in the negotiations.

This disclosure of agency requirement came out of public demand for assurance of representation in all real estate dealings. The uncertainty and suspicion that clouded the consumer/agent relationship in the past has been lifted by the openness of the disclosure of agency. Hopefully, with each use of the disclosure law, the real estate industry will earn greater confidence from the public, with past apprehension and distrust replaced by enlightenment and trust.

As a licensee, it is *not* optional for you to use and understand the agency disclosure document and be able to explain it to your clients and customers. The law is very clear about your responsibility for full disclosure. Misunderstanding or ignorance is not a defense and you will be held liable for failure to conform to the law.

Remember

Under the Disclosure of Agency Law:

- An agent is either the agent of the seller, the buyer, or both buyer and seller.

- A listing agent who is also a selling agent may not be the agent for a buyer only.

- A dual agent may not tell the seller that the buyer is willing to pay more, nor may a dual agent tell the buyer that the seller will take less without the express written consent of the party.

- An agency relationship can exist even though no compensation is to be received from the party with whom the agency relationship is established.

Ostensible Agency

A licensee must be aware that an agency relationship can result from one's conduct, even though no express employment contract has been signed, or possible payments established. This is a subject where great care must be taken to assure that the agent is operating correctly, under the law.

When a listing is taken by an agent, he or she promises to represent the seller while finding a buyer. The agent has a fiduciary duty to conduct negotiations in the best interest of the seller in dealing with buyers who are interested in the property. However, because of the way in which real estate is marketed in California, the distinction of who represents whom can get blurred unintentionally.

As the seller's agent, a licensee has the duty of utmost care, integrity, honesty and loyalty in dealings with the seller. Yet the law also requires that the agent exercise reasonable skill and care, honest and fair dealing, and full disclosure of all material facts to all parties. It is difficult for an agent to live up to fiduciary duty to a seller and at the same time meet general obligations to a buyer.

What services may a seller's agent provide to a buyer without becoming the ostensible or implied agent of the buyer?

Seller's Agent May:

1. Show the buyer properties meeting the buyer's requirements and describe to the buyer a property's amenities, attributes, condition and status

2. Complete a standard purchase contract by inserting the terms of the buyer's offer in the form's blanks and transmit all offers of the buyer to the seller on a timely basis

3. Inform the buyer about the availability of financing, legal service, inspection companies, title companies or other related services desired or required by the buyer to complete the transaction

While performing the above tasks, it is very difficult not to establish an implied agency. An agent must be very alert and conscious of his or her role at all times to avoid becoming a dual agent by implication or conduct.

Here are some common mistakes made by agents who are not aware they are violating their agency with the seller.

Common Mistakes that Violate Agency:

- "Leave it all up to me. I can get you the house at the price you want."

- "I'm sure I can get the seller to agree to this price and get the financing you need."

- "I know the sellers personally, and I'm sure they won't counter at that price."

- "The house has been for sale for more than eight months and I think it is listed too high. It's probably not worth more than $285,000. Let's make an offer to see if they take it."

- "If the sellers insist on the $200,000, I'll remind them that the heating system is old, the carpet is not exactly designer quality, and the whole place needs repainting. That should convince them to reduce their price".

- "I'll write up the offer for you and present it to the seller. If they don't like it, I can always try to find out their bottom line and we can go from there."

The important thing to remember is to act out of conscious knowledge of the law regarding agency, and you will be doing your job.

Dual Agency

A real estate agent who has an employment contract with a seller (a listing) may establish an agency with a buyer as well. In this case, whether the licensee is the actual agent of both the seller and the buyer, or the agent of the seller and the ostensible or implied agent of the buyer, the broker is acting as a **Dual Agent**.

A licensee can legally be the agent of both the seller and the buyer in a transaction, but must have the informed consent of both the seller and the buyer. The one thing an agent may not do, as a representative of buyer *and* seller is reveal any information to either about price that would influence an offer or acceptance.

http://www.rlsweb.com/
dual_agency_example.htm

A real estate license may be revoked or suspended for violation of the agency disclosure law.

Cooperating Agent and Subagent

Most property is sold through a local association of brokers called a multiple listing service (MLS). The MLS maintains an inventory of all the available properties in the area. A member agent can locate buyers and obtain offers for these properties even though he or she is not the listing agent. An agent who assists the listing agent in this way is called a cooperating agent. The cooperating agent receives a part of the commission at the close of escrow.

An issue that can be confusing is the question of whether the cooperating agent represents the seller or the buyer. Buyers commonly believe that the cooperating agent represents the buyer. Others assume that the cooperating agent is a subagent of the listing agent and represents the seller. A subagent is defined as the agent of someone who is already the agent of the principal. A subagent always represents the listing agent, who always represents the seller. If the cooperating agent is a subagent for the listing agent, then the cooperating agent owes a fiduciary duty and loyalty to the seller. If the cooperating agent represents the buyer, the fiduciary duty is to the buyer.

Nothing in the listing agreement compels the cooperating agent to represent the seller. A seller authorizes the listing agent to *cooperate* with other brokers in showing the property. The seller does not authorize the listing agent to designate a subagent. The listing agent may *offer* subagency to a cooperating agent, and the cooperating agent may accept or decline the offer. (Acceptance would be in writing or by the conduct of the cooperating agent.)

Thus a cooperating agent does not automatically become a subagent for the listing agent when he shows a property. As long as complete disclosure is made about agency relationships, the cooperating agent can represent either the seller or the buyer.

The Orange County Association of Realtors addresses the optional nature of subagency in this rule:

> 7.12 Unilateral Contractual Offer; Subagency Optional. In filing a property with the MLS, the broker participant makes a blanket unilateral contractual offer of compensation to the other MLS broker participants for their services in selling the property. A broker participant must specify some compensation to be paid to either a buyer's agent or a subagent and the offer of compensation must be stated in one, or a combination of the following forms (1) a percentage of the gross selling price; or (2) a definite dollar amount. At the broker participant's option, a broker participant may limit his or her offer of compensation to buyer's agents only, to subagents only, or make the offer of compensation to both. Any such limitations must be specified on the property data form and in the MLS. The amount of compensation offered to buyer's agents or subagents may be the same or different but must be clearly specified on the property data profile sheet. Broker participants wishing to offer subagency to the other MLS participants must so specify on the property data profile sheet and on the MLS; otherwise, the offer of compensation does not constitute an offer of subagency.

Cooperating agents should choose to be either the seller's agent or the buyer's agent, and make sure their actions conform to their choice. They should be aware of the practical and legal consequences of this choice to avoid a conflict of loyalties or a violation of Real Estate Law.

In general, if the cooperating agent is acting like the agent of the buyer, he or she *is* the agent of the buyer. An agency relationship is created between the agent and the buyer by implication. The buyer becomes the cooperating agent's principal and the seller becomes the third party. When the buyer makes an offer, he or she signs the Confirmation of Agency form and confirms the agency relationship in writing. Until that point, there is no clear rule about when the fiduciary relationship starts between the cooperating agent and the buyer. It is safe to assume that the agency relationship starts as soon as the cooperating agent begins acting in the best interest of the buyer.

Agent's Authority

http://www.leginfo.ca.gov

(Check California law, check Civil Code, type in agency at the bottom.)

There are certain restrictions on an agent's authority as described in a listing contract.

1. A principal is not responsible for the acts of the agent if those acts are beyond the agent's actual authority. If the principal has not given the agent actual or ostensible authority to do the act, a third party cannot hold the principal responsible.

2. An agent may have authority under a power of attorney, allowing him or her to conduct certain business for a principal. A special power of attorney authorizes the agent to do certain specific acts. A general power of attorney allows the agent to transact all the business of the principal. The agent is then known as an **Attorney in Fact**.

3. A broker cannot accept a deposit from a buyer unless specifically authorized to do so in the listing agreement. When an agent does so without authorization from the seller, he or she is acting as an agent of the buyer and not the seller. Any misappropriation of these funds by the broker would result in loss to the buyer and not the seller. Most listing agreements, however, do allow the agent to receive the buyer's deposit on behalf of the seller. This authority given to the agent also applies to any subagents, unless the subagent is working as the agent of the buyer.

4. An agent may not return a buyer's deposit after the seller accepts the offer, without the consent of the seller.

5. The acceptance of a check, rather than cash or a promissory note, as an earnest money deposit must be disclosed to the seller at the time the offer is presented. Also, if the buyer instructs the agent to hold the check uncashed until the offer is accepted, the fact must be disclosed to the seller when the offer is presented.

6. An agent who puts a client's money in his or her own personal bank account is guilty of **Commingling**. Checks must be deposited the next business day after receiving them, either into a trust account or a neutral escrow account. If an agent uses the client's money, it is known as **Conversion**.

Duties of an Agent Toward a Principal

A real estate agent owes loyalty and confidentiality to his or her principal. The agent is a fiduciary and may not personally profit from the agency relationship except through the agreed-upon commission. As a fiduciary, the agent, regarding the principal, is bound by law to show good faith, loyalty and honesty.

In addition to those duties to the seller, the listing agent owes a duty of fair and honest dealing to the buyer, including the duty of full disclosure. An agent may not withhold from a prospective buyer any material facts that are known to the seller or agent, but not to the buyer. The duty to disclose includes conducting a reasonably competent and diligent inspection of the property and noting anything that would affect its value or desirability.

As a result of the Easton decision (Easton v. Strassburger, 1984), real estate agents can be held liable, not only for defects they know about, but for defects about which they should have known as a result of careful investigation.

Easton v. Strassburger

A home built on a land fill that had not been properly compacted was listed for sale. The owner did not tell the listing broker about the landslide problem that had developed as a result of the poor engineering on the slope. The property was sold and the buyer suffered a substantial loss as a result of land slippage.

In a court action, the buyer proved that one of the listing agents noticed the netting that had been placed on the slope to keep it in place, and another agent had noticed an uneven floor in the house that had occurred as a result of the undisclosed soil problem. The court held that these **Red Flags** should have been seen as evidence of a problem and further investigated by the agents.

The court ruled that a broker has the duty to inspect a property and disclose any material facts affecting its value. A broker is required to uncover any "reasonably discoverable" problems and tell all interested parties. No property may be sold "as is" without a complete disclosure of the defect, even though a broker might possess a disclaimer of liability for the defect.

Senate Bill 453

The Easton decision has been modified by legislation (Senate Bill 453) to include these points.

1. The broker inspection requirement is limited to one-to-four residential units.

2. Brokers are only accountable for a reasonably competent visual inspection of a property.

3. The level of competence required for the property inspection is measured only by the degree of knowledge and experience required to obtain a real estate license.

4. A listing must be in writing for the broker or cooperating brokers to be liable for damages.

5. Inaccessible common areas need not be inspected.

6. There is a two-year statute of limitations from close of escrow, date of recording or occupancy.

7. Buyer must show adequate care and is held responsible for a reasonable personal inspection of the property.

8. Insurance companies may not exclude broker liability from their policy coverage, as a result of a breach of the obligation established by this bill.

Real Estate Transfer Disclosure Statement

The Real Estate Transfer Disclosure Statement is a document that must be provided to any buyer of property (one-to-four residential units) by the seller. It is a detailed statement telling what the seller knows about the condition of the property. Any defects must be mentioned as well as any potential problems that might affect the property value, that a buyer should know. Usually a broker obtains this statement at the time the listing is taken and provides a copy to a buyer before an offer is presented. If the disclosure statement is given after a buyer presents an offer, he or she may terminate the contract by written notice to the seller within three days after receiving the disclosure statement. A copy of this statement is included on the following page.

Real Estate Transfer Disclosure Statement Form (1 of 3)

CALIFORNIA
ASSOCIATION
OF REALTORS®

REAL ESTATE TRANSFER DISCLOSURE STATEMENT
(CALIFORNIA CIVIL CODE 1102, ET SEQ)
(C.A.R. Form TDS, Revised 10/01)

THIS DISCLOSURE STATEMENT CONCERNS THE REAL PROPERTY SITUATED IN THE CITY OF _____
_____, COUNTY OF _____, STATE OF CALIFORNIA,
DESCRIBED AS _____.
THIS STATEMENT IS A DISCLOSURE OF THE CONDITION OF THE ABOVE DESCRIBED PROPERTY IN COMPLIANCE
WITH SECTION 1102 OF THE CIVIL CODE AS OF (date)_____. IT IS NOT A WARRANTY OF ANY
KIND BY THE SELLER(S) OR ANY AGENT(S) REPRESENTING ANY PRINCIPAL(S) IN THIS TRANSACTION, AND IS
NOT A SUBSTITUTE FOR ANY INSPECTIONS OR WARRANTIES THE PRINCIPAL(S) MAY WISH TO OBTAIN.

I. COORDINATION WITH OTHER DISCLOSURE FORMS

This Real Estate Transfer Disclosure Statement is made pursuant to Section 1102 of the Civil Code. Other statutes
require disclosures, depending upon the details of the particular real estate transaction (for example: special study
zone and purchase-money liens on residential property).

Substituted Disclosures: The following disclosures have or will be made in connection with this real estate transfer,
and are intended to satisfy the disclosure obligations on this form, where the subject matter is the same:

☐ Inspection reports completed pursuant to the contract of sale or receipt for deposit.

☐ Additional inspection reports or disclosures._____
_____

II. SELLER'S INFORMATION

The Seller discloses the following information with the knowledge that even though this is not a warranty, prospective
Buyers may rely on this information in deciding whether and on what terms to purchase the subject property. Seller
hereby authorizes any agent(s) representing any principal(s) in this transaction to provide a copy of this statement to
any person or entity in connection with any actual or anticipated sale of the property.

**THE FOLLOWING ARE REPRESENTATIONS MADE BY THE SELLER(S) AND ARE NOT THE
REPRESENTATIONS OF THE AGENT(S), IF ANY. THIS INFORMATION IS A DISCLOSURE AND IS NOT
INTENDED TO BE PART OF ANY CONTRACT BETWEEN THE BUYER AND SELLER.**

Seller ☐ is ☐ is not occupying the property.

A. The subject property has the items checked below (read across)

☐ Range	☐ Oven	☐ Microwave
☐ Dishwasher	☐ Trash Compactor	☐ Garbage Disposal
☐ Washer/Dryer Hookups		☐ Rain Gutters
☐ Burglar Alarms	☐ Smoke Detector(s)	☐ Fire Alarm
☐ T.V. Antenna	☐ Satellite Dish	☐ Intercom
☐ Central Heating	☐ Central Air Conditioning	☐ Evaporator Cooler(s)
☐ Wall/Window Air Conditioning	☐ Sprinklers	☐ Public Sewer System
☐ Septic Tank	☐ Sump Pump	☐ Water Softener
☐ Patio/Decking	☐ Built-in Barbecue	☐ Gazebo
☐ Sauna		
☐ Hot Tub ☐ Locking Safety Cover*	☐ Pool ☐ Child Resistant Barrier*	☐ Spa ☐ Locking Safety Cover*
☐ Security Gate(s)	☐ Automatic Garage Door Opener(s)*	☐ Number Remote Controls _____
Garage: ☐ Attached	☐ Not Attached	☐ Carport
Pool/Spa Heater: ☐ Gas	☐ Solar	☐ Electric
Water Heater: ☐ Gas	☐ Water Heater Anchored, Braced, or Strapped*	☐ Private Utility or
Water Supply: ☐ City	☐ Well	Other _____
Gas Supply: ☐ Utility	☐ Bottled	
☐ Window Screens	☐ Window Security Bars ☐ Quick Release Mechanism on Bedroom Windows*	

Exhaust Fan(s) in _____ 220 Volt Wiring in _____ Fireplace(s) in _____
☐ Gas Starter _____ ☐ Roof(s): Type: _____ Age: _____ (approx.)
☐ Other: _____
Are there, to the best of your (Seller's) knowledge, any of the above that are not in operating condition? ☐ Yes ☐ No. If yes, then
describe. (Attach additional sheets if necessary): _____
_____

(*see footnote on page 2)

TDS-11 REVISED 10/01 (PAGE 1 OF 3) **Print Date BDC Jan 02**

Buyer and Seller acknowledge receipt of a copy of this page.

Buyer's Initials (_____)(_____)
Seller's Initials (_____)(_____)

Reviewed by
Broker or Designee _____ Date _____

EQUAL HOUSING
OPPORTUNITY

MASTER COPY
REAL ESTATE TRANSFER DISCLOSURE STATEMENT (TDS-11 PAGE 1 OF 3)

Real Estate Transfer Disclosure Statement Form (2 of 3)

Property Address: _____ Date: _____

B. Are you (Seller) aware of any significant defects/malfunctions in any of the following? ☐ Yes ☐ No. If yes, check appropriate space(s) below.

☐ Interior Walls ☐ Ceilings ☐ Floors ☐ Exterior Walls ☐ Insulation ☐ Roof(s ☐ Windows ☐ Doors ☐ Foundation ☐ Slab(s)
☐ Driveways ☐ Sidewalks ☐ Walls/Fences ☐ Electrical Systems ☐ Plumbing/Sewers/Septics ☐ Other Structural Components
(Describe:_____
_____)

If any of the above is checked, explain. (Attach additional sheets if necessary):_____
_____
_____

*This garage door opener or child resistant pool barrier may not be in compliance with the safety standards relating to automatic reversing devices as set forth in Chapter 12.5 (commencing with Section 19890) of Part 3 of Division 13 of, or with the pool safety standards of Article 2.5 (commencing with Section 115920) of Chapter 5 of Part 10 of Division 104 of, the Health and Safety Code. The water heater may not be anchored, braced, or strapped in accordance with Section 19211 of the Health and Safety Code. Window security bars may not have quick release mechanisms in compliance with the 1995 Edition of the California Building Standards Code.

C. Are you (Seller) aware of any of the following:
1. Substances, materials, or products which may be an environmental hazard such as, but not limited to, asbestos, formaldehyde, radon gas, lead-based paint, mold, fuel or chemical storage tanks, and contaminated soil or water on the subject property . . . . ☐ Yes ☐ No
2. Features of the property shared in common with adjoining landowners, such as walls, fences, and driveways, whose use or responsibility for maintenance may have an effect on the subject property . . . . ☐ Yes ☐ No
3. Any encroachments, easements or similar matters that may affect your interest in the subject property . . . . ☐ Yes ☐ No
4. Room additions, structural modifications, or other alterations or repairs made without necessary permits . . . . ☐ Yes ☐ No
5. Room additions, structural modifications, or other alterations or repairs not in compliance with building codes . . . . . . ☐ Yes ☐ No
6. Fill (compacted or otherwise) on the property or any portion thereof . . . . ☐ Yes ☐ No
7. Any settling from any cause, or slippage, sliding, or other soil problems . . . . ☐ Yes ☐ No
8. Flooding, drainage or grading problems . . . . ☐ Yes ☐ No
9. Major damage to the property or any of the structures from fire, earthquake, floods, or landslides . . . . ☐ Yes ☐ No
10. Any zoning violations, nonconforming uses, violations of "setback" requirements . . . . ☐ Yes ☐ No
11. Neighborhood noise problems or other nuisances . . . . ☐ Yes ☐ No
12. CC&R's or other deed restrictions or obligations . . . . ☐ Yes ☐ No
13. Homeowners' Association which has any authority over the subject property . . . . ☐ Yes ☐ No
14. Any "common area" (facilities such as pools, tennis courts, walkways, or other areas co-owned in undivided interest with others) . . . . ☐ Yes ☐ No
15. Any notices of abatement or citations against the property . . . . ☐ Yes ☐ No
16. Any lawsuits by or against the seller threatening to or affecting this real property, including any lawsuits alleging a defect or deficiency in this real property or "common areas" (facilities such as pools, tennis courts, walkways, or other areas, co-owned in undivided interest with others). . . . . ☐ Yes ☐ No

If the answer to any of these is yes, explain. (Attach additional sheets if necessary): _____
_____
_____

Seller certifies that the information herein is true and correct to the best of the Seller's knowledge as of the date signed by the Seller.

Seller_____ Date _____

Seller_____ Date _____

TDS-11 REVISED 10/01 (PAGE 2 OF 3)

Buyer and Seller acknowledge receipt of a copy of this page.
Buyer's Initials (_____)(_____)
Seller's Initials (_____)(_____)

Reviewed by
Broker or Designee _____ Date _____

EQUAL HOUSING OPPORTUNITY

MASTER COPY
REAL ESTATE TRANSFER DISCLOSURE STATEMENT (TDS-11 PAGE 2 OF 3)

Real Estate Transfer Disclosure Statement (3 of 3) is located in the back of the book.

Duties and Liabilities of an Agent Toward a Third Party

An agent has a duty of honesty and fairness in dealing with third parties. Occasionally, the line between truth and fiction is blurred, sometimes innocently, sometimes with malice intended. It is easy for an agent to misrepresent a fact to a third party if the agent is not careful.

A **Tort** is a violation of a legal right, or a civil wrong such as negligence, libel or nuisance. An agent is not liable for torts committed by the principal. For example, if a seller does not disclose to the agent that the shower floor has dry rot or that the roof leaks, the agent is not responsible for lack of disclosure by the seller. An agent is only responsible for his or her own torts.

Remember

Three types of misrepresentations:

- Innocent misrepresentations
- Negligent misrepresentations
- Fraudulent misrepresentations

Innocent Misrepresentations

These are statements not known to be untrue at the time they are made, and usually carry no legal liability for an agent. However, a buyer or seller could cancel a contract as a result.

Negligent Misrepresentations

These are untrue statements made without facts to back them up. The agent is not aware of the falseness of the statement at the time, but is liable for them.

Fraudulent Misrepresentations

Untrue statements made by an agent who knows he or she is not telling the truth. The agent may be liable for committing fraud.

Puffing is a term to describe a statement made by an agent who honestly believes the inflated statement about the condition of a property is just another innocent way to make a sale. If a prospective buyer believes it to be true, however, the agent may be guilty of misrepresentation and may be held liable.

Rights of an Agent Regarding a Principal

> ## Agents Earn a Commission if they:
>
> - Produce a ready, willing and able buyer to purchase on the terms and at the price asked by the seller
>
> - Secure from a prospective buyer a binding contract with terms and conditions that are accepted by the seller

A seller may not have a change of mind upon the occurrence of the above two events. Actually, a seller can opt out but must still pay a commission. An agent has earned a commission once the above tasks are accomplished. If the agent brings about a "meeting of the minds" of the buyer and seller on price and other terms for the transaction, the agent has earned the commission. So if a valid contract is entered into by buyer and seller, the agent is entitled to a commission even though the sale is never completed.

Agreements between cooperating brokers for dividing commissions are normally made. Usually the listing broker is the one who receives the commission as a result of his or her contract with the seller. Commonly, the broker agrees to a 50-50 split with the cooperating, or selling, broker. The payment ordinarily is made through escrow at the closing.

The amount of commission is decided by the seller and the broker, and included in the listing agreement. Usually it is a percentage of the sales price, but does not necessarily have to be mentioned in this manner. The amount of commission is not set by law and is always negotiable.

If a broker has produced a buyer during the term of the listing who presents an accepted offer to the seller, the broker has earned the commission. If, after a listing has expired, a buyer and seller complete a sale on the exact terms of those presented and rejected during the term of the listing, it is reasonable to say the broker has earned a commission.

There is a clause in most listing agreements called the safety, or protection, clause. It allows a broker to collect a commission if a prospective buyer, whose name has been supplied to the seller as a prospect for the property, comes to an agreement with the seller within so many proscribed days after the listing has terminated, regardless of whether or not the property has been relisted by another broker. This prevents a seller from simply waiting for a listing to end before accepting an offer, and then refusing to pay the original broker (the procuring cause), a commission.

Remember

About Commissions:

- The amount of commission is *not* set by law and is *always* negotiable

Termination of an Agency

An Agency can be Terminated by:

- Full performance

- Expiration of its term

- Agreement of the parties

- Acts of the parties

- Operation of law

- Death of the broker (not employed salesperson)

Acts of the Parties

A principal or agent always has the power to cancel a listing; whether it is a legal right to do so is another question. The principal or agent may be liable for breach of contract if the cancellation is without good reason.

Operation of Law

Operation of law can mean death of the broker or principal before a buyer is found, insanity, incapacity, destruction of the listed property or bankruptcy of the principal.

Multiple Listing Service

A multiple listing service is a cooperative listing service conducted by a group of brokers, usually members of a real estate association. A listing is submitted to a central bureau, where it is entered into a computerized system, and printed periodically in a multiple listing book that is available to the members.

Brokers then work cooperatively in selling each others' listings. Commission earned on such listings are shared between the cooperating brokers, with the listing broker providing for the division of commission in each listing sent to other participants.

A broker is entitled to a commission when he or she produces a buyer ready, willing and able to purchase the property for the price and on the terms specified by the seller, regardless of whether the sale is ever consummated. The broker must be the procuring cause of the sale to earn a commission.

Occasionally, a matter of great dispute becomes an issue between real estate agents. When more than one agent has shown a prospective buyer a property, with or without the knowledge of the other agent's involvement, each may feel they have earned the commission when the buyer finally authorizes one of them to write up an offer which is accepted by the seller.

The law says the agent who is the Procuring Cause of the sale, or the one who actually wrote the offer and presented it to the seller for acceptance, has earned the commission. The others were unable to bring the buyer to the point of sale, and therefore did not earn a commission.

This is the final chapter in the section about the legal aspects of real estate. Review the information that has been presented here carefully to make sure you have a clear understanding of real estate and the law.

Post Test

The following self test repeats the one you took at the beginning of this chapter. Now take the exam again—since you have read all the material— and check your knowledge of agency.

1. By authorizing an agent to perform particular acts in a listing, the seller is establishing a:
    - a. third party agency
    - b. special agency
    - c. ordinary agency
    - d. general agency

2. With whom do a principal and agent negotiate during the sale of a property?
    - a. broker
    - b. seller
    - c. third party
    - d. buyer

3. Ben put an ad in the local newspaper to sell his home. He only wanted legitimate buyers, and no agents, to respond to his advertisement. The phrase he would probably use is:
    - a. third parties only
    - b. buyers only
    - c. no general agents
    - d. principals only

4. Barbara, a broker, wrote an offer on a house that was not currently listed. The seller had not authorized her to act in his behalf, but said she could present her offer. The seller accepted the offer and agreed to pay the broker a commission as his agent. This is an example of:
    - a. ratification
    - b. specific agency
    - c. ostensible agency
    - d. estoppel

5. An agency is normally established between a broker and a principal by:
    - a. ostensible agreement
    - b. ratification
    - c. express contract
    - d. implied contract

6. Lonnie, an agent, has an exclusive agency listing with Keith and Sarah to sell their house. Her fiduciary duty is to:
    - a. the buyer and seller
    - b. the buyer
    - c. no one
    - d. the seller

7. Calvin, a homeowner, through carelessness led a third party to believe a broker named Harry was his agent, when in fact he was not. This is an example of:
    - a. ostensible agency
    - b. ratification
    - c. bilateral agency
    - d. express agency

8. Lori and Bryan listed their house with broker Jenny. The listing was an exclusive right to sell, and Jenny put it on the multiple listing service immediately. At an open house one weekend, a couple came in and made an offer on the house, and Jenny wrote up the offer. To whom does Jenny owe a fiduciary duty?
    - a. the seller and buyer
    - b. Lori and Bryan
    - c. primarily to the seller, secondarily to the buyer
    - d. the buyer

9. A listing is terminated by all of the following except:
    - a. death of the seller
    - b. destruction of the property
    - c. death of the listing salesperson
    - d. bankruptcy of the seller

10. The disclosure statement that must be signed by the seller and given to the buyer is known as a:
    - a. listing
    - b. deposit receipt
    - c. seller's disclosure of liens
    - d. real estate transfer disclosure statement

Vocabulary

Read the definition, find the matching term and write the corresponding term number on the line provided.

Terms

1. Agency	10. Estoppel
2. Agent	11. Fiduciary
3. Arm's Length Transaction	12. Principal
4. Attorney in Fact	13. Puffing
5. Client	14. Ratification
6. Commingling	15. Red Flag
7. Conversion	16. Subagent
8. Customer	17. Third Party
9. Dual Agent	18. Tort

Definitions

1. ___ A person who acts for and in the place of another, called a principal, for the purpose of effecting the principal's legal relationship with third persons

2. ___ A person who authorizes another to act in his or her place in regard to relations with third persons

3. ___ A person who may be affected by the terms of an agreement but who is not a party to the agreement

4. ___ A relationship in which one party (principal) authorizes another party (agent) to act as the principal's representative in dealing with third parties

5. ___ A transaction, such as a sale of property, in which all parties involved are acting in their own self-interest and are under no undue influence or pressure from the other parties

6. ___ The approval of a previously authorized act, performed on behalf of a person, which makes the act valid and legally binding

7. ___ A legal doctrine which prevents a person from denying something to be true or a fact which is contrary to previous statements made by that same person

8. ___ The person who employs an agent to perform a service for a fee

9. ___ A prospective buyer of real estate; not to be confused with a property seller, who is the listing broker's client

10. ___ A relationship that implies a position of trust or confidence

11. ___ An agent who represents both parties in a transaction

12. ___ An agent of a person who is already acting as an agent for a principal

13. ___ A competent and disinterested person who is authorized by another person to act in his or her place

14. ___ To deposit client funds in the broker's personal account

15. ___ Something that would warn a reasonably observant person of a potential problem, thus requiring further investigation

16. ___ Exaggerated comments or opinions not made as representations of fact, thus not grounds for misrepresentation

17. ___ A negligent or intentional wrongful act arising from breach of duty created by law and not contract; violation of a legal right

18. ___ The appropriation of property belonging to another; as in a broker using a client's funds

Answers

Pre-Test/Post Test

1. b
2. c
3. d
4. a
5. c
6. d
7. a
8. a
9. c
10. d

Vocabulary

1. 2
2. 12
3. 17
4. 1
5. 3
6. 14
7. 10
8. 5
9. 8
10. 11
11. 9
12. 16
13. 4
14. 6
15. 15
16. 13
17. 18
18. 7

SECTION THREE

FINANCIAL ASPECTS OF REAL ESTATE

CHAPTER

8

REAL ESTATE
FINANCE

Focus

- **Promissory note**
- **Trust deeds and mortgages**
- **Transfer of property by the borrower**
- **Special clauses in financing instruments**
- **Foreclosure**
- **Junior trust deeds**
- **Balloon payment loans**
- **Unsecured loans**
- **Alternative financing**
- **Closing those extra sales**
- **New type of mortgage**
- **Short pay**

Pre-Test

The following is a self test to determine how much you know about finance before reading this chapter. Take it without studying, then read the material presented in the text. At the end of the chapter you will find a repeat of this exam. Test your knowledge by answering the questions again, then check your improvement. (The answers are found at the end of this chapter.) Good luck!

1. When an owner uses a property as security for a loan, but does not give up possession, it is called:
   a. hypothecation
   b. pledge
   c. alienation
   d. amortization

2. A neutral third party is part of which of the following?
   a. contract of sale
   b. mortgage
   c. trust deed
   d. agreement of sale

3. In a trust deed, who of the following is the trustor?
   a. lender
   b. trustee
   c. beneficiary
   d. borrower

4. Who holds bare legal title to a property encumbered by a trust deed?
   a. beneficiary
   b. trustor
   c. escrow officer
   d. trustee

5. The purpose of a reconveyance deed is:
   a. to revert a life estate to the grantor
   b. to remove a cloud on a title
   c. to deed the property to the borrower after a note secured by a deed of trust has been paid in full
   d. to redeem a property after a foreclosure sale

6. An "or more" clause allows:
   a. a borrower to borrow as much as he or she wants
   b. a borrower to negotiate a new loan at the end of the term
   c. a borrower to pay off a loan early with no penalty
   d. a borrower to renegotiate his or her loan whenever the interest rate changes

7. Someone who buys an existing negotiable note is known as:
   a. the maker
   b. the holder
   c. the holder in due course
   d. the trustee

8. Which of the following is true about trust deeds and mortgages?
   a. foreclosure is the remedy for default
   b. there is a redemption period after foreclosure
   c. the cost to cure a default is the same
   d. the number of parties in the creation

9. Who must sign a reconveyance deed?
   a. the lender
   b. the buyer
   c. the trustor
   d. the trustee

10. Which of the following is inconsistent with the others?
    a. agreement of sale
    b. contract of sale
    c. all-inclusive trust deed (AITD)
    d. land contract

Terms

The following terms are the keys to your success in learning about real estate. Refer to them as you study this chapter for greater understanding of subjects presented here.

Acceleration Clause

A clause in a loan document describing certain events that would cause the entire loan to be due

Adjustable Rate Mortgage (ARM)

A note whose interest rate is tied to a flexible index

Agreement of Sale

A contract for the sale of real property where the seller gives up possession, but retains the title until the purchase price is paid in full

Alienation Clause

A clause in a loan document that would allow the lender to call the entire loan due upon the sale of the property

All-Inclusive Trust Deed

A purchase money deed of trust subordinate to—but still including—the original loan

Annual Percentage Rate (APR)

The relationship of the total finance charge to the total amount to be financed as required under the Truth-in-Lending Act

Assignment of Rents

An agreement between a property owner and the holder of a trust deed or mortgage by which the holder receives, as security, the right to collect rents from tenants of the property in the event of default by the borrower

Assumption Clause

A buyer takes over the existing loan and agrees to be liable for the repayment of the loan

Balloon Payment

Under an installment loan, a final payment that is substantially larger than any other payment and repays the debt in full

Beneficiary

The lender under a deed of trust

Blanket Loan

A loan secured by several properties

Collateral

Something of value given as security for a debt

Contract of Sale

A contract for the sale of real property where the seller gives up possession but retains title until the total of the purchase price is paid off

Default

Failure to pay a debt or on a contract

Deficiency Judgment

A personal judgment against a borrower for the balance of a debt owed when the sale of the security for the loan is not sufficient enough to pay the debt

Equal Credit Opportunity Act

A federal law that requires lenders to assure that credit is available with fairness, impartiality and without discrimination

Equitable Title

The interest held by the trustor or vendee

Equity of Redemption

Also known as the right of redemption; the right of a debtor, before a foreclosure sale, to reclaim property that had been given up due to mortgage default

Equity

The value remaining in a property after payment of all liens

Foreclosure

A legal procedure by which mortgaged property in which there has been default on the part of the borrower is sold to satisfy the debt

Foreclosure Sale

A sale where property is sold to satisfy a debt

Fully Amortized Note

A note that is fully repaid at maturity by periodic reduction of the principal

Grace Period

An agreed-upon time after the payment of a debt is past due, during which a party can perform without being considered in default

Graduated Payment Adjustable Mortgage (GPAM)

A loan in which the monthly payment graduates by a certain percentage each year for a specific number of years, then levels off for the remaining term of the loan

Hard Money Loan

The evidence of a debt that is given in exchange for cash

Holder

The party to whom a promissory note is made payable

Holder in Due Course

A person who has obtained a negotiable instrument (promissory note, check) in the ordinary course of business before it is due, in good faith and for value, without knowledge that it has been previously dishonored

Home Equity Loan

A cash loan made against the equity in the borrower's home

Hypothecation

A process which allows a borrower to remain in possession of the property while using it to secure a loan.

Interest

The cost of borrowing money

Judicial Foreclosure

Foreclosure by court action

Junior Trust Deed

Any trust deed that is recorded after a first trust deed, whose priority is less than the first trust deed

Land Contract

A contract for the sale of real property where the seller gives up possession, but retains the title until the purchase price is paid in full; also known as a contract of sale or agreement of sale

Legal Title

Title that is complete and perfect regarding right of ownership; may be held by a trustee under a deed of trust

Maker

The borrower who executes a promissory note and becomes primarily liable for payment to the lender

Mortgage

A legal document used as security for a debt

Mortgagee

The lender under a mortgage

Mortgagor

The borrower under a mortgage

Naked Legal Title

Title lacking the rights and privileges commonly associated with ownership

Negotiable Instrument

Any written instrument that may be transferred by endorsement or delivery

Notice of Default

A notice to a defaulting party that there has been a nonpayment of a debt

Notice of Trustee's Sale

Notice given, and published, that a trustee's sale will be held to sell a property to satisfy a debt

Novation

The substitution of a new obligation for an old one

Open End Loan

A loan where the borrower is given a limit up to which may be borrowed, with each advance secured by the same trust deed

"Or More" Clause

A clause in a promissory note that allows a borrower to pay it off early with no penalty

Package Loan

A loan on real property that can be secured by land, structure, fixtures and other personal property

Partially Amortized Installment Note

A promissory note with a repayment schedule that is not sufficient to amortize the loan over its term

Pledge

The transfer of property to a lender to be held as security for repayment of a debt; lender takes possession of property

Power of Sale

A clause in a trust deed or mortgage that gives the holder the right to sell the property in the event of default by the borrower

Prepayment Clause

A clause in a trust deed that allows a lender to collect a certain percentage of a loan as a penalty for an early payoff

Principal

The original amount borrowed

Promissory Note

A written promise or order to pay, evidence of a debt

Purchase Money Loan

A trust deed created as evidence of a debt at the time of the sale of real property

Reconveyance Deed

A deed used to transfer title to a property back to the trustor after a trust deed has been paid off

Reinstate

Bring current and restore

Release Clause

A provision found in many blanket loans enabling the borrower to obtain partial release from the loan of specific parcels

Request for Notice

A notice that is sent, upon request, to any parties interested in a trust deed, informing them of a default

Reverse Annuity Mortgage

A loan that enables elderly homeowners to borrow against the equity in their homes by receiving monthly payments from a lender, that are needed to help meet living costs

Rollover Mortgage

A loan that allows the rewriting of a new loan at the termination of a prior loan

Second Trust Deed

The evidence of a debt that is recorded after a first trust deed; a junior trust deed

Security

Evidence of obligations to pay money

Shared Appreciation Mortgage (SAM)

Lender and borrower agree to share a certain percentage of the appreciation in market value of the property

Sheriff's Deed

A deed given by a court; a proof of a sale to satisfy a judgment

Soldier's and Sailor's Relief Act

A federal law designed to protect persons in the military service from loss of property when their ability to make the payment has been affected by their entering military service

Statutory

Regarding laws created by the enactment of legislation as opposed to law created by court decisions

Straight Note

A promissory note in which payments of interest only are made periodically during the term of the note, with the principal payment due in one lump sum upon maturity; may also be a note with no payments on either principal or interest until the entire sum is due

"Subject-To" Clause

A buyer takes over the existing loan payments, but assumes no personal liability for the loan

Subordination Clause

A clause in which the holder of a trust deed permits a subsequent loan to take priority

Swing Loan

A short-term loan used to enable the purchaser of a new property to buy that property on the strength of the equity from the property the purchaser is now selling

Trust Deed

A document where title to property is transferred to a third party trustee as security for a debt owed by the trustor (borrower) to the beneficiary (lender)

Trustee's Deed

A deed given to a buyer of real property at a trustee's sale

Trustee's Sale

The forced sale of real property, by a lender, to satisfy a debt

Trustee

Holds naked legal title to property as a neutral third party where there is a deed of trust

Trustor

The borrower under a deed of trust

Truth in Lending Act (Regulation Z)

A law that requires borrowers to be informed about the cost of borrowing money

Usury

The act of charging a rate of interest in excess of that permitted by law

Variable Rate Mortgage (VRM)

Related to an adjustable rate loan

Vendee

The buyer under a contract of sale (land contract)

Vendor

The seller under a contract of sale (land contract)

Wrap-Around Loan

A method of financing where a new loan is placed in a secondary position; the new loan includes both the unpaid principal balance of the first loan and whatever sums are loaned by the lender; sometimes called an All-Inclusive Trust Deed (AITD)

Introduction

http://www.tmpmortgage.com/
others.html

Imagine buying a house and being required to pay the total price in cash. The sweet pleasure of home ownership probably would belong somewhere in the next century for most of us. With the average price of a single family home in California being so high, buying a home would be unthinkable without the practical benefit of financing.

http://www.dre.ca.gov
Reference Book, Ch. 12

By allowing a home buyer to obtain a loan for the difference between the sales price and the down payment, real estate lenders have provided the solution to the problem of how property can be bought and sold without the requirement of an all-cash sale.

What started out as a simple loan by a local bank—with an agreement that the borrower pay it all back in a timely manner—is now a complex subject. Buyers and sellers need to rely on experts to explain all the choices there are on financing the purchase or sale of property. You, as a real estate licensee, are one of the experts to whom they will turn.

This chapter on real estate finance is organized with each part building on what you have learned in the earlier sections of the chapter. Try to master each subject—promissory notes, trust deeds, mortgages, special financing clauses, foreclosure, junior trust deeds, other security instruments, miscellaneous provisions of finance and consumer protection—as you come to it. There is a thread that connects everything you are about to study in this chapter. Read with that in mind. Above all, use the list of terms at the beginning of the chapter to look up words you don't know.

Now that you know real estate finance is nothing more than lenders loaning money so people can buy property, let's start with an examination of the lending process.

How Does It Work?

When a loan is made, the borrower signs a promissory note, or note—as it is called, which states that a certain amount of money has been borrowed. The note, then, is the evidence of the debt.

When money is loaned for the purpose of financing real property, some kind of **Collateral** is usually required as well as the promise to pay the money back. That means the lender wants some concrete assurance of getting the money back beyond the borrower's written promise to pay. The property being bought or borrowed against is commonly used as **Security**, or collateral, for the debt. In other words, the lender feels more secure about making the loan if assured of the property ownership in case of **Default**, or nonpayment, of the loan. Then the lender can sell it to get the loan money back.

Commonly, in California, financing is secured with a trust deed or Deed of Trust. After signing the promissory note, the borrower is required to execute a trust deed at the same time, which is the security guaranteeing loan repayment. This is known as **Hypothecation**, a process which allows a borrower to remain in possession of the property while using it to secure the loan. If the borrower does not make payments per the agreement, he or she then loses the rights of possession and ownership.

The lender holds the trust deed, along with the note, until the loan is repaid.

Remember

About the Note and Trust Deed:

- The promissory note is the *evidence* of the debt, or the money borrowed, and the trust deed is the *security* for the debt.

The trust deed allows the lender, in case of loan default, to order the trustee to sell the property described in the deed. (More explanation of this process follows later in the chapter.)

When a buyer obtains a loan to purchase property, he or she is using the lender's money to finance the sale. This is known as leverage. The use of borrowed capital to buy real estate is a process that permits the buyer to use little of one's own money and large amounts of someone else's.

There are several reasons leverage is appealing to both the home buyer and the investor. The principal advantage to the home buyer is not having to amass the entire purchase price to become a home owner. The investor can use leverage to control several investments, rather than just one, each purchased with a small amount of personal funds, and a large amount of a lender's money. The investor can then earn a return on each property, therefore increasing the amount of yield on investment dollars.

Promissory Note

http://www.adnotes.com/
notes3.html

http://www.dre.ca.gov
Reference Book, Ch. 12
p. 228

A **Promissory Note** is a written promise to pay back a certain sum of money at specified terms at an agreed upon time. Sometimes it is simply called the note. Informally, it could be called an I.O.U. The **Maker** is the person borrowing the money, or making the note. It is a personal obligation of the borrower and a complete contract in itself, between the borrower and lender. The **Holder** is loaning the money, or the one holding the note.

According to the Uniform Commercial Code, to be valid or enforceable, a promissory note must meet certain requirements.

A Promissory Note Is:

1. An unconditional written promise to pay a certain sum of money

2. Made by one person to another, both able to legally contract

3. Signed by the maker, or borrower

4. Payable on demand or at a definite time

5. Paid to bearer or to order

6. Voluntarily delivered by the borrower and accepted by the lender

Note Secured by Deed of Trust

Do Not Destroy This Original Note: When paid the Original Note, together with the Deed of Trust securing same, must be surrendered to Trustee for cancellation and retention before reconveyance will be made.

NOTE SECURED BY DEED OF TRUST

$_____ _____, California,_____, 19___

_____after date, for value received, I promise to pay to

_____

_____, or order,

at _____

the sum of _____DOLLARS,

with interest from_____until paid at the rate of

_____per cent per annum, payable_____

In the event of any default in the payment of any installment of principal or interest as herein provided all sums so due including interest, shall bear interest at the rate set forth above but such unpaid interest so compounded shall not exceed an amount equal to simple interest on the unpaid principal at the maximum rate permitted by law. In the event of any default in the payment of any installment of principal or interest when due the whole sum of principal and interest shall become immediately due at the option of the holder of this note. Principal and interest payable in lawful money of the United States. If action be instituted on this note I promise to pay such sum as the Court may fix as attorney's fees. This note is secured by a Deed of Trust to Continental Lawyers Title Company a California corporation, Trustee.

_____   _____

_____   _____

TT-220 (Rev. 3/90)   THIS FORM FURNISHED BY CONTINENTAL LAND TITLE COMPANY
                                            DO NOT DESTROY THIS NOTE

A promissory note is a **Negotiable Instrument**. It is a written promise or order to pay money. The most common type of negotiable instrument is an ordinary bank check. A check is an order to the bank to pay money to the person named. A promissory note is the same thing. It can be transferred by endorsement (signature), just like a check. If correctly prepared, it is considered the same as cash.

Types of Notes

Commonly, a promissory note is referred to as "the note" and we shall do the same here as we study the basic types of notes in use with a trust deed.

> ### Promissory Notes
>
> #### Straight Note
>
> - Calls for payment of **Interest** only, or no payments, during the term of the note, with all accrued money (either **Principal** only, or principal and interest if no payments have been made) due and payable on a certain date
>
> #### Partially Amortized Installment Note
>
> - Calls for periodic payments on the principal, such payments not to include interest; usually demands a **Balloon Payment** at the end of the term to completely pay off debt
>
> #### Fully Amortized Installment Note
>
> - Calls for periodic payments of fixed amounts, to include both interest and principal, which will pay off the debt completely by the end of the term
>
> #### Adjustable Note
>
> - The interest rate in the note varies upward or downward over the term of the loan, depending on the money market conditions and an agreed upon index

Holder in Due Course

As we have seen, notes are negotiable instruments, easily transferable from one person to another. However, the transferee or buyer of a note must have confidence in getting the money when the note is paid.

A **Holder in Due Course** is someone who takes an existing note, and receives more benefits (more than just being paid) than the original holder of the note. This means if the holder of the instrument transfers it to a third party, that party enjoys a favored position, as long as that third party takes the note as a holder in due course. (It must be written on the note.)

Holder in Due Course Takes a Negotiable Instrument which is:

- Complete and regular in appearance and form

- Without notice that it is overdue, or has been dishonored or has any claim on it by any person

- Taken in good faith and for valuable consideration

The favored position that the holder in due course enjoys is a greater claim to the note's payment than the original holder. If a court action is necessary to bring payment on the note, the maker (debtor) cannot use any of the following defenses to refuse payment to a holder in due course, even though they could be used against the original lender.

Defenses Not Allowed by the Maker of a Note:

- The maker cannot claim non-receipt of what the payee promised in exchange for the note.

- The maker cannot claim the debt was already paid. Even if it was, with no proof (as in marking the note "paid"), and the original payee transfers the note to a holder in due course, the original maker might still be required to pay.

- The maker cannot use fraud (in the original making of the note) as a defense.

- The maker cannot claim a setoff. For example, if the amount owed is $10,000, but the payee owes $15,000 to the holder, the difference cannot be used as a defense against paying the note.

All the above defenses may be used against the original payee, or lender, but are not good against a holder in due course.

Indeed, some real defenses are good against any person, a payee or holder in due course.

Defenses Allowed Against Anyone:

- Forgery, if the maker didn't really sign the note

- Secret material changes in the note

- Incapacity, if the maker is a minor or an incompetent

- Illegal object, if the note is connected to an illegal act or if the interest rate is usurious

Conflict in Terms of Note and Trust Deed

As you recall, a note is the evidence of a debt. A **Trust Deed** is only an incident of the debt. As we shall see in the next section, a trust deed must have a note to secure, but a note does not need a trust deed to stand alone. If there is a conflict in the terms of a note and the trust deed used to secure it, the provisions of the note will control. If a note is unenforceable, the presence of a trust deed will not make it valid. However, if a note contains an acceleration clause (due on sale), the trust deed must mention it as well for the clause to be enforceable.

Remember

About Notes and Trust Deeds:

- A trust deed must have a note to secure, but a note does not need a trust deed to stand alone.

- If the conditions of a note and trust deed are in conflict, the terms of the note have the authority.

Trust Deed Jurisdiction

Trust deeds are commonly used as security instruments in the following states: Alaska, Arizona, California, Colorado, the District of Columbia, Idaho, Maryland, Mississippi, Missouri, North Carolina, Oregon, Tennessee, Texas, Virginia, and West Virginia. Different variations on trust deeds as security instruments may be found in a few other states as well.

Trust Deeds and Mortgages

http://www.bradevans.com/ 37full.html

http://www.dre.ca.gov Reference Book, Ch. 12 p. 231

The term that describes the interest of a creditor (lender) in the property of a debtor (borrower), is security interest. The security interest allows certain assets of a borrower to be used to pay off a loan if the borrower defaults. Proceeds from the sale of that property can be taken to pay off the debt. The rights and duties of lenders and borrowers are described in a document called a security instrument. In California, trust deeds are the principal instruments used to secure loans on real property.

Mortgages accomplish the same thing as trust deeds, and are used in other states as security for real property loans. You will hear the term mortgage used loosely in California, as in mortgage company, mortgage broker and mortgage payment—but the mortgage reference here really is a trust deed.

Trust Deeds (Deeds of Trust)

As we mentioned, a trust deed is used to secure a loan on real property. It describes the property being used as security for a debt, and usually includes a power of sale and assignment of rents clause.

Trust Deeds Can Include:

Power of Sale Clause

- Trustor gives trustee the right (by signing the trust deed) to foreclose, sell and convey ownership to a purchaser of the property if the borrower defaults on the loan

Assignment of Rents Clause

- Upon default by the borrower, the lender can take possession of the property and collect any rents being paid

---

The thing to remember about a trust deed is that it is the security for a loan. If the borrower fails to pay, the lender can use the proceeds from sale of the property used as collateral (or secured by the trust deed) for payment. **Foreclosure** is the procedure used by the lender who must exercise the right to collect what is owed if the borrower defaults on payments. Under a deed of trust, it normally takes no more than four months. We will study foreclosure later in this chapter.

Once recorded, a trust deed places a lien on a certain described property to secure the repayment of a debt. It does not have to be recorded to be valid. Since trust deeds, and rarely mortgages, are used to secure real property loans in California, we will examine the trust deed in detail.

Deed of Trust

WOLCOTTS FORM 847—DEED OF TRUST AND ASSIGNMENT OF RENTS WITH INSTALLMENT NOTE—INTEREST INCLUDED (attached)—Rev. 1-93

©1993 WOLCOTTS FORMS, INC.

RECORDING REQUESTED BY

WHEN RECORDED MAIL TO

NAME
STREET
ADDRESS
CITY
STATE
ZIP

(SPACE ABOVE THIS LINE FOR RECORDER'S USE)

DEED OF TRUST AND ASSIGNMENT OF RENTS

THIS DEED OF TRUST, made this _____ day of _____, 19____

BETWEEN _____

_____

_____

_____, herein called Trustor,

whose address is _____
(Number and Street)   (City)   (State)   (Zip Code)

_____, herein called Trustee, and

_____

_____, herein called Beneficiary.

Trustor irrevocably grants, transfers and assigns to Trustee, in trust, with power of sale, all that real property in the City of _____

_____, County of _____, State of California, described as:

TOGETHER with all the rights, privileges, title and interest which Trustor now has or may hereafter acquire in or to said property, including, without limitation, the rents, issues and profits thereof, and with the appurtenances and all buildings and improvements now or hereafter placed thereon, it being understood and agreed that all classes of property, attached or unattached, used in connection therewith shall be deemed fixtures and subject to the property above described;

SUBJECT, HOWEVER, to the right, power and authority given to and conferred upon Beneficiary hereinbelow to collect and apply such rents, issues and profits;

(For the purposes of this instrument all of the foregoing described real property, property rights and interests shall be referred to as "the property.")

Parties

There are three parties to a trust deed: the trustor, the trustee and the beneficiary.

<u>**Three Parties to a Trust Deed:**</u>

- **Trustor**, or borrower; holds **Equitable Title** while paying off the loan; conveys **Bare Legal Title** to trustee by way of the trust deed

- **Trustee**, or neutral third party; holds bare legal title until reconveyance or foreclosure occurs; normally is not involved with the property until asked to reconvey or foreclose

- **Beneficiary**, or lender; holds the note and trust deed until reconveyance, or until the debt is paid off

---

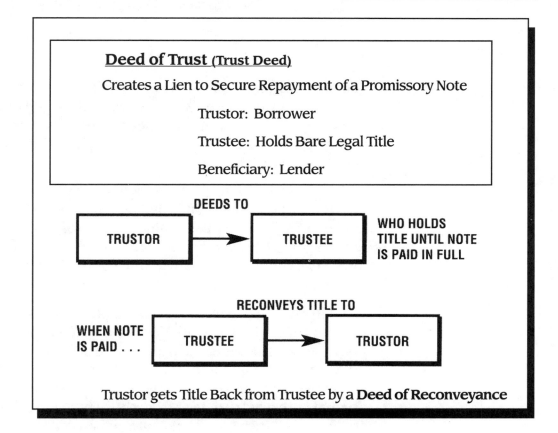

Deed of Trust (Trust Deed)

Creates a Lien to Secure Repayment of a Promissory Note

Trustor: Borrower

Trustee: Holds Bare Legal Title

Beneficiary: Lender

DEEDS TO

| TRUSTOR | → | TRUSTEE | **WHO HOLDS TITLE UNTIL NOTE IS PAID IN FULL** |

RECONVEYS TITLE TO

| **WHEN NOTE IS PAID . . .** | TRUSTEE | → | TRUSTOR |

Trustor gets Title Back from Trustee by a **Deed of Reconveyance**

Leon and Betty bought a house. They signed a note secured by a deed of trust and were given a grant deed, as proof of conveyance, from the seller. The beneficiary, Bank of America, held the note and trust deed. Commonwealth Land Title Company was named as the trustee. When they signed the trust deed, Leon and Betty granted Commonwealth Title naked legal title so they could conduct duties as a trustee. Years went by, and the loan was paid off. Upon notifica-

*tion by Bank of America (the beneficiary), Commonwealth Title (trustee) signed a **Reconveyance Deed**, giving clear **Legal Title** to Leon and Betty.*

Quentin and Kate bought their first house with a 90% loan from First Interstate Bank. As trustors, or borrowers, they were given a grant deed by the seller, which conveyed title to them. First Interstate, the beneficiary, or lender, held the note Quentin and Kate had signed promising to pay back the money loaned, and trust deed which secured the loan. Commonwealth Title Company was named as the trustee, and held naked legal title until the loan was paid off.

The payments were high, but both Quentin and Kate had good jobs, and were confident they could afford the house. After a few years, Kate was laid off, and they fell behind in their payments. They weren't getting along, and finally Kate left Quentin.

Sadly, he notified the beneficiary (First Interstate) that he could no longer make the payments, and the trustee was notified to start foreclosure procedures. A trustee's sale was held, and the house was sold, with the proceeds going to First Interstate to pay off the debt.

Title

The most distinguishing feature of a trust deed is the conveyance of title to a trustee by the borrower, until the debt is paid off. When a trust deed is used to secure a loan, even though the borrower technically owns the property, naked—or bare—legal title is transferred to the trustee by the deed of trust.

The trustee is only given the right to do what is necessary to carry out the terms of the trust. The trustee can foreclose or reconvey, but does not have any other rights relating to the property, such as the right to use or the right to sell. Commonly, the trustee is not even notified until either foreclosure (in case of loan default) or reconveyance (when the loan is paid in full) is required.

Think of the trustee as a neutral party, holding the title for the borrower until the loan is paid off, and foreclosing for the lender if the borrower defaults. Neither the trustor (borrower) nor the beneficiary (lender) holds the title until all terms of their agreement have been met. Upon payment of the debt in full and within 21 calendar days after receiving the original note and trust deed from the beneficiary, along with instructions and fees, the trustee must execute and record the reconveyance.

Full Reconveyance Deed

```
RECORDING REQUESTED BY

WHEN RECORDED MAIL TO:
NAME
STREET ADDRESS
CITY STATE ZIP

                              SPACE ABOVE THIS LINE FOR RECORDER'S USE

AL1        Title Order No. _____
P'N        Escrow or Loan No. _____

          FULL RECONVEYANCE          Recon No. _____

_____ a Corporation, as Trustee under Deed of Trust,
dated _____ , 19 ____ , made by _____
_____
Trustor; and recorded as Instrument No. _____ on _____ , 19 ____ ,
in Book _____ , Page _____ , of Official Records in the office of the County Recorder of
_____ County, California, describing land therein as

having received from holder of the obligations thereunder a written request to reconvey, reciting that all
sums secured by said Deed of Trust have been fully paid, and said Deed of Trust and the note or notes
secured thereby having been surrendered to said Trustee for cancellation, does hereby RECONVEY without
warranty, to the person or persons legally entitled thereto, the estate now held by it thereunder.

     IN WITNESS WHEREOF, _____ , as Trustee, has caused its
corporate name and seal to be hereto affixed by its duly authorized officer.

Dated _____
State of ____ CALIFORNIA ____        as Trustee
                              } SS.  By _____
County of _____                   Assistant Secretary
On _____ before me.

Notary Public, personally appeared _____

personally known to me (or proved to me on the basis of
satisfactory evidence) to be the person(s) whose name(s) is/are
subscribed to the within instrument and acknowledged to me
that he/she/they executed the same in his/her/their authorized
capacity(ies), and that by his/her/their signature(s) on the
instrument the person(s), or the entity upon behalf of which the
person(s) acted, executed the instrument.
WITNESS my hand and official seal.

Signature _____
        Name (Typed or Printed)          (This area for official notarial seal)
```

After being signed by the trustor (borrower), the trust deed—not the note—is recorded in the county where the property is located, then is sent to the lender to hold for the life of the loan. Recording of the trust deed gives public notice of the lien against the property for anyone interested in searching the title of the property.

The reconveyance deed is also recorded, after being signed by the trustee, to give public notice of the lien payment.

Statute of Limitations

The rights of the lender (beneficiary) under a deed of trust do not end when the statute has run out on the note. The trustee has the bare legal title with power of sale and can still sell the property to pay off the debt. The power of sale in a trust deed never expires.

Remedy for Default

Under a deed of trust, the lender may choose between a trustee's sale or **Judicial Foreclosure**.

Reinstatement

When a trust deed debtor is in default on a loan, the loan may be reinstated if all delinquencies and fees are paid prior to five business days before the trustee's sale.

Redemption

Under a trust deed with a power of sale, there is no right of redemption after the trustee's sale. The sale is final.

Deficiency Judgment

A **Deficiency Judgment** is a personal judgment against a borrower for the difference between the unpaid amount of the loan, plus interest, costs and fees of the sale, and the amount of the actual proceeds of the **Foreclosure Sale**. This means if the property sells for less than what is owed to the lender, the borrower will be personally responsible for repayment after the deficiency judgment is filed.

When a loan is secured by a trust deed and the lender forecloses under a power of sale (trustee's sale), a deficiency judgement is not allowed in most cases. Since trust deeds are used almost exclusively in California to secure loans, the only security for a beneficiary is the property itself. Any other personal assets of the borrower in default are protected from judgment under the trust deed.

Peter fell on hard times and lost his house, which was financed with a note secured by a deed of trust, to foreclosure. He owed $250,000 which included the costs of the foreclosure. However, the proceeds of the trustee's sale only amounted to $200,000. The lender lost the deficient $50,000, unable to obtain a deficiency judgment against Peter.

Reconveyance

When payment in full is made, the trustee issues a deed of reconveyance upon request from the beneficiary.

Benefits of a Trust Deed to a Lender

- In case of default, lender takes possession, after trustee sale collects rents

- Relatively short and simple foreclosure process

- Trustee holds title and can easily grant title to buyer at foreclosure sale

- No redemption after foreclosure

- A trust deed never expires

Benefits of a Trust Deed to a Borrower

- Property is the only security for a loan; no deficiency judgment allowed in most cases

Mortgage

A **Mortgage** is a financial instrument that is used to secure a property for the payment of a promissory note. It serves the same purpose as a trust deed by acting as the security for a debt. A mortgage is a lien against a described property until payment of the debt.

Do not get confused when you hear the word mortgage to describe some financial transactions. As mentioned earlier, a mortgage is not commonly used in California, even though you will hear reference to home mortgage, mortgage loan broker and mortgage banker. In reality, a trust deed is the instrument used.

A mortgage is held by the lender for the life of a loan, or until the borrower pays it off. There are some similarities to a trust deed, and some differences, as we shall see in the following examination of mortgages.

Parties

In a mortgage there are two parties: a **Mortgagor** and a **Mortgagee**. The mortgagor (borrower) receives a loan from the mortgagee (lender) and signs a promissory note and mortgage. The mortgage becomes a lien in favor of the mortgagee until the debt is paid in full.

The Two Parties to a Mortgage are:

- Mortgagor (borrower)
- Mortgagee (lender)

Title

A mortgage creates a lien on real property. Title is vested in the borrower, unlike a trust deed, where technically a deed of trust gives limited title (naked legal title) to a trustee, even though it is also spoken of as a lien. In both cases, possession of the property remains with the borrower.

Statute of Limitations

The Statute of Limitations runs out on a note secured by a mortgage in four years. This means a lender must sue within four years of nonpayment to get his or her money back, or the mortgage expires.

Remedy

The common remedy for default of a mortgage is judicial foreclosure, or a court action. If the mortgage contains a power of sale clause, a nonjudicial foreclosure is possible.

Reinstatement

Under a mortgage, a borrower in default may reinstate the loan by paying all delinquencies, plus all costs of the foreclosure action, at any time before the court approves the foreclosure.

Redemption

The right of redemption, or **Equity of Redemption** as it is known in those states using mortgages rather than trust deeds, usually allows a borrower in default to redeem the property within three months after foreclosure sale if the proceeds are sufficient to pay off all indebtedness plus any other foreclosure costs. If the sale does not bring enough money to pay off the debt, the mortgagor has one year to redeem the property by paying off the amount owed, plus costs.

Deficiency Judgment

A lender who forecloses against a defaulted mortgage may obtain a deficiency judgment against the debtor. Because a court action is required in order to foreclose against a mortgage, a deficiency judgment is allowed.

As you recall, a deficiency judgment may be filed against a borrower for the difference between the unpaid amount of the loan, plus foreclosure costs, and the amount of the proceeds of the foreclosure sale. In that case, the lender may get a personal judgment against the borrower that will be effective for 10 years.

Satisfaction

Satisfaction of a mortgage, or payment in full, requires that the lender deliver the original note and mortgage to the party making the request.

Basic Differences Between Trust Deeds and Mortgages	
Parties	Reinstatement
Title	Redemption
Statute of Limitations	Deficiency Judgment
Remedy	Satisfaction

Transfer of Property by the Borrower

Under certain circumstances, a property owner may transfer responsibility for the loan to the buyer when he or she sells the property to another party. A buyer may "assume" an existing loan, or may buy a property "subject to" an existing loan.

Loan Assumption

When a property is sold, a buyer may assume the existing loan. Usually with the approval of the lender, the buyer takes over primary liability for the loan, with the original borrower secondarily liable if there is a default.

What that means in California is that even though the original borrower is secondarily responsible, according to the loan assumption agreement, no actual repayment of the loan may be required of that person. If the new owner defaults, the property is foreclosed, and no deficiency judgment is allowed beyond the amount received at the trustee's sale, even though the original borrower's credit is affected by the foreclosure.

"Subject To"

A buyer may also purchase a property "subject to" the existing loan. The original borrower remains responsible for the loan, even though the buyer takes title and makes the payments. In this case, also, the property remains the security for the loan. In the case of default, it is sold and the proceeds go to the lender, with no recourse to the original buyer other than the foreclosure going against the borrower's credit.

However, a deficiency judgment is allowed if the loan was not a **Purchase Money Loan**, or one made specifically upon purchase of the property. If the loan was a **Hard Money Loan**, or a loan made to get cash, the original borrower could be held personally liable until the loan is paid off, if the trustee forecloses judicially.

Roberto bought his home 20 years ago, and refinanced it after 10 years for money to add on a room. His first deed of trust was a purchase money loan in the amount of $10,000, and the second loan was a hard money loan, secured by the property.

Roberto sold the property to Vicki, who bought the property "subject to" the two existing loans. When she defaulted on the loans and the property went into foreclosure, Roberto was responsible for the second loan, even though he no longer owned the property.

What Roberto should have done, in this case, was to ask the lender, upon sale of the property, for a substitution of liability and agreement to pay (Novation), relieving himself of any liability.

Special Clauses in Financing Instruments

When a borrower signs a note promising to repay a sum, the lender usually will include some specific requirements in the note regarding repayment. These are special clauses meant to protect the lender and the lender's interests.

An **Acceleration Clause** allows a lender to call the entire note due, on occurrence of a specific event such as default in payment, taxes or insurance, or sale of the property.

Another clause, known as an **Alienation** or due-on-sale clause, is a kind of acceleration clause. A lender may call the entire note due if there is a transfer in property ownership from the original borrower to someone else. This clause protects the lender from an unqualified, unapproved buyer taking over a loan. Justifiably, the lender fears possible default, with no control over who is making the payments.

An **Assumption Clause** allows a buyer to assume responsibility for the full payment of the loan with the lender's knowledge and consent.

A **"Subject To" Clause** allows a buyer to take over a loan, making the payments without the knowledge or approval of the lender. The original borrower remains responsible for the loan.

A **Subordination Clause** is used to change the priority of a financial instrument. Remember, the priority of a trust deed is fixed by the date it is recorded: the earlier the date, the greater the advantage. When a note and trust deed includes a subordination clause, a new, later loan may be recorded, and because of the subordination clause, assume a higher priority. This clause is used mainly when land is purchased for future purposes of construction that will require financing. The lender on the new financing would want to be in first position to secure his or her interest, so the trust deed on the land would become subordinate to a new loan on the structure when the new loan was funded and recorded.

Occasionally, a trust deed will include a **Prepayment Clause** in case a borrower pays off a loan early. When lenders make loans, they calculate their return, over the term of the loan. If a loan is paid off before that time, the lender gets less interest than planned, thus the return on investment is threatened. So the borrower has to make it up by paying a penalty. It may not make a lot of sense to us as consumers, but that's the banking business.

For residential property, the prepayment penalty cannot exceed six month's interest. A borrower may prepay up to 20% of the loan amount in any 12 month period without a penalty. A prepayment penalty can then be charged only on the amount in excess of 20% of the original loan amount. Other rules apply for non-residential property.

An **"Or More" Clause** allows a borrower to pay off a loan early, or make higher payments without penalty.

Foreclosure

http://www.dre.ca.gov
Reference Book, Ch. 12
p. 245

When a borrower defaults or stops making payments on a loan secured either by a trust deed or a mortgage, the lender can use the legal process of foreclosure. That terminates the rights and title of the borrower by selling the encumbered property and using the proceeds to pay off the loan and other liens.

Generally, a mortgage can only be foreclosed through a court procedure. However, a trust deed containing a power of sale may be foreclosed by trustee's sale, or judicially.

Trustee's Sale

A **Trustee's Sale** occurs when there is a power of sale included in the trust deed. The power of sale is given to the trustee by the buyer (borrower, trustor) in the trust deed he or she signs at the time of closing. This is commonly part of all trust deeds, and a trustee's sale is the most usual way to foreclose in California. In a trustee's sale, as we have seen, normally no deficiency judgments are allowed. Nor does the debtor have any rights of redemption after the sale.

During the **Statutory** reinstatement period, which runs until five days before the date of sale, the debtor or any other party with a junior lien may **Reinstate** (bring current and restore) the loan in default. After the statutory reinstatement period, the debtor may still redeem the property and stop the foreclosure sale by paying off the entire debt, plus interest, costs and fees, prior to the date of the sale.

The Procedure

http://www.bob-taylor.
com/timetabl.htm

When a borrower is behind in payments, usually a lender will work toward avoiding a foreclosure by allowing a **Grace Period**, usually 10 to 15 days. The lender does not want the property, but just wants to get repaid for the loan. At some point, however, the lender must decide to foreclose, notify the trustee of the borrower's failure to pay (default), and deliver the original note and trust deed to the trustee with instructions to prepare and record a **Notice of Default** against the debtor.

Notice of Default and Election to Sell Under Deed of Trust

Notice of Default and Election to Sell Under Deed of Trust
IMPORTANT NOTICE
IF YOUR PROPERTY IS IN FORECLOSURE BECAUSE YOU ARE BEHIND IN YOUR PAYMENTS, IT MAY BE SOLD WITHOUT ANY COURT ACTION, and you may have the legal right to bring your account in good standing by paying all of your past due payments plus permitted costs and expenses within the time permitted by law for reinstatement of your account, which is normally five business days prior to the date set for the sale of your property. No sale date may be set until three months from the date this notice of default may be recorded (which date of recordation appears on this notice). This amount is _____
as of _____, and will increase until your account becomes current.
      (Date)

You may not have to pay the entire unpaid portion of your account, even though full payment was demanded, but you must pay the amount stated above. However, you and your beneficiary or mortgagee may mutually agree in writing prior to the time the notice of sale is posted (which may not be earlier than the end of the three-month period stated above) to, among other things, (1) provide additional time in which to cure the default by transfer of the property or otherwise: (2) establish a schedule of payments in order to cure your default; or both (1) and (2).

    Following the expiration of the time period referred to in the first paragraph of this notice, unless the obligation being foreclosed upon or a separate written agreement between you and your creditor permits a longer period, you have only the legal right to stop the sale of your property by paying the entire amount demanded by your creditor.

    To find the amount you must pay, or to arrange for payment to stop the foreclosure, or if your property is in foreclosure for any other reason, contact:

_____
(Name of beneficiary or mortgagee)

_____
(Mailing address)

_____
(Telephone)

    If you have any questions, you should contact a lawyer or the government agency which may have insured your loan.

    Notwithstanding the fact that your property is in foreclosure, you may offer your property for sale, provided the sale is concluded prior to the conclusion of the foreclosure.

    Remember, **YOU MAY LOSE LEGAL RIGHTS IF YOU DO NOT TAKE PROMPT ACTION.**

NOTICE IS HEREBY GIVEN, THAT   a corporation, is duly appointed Trustee under a Deed of Trust dated   executed by
                 as Trustor; to secure certain obligations
in favor of

                         , as beneficiary,
recorded   , as instrument no.   , in book   , page   , of Official Records
                        in the Office of the
Recorder of   County, California, describing land
therein as:
                        said obligations
including   note   for the   sum of $

that the beneficial interest under such Deed of Trust and the obligations secured thereby are presently held by the undersigned; that a breach of, and default in, the obligations for which such Deed of Trust is security has occurred in that payment has not been made of:

that by reason thereof, the undersigned, present beneficiary under such Deed of Trust, has executed and delivered to said duly appointed Trustee, a written Declaration of Default and Demand for Sale, and has deposited with said duly appointed Trustee, such Deed of Trust and all documents evidencing obligations secured thereby, and has declared and does hereby declare all sums secured thereby immediately due and payable and has elected and does hereby elect to cause the trust property to be sold to satisfy the obligations secured thereby.

_____

_____

Dated _____

Notice of Default

The Notice of Default must be executed by the beneficiary or trustee and must be recorded in the office of the county recorder where the property is located at least three months before Notice of Sale is given. Within 10 days after recording the Notice of Default, a copy of the notice must be sent by certified or registered mail to all persons who have recorded a request for notice. A copy must also be sent within one month after recording to parties who have recorded interests in the property.

Notice of Default must be sent to:

- Successors in interest to the trustor
- Junior lien holders
- Vendee of any contract of sale
- State Controller if there is a tax lien against the property

---

Anyone interested in a particular deed of trust may ensure being informed of a Notice of Default and Notice of Sale by recording a **Request for Notice** with the county recorder where the property is located.

Request for Notice

RECORDING REQUESTED BY

AND WHEN RECORDED MAIL TO:

NAME

STREET
ADDRESS

CITY
STATE
ZIP

SPACE ABOVE THIS LINE FOR RECORDER'S USE

REQUEST FOR NOTICE

UNDER SECTION 2924b CIVIL CODE

| | | | | ALL | |
| | | | | PTN. | |

Escrow or Loan No.

Title Order No.

In accordance with section 2924b, Civil Code, request is hereby made that a copy of any Notice of Default and a copy of any Notice of Sale under the Deed of Trust recorded as Instrument No. _____ on _____ , in book _____ , page _____ , Official Records of _____ County, California, and describing land therein as

Executed by _____ , as Trustor,
in which _____ is named as
Beneficiary, and _____ , as Trustee,
be mailed to _____
at _____
    Number and Street

    City and State

NOTICE: A copy of any notice of default and of any notice of sale will be sent to the address contained in this recorded request. If your address changes, a new request must be recorded.
Signature _____

Dated _____

State of _____ **CALIFORNIA** _____ } SS.

County of _____

On _____ before me,

Notary Public, personally appeared _____

personally known to me (or proved to me on the basis of satisfactory evidence) to be the person(s) whose name(s) is/are subscribed to the within instrument and acknowledged to me that he/she/they executed the same in his/her/their authorized capacity(ies), and that by his/her/their signature(s) on the instrument the person(s), or the entity upon behalf of which the person(s) acted, executed the instrument.
WITNESS my hand and official seal.

Signature _____

TI-403 (Rev. 12/92)   Ω

Notice of Sale

After recording the Notice of Default, a trustee must wait three months before recording a Notice of Trustee's Sale if the loan is not reinstated by the borrower.

The Notice of Sale must contain a description of the property, and must be published in a newspaper of general circulation in the area where the property is located. The notice must appear at least once a week for 20 days, not more than seven days apart, and must be posted publicly in the city where the sale will be held.

Remember

Foreclosure Facts:

- Reinstatement period: until five days before the sale

- Trustee's sale may be held 20 days after Notice of Trustee's Sale is issued

- Notice of Sale must be published in local newspaper once weekly for 20 days prior to sale

The Sale

The sale is conducted at public auction by the trustee in the county where the property is located, approximately four months after the Notice of Default is recorded.

Remember

Foreclosure Timeframe Under a Trustee Sale:

- Minimum of Three Months and 21 Days

Until the auction bidding is over, the debtor or any junior lienholder may still redeem the property by paying off the defaulted loan in full, plus all fees, costs and expenses permitted by law. Reinstatement of the loan by bringing all delinquent payments up to date and paying all fees may be made at any time until five business days prior to the date of sale.

> ### Trustee Applies Foreclosure Sale Proceeds in This Order:
>
> 1. Trustee's fees, costs and sale expenses
> 2. Beneficiary—to satisfy the full amount of unpaid principal and interest, charges, penalties, costs and expenses
> 3. Junior lien holders in order of priority
> 4. Debtor—any money left over

Anyone may bid at the auction, but the first lien holder, or holder of the debt being foreclosed, is the only one who may "credit bid," or bid the amount that is owed the holder on the defaulted loan without having to actually pay the money. All other bids must be in cash or cashier's checks.

The sale is made to the highest bidder, and the buyer receives a **Trustee's Deed** to the property. The debtor no longer has any interest in, nor the right to, redeeming the foreclosed property.

Steps in a Trustee's Sale

1. Beneficiary Notifies Trustee to Foreclose
2. Trustee Records Notice of Default
3. Reinstatement Period (Up to Five Days before the Sale)
4. Notice of Trustee's Sale and Publication of Date, Time and Place of Sale (Three Weeks)
5. Sale is Held; Highest Cash Bidder Wins
6. Trustee's Deed is Given to Buyer (Sale is Final, Borrower has No Right of Redemption)

The sale is subject to certain liens of record that do not get eliminated by a foreclosure sale. That means the new buyer is responsible for payment of those liens.

> ### Liens Not Eliminated by Foreclosure
>
> * Federal tax liens
> * Assessments and real property taxes

The sale of a property at a trustee's sale will extinguish the trust deed lien securing the debt to the beneficiary (lender) and will also extinguish any junior liens. That means the holder of a junior lien (a second, third or fourth trust deed), in order to protect his or her interest, had better make a bid for the property, or possibly lose the right to collect on the loan if the sale amount is not enough for a pay-off.

Judicial Foreclosure

A trustee may choose a judicial foreclosure instead of the statutory trustee sale. That means instead of the automatic, defined by statute, three month and 21 days minimum foreclosure period, a lengthly court action may take place. The reason a beneficiary would choose a judicial foreclosure under a trust deed is that a deficiency judgment is allowed and the lender has the right to collect any unpaid amount.

Soldier's and Sailors' Civil Relief Act

Persons in the military, under this law known as the **Soldiers' and Sailors' Civil Relief Act**, are protected from foreclosure on their homes while serving time in the military service.

Junior Trust Deeds

http://www.tmpmortgage.
com/others.html

http://www.dre.ca.gov
Reference Book, Ch. 12
p. 236

Another way to finance a property, either at the time of a sale, or afterward, is by using a **Junior Trust Deed**, which is any loan recorded after the first trust deed, secured by a second, third or subsequent trust deed. Many times in a sale, where the first trust deed loan plus the buyer's down payment are not enough to meet the purchase price, additional money is needed.

Outside Financing

One way to get the needed financing is for the buyer to obtain a secondary loan through an outside source, such as a mortgage banker, or private investor. At the same time the buyer is applying for a loan secured by a first trust deed from a conventional lender, a second—or junior—loan is arranged to complete the financing.

As you recall, any loan made at the time of a sale, as part of that sale, is known as a purchase money loan. At the close of escrow, then, the loan from the first trust deed is funded and sent to the escrow holder to be given to the seller after all necessary loan documents have been signed by the buyer.

The same is true of the new purchase money loan secured by a second trust deed. That loan is also funded and the money sent to the escrow holder to be given to the seller after all loan documents have been signed by the buyer. At the same time, the escrow holder asks the buyer to bring in the down payment. The net proceeds after costs of sale from both the first and the second loan, plus the down payment, are then given to the seller at the close of escrow.

Seller Financing

Another common source for secondary financing of a sale is the seller. If the seller is going to be the lender, he or she agrees to "carry back," or act as a banker, and make a loan to the buyer for the needed amount. That loan is secured by a trust deed, in favor of the seller, recorded after the first trust deed.

When a seller "carries the paper" on the sale of his or her home, it is also called a purchase money loan, just like the loan made by an outside lender. If a seller receives a substantial amount from the proceeds of a first loan, plus the buyer's down payment, it may be in the seller's interest to carry a second trust deed—possibly for income or to reduce tax liability by accepting installment payments.

Dominick made an offer on a house owned by Bruno, who accepted an offer of $275,000, with $27,500 as the down payment. The buyer qualified for a new first loan in the amount of $220,000, and asked Bruno to carry a second loan in the amount of $27,500 to complete the purchase price.

When the seller extends credit in the form of a loan secured by a second deed of trust, the note may be written as a straight note, with interest-only payments, or even no payments. Or it could be an installment note with a balloon payment at the end, or **Fully Amortized Note** with equal payments until it is paid off. The term of the loan is decided by the buyer and seller. The instructions of the buyer and seller regarding the seller financing are usually carried out through escrow.

A trust deed held by the seller may be sold by the seller to an outside party, usually a mortgage broker. The note and trust deed will be discounted, or reduced in value by the mortgage broker, but it is one way a seller can get cash out of a trust deed that was carried back.

Ben and Jerry owned a house together as investors. After several years, they put the house on the market for $350,000 and hoped to get a full-price offer so they could go their separate ways with the profit from the house.

After a short time, they did get a full price offer. The buyer offered to put $70,000 down, get a $240,000 new first loan and asked Ben and Jerry to carry $40,000 for five years, as a second trust deed. Ben and Jerry would have turned the offer down if their agent hadn't suggested they accept and sell the second trust deed after the close of escrow. Even though it would be discounted, it was one way they could get most of the cash out of their investment.

If the second trust deed was sold at a discounted 20%, or $8,000, Ben and Jerry would end up with $40,000, less $8,000, or $32,000. In that way they would get the cash out of the sale, though they would be netting less than they originally planned because of the discount. They followed their agent's suggestion, and were satisfied with the result.

Whenever there is seller financing in a real estate transaction, the law requires the buyer and seller to complete a Seller Financing Disclosure Statement. It gives both the seller and buyer all the information needed to make an informed decision about using seller financing to complete the sale.

The seller can see from the disclosure whether or not the buyer has the ability to pay off the loan by looking at the buyer's income, and whether or not the buyer has a good credit history. The buyer can see what the existing loans are, as well as such things as due date and payments on existing loans that would be senior to the loan in question.

Disclosures Regarding the Borrower's Credit-worthiness Needed in Transactions Involving:

- A purchase money loan on one-to-four units
- Seller financing to the purchaser
- "An arranger of credit" (real estate agent)

If there is a real estate agent involved, that agent is known as the arranger of credit. There is a place on the disclosure for the agent to sign, signifying that he or she has complied with the law regarding the transaction. A copy of the required seller financing disclosure statement is included here.

Seller Financing Disclosure Statement (1 of 2)

SELLER FINANCING DISCLOSURE STATEMENT
(California Civil Code 2956-2967)
CALIFORNIA ASSOCIATION OF REALTORS® (CAR) STANDARD FORM

This two page disclosure statement from the Purchaser (Buyer) and Vendor (Seller) is prepared by an arranger of credit [defined in Civil Code 2957 (a)] and provided to **both** the Purchaser (Buyer) and Vendor (Seller) in a residential real estate transaction involving four or fewer units whenever the Seller has agreed to extend credit to the Buyer as part of the purchase price.

Buyer: _____

Seller: _____

Arranger of Credit: _____

Real Property: _____

A. Credit Documents: This extension of credit by the Seller is evidenced by ☐ note and deed of trust, ☐ all-inclusive note and deed of trust, ☐ installment land sale contract, ☐ lease/option (when parties intend transfer of equitable title), ☐ other (specify) _____

B. Credit Terms:
1. ☐ See attached copy of credit documents referred to in Section A above for description of credit terms; **or**
2. ☐ The terms of the credit documents referred to in Section A above are: Principal amount $_____ interest at _____% per annum payable at $_____ per _____ (month/year/etc.) with the entire unpaid principal and accrued interest of approximately $_____ due _____ 19____ (maturity date).

Late Charge: If any payment is not made within _____ days after it is due, a late charge of $_____ or _____% of the installment due may be charged to the Buyer.

Prepayment: If all or part of this loan is paid early, the Buyer ☐ will, ☐ will **not**, have to pay a prepayment penalty as follows: _____

Due on Sale: If any interest in the property securing this obligation is sold or otherwise transferred, the Seller ☐ has, ☐ does **not** have, the option to require immediate payment of the entire unpaid balance and accrued interest.

Other Terms: _____

C. Available information on loans/encumbrances * that will be **senior** to the Seller's extension of credit:

	1st	2nd	3rd
1. Original Balance	$_____	$_____	$_____
2. Current Balance	$_____	$_____	$_____
3. Periodic Payment (e.g. $100/month)	$_____ / _____	$_____ / _____	$_____ / _____
4. Amt. of Balloon Payment	$_____	$_____	$_____
5. Date of Balloon Payment	_____	_____	_____
6. Maturity Date	_____	_____	_____
7. Due On Sale ('Yes' or 'No')	_____	_____	_____
8. Interest Rate (per annum)	_____%	_____%	_____%
9. Fixed or Variable Rate: If Variable Rate:	☐ a copy of note attached ☐ variable provisions are explained on attached separate sheet	☐ a copy of note attached ☐ variable provisions are explained on attached separate sheet	☐ a copy of note attached ☐ variable provisions are explained on attached separate sheet
10. Is Payment Current?			

☐ SEPARATE SHEET WITH INFORMATION REGARDING OTHER SENIOR LOANS/ENCUMBRANCES IS ATTACHED.

*IMPORTANT NOTE: Asterisk (*) denotes an estimate.

D. Caution: If any of the obligations secured by the property calls for a balloon payment, then Seller and Buyer are aware that refinancing of the balloon payment at maturity may be difficult or impossible depending on the conditions in the mortgage marketplace at that time. There are no assurances that new financing or a loan extension will be available when the balloon payment is due.

E. Deferred Interest:
"Deferred interest" results when the Buyer's periodic payments are less than the amount of interest earned on the obligation, or when the obligation does not require periodic payments. This accrued interest will have to be paid by the Buyer at a later time and may result in the Buyer owing more on the obligation than at origination.
☐ The credit being extended to the Buyer by the Seller does **not** provide for "deferred interest," **or**
☐ The credit being extended to the Buyer by the Seller does provide for "deferred interest."
The credit documents provide the following regarding deferred interest:
☐ All deferred interest shall be due and payable along with the principal at maturity (simple interest); **or**
☐ The deferred interest shall be added to the principal _____ (e.g., annually, monthly, etc.) and thereafter shall bear interest at the rate specified in the credit documents (compound interest); **or**
☐ Other (specify) _____

F. All-Inclusive Deed of Trust or Installment Land Sale Contract:
☐ This transaction does **not** involve the use of an all-inclusive (or wraparound) deed of trust or an installment land sale contract; **or**
☐ This transaction **does** involve the use of either an all-inclusive (or wraparound) deed of trust or an installment land sale contract which provides as follows:
1) In the event of an acceleration of any senior encumbrance, the responsibility for payment or for legal defense is:
☐ **Not** specified in the credit or security documents; **or**
☐ Specified in the credit or security documents as follows:
_____

Buyer and Seller acknowledge receipt of copy of this page, which constitutes Page 1 of 2 Pages.
Buyer's Initials (_____) (_____) Seller's Initials (_____) (_____)

BUYER'S COPY

OFFICE USE ONLY
Reviewed by Broker or Designee _____
Date _____

Seller Financing Disclosure Statement (2 of 2)

☐

2) In the event of the prepayment of a senior encumbrance, the responsibilities and rights of Seller and Buyer regarding refinancing, prepayment penalties, and any prepayment discounts are:
☐ **Not** specified in the credit or security documents; **or**
☐ Specified in the credit or security documents as follows:
_____
_____

3) The financing provided that the Buyer will make periodic payments to _____
[e.g., a collection agent (such as a bank or savings and loan); Seller; etc.] and that _____
will be responsible for disbursing payments to the payee(s) on the senior encumbrance(s) and to the Seller.

CAUTION: The parties are advised to consider designating a neutral third party as the collection agent for receiving Buyer's payments and disbursing them to the payee(s) on the senior encumbrance(s) and to the Seller.

G. **Buyer's Creditworthiness:** Section 580(b) of the California Code of Civil Procedure generally limits a Seller's rights in the event of a default by the Buyer in the financing extended by the Seller, to a foreclosure of the property.
☐ No disclosure concerning the Buyer's creditworthiness has been made to the Seller; **or**
☐ The following representations concerning the Buyer's creditworthiness have been made by the Buyer(s) to the Seller:

1. Occupation: _____   1. Occupation: _____
2. Employer: _____   2. Employer: _____
3. Length of Employment: _____   3. Length of Employment: _____
4. Monthly Gross Income: _____   4. Monthly Gross Income: _____
5. Buyer ☐ has, ☐ has **not**, provided Seller a current credit report issued by: _____   5. Buyer ☐ has, ☐ has **not**, provided Seller a current credit report issued by: _____
6. Buyer ☐ has, ☐ has **not**, provided Seller a completed loan application.   6. Buyer ☐ has, ☐ has **not**, provided Seller a completed loan application.
7. Other (specify): _____   7. Other (specify): _____

H. **Insurance:**
☐ The parties' escrow holder or insurance carrier has been or will be directed to add a loss payee clause to the property insurance protecting the Seller; **or**
☐ No provision has been made for adding a loss payee clause to the property insurance protecting the Seller. Seller is advised to secure such clauses or acquire a separate insurance policy.

I. **Request for Notice:**
☐ A Request for Notice of Default under Section 2924(b) of the California Civil Code has been or will be recorded; **or**
☐ No provision for recording a Request for Notice of Default has been made. Seller is advised to consider recording a Request for Notice of Default.

J. **Title Insurance:**
☐ Title insurance coverage will be provided to **both** Seller and Buyer insuring their respective interests in the property; **or**
☐ No provision for title insurance coverage of **both** Seller and Buyer has been made. Seller and Buyer are advised to consider securing such title insurance coverage.

K. **Tax Service:**
☐ A tax service has been arranged to report to Seller whether property taxes have been paid on the property. _____ (e.g., Seller, Buyer, etc.) will be responsible for the continued retention and payment of such tax service; **or**
☐ No provision has been made for a tax service. Seller should consider retaining a tax service or otherwise determine that the property taxes are paid.

L. **Recording:**
☐ The security documents (e.g., deed of trust, installment land contract, etc.) will be recorded with the county recorder where the property is located; **or**
☐ The security documents will **not** be recorded with the county recorder. Seller and Buyer are advised that their respective interests in the property may be jeopardized by intervening liens, judgments or subsequent transfers which **are** recorded.

M. **Proceeds to Buyer:**
☐ Buyer will **NOT** receive any cash proceeds at the close of the sale transaction; **or**
☐ Buyer will receive approximately $_____ from _____ (indicate source from the sale transaction proceeds of such funds). Buyer represents that the purpose of such disbursement is as follows: _____

N. **Notice of Delinquency:**
☐ A Request for Notice of Delinquency under Section 2924(e) of the California Civil Code has been or will be made to the Senior lienholder(s); **or**
☐ No provision for making a Request for Notice of Delinquency has been made. Seller should consider making a Request for Notice of Delinquency.

The above information has been provided to: (a) the Buyer, by the arranger of credit and the Seller (with respect to information within the knowledge of the Seller); (b) the Seller, by the arranger of credit and the Buyer (with respect to information within the knowledge of the Buyer).

Arranger of Credit _____
Date _____, 19____   By _____

Buyer and Seller acknowledge that the information each has provided to the arranger of credit for inclusion in this disclosure form is accurate to the best of their knowledge.

Buyer and Seller hereby acknowledge receipt of a completed copy of this disclosure form.

Date _____, 19____   Date _____, 19____

Buyer _____   Seller _____

Buyer _____   Seller _____

OFFICE USE ONLY
Reviewed by Broker or Designee _____
Date _____

BUYER'S COPY
Page 2 of _____ Pages.

M-PM-2/93

Home Equity Loans

Another way a junior loan can be created is by a **Home Equity Loan**. Assuming there is enough **Equity**, or the difference between the value of a home and the money that is owed against it, a homeowner can apply for a cash loan for any purpose.

A lender uses strict standards about the amount of equity required in a property before loaning money, and particularly for a junior loan. The reason is simple. All a lender wants is to get his or her money back in a timely manner, along with the calculated return on the investment. Care must be taken, in case of a decrease in the value of the subject property, to make sure there is enough of a margin between the total amount owed and the value of the property. If the lender has to sell the property at a foreclosure sale, he or she will be assured of getting the money back. By only loaning up to 80% or 90% of the property value, the lender leaves some room for loss.

Michael's home was appraised at $100,000, with a $40,000 first trust deed recorded against it. Michael wants a $40,000 home equity loan. To determine whether or not to make the loan, the lender adds the amount owed to the amount desired in the loan to determine the percentage that would be encumbered by the existing first trust deed, and the desired second trust deed. If the lender would only loan up to 80% of the appraised value of the property, would Michael get his loan?

The priority of the loan will depend on what other instruments are recorded ahead of it, but it will be known as a hard money loan and will be secured by a deed of trust against the property. (Of course Michael does get his loan because the figures work out.)

Alberta, a homeowner, wanted to modernize her home. She owed $50,000 on a first trust deed, and the house was worth about $250,000. She had no trouble obtaining a home equity loan, secured by a second deed of trust, for her improvements.

Balloon Payment Loans

Often, when a hard money lender makes a first trust deed loan for $30,000 or more, or a junior trust deed loan for $20,000 or more, or when a seller takes back a junior purchase money note and trust deed, the monthly installment payments required do not amortize the loan over the term. The result is a large payment of principal (balloon payment), due on the last payment.

In the interest of consumer welfare, the law requires the holder of a balloon note secured by an owner-occupied building of one-to-four units to give 90- to 150-days' warning of the balloon payment due date.

About Balloon Payment Loans

- A final payment on a loan that is substantially larger than any other payment and repays the debt in full.

Regarding hard money junior loans negotiated by loan brokers (under $20,000), if payments are made in installments and the term is less than three years, the final payment may not be more than twice the amount of the smallest payment.

The law dealing with balloon payments is for loans other than purchase money loans extended by a seller to help a buyer finance a sale.

Hard Money Loan

- A hard money loan is one made in exchange for cash, as opposed to a loan made to finance a certain property.

Other Types of Loans Secured by Trust Deeds

Package Loan

http://www.dre.ca.gov
Reference Book, Ch. 12
p. 238

A loan on real property that is secured by more than the land and structure is known as a package trust deed, or package loan. It includes fixtures attached to the building (appliances, carpeting, drapes, air conditioning) and other personal property.

Blanket Loan

http://jrfunding.com/
p23_balloon_payment.htm

A trust deed that covers more than one parcel of property may be secured by a **Blanket Loan**. It usually contains a **Release Clause** that provides for the release of any particular parcel upon the repayment of a specified part of the loan. Commonly, it is used in connection with housing tracts, or construction loans.

Open-End Loan

An additional amount of money may be loaned to a borrower in the future under the same trust deed. The effect is to preserve the original loan's priority claim against the property.

Swing Loan

A **Swing Loan** is a temporary loan made on a borrower's equity in his or her present home. It is used when the borrower has purchased another home, with the present home unsold, and needs the cash for the new home's down payment.

Wrap-Around Loan

Also known as an **All-Inclusive Trust Deed** (AITD), this type loan wraps an existing loan with a new loan, and the borrower makes one payment for both. In other words, the new trust deed (the AITD) includes the present encumbrances, such as first, second, third, or more trust deeds, plus the amount to be financed by the seller.

The AITD is subordinate to existing encumbrances because the AITD is created at a later date. This means any existing encumbrances have priority over the AITD, even though they are included, or wrapped, by the new All-Inclusive Trust Deed. At the closing the buyer receives title to the property, as opposed to a contract of sale where the seller retains title until the debt is paid in full.

http://www.noteandpapertrader.
com/888/AITD.html

Typically an AITD is used in a transaction between buyer and seller to make the financing attractive to the buyer and beneficial to the seller as well. Instead of the buyer assuming an existing loan and the seller carrying back a second trust deed, the AITD can accomplish the same purpose with greater benefit to both parties.

Benefits of a Wrap-Around-Loan

Seller:
- Usually gets full-price offer
- Increased percent on amount carried

Buyer:
- Low down payment
- No qualifying for a loan or payment of loan fees

The AITD does not disturb the existing loan. The seller, as the new lender, keeps making the payments while giving a new increased loan at a higher rate of interest to the borrower. The amount of the AITD includes the unpaid principal balance of the existing (underlying) loan, plus the amount of the new loan being made by the seller. The borrower makes payment on the new larger loan to the seller, who in turn makes payment to the holder of the existing underlying loan. The new loan "wraps around" the existing loan.

A seller usually will carry back a wrap-around trust deed at a higher rate of interest than the underlying trust deed, thereby increasing the yield. The seller continues to pay off the original trust deed from the payments on the wrap-around, while keeping the difference. This type of financing works best when the underlying interest rate is low, and the seller can then charge a higher rate on the wrapped loan.

A wrap-around loan isn't for everyone. If a seller needs to cash out, it won't work. Also, most loans contain a due-on-sale clause, and cannot be wrapped without the lender's knowledge and approval. Depending on the buyer's and seller's motivation, sometimes an AITD will be created, with full knowledge of the risk. This is how the term "creative financing" came into being.

Generally, these payments are collected by the note department of a bank or a professional collection company and sent on to the appropriate parties. This assures the maker (borrower) of the AITD that all underlying payments are being forwarded and are kept current by a neutral party.

Arthur wanted to sell his house, and listed it for $100,000. The existing first trust deed was for $50,000 at 8%, payable at $377 monthly. He thought about carrying a second trust deed at 10%, counting on the income from the note. However, Bonnie, his listing agent, explained he could get a greater return from carrying an all-inclusive trust deed (AITD) instead of just a note and second trust deed from a buyer. She also told him any offer that included an AITD should be referred to an attorney. Arthur, with his attorney's approval, accepted the following offer soon after listing the house:

Arthur's Offer

Sales price $100,000

Cash by buyer (down payment) 20,000

AITD in favor of Arthur $80,000

- Payments on new AITD of $80,000 at 10% to be $702 made monthly to Arthur
- Payments on existing first trust deed of $50,000 at 8%, in the amount of $377 monthly, to be paid by Arthur to original lender

AITD payment to Arthur $702

Existing First Trust Deed payment .... -377

Monthly difference to Arthur $325

All-Inclusive Note Secured by Deed of Trust

UNSECURED NOTE

$ _____   California, _____ , 19 ___

In installments as herein stated, for value received, _____

_____

_____ promise ___ to pay to

_____ or order, at

_____ . California,

the principal sum of _____ DOLLARS,

with interest from _____ on unpaid principal at the

rate of _____ per cent per annum; principal and interest payable in installments of

_____ Dollars,

or more on the _____ day of each _____ month, beginning

on the _____ day of _____ , 19 ___ _____

_____

_____

_____

and continuing until said principal and interest have been paid. Each payment shall be credited first on interest then due; and the remainder on principal; and interest shall thereupon cease upon the principal so credited. In the event of any default in the payment of any installment of principal or interest as herein provided all sums so due including interest, shall bear interest at the rate set forth above but such unpaid interest so compounded shall not exceed an amount equal to simple interest on the unpaid principal at the maximum rate permitted by law. Should default be made in payment of any installment when due, the whole sum of principal and interest shall, at the option of the holder of this note, become immediately due. Principal and interest payable in lawful money of the United States. If suit or action shall be instituted in any Court to collect any sum becoming due on this note, the undersigned promise ___ to pay such sum as the Court may adjudge reasonable as attorney's fees in said suit or action.

_____   _____

_____   _____

T-223 (Rev. 1/86)

Remember

<u>Wrap-Around Loans (AITD's)</u>

- Secured by a trust deed that "wraps," or includes existing financing plus the amount to be financed by the seller

Unsecured Loan

The lender receives a promissory note from the borrower, without any assurance of payment. The only recourse is a lengthy court action to force payment. This is truly the traditional I.O.U.

UNSECURED NOTE

$ _____   California, _____ , 19 ___

In installments as herein stated, for value received, _____

_____

_____ promise ___ to pay to

_____

_____ or order, at

_____ California,

the principal sum of _____ DOLLARS,

with interest from _____ on unpaid principal at the

rate of _____ per cent per annum; principal and interest payable in installments of

_____ Dollars

or more on the _____ day of each _____ month, beginning

on the _____ day of _____ , 19 ___ _____

_____

_____

_____

and continuing until said principal and interest have been paid. Each payment shall be credited first on interest then due; and the remainder on principal; and interest shall thereupon cease upon the principal so credited. In the event of any default in the payment of any installment of principal or interest as herein provided all sums so due including interest, shall bear interest at the rate set forth above but such unpaid interest so compounded shall not exceed an amount equal to simple interest on the unpaid principal at the maximum rate permitted by law. Should default be made in payment of any installment when due, the whole sum of principal and interest shall, at the option of the holder of this note, become immediately due. Principal and interest payable in lawful money of the United States. If suit or action shall be instituted in any Court to collect any sum becoming due on this note, the undersigned promise _____ to pay such sum as the Court may adjudge reasonable as attorney's fees in said suit or action.

_____   _____

_____   _____

TT-223 (Rev. 1/86)

Alternative Financing

Alternative financing is one way lenders and borrowers can respond to the realities of today's unsteady economy. Because there are different kinds of lenders and different kinds of borrowers who are in need of credit to buy homes, there is no single type of financing that fits everyone.

The changing needs of consumers have caused lenders to respond by offering various solutions to credit demands. In the past, the only way people could buy a home was to use the fixed-rate loan. Today, any number of variable-rate loans are available to serve consumers.

After the public began to see the benefits of these "alphabet soup" loans, they realized this was one solution to the uncertainty of a rapidly changing marketplace. As a real estate agent, it will be your job to help consumers understand these new types of loans and to select the one that best suits their needs.

Graduated Payment Adjustable Mortgage

The loan known as a **Graduated Payment Adjustable Mortgage** (GPAM) has partially deferred payments of principal at the start of the term, increasing as the loan matures. This loan is for the buyer who expects to be earning more after a few years and can make a higher payment at that time. It is also known as a Flexible Rate Mortgage.

Variable or Adjustable Rate Mortgage

The **Variable Rate Mortgage** (VRM) or **Adjustable Rate Mortgage** (ARM) loan provides for adjustment of its interest rate as market interest rates change. The interest rate is tied to some reference index that reflects changes in market rates of interest. Changes in the interest rate may be reflected in the changing payment, the term of the loan, or a combination of both.

Shared Appreciation Mortgage

Under a **Shared Appreciation Mortgage** (SAM), the lender and the borrower agree to share a certain percentage of the appreciation in the market value of the property which is security for the loan. In return for the shared equity, the borrower is offered beneficial loan terms.

Rollover Mortgage

The **Rollover Mortgage** (ROM) is a loan where the interest rate and monthly payment is renegotiated, typically every five years.

Reverse Annuity Mortgage

This type of loan—the **Reverse Annuity Mortgage** (RAM)—is used by older homeowners who have owned their homes for a long time and have a large amount of equity but not much of a monthly income. This loan uses their built-up equity to pay the borrower a fixed annuity, based on a percentage of the property value.

The borrower is not required to repay the loan until a specified event such as death or sale of the property, at which time the loan is paid off. A retired couple can draw on their home equity by increasing their loan balance each month.

Contract of Sale

The **Contract of Sale** is the financing instrument with many names. It may be called an installment sales contract, a contract of sale, an **Agreement of Sale**, a conditional sales contract or a land sales contract.

In this type of agreement, the seller retains legal ownership of the property until the buyer has made the last payment, much like the buying of a car. This is a contract between a buyer and seller, and can be used during times when usual financing is difficult.

The buyer, or **Vendee**, holds what is known as equitable title. The vendee may enjoy possession and use of the property even though legal title is held by the seller, or **Vendor**. Like the holder of an AITD, the vendor pays off the original financing while receiving payments from the vendee on the contract of sale. Indeed, a contract of sale and an AITD are very similar. The most important distinction is that with the AITD—title passes to the buyer; under a contract of sale—title stays with the seller until the contract is paid off.

Remember

Difference Between AITD and Contract of Sale

- AITD: buyer gets title to property

- Contract of sale: seller keeps title until loan is paid off

Long Form Security (Installment) Land Contract with Power of Sale

RECORDING REQUESTED BY

AND WHEN RECORDED MAIL TO:

NAME

STREET
ADDRESS

CITY
STATE
/IP

FORM 2

SPACE ABOVE THIS LINE FOR RECORDER'S USE

ALL   PIN.

LONG FORM SECURITY (INSTALLMENT) LAND CONTRACT
WITH POWER OF SALE

THIS AGREEMENT, made and entered into this _____ day of _____ , 19 ____ , by and

between _____ (Vendor's name),

whose address is _____

(hereinafter sometimes referred to as "Vendor"), and _____

_____ (Vendee's name), whose address is _____

_____ (hereinafter sometimes referred to as "Vendee"); and

CONTINENTAL LAND TITLE COMPANY (hereinafter sometimes referred to as "Trustee")

W I T N E S S E T H :

WHEREAS, Vendor is now the owner of certain real property situated in the County of _____

State of California, commonly known as _____

_____ (Property street address), and described as follows:

WHEREAS, Vendor has agreed to sell, and Vendee has agreed to buy said real property on the terms and conditions hereinafter set forth;

Whereas, Vendor shall retain legal title as a security interest in said real property until the payment of the balance of the purchase price has been paid by Vendee to Vendor as set forth below.

NOW, THEREFORE, THE PARTIES HERETO DO HEREBY AGREE AS FOLLOWS:

PURCHASE PRICE

1. Vendor agrees to sell, and Vendee agrees to buy all of the aforedescribed real property for the sum of

_____ (Total purchase price) (_____).

lawful money of the United States, as hereinafter more fully set forth.

REQUEST FOR NOTICE OF DEFAULT

2. In accordance with Section 2924b, Civil Code, request is hereby made by the undersigned Vendor and Vendee that a copy of any Notice of Default and a copy of any Notice of Sale under Deed of Trust recorded _____ in Book _____ , Page _____ , Official Records of _____ County, California, as affecting above described property, executed by _____ as Trustor in which _____

is named as beneficiary, and _____ as Trustee, be mailed to Vendor and Vendee at address in paragraph 3 below.

NOTICES AND REQUEST FOR NOTICE

3. Notices required or permitted under this agreement shall be binding if delivered personally to party sought to be served or if mailed by registered or certified mail, postage prepaid in the United States mail to the following:

Vendor: _____

_____

Vendee: _____

_____

_____

Vendor and Vendee hereby request that notice of default and notice of sale hereunder be mailed to them at the above address.

PAYMENT OF PURCHASE PRICE

4. Vendee shall pay the purchase price of $ _____ as follows:

(a) Vendee shall pay to Vendor the sum of $ _____ (down payment) as and for a down payment.

(b) The balance of purchase price of $ _____ shall be paid by Vendee to Vendor and shall bear interest at the rate of _____ percent per annum of any balance unpaid. Said sum shall be paid in installments of $ _____ on the _____ day of each and every month commencing _____ and continuing thereafter until paid in full; each payment first to be credited to interest with balance to principal. This agreement will require _____ years and _____ months to complete payment in accordance with its terms. Vendor shall make payment of any installments on existing first, second and/or third deeds of trust in accordance with paragraph (c) hereinbelow.

Title Order No. _____   Escrow or Loan No. _____

TT-281

Closing Those Extra Sales

Many times in your real estate career you will have the opportunity to make a sale that seems to be impossible because some part of the finance equation is missing or invisible at first glance. Those are the sales, however, that you may be able to put together with your knowledge of real estate finance. Solving what looks like a hopeless problem and a dead real estate deal by using your new familiarity with resourceful finance techniques can lead to a happy buyer with a grant deed, a grateful seller with the money and you with a well-deserved commission.

Once you have mastered the basic concepts of finance, you are ready to use them in different combinations for the desired outcome. One of the keys to success in putting real estate transactions together using finance is knowing how to use other people's money. The following are a few ways this can be done to benefit you or your client or to simply save a deal that isn't pulling together.

1. Use something other than cash as a down payment (bonds, boats, cars)

2. Buy with no cash down; take over all existing loans

3. Trade, using several lesser valued properties as a down payment on a greater valued property

4. Use a contract of sale to take over existing loans with little or no down payment

5. Ask the seller carry to back a note as a second or third trust deed

6. Use an option

7. Lease with the right to buy

8. Refinance up to the maximum amount, taking out cash which can then be used for another purchase

9. Wrap the existing loans with an AITD

10. Pool resources of several investors to buy a property of greater value than any one partner could purchase alone

11. Carry your commission for a short time, secured by a note and trust deed against the property

12. Use a note and trust deed held by the buyer as a down payment to purchase another property, assigning the note and trust deed, through escrow, to the seller

13. Seller accepts a trust deed as a down payment and in turn uses it as the down payment on property the seller wants to purchase.

New Type of Mortgage

A new type of mortgage was approved by the Federal National Mortgage Association (Fannie Mae) in the summer of 1994. The Asset Integrated Mortgage—AIM for short—promises to help consumers save while paying off their mortgage.

AIM, originally available in 50 metropolitan areas around the country, is one of numerous new types of mortgages that combines home loans with investments. Lenders are test-marketing similar loans, like the Money Back Home Loan (described later) and others.

With Fannie Mae's approval of the AIM loan, many banks are using such practices to boost loan demand in a rising-interest-rate environment. Fannie Mae's approval is important because it buys the loans from bankers, giving the banks cash to make more loans.

But consumers need to be careful of the new loans. They are complicated because they combine a home loan with an insurance product. A borrower must examine the terms of both the mortgage and the insurance "investment" to determine whether they're a good deal. Sometimes they are not.

One of the good things about these types of loans is that they provide forced savings for the borrower who might have difficulty saving on his or her own. But the knowledgeable and disciplined borrower could probably do better alone.

The two recently introduced loans—the AIM loan and the Money Back Home Loan—illustrate why these types of loans are not good for everyone.

The AIM loan works this way: The borrower puts 5% down on a property and another 15% normally needed for a 20% down payment into an insurance annuity, which is pledged as security for the loan.

Assuming the borrower does not default and keeps the loan and insurance annuity for the full 30-year term, he or she will have paid off the house and will have an annuity worth at least the original mortgage amount at the end of the term. However, because the borrower has used a major part of the down payment on an insurance annuity, the home loan is larger, as are the monthly payments.

Assuming the borrower is buying a $100,000 home, the payment would be $730.47 a month on a $95,000 loan at an 8.5% fixed interest rate. With a traditional loan, requiring a 20% down payment, the borrower would pay only $615.13 monthly, or about $115 a month less.

However, consider what would happen instead if the borrower put the 10% down on the house and invested the $115 a month difference—the $730 monthly cost of the AIM minus the $615 monthly payment for the conventional loan—in a 401(K) plan, which gives tax benefits much like the annuity. Assuming the borrower earns 6% on the investments, he or she would have accumulated more than $115,000 at the end of 30 years— $20,000 more than AIM promises.

Also, AIM doesn't guarantee that the borrower will have $95,000 saved in 30 years. It estimates that much, based on the assumption that annual earnings are at least 6% on the $15,000 investment in the insurance annuity. The "guaranteed" rate—the amount the borrower will earn regardless of market conditions—is just 4%. If the borrower earns only 4% on the $15,000, the nest egg will be worth less than $50,000.

Furthermore, if the borrower wants to get rid of the insurance policy early, he or she may have to refinance the house. The policy and the loan are separate, but because the policy secures the loan, the borrower would have to add cash, refinance or prove an equity build-up in the home of more than 20%.

One other loan, the Money Back Home Loan, presents yet another troubling worst-case scenario. With this loan, the borrower makes the traditional 20% down payment. But the monthly payments don't pay down principal: They pay interest on the loan balance and they buy an insurance policy.

Assuming the borrower buys a $100,000 home and makes a down payment of 20%, payment would be $566.67 on an interest-only 8.5% loan. Then add the cost of the insurance policy, which in this case would be roughly $83 a month. In total, the Money Back loan would cost $650 a month, compared to $615 for a traditional loan.

If the $83 the borrower pays monthly to the insurer earns an average of 8% annually, he or she will have $123,700 accumulated in the policy at the end of 30 years. The homeowner "borrows" out $80,000 to pay off the loan. Tax penalties are avoided by borrowing against the policy rather than cashing it in—and has $43,700 left. And all for just $35 extra a month.

But what happens if the insurance policy pays just the guaranteed rate of 4%? The borrower has only $57,606 accumulated in 30 years, and still owes $80,000 on the mortgage. The numbers don't add up to the anticipated prospect of a paid-up mortgage.

Also, what happens if the borrower obtains a traditional mortgage and invests the $35 difference in a 401(k) plan at an average annual return of 8%? In addition to a paid-off mortgage, the borrower has $52,162 at the end of 30 years—or $8,462 more than with the comparable Money Back Home Loan option.

The above new types of loans probably will appeal only to the few who are unable to save any other way, and need a forced savings plan.

Short Pay

In the discussion of alternate and creative financing, we have been focusing on buyers and sellers. There is, however, a movement on the part of lenders toward a non-traditional, or creative, method of dealing with loans that are in default and require foreclosure.

What is known as a "short payoff" or "short pay" is an alternative to foreclosure that has been explored by some lenders. By accepting a "short pay," a lender allows a borrower to sell the home at market value or whatever he or she can get for it. The lender agrees to take the proceeds, even though the amount is less than is owed against the property, and call the loan paid in full.

There are severe guidelines used to determine if a property and borrower qualify for this substitute for foreclosure, but it is an option for lenders to minimize loss when a borrower defaults and loses the property to the bank.

Normally, when a lender takes a property back through foreclosure, the costs for the trustee sale and maintenance on the property add to the amount already in arrears on the loan amount. If the lender has to keep the property for awhile until a buyer is found, it further adds to the cost of the default.

By accepting a payoff less than the loan amount, lenders can cut their losses by not having to foreclose and maintain real estate. Not all lenders are willing to do that, however. Some insist on foreclosing, saying that a short pay is just a way for a borrower to step out of a loan simply because circumstances have changed, such as a job transfer or divorce.

James and Eileen made a reasonable proposal to the mortgage lenders on their West Los Angeles home. Desperate to move their family to Oregon after the recent devastating earthquake, they were trapped in a home that was worth less than 75% of what they had paid for it three years ago, well below what was still owed on two mortgages.

Their solution was simple. They would ask the lenders to share the loss by accepting less than was owed to close out the mortgages. By James figuring the two lenders would suffer a combined loss of about $75,000, he still would have a personal loss of more than $70,000 in equity and cash on the sale.

Because California law makes it nearly impossible for the lenders to attach any of James' and Eileen's personal property to cover the mortgage shortfall, he thought they would leap at the chance to avoid the even greater losses they would suffer by foreclosing.

Both lenders rejected the offer, saying foreclosure was the only acceptable solution to them.

James' and Eileen's experience illustrates a cruel new reality in the real estate market. With thousands of homes now worth far less than their mortgage balances due to many years of falling housing values, homeowners are trying to persuade their lenders to share their losses in what traditionally has been the largest and most secure investment anyone makes in a lifetime.

Many real estate agents now specialize in negotiating short pays. Banks and other lenders have set up special offices to field the requests and have re-examined their guidelines in an attempt to balance the pros and cons of accepting such deals rather than foreclosing—an option that usually leaves lenders with larger losses than would granting homeowners a short sale.

Once the beneficiaries of California's inflated housing market, lenders now find themselves in the position of asking home sellers to write a check to unload property that would have sold at a large profit five years ago.

The scale of the problem is hard to evaluate because most of the negotiations are done behind closed doors, in intense but secret talks between seller and lender. The borrowers who obtain a short payoff on their loans are those with $1,500 left in an account for food—and not much else. Most homeowners who have successfully negotiated short pays find the experience so humiliating that they don't want to talk about it.

Lenders and realtors both say short payoffs tend to be accepted only when indisputable and unavoidable hardships are certain to cause a default in the loan. Unemployment, business failures and unexpected medical bills are some of the misfortunes that trigger loss of ability to pay on the part of the borrower. Where the difficulties are self imposed or simply an inconvenience, lenders will still foreclose rather than let defaulting borrowers walk away from their loans.

Many people believe that California law allows them to walk away without consequences from a home whose sale won't cover the outstanding mortgage.

It is true that under state law a lender usually cannot attach the borrower's personal assets to cover any deficiency from a foreclosure sale. Borrowers generally lose that protection, however, for all subsequent loans on the property, such as second and third mortgages and refinances of the original loan.

Furthermore, even protected borrowers can be penalized in other ways for failing to pay a mortgage in full. Foreclosures, a lender's ultimate remedy against the holder of an original mortgage, is a ding on a borrower's credit history that can prevent the homeowner from getting credit for as long as seven years.

The number of homeowners whose home values are lower than their outstanding mortgage balance is hard to calculate. But with prices in some areas of California having dropped from their 1990 peak by more than 30 to 50%, brokers and bankers estimate that the figure may be in the hundreds of thousands.

Bankers know that foreclosing rather than negotiating a short payoff looks like a money-losing policy in the short term. But they feel that maintaining the intent of the contract will protect them from more loss in the future. They feel that an overly liberal short-sale policy would invite thousands of customers to walk away from inconvenient loans.

The aversion to making it too easy to short pay has kept many lenders from accepting propositions that look like rational compromises to homeowners. James and Eileen offered to continue paying down the mortgages and setting aside taxes on the earthquake-damaged house until it could be sold. James would even consider turning over an expected insurance payment of $50,000 to $60,000 to reduce the shortfall.

It is more difficult than ever to work out problem loans because of the changes in the home-mortgage market over the last two decades.

Today, if a bank approves and funds a mortgage, it often sells the loan to investors, often through Fannie Mae or other intermediaries. The originating bank keeps a fee for servicing the loan and collecting monthly payments, keeping records and pursuing non-payers. But before it can reach agreement with a borrower who is behind in payments, it must get approval from the loan's owner, which may be another bank, an investment company, Fannie Mae or even an individual investor.

So, many times homeowners find themselves negotiating with bankers who have no vested interest in coming to a mutually satisfactory deal. Banking professionals say investors who bought mortgages in the secondary market are much more rigid about rejecting short pay agreements than are banks negotiating over a loan in their own portfolios.

Even so, short sales can be negotiated in many cases—but they are far from routine transactions. A borrower who is current with loan payments is not even considered a candidate for a short sale. The degree of hardship is the main factor in whether a bank will accept a short pay. Many times, more documentation is required by the lender than was requested for the original loan: as much as three years' tax returns, pay stubs, business records if the borrower is self employed, and detailed information about personal assets.

Even though the lender may have no legal recourse against a borrower's personal assets, banks are likely to insist that the applicant commit all financial holdings to the shortfall. The lender who sees a borrower with any amount of money in savings, stocks, bonds or other property will want everything turned over to assure that the borrower is paying all he or she can on the shortfall.

Post Test

The following self test repeats the one you took at the beginning of this chapter. Now take the exam again—since you have read all the material—and check your knowledge of real estate finance.

1. When an owner uses a property as security for a loan, but does not give up possession, it is called:
   a. hypothecation
   b. pledge
   c. alienation
   d. amortization

2. A neutral third party is part of which of the following?
   a. contract of sale
   b. mortgage
   c. trust deed
   d. agreement of sale

3. In a trust deed, who of the following is the trustor?
   a. lender
   b. trustee
   c. beneficiary
   d. borrower

4. Who holds bare legal title to a property encumbered by a trust deed?
   a. beneficiary
   b. trustor
   c. escrow officer
   d. trustee

5. The purpose of a reconveyance deed is:
   a. to revert a life estate to the grantor
   b. to remove a cloud on a title
   c. to deed the property to the borrower after a note secured by a deed of trust has been paid in full
   d. to redeem a property after a foreclosure sale

6. An "or more" clause allows:
   a. a borrower to borrow as much as he or she wants
   b. a borrower to negotiate a new loan at the end of the term
   c. a borrower to pay off a loan early with no penalty
   d. a borrower to renegotiate his or her loan whenever the interest rate changes

7. Someone who buys an existing negotiable note is known as:
   a. the maker
   b. the holder
   c. the holder in due course
   d. the trustee

8. Which of the following is true about trust deeds and mortgages?
   a. foreclosure is the remedy for default
   b. there is a redemption period after foreclosure
   c. the cost to cure a default is the same
   d. the number of parties in the creation

9. Who must sign a reconveyance deed?
   a. the lender
   b. the buyer
   c. the trustor
   d. the trustee

10. Which of the following is inconsistent with the others?
    a. agreement of sale
    b. contract of sale
    c. all-inclusive trust deed (AITD)
    d. land contract

Vocabulary

Read the definition, find the matching term and write the corresponding term number on the line provided.

Terms

1.	Acceleration Clause	17.	Judicial Foreclosure
2.	Adjustable Rate Note	18.	Junior Trust Deed
3.	Alienation Clause	19.	Maker
4.	Balloon Payment	20.	Mortgagee
5.	Beneficiary	21.	Mortgagor
6.	Blanket Loan	22.	Novation
7.	Collateral	23.	Pledge
8.	Contract of Sale	24.	Principal
9.	Default	25.	Reconveyance Deed
10.	Deficiency Judgment	26.	Statutory
11.	Equity	27.	Subordination Clause
12.	Hard Money Loan	28.	Trustee
13.	Holder	29.	Trustor
14.	Holder in Due Course	30.	Usury
15.	Home Equity Loan	31.	Vendee
16.	Interest	32.	Vendor

Definitions

1. ___ Failure to pay a debt or on a contract

2. ___ Under an installment loan, a final payment that is substantially larger than any other payment and repays the debt in full

3. ___ Foreclosure by court action

4. ___ The transfer of property to a lender to be held as security for repayment of a debt; lender takes possession of property

5. ___ Holds naked legal title to property as a neutral third party where there is a deed of trust

6. ___ The seller under a contract of sale (land contract)

7. ___ A clause in a loan document describing certain events that would cause the entire loan to be due

8. ___ The value remaining in a property after payment of all liens

9. ___ The cost of borrowing money

10. ___ The substitution of a new obligation for an old one

11. ___ A deed used to transfer title to a property back to the original owner after a trust deed has been paid off

12. ___ A clause in which the holder of a trust deed permits a subsequent loan to take priority

13. ___ The buyer under a contract of sale (land contract)

14. ___ A note whose interest rate is tied to a flexible index

15. ___ The lender under a deed of trust

16. ___ A contract for the sale of real property where the seller gives up possession but retains title until the total of the purchase price is paid off

17. ___ The evidence of a debt that is given in exchange for cash

18. ___ A person who has obtained a negotiable instrument (promissory note, check) in the ordinary course of business before it is due, in good faith and for value, without knowledge that it has been previously dishonored

19. ___ The borrower who executes a promissory note and becomes primarily liable for payment to the lender

20. ___ The original amount borrowed

21. ___ Regarding laws created by the enactment of legislation as opposed to law created by court decisions

22. ___ The act of charging a rate of interest in excess of that permitted by law

23. ___ A clause in a loan document that would allow the lender to call the entire loan due upon the sale of the property

24. ___ A loan secured by several properties

25. ___ A judgment against a borrower for the balance of a debt owed when the security for the loan is not sufficient enough to pay the debt

26. ___ The party to whom a promissory note is made payable

27. ___ A cash loan made against the equity in the borrower's home

28. ___ Any trust deed that is recorded after a first trust deed, whose priority is less than that first trust deed

29. ___ The lender under a mortgage

30. ___ The borrower under a mortgage

31. ___ The borrower under a deed of trust

32. ___ Something of value given as security for a debt

Answers

Pre-Test/Post Test

1. a
2. c
3. d
4. d
5. c
6. c
7. c
8. a
9. d
10. c

Vocabulary

1. 9
2. 4
3. 17
4. 23
5. 28
6. 32
7. 1
8. 11
9. 16
10. 22
11. 25
12. 27
13. 31
14. 2
15. 5
16. 8
17. 12
18. 14
19. 19
20. 24
21. 26
22. 30
23. 3
24. 6
25. 10
26. 13
27. 15
28. 18
29. 20
30. 21
31. 29
32. 7

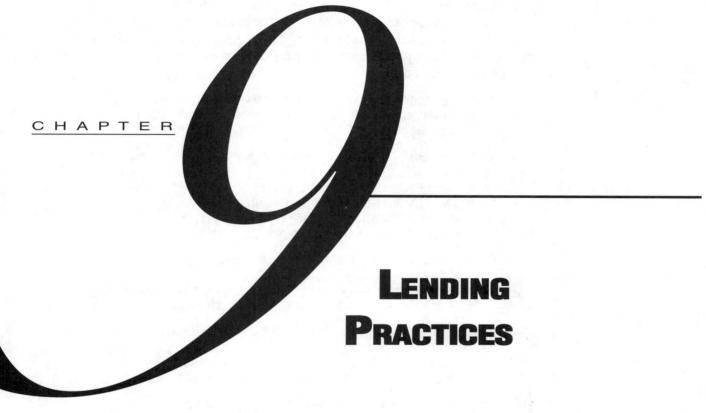

LENDING
PRACTICES

Focus

- **Importance of real estate finance**
- **The national economy**
- **The role of federal agencies in real estate finance**
- **The money mortgage market**
- **Government participation in real estate finance**
- **Real Estate Settlement Procedures Act (RESPA)**
- **Truth in Lending Act (Regulation Z)**
- **Equal Credit Opportunity Act**
- **Personal property secured transactions**

Pre-Test

The following is a self test to determine how much you know about lending practices before reading this chapter. Take it without studying, then read the material presented in the text. At the end of the chapter you will find a repeat of this exam. Test your knowledge by answering the questions again, then check your improvement. (The answers are found at the end of this chapter.) Good luck!

1. When the money supply is limited and the demand is great, it is known as:
   a. inflation
   b. tight money
   c. disintermediation
   d. leverage

2. When a group of investors pools its money to buy real estate it is known as:
   a. Real Estate Investment Trust (REIT)
   b. Real Estate Settlement Procedures Act (RESPA)
   c. Federal Deposit Insurance Corporation (FDIC)
   d. Federal Home Loan Insurance Corporation (FHLIC)

3. The instrument commonly used to secure a loan on personal property is known as a:
   a. pledge agreement
   b. financing statement
   c. security agreement
   d. trust deed

4. Which of the following is related to the Federal Housing Administration (FHA)?
   a. loan origination
   b. insurance
   c. guarantee
   d. contract of sale

5. The process of depositors removing funds from savings is called:
   a. disintermediation
   b. reapportionment
   c. intermediation
   d. disinterment

6. The maximum amount that an eligible and qualified veteran can pay for a home is:
   a. no maximum limitation
   b. $23,900
   c. $184,000
   d. $174,000

7. Which of the following lenders is most likely to make large commercial loans to developers?
   a. national banks
   b. insurance companies
   c. private parties
   d. credit unions

8. The major role of a mortgage company is to originate:
   a. construction loans
   b. loans which are sold on the secondary mortgage market
   c. loans for the primary market
   d. loans for sale to private individuals

9. Secondary mortgage markets redistribute funds from:
   a. money-poor areas to money-rich areas
   b. money-poor areas to money-poor areas
   c. money-rich areas to money-poor areas
   d. money-rich areas to money-rich areas

10. Conventional first trust deeds in California are mostly financed by:
    a. banks
    b. mortgage companies
    c. insurance companies
    d. savings banks

Terms

The following terms are the keys to your success in learning about real estate. Refer to them as you study this chapter for greater understanding of subjects presented here.

Adjustable Rate Mortgage (ARM)

A loan which allows for the interest rate to adjust periodically in relationship to a predetermined index based on the maintenance of a pre-established margin

Deregulation

A process where financial institutions that formerly had been restrained in their lending activities by the law are allowed to compete freely for profits in the marketplace

Disintermediation

The process of depositors removing funds from savings

Financial Intermediary

An organization that obtains funds through deposits and then lends those funds to earn a return—such as savings banks, commercial banks, credit unions and mutual savings banks

Financing Statement

The instrument which is recorded in order to give public notice of the security interest, thus protecting the interest of the secured party in the collateral

Intermediation

The process of transferring capital from those who invest funds to those who wish to borrow

Mortgage Loan Disclosure Statement

A statement that informs the buyer of all charges and expenses related to a particular loan

Real Estate Investment Trust (REIT)

A way investors with a small amount of capital can pool their resources to buy real estate

Security Agreement

The device commonly used to secure a loan on personal property

Tight Money

An economic situation in which the supply of money is limited, and the demand for money is high, as evidenced by high interest rates

Variable Rate Mortgage (VRM)

A mortgage where the interest rate varies according to an agreed-upon index, thus resulting in a change in the borrower's monthly payments

Warehousing

The process of assembling into one package a number of mortgage loans, prior to selling them to an investor

Introduction

http://www.
national-mortgages.net

At the center of nearly all real estate transactions is some kind of financing. Without an understanding of how the transfer of real property is financed, the developer, the contractor, the real estate broker and the property manager would find themselves out of a job. Most sellers would not be able to sell, because most buyers would be financially unable to pay cash, or unwilling to purchase unless a large part of the purchase price could be borrowed.

Proven sources of funds include lending institutions such as savings banks, mortgage lenders, banks and insurance companies. Other proven sources are non-institutional, such as mortgage bankers, mortgage brokers, private individuals, pension funds, mortgage trusts and investment trusts. The real estate licensee must stay alert to the changing credit markets, mortgage sources and mortgage methods to be competitive in the real estate industry.

The Importance of Real Estate Finance

http://www.dre.ca.gov
Reference Book, Ch. 12

During the past decade, traditional lending institutions have been under great pressure. As the economy shifted and stalled, lenders had to become responsive to the public's need if they were going to survive. As a result of the changing economy and different demands put upon the banking industry, adjustments were made in lending practices. Drift and deadlock were replaced with renewal and reform.

Some of the events that have put pressure on the real estate and lending industry are: the energy crisis, technological growth, worldwide economic stress, capital shortages, growing inflation with unreliable drift in interest rates, tight money and credit for the private sector, soaring deficit spending and borrowing by government, high unemployment and depressed major industries.

Remember

Hedges Against Inflation

- An equity asset such as bonds, diamonds or gold
- Ownership of real estate
- Income-producing property that will maintain its value

http://www.westegg.
com/inflation

In the aftermath of a decade of negative forces at work in the economy, the real estate industry, and particularly government-regulated financial institutions that supplied most of the funds, had to find new ways to compete and serve the consumer.

These government-regulated depository institutions, known as **Financial Intermediaries** (savings banks, commercial banks, credit unions and mutual savings banks), lost customers—and their savings accounts— to the unregulated nondepository institutions such as the uninsured money-market funds. The reason: Customers could get a higher interest rate on their savings from the unregulated institutions than the regulated lenders were allowed to pay under the law.

The process of depositors removing funds from savings is called **Disintermediation**. That savings account money was what the financial institutions used to make home loans. The less available money there was, like all scarce goods, the more it cost. And the more it cost, the fewer there were who could afford it. The downward spiral of the economy fed upon itself.

Institutional lenders holding existing, low-interest-rate loan portfolios that were declining in value could not make enough new higher-interest-rate loans to make up for their losses. There were several reasons for their lack of profits. As we have seen, money was disappearing from personal savings accounts and interest rates were rising. Potential home buyers could not qualify for the high monthly payments required on the new loans, nor could they come up with the downpayment to buy the expensive new homes whose prices were inflated by rapid appreciation.

Home ownership often was postponed by the crisis in the banking industry, which caused a crisis in the real estate industry. If no one could buy, no one could sell. Builders and developers stopped operations and the economy was stuck. **Tight Money** and credit, plus high interest rates, made money scarce for mortgage loans and expensive in the nation's financial services marketplace. The viable borrowers had to compete for whatever funds were available, and had to pay top dollar.

Deregulation is a process where financial institutions that formerly had been restrained in their lending activities by the law, are allowed to compete freely for profits in the marketplace. Controls on lending practices still exist, but loans can now be marketed competitively by all lending institutions.

Now the question was how to make mortgage funds available and affordable to the consumer, and allow financial institutions to make a profit. The deregulation efforts of the federal government, along with alternative mortgage plans, have worked together to restructure the housing finance system throughout the nation.

Traditionally, fixed-rate loans have been the only choice for a home buyer. In an attempt to offer alternatives to consumers, and renew their faith in their ability to borrow money for homes, lenders found new ways to make loans consumer friendly.

What lenders offered were newly designed **Variable Rate Mortgages** (VRM's) that made it possible for everyone to win. Lenders could offer loans at a rate that was affordable to the borrower, yet not be tied to that original interest rate for the life of the loan. They were loans connected to movable indexes that reflected changes in the economy, and allowed a safety net for the lending institutions. Lenders wouldn't be stuck with old, unprofitable, low-interest-rate loans, and could be reasonably sure that the new loans would stimulate the real estate industry by creating new buyers, which in turn would create more borrowers.

As the banking industry continued to correct itself with more alternatives for borrowers, the **Adjustable Rate Mortgage** (ARM) was offered as an improvement on the VRM loans. The ARM allows for the interest rate to adjust periodically in relationship to a predetermined index plus a pre-established margin. For example, if a loan was tied to an index, such as the 11th District cost of funds, and that rate was 5% at the time the loan was originated, the interest rate on the loan might be quoted as 5% plus a margin of 2%, to make the interest rate to the consumer 7% upon origination of the loan.

Generally, the way adjustable rate financing works to the benefit of the bankers is that it allows, contractually, for an inflow of extra money during times of tight money and higher interest rates. In other words, the borrower's payments will increase because the interest rate will go up, therefore more money will flow into the financial institution.

Historically, the role of financial institutions has been intertwined with that of real estate in ways that may or may not benefit all parties. What has taken place during the past decade is a learning curve toward mutually acceptable goals by bankers and consumers alike.

Leverage

- Using borrowed money to the greatest extent possible

The National Economy

http://www.dre.ca.gov
Reference Book, Ch.12
p. 214

The economic system in America is a mixed capitalistic system. The government is asked by its citizens to influence the general economic direction, and assure reasonable stable competition. However, private citizens have the right to own, control and dispose of property and make the majority of decisions about the overall economy themselves. Our economy is the result of millions of decisions we all make every day about producing, earning, saving, investing and spending.

Real Estate's Four Major Roles in the U.S. Economy

Net Worth

- Real estate in the form of land and improvements makes up a very large portion of the total net worth of the United States as a nation (not to be confused with the government).

Income Flow

- Money is paid for the use of real estate and for the raw materials, labor, capital and management used in real estate focussed work of all kinds.

Major Employer

- The real estate industry (brokerage, construction, management, finance) is a major employer in this country. It provides employment for a large segment of the population, accounting for billions of dollars in national income.

Appreciation and Inflation

- In recent years appreciation in the value of real estate has overtaken the annual rate of inflation and is the single largest indicator of inflation. As the value of the dollar has decreased, passbook savings accounts and other forms of financial savings have lost their appeal as ways to save and invest for the future. Real estate has become a major means by which people save. Particularly in California where property has historically appreciated at such an alarmingly fast rate, it has been common for homeowners to consider their home as "money in the bank."

The Circular Flow of the National Economy

The money that pays for the use of various components of production.

Personal Income
The people who own the various components needed to produce goods and services, sell them. They are paid for these components in the form of: Wages, or Rents, or Profits, or Interest.
In return for such payment, they supply these components to the economy so that goods and services can be produced.

Taxes
Payment to government for services it provides.

Consumer Demand
Payment for what people want such as food, clothing and shelter.

The Marketplace

Supply of Goods and Services
Food
Clothing
Shelter
Services

Production
Goods and services are produced by combining:
Labor
Raw Materials
Management
Capital
For each of these components, something is paid. Labor gets wages, capital gets interest, etc.

Savings
Income not needed at the moment it is earned.

Financial Intermediaries
Institutions (banks, etc.) that pool the savings of many people to invest in factors of production.

The supply of components needed for the production of goods and services.

The Role of Federal Agencies in Real Estate Finance

Financial Institutions Reform, Recovery and Enforcement Act (FIRREA)

In 1989, as a result of abuses of the banking system, Congress passed the Financial Institutions Reform, Recovery and Enforcement Act (FIRREA). This was an attempt to rebuild an industry which had disgraced itself by disregarding the welfare of consumers and nurturing greed and profiteering within the banking business.

Under FIRREA, the Office of Thrift Supervision (OTS) and the Housing Finance Board were authorized to oversee the savings and loan regulation responsibilities that had belonged to the Federal Home Loan Bank Board (FHLBB) under the old system. The Federal Deposit Insurance Corporation (FDIC) now insures deposits in all federally chartered banks and savings institutions up to $100,000 per account for commercial and savings banks. The FDIC also supervises the Savings Association Insurance Fund (SAIF) and the Resolution Trust Corporation (RTC). Other new government agencies were created to unravel the banking crisis and regulate banking transactions in the future.

Other New Agencies Created For Bank Reorganization

Savings Association Insurance Fund (SAIF)

This agency, now managed by FDIC, replaced the Federal Savings and Loan Insurance Corporation (FSLIC) that was dissolved in 1988. This fund collects premiums to produce the money needed to insure accounts at savings banks.

Federal Housing Finance Board (FHFB)

Mortgage lending by the twelve regional Federal Home Loan Banks is supervised by the FHFB, replacing the now lifeless Federal Home Loan Bank Board (FHLBB). If a savings bank can't meet "Qualified Thrift Lender" (QTL) guidelines, they may not borrow funds from any of the Federal Home Loan Banks. The FHFB may close a bank which is in trouble and transfer management of the institution to the Resolution Trust Corporation (RTC).

Department of Housing and Urban Development (HUD)

http://www.hud.gov

The Department of Housing and Urban Development (HUD) was created to bring together under one authority many federal agencies that already existed. Some of those agencies are explained here.

Federal Housing Administration (FHA)

The Federal Housing Administration (FHA) insures loans made by approved lenders. The FHA does not make loans, but only insures loans made by approved lenders who hold and service the loans or sell them on the secondary mortgage market.

Federal Reserve Bank System (the Fed)

http://www.federalreserve.gov

http://www.dre.ca.gov
Reference Book, Ch 12
p. 214

This is the nation's central bank, whose job it is to regulate the flow of money and credit to promote economic growth with stability. The Fed develops national monetary policy and shares responsibility with the 12 Federal Reserve Banks for applying that policy and setting money supply goals.

In an effort to avoid the peaks and valleys of the business cycle that cause liquidity and credit crises, the Fed monitors changing economic conditions and applies appropriate controls. The Fed influences the sup-

263

ply of money and credit available, thus controlling the behavior of lenders and borrowers. These controls are far reaching, often affecting interest rates, jobs and economies worldwide. To accomplish its goals, the Fed uses three basic tools.

Basic Tools of the Federal Reserve System

1. *Reserve requirements*: The Fed increases or decreases the amount of money in circulation by raising or lowering reserve requirements for member banks. A certain percentage of each deposit must be set aside as a reserve, and when the Fed requires a larger reserve, the banks have less to lend, thus interest rates increase while borrowing and spending decrease. By lowering the reserve requirement, the banks have more money to lend, interest rates may decrease, and borrowing and spending increase.

2. *Discount rates*: This is the interest rate a bank is charged by the Fed to borrow money. A decrease in the discount rate allows more bank borrowing from the Fed. Bank borrowing increases money available for lending. Raising the discount rate produces less money available for lending to the consumer.

3. *Open market operations*: The Fed also buys and sells government securities to influence the amount of available credit. When the Fed buys securities, more money is available in the banks to lend. When the Fed sells securities, the opposite is true. Open market operations is the most flexible and widely used technique for expanding or slowing the economy.

Remember

Three Tools of the Fed to Regulate the Money Supply

- Reserve requirements
- Discount rate
- Open market operations

The following three federal agencies, all under the authority of HUD, have been created to operate in the secondary money market. Each will be discussed in more detail later in this chapter.

<u>Federal Agencies Involved In Secondary Mortgage Market:</u>

- Federal National Mortgage Association (FNMA or Fannie Mae)

- Government National Mortgage Association (GNMA or Ginnie Mae)

- Federal Home Loan Mortgage Corporation (FHLMC or Freddie Mac)

The Money Mortgage Market

The main source of all mortgage money is the money people save from the wages, profit, interest, or any other source of income paid to them in exchange for the services and goods they produce. Money used for home mortgages comes from surplus money that people put in savings accounts in banks.

Primary Mortgage Market

The primary mortgage market is where lenders make mortgage loans directly to borrowers. As you recall from our study of security instruments in California, the document used most often to secure a home loan is a trust deed, rather than a mortgage. Any reference to mortgage lending here refers to loans secured by trust deed, not mortgage. The primary mortgage market includes both institutional lenders and non-institutional lenders.

Institutional Lenders

Earlier in our study of real estate lending, the term financial intermediary was used to describe certain institutions that make real estate loans. They are known as conventional lenders who make money available to borrowers. Institutional lenders, such as savings banks, commercial banks, insurance companies, credit unions and mutual savings banks are financial intermediaries whose main job is to transfer money from the people who invest money to those who want to borrow it. This is called **Intermediation**.

As a liaison, the financial intermediary combines funds from many sources (individual savers, or short-term or long-term investors) and adapts them into loans for the consumer.

Savings Banks (Formerly known as Savings and Loans)

http://www.fdic.gov

The financial institution which collects savings from individuals and invests those savings primarily in trust deeds and mortgages is now called a savings bank. Of all the institutional lenders, savings banks make the majority of home loans. They can be federally or state chartered. The main purpose of savings banks is to encourage thrift by providing an easy place for people to save and invest money, and to provide for simple economical financing of homes.

Remember

- Savings Banks are the main source for home loans.

Commercial Banks

The commercial banks are the all purpose lenders. They make the widest range of loans, including loans for buying real estate, home equity loans, business loans and other short-term loans. Typically, a commercial bank will make short term, or interim, loans to finance construction. Long-term, take-out loans may be available after a construction loan is paid off.

Remember

- Commercial banks prefer short-term loans and are a primary source of construction loans.

Insurance Companies

Insurance companies generally invest in real estate by making large commercial loans to developers and builders. They don't usually get involved with the single home residential market, but can buy loans from mortgage companies and invest in government insured or guaranteed loans.

Credit Unions

A credit union is an association whose members usually have the same type of occupation. The members join together for mutual benefit by saving money in their own bank and receiving better interest rates. Both secured and unsecured loans are made at rates lower than other lenders can offer. Because of the low overhead and other costs of doing business, credit unions are a growing source of funds for consumers.

Mutual Savings Banks

Depositors in mutual savings banks share in the earnings of the bank after expenses, reserves and contributions to surplus. Recently, mutual savings banks have been permitted to convert to savings bank status. These banks are located mostly in the northeastern U.S.

Remember

Institutional Lenders Include:

- Savings Banks (formerly known as Savings and Loans)
- Commercial Banks
- Insurance Companies
- Credit Unions
- Mutual Savings Banks

Non-Institutional Lenders

In addition to institutional lenders, there is another group of lenders referred to as non-institutional lenders. This group includes mortgage companies and private individuals, as well as others—like pension funds and title companies—who are non-financial lenders.

Mortgage Companies

Mortgage companies, or mortgage bankers, make mortgage loans to consumers and sell them to institutional investors. Some mortgage companies have funds of their own, and others act as a go-between for the institutions who have the money and the borrowers who need it.

Many companies get their funding from commercial banks on short-term lines of credit while arranging to sell pools of loans they have originated. The process of assembling into one package a number of mortgage loans, prior to selling them to an investor, is called **Warehousing**. The sale of these loan packages provides added capital with which to make more loans, which can then be packaged and sold, thus repeating the cycle.

Remember

About Mortgage Bankers and Brokers

- Mortgage bankers loan their own funds and service their loans, as well as broker loans for others.

- Mortgage brokers mainly put borrowers and lenders together, and do not normally loan their own money, or service loans.

The mortgage banker often acts as a mover of funds from one area of the country with an abundance of money to be loaned, to another area that is capital deficient.

The biggest role of mortgage companies, however, is to originate and service loans which they then sell in the secondary mortgage market. As the person in the middle who stirs the pot, the mortgage banker is careful to follow guidelines established by those who will be buying the loans.

Generally, a mortgage company prefers loans that are most readily saleable in the secondary market, such as government-insured or government-guaranteed mortgages (FHA, VA), or conventional mortgages for which it has advance purchase commitments.

When a borrower applies for a loan from a mortgage broker or banker, there are certain procedures followed to assure the loan will be saleable in the secondary market.

Loan Application Procedures

1. The customer fills out a loan application.
2. A credit report is ordered.
3. The subject property is appraised
4. The application package, including application form, borrower's financial statement, appraisal and copy of the sale agreement is presented to the investor.
5. The investor decides whether or not to accept.
6. Approval is sent to the mortgage company.
7. When loan conditions are met, the mortgage banker sends funds to escrow for closing.
8. After closing, documents are sold to the investor and the mortgage banker services the loan (accepts and keeps track of payments, tracks the life of the loan).

Private Individuals

Private individuals can be lenders, also. The most common way is by carrying back a trust deed on the sale of their own home, or they can go through a mortgage broker, who will then find them a borrower. Usually, private loans are short term, with the main motivation of the lender being safety of the loan, and a high return on the investment.

Another way private individuals can operate in the real estate market is by joining together in a **Real Estate Investment Trust**, known as an REIT. This is a way investors with a small amount of capital can pool their resources to buy real estate. REITs invest in an assorted mix of real estate and mortgage investments as a group, with a minimum of 100 investors required. There are serious legal requirements to qualify as a trust and for special tax treatment which will not be discussed here.

Remember

• An REIT requires 100 or more investors.

Non-Financial Institutions

Universities, pension funds, trust departments of banks, title companies and mortgage investment companies all hold real estate loans as investments.

Remember

Non-Institutional Lenders Include:

• Mortgage Companies
• Private Individuals
• Non-financial Institutions

Secondary Mortgage Market

The secondary mortgage market consists of the system of lending institutions, private investors and government credit agencies that buy pools of loans from loan-originator sellers (primary markets). They later buy from—and sell to—each other the existing mortgage loans originated in the primary mortgage market.

The Three Major Participants in the Secondary Mortgage Market

http://www.fanniemae.com

Federal National Mortgage Association (FNMA or Fannie Mae)

- Originally created as a secondary market for FHA-insured and VA-guaranteed loans and the private residential mortgage market. That means FNMA buys loans from lenders who conform to FNMA guidelines, and by doing so, puts mortgage money back into the system so lenders can make more loans. FNMA is the largest investor in the secondary market. In 1968 FNMA was divided into two separate systems: FNMA and GNMA. FNMA became a privately owned corporation, while GNMA remained government owned.

http://www.hud.gov

Government National Mortgage Association (GNMA or Ginnie Mae)

- Established as a government corporation within the Department of Housing and Urban Development (HUD) to participate in the secondary mortgage market.

Federal Home Loan Mortgage Corporation (FHLMC or Freddie Mac)

http://www.freddiemac.com

- Freddie Mac was created to increase the availability of mortgage credit by developing and maintaining a nationwide secondary market for residential conventional mortgage loans. Approved existing mortgage loans are bought and resold to individual investors or financial institutions.

SECONDARY MORTGAGE MARKET

FEDERAL NATIONAL MORTGAGE ASSOCIATION
(Fannie Mae)

- Issues stock to general public
- Provides adjustable rate mortgages
- Issues mortgage-backed securities

GOVERNMENT NATIONAL MORTGAGE ASSOCIATION
(Ginnie Mae)

- Guarantees securities issued by FHA-approved home mortgage lenders

FEDERAL HOME LOAN MORTGAGE CORPORATION
(Freddie Mac)

- Issues stock to general public
- Buys and resells residential conventional mortgage loans

This important market is the foundation of the lending process and an essential part of our national economy's health. Once again, the market's main function is to get the money to primary lenders who then loan it to consumers, who make loan commitments which are then sold on the secondary market, with the money paid back into the primary market.

Remember

About Loan Markets:

- The primary mortgage market initiates loans directly with borrowers.
- The secondary mortgage market buys and sells existing loans which have originated in the primary market.

Real Property Loan Law

The Real Estate Law requires anyone negotiating a loan to have a real estate license. In the past, abuses have occurred in the form of excessive commissions, inflated costs and expenses, the negotiating of short-term loans with large balloon payments, and misrepresentation or concealment of material facts by licensees negotiating these loans.

As a result of this mistreatment of consumers by corrupt agents, legislation was passed to correct the situation. The Real Property Loan Law now applies to loans secured by first trust deeds under $30,000 and by junior trust deeds under $20,000.

The law requires anyone negotiating a loan to provide a Mortgage Loan Broker's Statement (sometimes called a **Mortgage Loan Disclosure Statement**) to a prospective borrower, with information concerning all important features of a loan to be negotiated for the borrower.

From time to time, a real estate agent, as part of a transaction, will be involved in negotiating a loan for the borrower. A completed Mortgage Loan Disclosure Statement must be presented to the prospective borrower, and the borrower must sign the statement prior to signing loan documents.

Mortgage Loan Disclosure Statement (Borrower) (1 of 2)

MORTGAGE LOAN DISCLOSURE STATEMENT (BORROWER)
CALIFORNIA ASSOCIATION OF REALTORS® (CAR) STANDARD FORM
(As required by the Business and Professions Code Section 10240 and Title 10, California Administrative Code, Section 2840)

_____
(Name of Broker/Arranger of Credit)

_____
(Business Address of Broker)

I. SUMMARY OF LOAN TERMS

A. PRINCIPAL AMOUNT OF LOAN .... $ _____

B. ESTIMATED DEDUCTIONS FROM PRINCIPAL AMOUNT
 1. Costs and Expenses (See Paragraph III-A) .... $ _____
 *2. Commission/Loan Origination Fee (See Paragraph III-B) ...... $ _____
 3. Liens and Other Amounts to be Paid on Authorization of Borrower
 (See Paragraph III-C) .... $ _____

C. ESTIMATED CASH PAYABLE TO BORROWER (A less B) .... $ _____

II. GENERAL INFORMATION ABOUT LOAN

A. If this loan is made, you will be required to pay the principal and interest at _____ % per year, payable as follows: _____ _____ payments of $_____
 (number of payments) (monthly/quarterly/annually)
 and a FINAL/BALLOON payment of $_____ to pay off the loan in full.

NOTICE TO BORROWER: If you do not have the funds to pay the balloon payment when it comes due, you may have to obtain a new loan against your property to make the balloon payment. In that case, you may again have to pay commissions, fees, and expenses for the arranging of the new loan. In addition, if you are unable to make the monthly payments or the balloon payment, you may lose the property and all of your equity through foreclosure. Keep this in mind in deciding upon the amount and terms of this loan.

B. This loan will be evidenced by a promissory note and secured by a deed of trust in favor of lender/creditor on property located at (street address or legal description):

C. 1. Liens presently against this property (do not include loan being applied for):

Nature of Lien	Priority	Lienholder's Name	Amount Owing

 2. Liens that will remain against this property after the loan being applied for is made or arranged (include loan being applied for):

Nature of Lien	Priority	Lienholder's Name	Amount Owing

NOTICE TO BORROWER: Be sure that the amount of all liens is stated as accurately as possible. If you contract with the broker for this loan, but it cannot be made or arranged because you did not state these lien amounts correctly, you may be liable to pay commissions, fees, and expenses even though you did not obtain the loan.

D. If you wish to pay more than the scheduled payment at any time before it is due, you may have to pay a PREPAYMENT PENALTY computed as follows:

E. The purchase of credit life or credit disability insurance is not required of the borrower as a condition of making this loan.

F. The real property which will secure the requested loan is an "owner-occupied dwelling." YES _____ NO _____
 (Borrower initial opposite YES or NO)

"For purposes of restrictions on scheduled balloon payments and unequal payments, an "owner-occupied dwelling" means a single dwelling unit in a condominium or cooperative or a residential building of less than three separate dwelling units, one of which will be owned and occupied by a signatory to the mortgage or deed of trust for this loan within 90 days of the signing of the mortgage or deed of trust. For certain other purposes relating to this loan, "dwelling" means a single dwelling unit in a condominium or cooperative, or any parcel containing only residential buildings if the total number of units on the parcel is four or less, which is owned by a signatory to the mortgage or deed of trust."

Borrower hereby acknowledges the receipt of a copy of this page, which constitutes page 1 of 2 pages.
Borrower's Initials (_____) (_____)

OFFICE USE ONLY
Reviewed by Broker or Designee _____
Date _____

BROKER'S COPY

Mortgage Loan Disclosure Statement (Borrower) (2 of 2)

MORTGAGE LOAN DISCLOSURE STATEMENT (BORROWER)

CALIFORNIA ASSOCIATION OF REALTORS® (CAR) STANDARD FORM

(As required by the Business and Professions Code Section 10240 and Title 10, California Administrative Code, Section 2840)

_____
(Name of Broker/Arranger of Credit)

_____
(Business Address of Broker)

I. SUMMARY OF LOAN TERMS
- A. PRINCIPAL AMOUNT OF LOAN . . . . S _____
- B. ESTIMATED DEDUCTIONS FROM PRINCIPAL AMOUNT
  1. Costs and Expenses (See Paragraph III-A) . . . . S _____
  * 2. Commission/Loan Origination Fee (See Paragraph III-B) . . . . S _____
  3. Liens and Other Amounts to be Paid on Authorization of Borrower
  (See Paragraph III-C) . . . . S _____
- C. ESTIMATED CASH PAYABLE TO BORROWER (A less B) . . . . S _____

II. GENERAL INFORMATION ABOUT LOAN
- A. If this loan is made, you will be required to pay the principal and interest at _____% per year, payable as
  follows: _____ _____ payments of $_____
  (number of payments)   (monthly/quarterly/annually)
  and a FINAL/BALLOON payment of $_____ to pay off the loan in full.

    **NOTICE TO BORROWER: If you do not have the funds to pay the balloon payment when it comes due, you may
    have to obtain a new loan against your property to make the balloon payment. In that case, you may again have
    to pay commissions, fees, and expenses for the arranging of the new loan. In addition, if you are unable to
    make the monthly payments or the balloon payment, you may lose the property and all of your equity through
    foreclosure. Keep this in mind in deciding upon the amount and terms of this loan.**

- B. This loan will be evidenced by a promissory note and secured by a deed of trust in favor of lender/creditor on property located at
  (street address or legal description):

  _____
  _____

- C. 1. Liens presently against this property (do not include loan being applied for):

Nature of Lien	Priority	Lienholder's Name	Amount Owing

  2. Liens that will remain against this property after the loan being applied for is made or arranged (include loan being applied for):

Nature of Lien	Priority	Lienholder's Name	Amount Owing

    NOTICE TO BORROWER: Be sure that the amount of all liens is stated as accurately as possible. If you contract with the broker
    for this loan, but it cannot be made or arranged because you did not state these lien amounts correctly, you may be liable to
    pay commissions, fees, and expenses even though you did not obtain the loan.

- D. If you wish to pay more than the scheduled payment at any time before it is due, you may have to pay a PREPAYMENT PENALTY
  computed as follows:

  _____
  _____
  _____

- E. The purchase of credit life or credit disability insurance is not required of the borrower as a condition of making this loan.
- F. The real property which will secure the requested loan is an "owner-occupied dwelling."   YES _____ NO _____
  (Borrower initial opposite YES or NO)

    "For purposes of restrictions on scheduled balloon payments and unequal payments, an "owner-occupied dwelling" means a single
    dwelling unit in a condominium or cooperative or a residential building of less than three separate dwelling units, one of which will
    be owned and occupied by a signatory to the mortgage or deed of trust for this loan within 90 days of the signing of the mortgage
    or deed of trust. For certain other purposes relating to this loan, "dwelling" means a single dwelling unit in a condominium or
    cooperative, or any parcel containing only residential buildings if the total number of units on the parcel is four or less, which is
    owned by a signatory to the mortgage or deed of trust."

    Borrower hereby acknowledges the receipt of a copy of this page, which constitutes page 1 of 2 pages.

    Borrower's Initials (_____) (_____)

OFFICE USE ONLY

Reviewed by Broker or Designee _____
Date _____

EQUAL HOUSING
OPPORTUNITY
M-SC-JAN-92

BROKER'S COPY

A real estate broker negotiating or making loans subject to the Real Property Loan Law is limited by law in the amount that may be charged as a commission.

Maximum Commissions Allowed Under Real Property Loan Law:

First Trust Deeds

- 5% of loan amount if term is less than three years

- 10% of loan amount if term is three years or more

Second or other Junior Trust Deeds

- 5% of loan amount if term is less than two years

- 10% of loan amount if term is at least two years, but less than three years

- 15% of loan amount if term is three years or more

On loans $30,000 and over for first trust deeds, and $20,000 or more for junior trust deeds, the broker may charge as much as the borrower will agree to pay.

No balloon payment is allowed for loans on owner-occupied homes where a broker has been involved in the negotiation if the term is six years or less. This requirement does not apply when a seller carries back a trust deed as part of the purchase price.

Remember

REAL PROPERTY LOAN LAW ONLY APPLIES TO:

1st Trust Deed less than $30,000

2nd Trust Deed less than $20,000

Remember

> **About Loans**
>
> * A conventional loan is a loan that is not a government- sponsored or private loan.

Government Participation in Real Estate Finance

http://www.dre.ca.gov
Reference Book, Ch. 13

The two federal agencies that participate in real estate financing are the Federal Housing Administration (FHA) and the Veterans Administration (VA). Together, they make it possible for people to buy homes they would never be able to purchase without government involvement. The California Farm and Home Purchase Program, or Cal-Vet loan, is a state program that helps eligible veterans.

Federal Housing Administration (FHA)

http://www.hud.gov

The FHA program, a part of HUD since 1934, has caused the greatest change in home mortgage lending in the history of real estate finance. The FHA was established to improve the construction and financing of housing.

As a licensee, you must be familiar with the operation, purposes and advantages of the program to best serve your clients and customers. Regulations change from time to time, and up-to-date information on loan programs is usually available through a mortgage broker who specializes in government insured or guaranteed loans.

The FHA does *not* make loans. It *insures* loans made by authorized lending institutions such as banks, savings banks, and independent mortgage companies. As long as FHA guidelines are used in funding the loan, the FHA, upon default by the borrower, insures the lender against loss. If the borrower does default, the lender may foreclose and the FHA will pay cash up to the established limit of the insurance.

Any consumer may qualify for an FHA loan. A borrower does not apply to the FHA for a mortgage loan, but application is made through an approved lender who processes the application and submits it to FHA for approval.

The lender is protected, in case of foreclosure, by charging the borrower a fee for an insurance policy called Mutual Mortgage Insurance. The insurance requirement is how the FHA finances its program. The premium may be financed as part of the loan or paid in cash at the close of escrow.

Remember

- An FHA Loan will be based on the selling price when it is lower than the appraisal.

Section 203-B

FHA offers financing on the purchase or construction of an owner-occupied residence of one-to-four units under Section 203-B.

Section 245 GPM

A graduated payment mortgage (GPM) is offered by the FHA to borrowers who might have trouble qualifying for regular loan payments, but who expect their income to increase. Payments for the first five years are low, and cover only part of the interest due, with the unpaid amount added to the principal balance. After that time the loan is recalculated, with the new payment remaining steady for the term of the loan.

Remember

- The FHA insures loans.

Veterans Administration

http://www.va.gov

The Veterans Administration does *not* make loans. It *guarantees* loans made by an approved institutional lender, much like the FHA. The main differences between the two government programs are: Only an eligible veteran may obtain a VA loan, and the VA does not require a down payment up to a certain loan amount. Both programs were created to assist people in buying homes when conventional loan programs did not fit their needs.

When a veteran finds a house he or she wants to purchase, a VA approved conventional lender will take the loan application and process the loan according to VA guidelines.

Remember

- The VA guarantees loans.

Important Facts About VA Loans

A veteran must possess a Certificate of Eligibility, which is available from the Veteran's Administration, before applying for a VA loan. The certificate will show the veteran's entitlement, or right to obtain the loan.

A major benefit of a loan guaranteed by the Veterans Administration is that no down payment is required for some VA loans. There is a maximum loan amount allowed for a no-down payment transaction, and a formula to establish the amount of down payment for a larger loan amount.

If a veteran sells his or her home, and the buyer gets a new loan which pays off the old VA loan, the Veteran may restore eligibility and apply for a new VA loan.

If a veteran sells his or her home and the buyer takes it "subject to" the existing VA loan, the veteran remains personally liable for the loan. A VA loan is a purchase-money loan that may result in a deficiency judgment in the case of foreclosure, and the original borrower (the veteran) would be liable for the deficient amount.

A VA appraisal is called the Certificate of Reasonable Value (CRV). A loan may not exceed the value established by the CRV.

Maximum loan amounts vary in different areas of the state depending on local economies. There is no maximum sales price a veteran may pay.

Certain specific criteria apply to these loans, however. All property secured by a VA loan must be owner-occupied. Points charged to the seller, and interest rates, are subject to change depending on economic conditions. No prepayment penalty is allowed on a VA loan. The seller usually pays loan discount points, unless the loan is a refinance.

There are a variety of loan types available, including fixed-term loans, adjustable-rate loans and graduated payment loans.

Quick Facts About VA Loans

- No down payment required in some cases
- Certificate of Eligibility required
- Loan amount may not be more than the appraised value
- Certificate of Reasonable Value (VA appraisal) required
- Property must be owner occupied
- Seller usually pays discount points
- No maximum sales price

California Veteran Loans (Cal-Vet)

The California Department of Veterans Affairs administers the Cal-Vet loan program to assist California veterans in buying a home or farm. Unlike other government financing, the Cal-Vet program funds and services its own loans. Funds are obtained through the sale of State General Obligation Bonds.

Upon application for a Cal-Vet loan and approval of the borrower and property, the Department of Veterans Affairs purchases the property from the seller, takes title to the property and sells to the veteran on a contract of sale. The department holds legal title, with the veteran holding equitable title, until the loan is paid off. The veteran has an obligation to apply for life insurance, with the Department of Veterans Affairs as beneficiary, to pay off the debt in case of the veteran's death.

Remember

- A veteran does not get title to property bought with a Cal-Vet loan until the loan is paid in full.

Important Facts About Cal-Vet Loans

The Department of Veterans Affairs buys the home selected by the veteran and sells it to him or her, using a contract of sale (land contract). The state is the vendor and the veteran becomes the vendee. Title is held by the California Department of Veterans Affairs until the loan is paid off.

Qualified veterans living in California are eligible for Cal-Vet loans, regardless of where they were born or where they lived when they entered military service. A veteran who accepted a benefit from another state can be eligible for a Cal-Vet loan. A 17-year-old California veteran is eligible, and can sign Cal-Vet documents.

Eligibility is returned to the veteran after an original loan is paid in full.

Remember

- The same person could be eligible for an FHA, a VA and a Cal-Vet loan.

The Real Estate Settlement Procedures Act (RESPA)

http://www.eldoradoinc.com/
edupage.htm

The Real Estate Settlement Procedures Act (RESPA) applies to all federally related mortgage loans. The act requires special disclosures for certain lenders who provide loan funds for transactions involving one-to-four residential units.

http://www.dre.ca.gov
Reference Book, Ch. 12
p. 225

Special procedures and forms for settlements (closing costs) must be used for most home mortgage loans, including FHA and VA loans, and those from financial institutions with federally-insured deposits.

The lender must furnish a copy of a Special Information Booklet, together with a Good Faith Estimate of the amount or range of closing costs to every person from whom the lender receives a written application for any federally related loan.

Truth-In-Lending Act (Regulation Z)

http://www.alumninational.
com/TIL.html

The main purpose of the Truth-In-Lending Law is to promote the informed use of consumer credit by requiring creditors to disclose credit terms so consumers can make comparisons between various credit sources. To accomplish the objectives of the act the Board of Governors of the Federal Reserve System issued a directive known as Regulation Z.

After years of experience with Regulation Z (or Reg Z as it is known), it became clear that the requirements put too great a burden on creditors, offered too many disclosures for consumers and invited too many lawsuits. In 1980 the congress amended the act by passing the Truth in Lending Simplification and Reform Act. To reflect the amendments to the act, the Federal Reserve Board substantially revised Regulation Z. Compliance with the simplified act and revised Regulation Z became mandatory on October 1, 1982.

At the same time, the Federal Reserve Board adopted model disclosures for closed-end transactions such as the purchase of real property and model language for certain other disclosures. The Federal Reserve Board also announced that its staff would no longer provide written answers to individuals requesting interpretations of Regulation Z, but would issue statements from time to time to answer questions of interpretation.

Creditor

The creditor is responsible for giving Truth in Lending disclosures to the borrower. Regulation Z defines a creditor as someone who gives consumer credit more than 25 times a year or more than five times a year for transactions secured by a dwelling. The credit extended must be subject to a finance charge or be payable by written agreement in more than four installments. Also, a creditor is someone to whom a debt is initially payable, rather than an assignee.

In its definition of "creditor," Regulation Z includes "arranger of credit," which it defined as a person who initially arranged for the extension of credit by persons who did not meet the "creditor" definition. The Federal Reserve Board, in considering the need for a more specific description of the type of activity that would describe an "arranger of credit," examined whether real estate brokers who arrange seller financing of homes should be considered in that category. In passing the Garn-St. Germain Despository Institutions Act, Congress amended the Truth in Lending Simplification and Reform Act of 1980 by deleting "arranger of credit" from the definition of "creditor." The Federal Reserve Board then removed "arranger of credit" from the "creditor" definition in Regulation Z as of October 1, 1982. The effect of the Fed's action is to release real estate brokers or other arrangers of credit from the responsibility for providing Truth in Lending disclosures, unless such persons otherwise come within the definition of "creditors."

Exempt Transactions

Two types of transactions are exempt from Regulation Z. The first is for credit extended mainly for business, commercial or agricultural reasons. If property is not—or is not intended to be—owner-occupied, and the creditor extends credit to acquire, improve or maintain a rental property regardless of the number of family units, the transaction will be considered a business activity.

There are special rules when application is made to acquire, improve or maintain rental property that is—or will be— owner-occupied within a year. If there are more than two family units and the purpose of the credit is to purchase the property, the credit is considered to be for a business purpose. If the credit is given to improve or maintain a property, however, it is considered to be for a business purpose only if it contains more than four housing units. These rules should not be used to prevent an extension of business credit for property with fewer than the prescribed number of units, depending on the circumstances of the transaction.

Also exempt from Regulation Z is credit over $25,000. The dollar limitation does not apply if the loan is secured by real property, or by personal property which is used or expected to be used as the consumer's principal residence.

Form of Disclosure

Under Regulation Z, all Truth in Lending disclosures concerning the credit sale or loan are to be grouped together and separated from other information. The inclusion of any information not directly related to the disclosures required by Regulation Z is prohibited. Also, any itemization of the amount financed must be made separately from the other required disclosures. The terms "finance charge" and "annual percentage rate" must be more conspicuous than other required disclosures.

The disclosures may be segregated by putting them on a separate document. If they are on a contract or other document, they may be set off from other information by outlining them in a box or by printing them in a different type style, with bold print dividing lines, or with a different color background. The portion of the sale or loan document containing these disclosures is commonly called "the federal box."

Regulation Z contains several model forms, including forms which contain disclosures required for transactions involving loan assumptions, variable rate mortgages and graduated payment mortgages. Lenders may duplicate these forms or modify them by including disclosures required for particular transactions.

Required Disclosures

For closed-end credit transactions such as mortgage loans there are at least 18 disclosures required by Regulation Z. A creditor must only make those disclosures that are relevant to a particular transaction. The disclosure statement must have simple descriptive phrases next to five of the most important items disclosed.

Five Most Important Regulation Z Disclosures

1. Amount financed

2. Finance charge

3. Annual percentage rate

4. Total of payments

5. Total sale price (for credit sales)

The following is a summary of other disclosures required under Regulation Z:

1.   Identity of Creditor

2.   Amount Financed

The term "amount financed," together with a brief description of the term, must be included in the disclosure. The suggested phrase is "...the amount of credit provided to you or on your behalf."

3.   Itemization of Amount Financed

This may be eliminated in cases where good faith estimates of settlement costs have been supplied for transactions subject to RESPA. If the transaction is not subject to RESPA, the creditor must either provide a written itemization of the amount financed, or offer a statement that the consumer has the right to receive a written explanation of the amount financed, together with a space for the consumer to indicate whether a detailed list is desired. The itemization must be separate from the "federal box."

4.   Finance Charge

The term "finance charge" and a brief description, such as "the dollar amount the credit will cost you," must appear. Finance charges may not be itemized with other disclosures, and only the total dollar amount may be given. Also, Regulation Z requires the disclosure of the finance charge in all real estate transactions.

Any charge payable directly or indirectly by the consumer and imposed directly or indirectly by the creditor as an incident to or a condition of the extension of credit must be included in the disclosure.

Good Faith Estimate

MILLENNIA FUNDING COMPANY

Borrower Name(s): _____

Property Address: _____

This Mortgage Loan Disclosure Statement/Good Faith Estimate is being provided by Millennia Funding, a real estate broker acting as a mortgage loan broker, pursuant to the Federal Real Estate Settlement Procedures Act (RESPA) and similar California law. In the following, Investor implies the ultimate lender to which the Broker submits the loan application. In a transaction subject to RESPA, an ultimate lender will provide you with an additional Good Faith Estimate within three business days of the receipt of your loan application. You will also be informed of material changes before settlement/close of escrow.

GOOD FAITH ESTIMATE OF CLOSING COSTS

The information provided below reflects estimates of the charges you are likely to incur at the settlement of your loan. The fees, commissions, costs and expenses listed are estimates; the actual charges may be more or less. Your transactions may not involve a charge for every item listed and any additional items charged will be listed. The number listed beside the estimate generally corresponds to the numbered lines contained in the HUD-1 Settlement Statement which you will receive at settlement if this transaction is subject to RESPA, which contains the actual costs for the items paid at settlement. When this transaction is subject to RESPA, by signing the page for Additional California Disclosure, you are also acknowledging receipt of the HUD-1 guide to Settlement Costs.

HUD-1 ITEMS	Paid to Others	Paid to Broker
0800 Items Payable in Connection with Loan		
0801 Broker's Loan Origination Fee ... *(see comment below)*		
0802 Investor's Loan Discount Fee ... *(floating unless blocked)*		
0803 Appraisal Fee ... *($300 or higher)*		
0804 Credit Report ... *($55)*	55	
0805 Lender's Inspection Fee		
0808 Mtg Broker Processing Fee ... *($400 waived)*		Waived
0809 Tax Service Fee ... *($62- 75)*	70	
0810 Administration Fee		
0811 Underwriting Fee ... *(including adm; industry 500 - 700)*	600	
0812 Wire Transfer Fee ... *($25 waived by some banks)*	25	
0813 Flood Certificate Fee ... *($25)*	25	
0900 Items Required by Lender to be Paid in Advance ... *(recurring)*		
0901 Interest for____ days at $____ per day		
0902 Mortgage Insurance Premiums		
0903 Hazard Insurance Premiums		
0904 County Property Taxes		
0905 VA Funding Fee		
1000 Reserves Deposited with Lender ... *(recurring)*		
1001 Hazard Insurance: ____ months at $ ____/mo.		
1002 Mortgage Insurance: ____ months at $ ____ /mo.		
1004 Co Property Taxes: ___ months at $ ___ /mo.		
1100 Title Charges		
1101 Escrow Fees ... *(NO COST REFI: 300 jumbo)*	480	
1105 Document Preparation Fee ... *($100 express/courier)*	100	
1106 Notary Fee ... *($40, counted $10 per signature)*	40	
1108 Title Insurance ... *(PURCHASE offers joint policy discount)*		
- Owner's Policy ... *(Required of PURCHASE)*		
- Lender's Policy ... *(REFI: based on loan amount)*	825	
1200 Government Recording and Transfer Charges		
1201 Recording Fees ... *($35 or higher, based on pages)*	35	
1202 City/County Tax/Stamps ... *(PURCHASE: transfer tax)*		
1300 Additional Settlement Charges		
1302 REFI: payoff statement & reconveyance $100		

- **Subtotal of Fees, Commissions, Costs & Expenses** _____
- **Total of Initial Fees, Commissions, Costs & Expenses** _____
- **Compensation to Broker (Not Paid Out of Loan Proceeds):**
  ( ) Mortgage Broker Origination/Processing Fees:
  ( ) Any Compensation from Investor Yes ____ No ____ (If known) _____

  0.25 pt off retail 1 pt applies. Any yield spread from Investor beyond 0.75 pt to be applied to borrowers' NRCC.

Co-Borrower's Signature: _____

Borrower's Signature: _____ Date: _____

Itemization of Amount Financed

Ed Becker & Associates

NOTICE TO CUSTOMER REQUIRED BY FEDERAL LAW AND FEDERAL RESERVE REGULATION Z

LENDER NAME AND ADDRESS	DATE:	Aug 3rd, 1994
Ed Becker & Associates 111 Avenida Del Mar, Suite 222 San Clemente, CA 92672	LOAN NUMBER:	
	LOAN AMOUNT:	$198,000.00
	NOTE RATE:	5.125%
NAME OF BORROWERS AND ADDRESS		
	PROPERTY ADDRESS	

ANNUAL PERCENTAGE RATE: The cost of your credit as a yearly rate:	FINANCE CHARGE The dollar amount the credit will cost you.	AMOUNT FINANCED The amount of credit provided to you or on your behalf	TOTAL OF PAYMENTS The amount you will have paid after you have made all payments as scheduled
6.588%	$ 256,614.96	$ 197,154.36	$ 453,769.32

********** ALL NUMERICAL DISCLOSURES ARE ESTIMATES **********

YOUR PAYMENT SCHEDULE IS ESTIMATED TO BE:

6 MONTHLY PAYMENTS OF $ 1,078.08 AT 5.125% BEGINNING 10-01-94
6 MONTHLY PAYMENTS OF $ 1,201.60 AT 6.125% BEGINNING 04-01-95
348 MONTHLY PAYMENTS OF $ 1,264.63 AT 6.623% BEGINNING 10-01-95

ADJUSTABLE: THE ANNUAL PERCENTAGE RATE MAY FLUCTUATE DURING THE TERM OF
RATE: THIS TRANSACTION IF THE 1 YEAR TREASURY INDEX CHANGES.
THE INDEX AS OF 07-14-94 IS 3.998%.
THE MARGIN/SPREAD ON THIS LOAN IS 2.625%.
YOUR INTEREST RATE MAY ADJUST EVERY 6 MONTHS BY 2.000%.
YOUR INTEREST RATE SHALL NOT EXCEED 11.000%.

INSURANCE: YOU MAY OBTAIN PROPERTY INSURANCE FROM ANYONE YOU WANT THAT
IS ACCEPTABLE TO THE LENDER. CREDIT LIFE AND CREDIT
DISABILITY INSURANCE ARE NOT REQUIRED TO OBTAIN CREDIT.

SECURITY: YOU ARE GIVING A SECURITY INTEREST IN REAL PROPERTY LOCATED
AT:

LATE CHARGE: IF A PAYMENT IS MORE THAN 15 DAYS LATE, YOU MAY BE CHARGED
5% OF THE PAYMENT.

PREPAYMENT: IF YOU PAYOFF EARLY, YOU MAY HAVE TO PAY A PENALTY. YOU
WILL NOT BE ENTITLED TO A REFUND OF THE PREPAID FINANCE CHARGE.

ASSUMPTION: SOMEONE BUYING YOUR PROPERTY MAY, SUBJECT TO CONDITIONS
ASSUME THE REMAINDER OF THE MORTGAGE ON THE ORIGINAL TERMS.

Loan Amount: $ 198,000.00

Prepaid Finance Charges:

801 Loan Origination Fee To: Ed Becker & Associates	(0 Points + $ 0.00)	$	0.00
802 Loan Discount Fee	(0 Points + $ 0.00)	$	0.00
813 Lender Rebates To: Ed Becker & Associates	(1.000 Points + $ 0.00) Paid from Lender $ 1,980.00)	$	0.00
901 Prepaid Interest	(30 Days @ % 5.125)	$	845.64

Total Prepaid Finance Charge: $ 845.64

Total Amount Financed: $ 197,154.36

See your contract documents for any additional information about nonpayment, default, any required repayment in full before the scheduled
date, and prepayment refunds and penalties, and security interest and the policy of the lender regarding assumption of the mortgage.

By signing below - I acknowledge receipt of a copy of this disclosure on the date indicated above.

_____   _____   _____

Good Faith Estimate of Loan Closing Costs

Ed Becker & Associates

GOOD FAITH ESTIMATE OF LOAN CLOSING COSTS

LENDER NAME AND ADDRESS	
Ed Becker & Associates 111 Avenida Del Mar, Suite 222 San Clemente, CA 92672	DATE: Aug 3rd, 1994 LOAN NUMBER: LOAN AMOUNT: $198,000.00 NOTE RATE: 5.125%

NAME OF BORROWERS AND ADDRESS

PROPERTY ADDRESS

This Good Faith Estimate is being provided by _____ Ed Becker & Associates _____, a mortgage broker, and no lender has yet been obtained. A lender will provide you with an additional Good Faith Estimate within three Business Days of the receipt of your loan application.

The information provided below reflects estimates of the charges which you are likely to incur at the settlement of your loan. The fees listed are estimates - the actual charges may be more or less. Your transaction may not involve a fee for every item listed. The numbers listed inside the estimates generally correspond to the numbered lines contained in the HUD-1 settlement statement which you will be receiving at settlement. The HUD-1 settlement will show you the actual cost for items paid at settlement.

800   ITEMS PAYABLE IN CONNECTION WITH LOAN

801	Loan Origination Fee	(0 Points + $ 0.00) $	0.00
	To: Ed Becker & Associates		
802	Loan Discount Fee	(0 Points + $ 0.00) $	0.00
803	APPRAISAL	Paid $ 325.00) $	325.00 *
	To: SCOTT COEN		
804	Credit Report Fee	Paid $ 50.00) $	50.00 *
	To: Ed Becker & Associates		
809	Tax Service Fee	$	58.00
	To: BANK OF AMERICA		
810	Processing Fee	$	250.00
	To: Ed Becker & Associates		
813	Lender Rebates	(1.000 Points + $ 0.00) $	0.00
	To: Ed Becker & Associates	Paid from lender $ 1,980.00)	

900   ITEMS REQUIRED BY LENDER TO BE PAID IN ADVANCE

901	Prepaid Interest	(30 Days @ % 5.125) $	845.64

1000   RESERVES DEPOSITED WITH LENDER

1002	Mortgage Insurance	(2 Mos @ $ 74.25) $	148.50

1100   TITLE CHARGES

1101	Settlement or Closing Fee	$	600.00
	To: SPRING MOUNTAIN		
1102	Loan Tie In Fee	$	100.00
	To: SPRING MOUNTAIN		
1108	Title Insurance	(Coverage $ 0.00) $	357.00
1111	SUB ESCROW	$	100.00
	To: 1ST AMERICAN		
1112	MISC/FED EX - NOTARY	$	200.00
	To: SPRING MOUNTAIN		

1200   GOVERNMENT RECORDING & TRANSFER CHARGES

1201	Recording Fee	$	100.00

TOTAL ESTIMATED SETTLEMENT CHARGES: $ 3,134.14

* Seller / Broker / Lender Reimbursed Fees

THESE ESTIMATES ARE PROVIDED PURSUANT TO THE REAL ESTATE SETTLEMENT PROCEDURES ACT OF 1974, AS AMENDED (RESPA). ADDITIONAL INFORMATION CAN BE FOUND IN THE HUD SPECIAL INFORMATION BOOKLET, WHICH IS TO BE PROVIDED TO YOU BY YOUR MORTGAGE BROKER OR LENDER.

By signing below - I acknowledge receipt of a copy of this disclosure on the date indicated above.

Summary of Mortgage Loan Transaction

Ed Becker & Associates

SUMMARY OF MORTGAGE LOAN TRANSACTION

LENDER NAME AND ADDRESS	DATE:	Aug 3rd, 1994
Ed Becker & Associates 111 Avenida Del Mar, Suite 222 San Clemente, CA 92672	LOAN NUMBER:	
	LOAN AMOUNT:	$198,000.00
	NOTE RATE:	5.125%
NAME OF BORROWERS AND ADDRESS		
	PROPERTY ADDRESS	

I. LOAN TERMS

Sales Price	$ 220,000.00	$ 220,000.00
Down Payment	$ 22,000.00	
Appraised Value	$ 0.00	
Loan Term	360 months	
Loan Amount	$ 198,000.00	$ 198,000.00

II. SETTLEMENT CHARGES

A) Total Settlement Charges (from Good Faith Estimate)		
	$ 3,134.14	
C) Settlement Charges Paid by Lender		
APPRAISAL	$ 325.00	
Credit Report Fee	$ 50.00	
E) Total Settlement Charges Paid by Borrower		$ 2,759.14

III. ITEMS TO BE PAID OFF

A) Mortgage Loan	$ 0.00	
	$ 0.00	
B) Other Liabilities		
C) Total Amount of Items to be Paid Off		$ 0.00

IV. ESTIMATED CASH REQUIRED AT CLOSING

A) Fees Paid by Borrower		$ 375.00
B) Estimated Cash Required from Borrower to Close (I-II-III)		$ 24,384.14
C) Estimated Cash on Deposit for Closing Costs	$ 36,091.00	
D) Estimated Profit from Pending Sales	$ 0.00	
E) Estimated Additional Cash Reserves Required Prior to Close	$ 0.00	

V. PROPOSED MONTHLY PAYMENTS

A) Principal and Interest	$ 1,078.08
B) Other Financing	$ 0.00
C) Hazard Insurance	$ 0.00
D) Real Estate Taxes	$ 229.00
E) Mortgage Insurance	$ 74.25
F) Homeowner Association Dues	$ 179.00
G) Lease/Ground Rent	$ 0.00
H) Other	$ 0.00
TOTAL PROPOSED MONTHLY PAYMENTS	$ 1,560.33

THE ABOVE LISTED FIGURES ARE ESTIMATES BASED ON INFORMATION PROVIDED BY YOU AND OTHER SOURCES. PLEASE REFER TO THE GOOD FAITH ESTIMATE OF CLOSING COSTS AND/OR OTHER DISCLOSURES FOR ADDITIONAL INFORMATION ON THIS MORTGAGE LOAN TRANSACTION.

Charges of Particular Importance in Real Estate and Residential Mortgage Transactions

- Interest

- Loan fees, assumption fees, finder's fees and buyer's points

- Investigation and credit-report fees

- Premiums for mortgage guaranty or similar insurance

Costs that are not finance charges include:

- Seller's points

- Fees for title examination

- Fees for preparing deeds, mortgages and reconveyance, settlement and similar documents

- Notary, appraisal and credit report fees

- Amounts required to be paid into escrow or trustee accounts if the amounts would not otherwise be included in the finance charge

---

5. Annual Percentage Rate (APR)

That particular term and a brief description such as "the cost of your credit as a yearly rate" must be used in the disclosure of the annual percentage rate. The disclosed annual percentage rate is considered accurate if it is not more than 1/8 of 1 percentage point above or below the actual annual percentage rate determined, in a normal transaction. If the transaction is irregular, however, the annual percentage rate is considered accurate if it is not more than 1/4 of 1 percentage point above or below the actual annual percentage rate determined. Irregular transactions include multiple advances, irregular payment periods or irregular payment amounts.

6. Variable Rate

There must be a disclosure of the following items for the annual percentage rate to increase after closing in a transaction secured by the consumer's principal dwelling, within one year or less.

<u>**Required Disclosures**</u>

- Circumstances under which the rate may increase

- Any limitations on the increase

- The effect of an increase

- An example of the payment terms resulting from an increase in the APR

If the APR is to increase after closing in a transaction secured by the consumer's principal dwelling within a term greater than one year:

<u>**There must be a Disclosure of:**</u>

- The fact that the transaction contains a variable-rate feature

- A statement that variable-rate disclosures have been provided to the borrower

<u>7. Payment Schedule</u>

The number, amounts and timing of payments required to repay the obligation must be disclosed by the creditor. A brief disclosure must be made of the payment schedule for transactions in which a series of payments vary solely because of the application of a finance charge to the unpaid principal balance. This usually can be found in graduated payment mortgages or in those where mortgage insurance premiums are based on the unpaid principal balance. In these transactions, creditors must disclose only the amount of the largest and smallest payments in the series, and that the other payments may vary.

<u>8. Total of Payments</u>

The creditor must use the term "total of payments" as well as a brief description such as "the amount you will have paid when you have made all scheduled payments." The sum of the payments noted in the payment schedule must be disclosed for all real estate transactions under Regulation Z.

<u>9. Total Sale Price</u>

In a sale where the seller is a creditor, Regulation Z requires the use of the term "total sale price" along with a brief description such as "the total price of your purchase on credit, including your downpayment of $_____."

10. Prepayment Penalties and Rebates

Creditors must make a disclosure of the existence of a penalty on pre-payment in full. Even if a creditor does not charge a pre-payment penalty, a statement to that effect must be included. This disclosure is only required, however, if the finance charge is computed from time to time by application of a rate to the unpaid principal balance. Any other type of transaction must include a statement indicating whether the consumer is entitled to a rebate of any portion of the finance charge in the event of pre-payment.

11. Late Payment Charge

Any charges due to a late payment must be disclosed. The disclosure may reflect the fact that late charges may be determined as either a percentage or a specified dollar amount.

12. Security Interest

A creditor must disclose what security interest is or will be retained in the property purchased in the transaction. Where credit is being used to purchase the collateral the creditor is required to give only a general identification such as "the property purchased in this transaction."

13. Insurance

The amount of the premium and a statement that the insurance is not required to obtain credit must be disclosed if charges for credit life, accident, health or loss-of-income insurance are excluded from the finance charge. If the charges for property insurance are excluded from the finance charge, there must be a disclosure stating the cost of the insurance if obtained from the creditor and declaring that the insurance may be obtained from a person of the consumer's choice.

14. Assumption Policy

A creditor must state, in a residential mortgage transaction, whether a subsequent buyer of a dwelling from the borrower may be permitted to assume the remaining debt on its original terms.

15. Required Deposit

An example of a required deposit is a savings account created as a condition of a loan. If a creditor requires the consumer to maintain the deposit as a condition of the extension of credit, the creditor must state that the annual percentage rate does not reflect the effect of the required deposit.

Time of Disclosures

Disclosures must be made before consummation of the credit transaction, which is usually the time of closing. Consummation is defined as the time a consumer becomes liable for a credit obligation.

Certain Residential Mortgage Transactions

Creditors have been encouraged to use early disclosures in order to give borrowers ample time to shop for credit. Creditors involved in residential mortgage transactions subject to RESPA, however, are required to make Regulation Z disclosures before closing, or deliver or place them in the mail within three business days after receiving the consumer's written application, whichever is earlier.

Certain Variable-Rate Transactions

The following disclosures must be made if the annual percentage rate may increase after closing in a transaction secured by the consumer's principal dwelling with a term greater than one year.

Required Disclosures for some Variable-Rate Loans

- The booklet titled *Consumer Handbook on Adjustable Rate Mortgages*, published by the Fed and the Federal Home Loan Bank Board, or a suitable substitute

- A loan program disclosure for each variable-rate program in which the consumer expresses an interest

---

Redisclosure

Generally, an event occurring after delivery of the disclosures to the consumer, which makes the disclosures inaccurate, does not result in a violation of Regulation Z and does not require redisclosure. But if disclosures are given before the date of closing, redisclosure is required before the closing, if the actual annual percentage rate is above or below the disclosed rate by more than 1/8 of 1% in a regular transaction, or more than 1/4 of 1% in an irregular transaction.

The creditor has the option of providing the consumer with either a complete set of new disclosures or a disclosure of only the terms that have changed.

Subsequent Disclosure

Three events require the creditor to make disclosures after the closing; refinancing, assumption and variable-rate adjustments.

Refinancing

Refinancing is a new transaction requiring new disclosures to the borrower. Refinancing occurs when an existing obligation is paid in full and replaced by a new one. Regulation states what is not considered a refinance:

1. A renewal of a single payment obligation with no change in the original terms

2. A reduction in the annual percentage rate with a corresponding change in the payment schedule

3. A change in the payment schedule or a change in collateral requirements as a result of the borrower's default or delinquency

Assumption

An assumption is a new transaction requiring new disclosures to the borrower. An assumption occurs when a new party becomes obligated on an existing debt. Whenever a creditor agrees to accept a new borrower as a primary obligor on an existing residential mortgage transaction, before the assumption occurs, the creditor must make new disclosures to the new obligor based on the remaining debt.

Variable-Rate Adjustments

When an adjustment is made to the interest rate in a variable rate loan secured by the borrower's principal dwelling and with a term greater than one year, certain new disclosures are required. The following information must be provided by the creditor at least once each year during which an interest rate adjustment is made without an accompanying payment change, and at least 25 but not more than 120 calendar days before a payment is due at a new level:

1. The current and prior interest rates

2. The index values on which the current and prior interest rates are based

3. The extent to which the creditor has foregone any interest rate increase

4. The contractual effects of the adjustment, including the new payment amount and the loan balance

5. The payment (if different from the payment disclosed above) that would be required to fully amortize the loan at the new interest rate over the remaining loan term

Consumer's Right to Rescind

Generally, the right to rescind applies to all consumer credit transactions where the debt is secured by a lien against the borrower's principal dwelling. A transaction involving a mobile home can be rescinded, even if it is considered personal property because the definition of a dwelling is not limited to real property.

Exemptions

A number of important exemptions to the right to rescind exist in loans on residential real estate. A residential mortgage transaction is one of those exemptions. The right to rescind does not apply to transactions made to finance the purchase or construction of a borrower's principal dwelling, no matter what the priority of the lien.

Another exemption is for a refinance, by the same lender, of a loan already secured by the principal dwelling if no new money is advanced. If the borrower receives money from the refinance, the transaction is rescindable to the extent of the new money if the loan is secured by the borrower's principal dwelling. An example of when this exemption is likely is when balloon notes are renewed, extended or refinanced.

The right of rescission is not applicable on loans for a primary residence. However, loans secured by property that is to be used other than as a principal dwelling may be rescinded within the guidelines for rescission.

Notice of Right to Rescind

Each consumer must be provided with two copies of the notice of right to rescind if the transaction qualifies under the guidelines for rescission.

Rescission Period

A borrower has the right to rescind until midnight of the third business day following the last of these events to occur:

1. Closing of the transaction

2. Delivery of all material Truth in Lending disclosures

3. Delivery of the notice of the right to rescind

Equal Credit Opportunity Act

This federal law protects borrowers from discrimination based on their race, sex, color, religion, national origin, age or marital status or on the grounds of receiving income from a public welfare program. Under this law, all qualified people will be assured of an equal right to credit.

Important Guidelines of the Equal Credit Opportunity Act

- A borrower may not be required, nor asked, to reveal whether they are divorced or widowed. A lender may require information regarding marital status, however.

- A borrower may not be required, nor asked, about receiving alimony or child support unless he or she is told there is no requirement to reveal that information. An obligation to pay alimony or child support may be discussed, however, and information may be requested by the lender.

- A borrower is not required to answer questions about birth control practices or intent to become parents.

- A borrower must be notified within 30 days whether or not he or she has qualified for a loan. If the loan is turned down, a reason must be given by the lender.

- A lender must use information provided by a borrower that explains a bad credit history, as a result of a joint account, showing that it does not reflect on the borrower.

Personal Property Secured Transactions

A **Security Agreement** is the device commonly used to secure a loan on personal property, much as a trust deed secures a loan on real property. As you recall, personal property is something that is movable, and is not real property. Jewelry and bulk items—such as retail inventory, autos and boats—are examples of personal property that might be used to secure a debt. The Security Agreement is the document used to create the security interest in personal property.

To protect, or "perfect"—as it is called, the interest created by the security agreement, or prevent the security from being sold or liened by someone else, a **Financing Statement** must be filed. A security interest is "perfected" when it has "attached"—or finalized, and the Financing Statement has been properly recorded in the office of the Secretary of State in Sacramento.

> ### A Security Interest "Attaches" When:
>
> - There is agreement by the parties
>
> - Value has been given
>
> - The debtor has acquired rights in the collateral

The Financing Statement is only the form used to record the debt, not actual evidence of the debt. The Security Agreement contains all the details of the agreement, and is the document that describes the obligation. Once the interest created by the security agreement is perfected, the secured party's interest is protected against the debtor's other creditors.

Now that you are acquainted with the exciting possibilities in real estate finance, you are ready to move on to the new challenge of how property is valued, in the next chapter.

Post Test

The following self test repeats the one you took at the beginning of this chapter. Now take the exam again—since you have read all the material— and check your knowledge of lending practices.

1. When the money supply is limited and the demand is great, it is known as:
   a. inflation
   b. tight money
   c. disintermediation
   d. leverage

2. When a group of investors pools its money to buy real estate it is known as:
   a. Real Estate Investment Trust (REIT)
   b. Real Estate Settlement Procedures Act (RESPA)
   c. Federal Deposit Insurance Corporation (FDIC)
   d. Federal Home Loan Insurance Corporation (FHLIC)

3. The instrument commonly used to secure a loan on personal property is known as a:
   a. pledge agreement
   b. financing statement
   c. security agreement
   d. trust deed

4. Which of the following is related to the Federal Housing Administration (FHA)?
   a. loan origination
   b. insurance
   c. guarantee
   d. contract of sale

5. The process of depositors removing funds from savings is called:
   a. disintermediation
   b. reapportionment
   c. intermediation
   d. disinterment

6. The maximum amount that an eligible and qualified veteran can pay for a home is:
   a. no maximum limitation
   b. $23,900
   c. $184,000
   d. $174,000

7. Which of the following lenders is most likely to make large commercial loans to developers?
   a. national banks
   b. insurance companies
   c. private parties
   d. credit unions

8. The major role of a mortgage company is to originate:
   a. construction loans
   b. loans which are sold on the secondary mortgage market
   c. loans for the primary market
   d. loans for sale to private individuals

9. Secondary mortgage markets redistribute funds from:
   a. money-poor areas to money-rich areas
   b. money-poor areas to money-poor areas
   c. money-rich areas to money-poor areas
   d. money-rich areas to money-rich areas

10. Conventional first trust deeds in California are mostly financed by:
    a. banks
    b. mortgage companies
    c. insurance companies
    d. savings banks

Vocabulary

Read the definition, find the matching term and write the corresponding term number on the line provided.

Terms

1. Adjustable Rate Mortgage (ARM)
2. Deregulation
3. Financial Intermediary
4. Financing Statement
5. Intermediation
6. Mortgage Loan Disclosure Statement
7. Real Estate Investment Trust
8. Security Agreement
9. Tight Money
10. Variable Rate Mortgage (VRM)
11. Warehousing

Definitions

1. ___ An economic situation in which the supply of money is limited, and the demand for money is high, as evidenced by high interest rates

2. ___ An organization that obtains funds through deposits and then lends those funds to earn a return—such as savings banks, commercial banks, credit unions and mutual savings banks

3. ___ The process of transfer capital from those who invest funds to those who wish to borrow

4. ___ A loan which allows for the interest rate to adjust periodically in relationship to a predetermined index based on the maintenance of a pre-established margin

5. ___ A way investors with a small amount of capital can pool their resources to buy real estate

6. ___ A mortgage where the interest rate varies according to an agreed-upon index, thus resulting in a change in the borrower's monthly payments

7. ___ A process where financial institutions that formerly had been restrained in their lending activities by the law are allowed to compete freely for profits in the marketplace

8. ___ The device commonly used to secure a loan on personal property

9. ___ A statement that informs the buyer of all charges and expenses related to a particular loan

10. ___ The instrument which is recorded in order to give public notice of the security interest, thus protecting the interest of the secured party in the collateral

11. ___ The process of assembling into one package a number of mortgage loans, prior to selling them to an investor

Answers

Pre-Test/Post Test

1. b
2. a
3. c
4. b
5. a
6. a
7. b
8. b
9. c
10. d

Vocabulary

1. 9
2. 3
3. 5
4. 1
5. 7
6. 10
7. 2
8. 8
9. 6
10. 4
11. 11

ECONOMIC AND POLITICAL ASPECTS OF REAL ESTATE

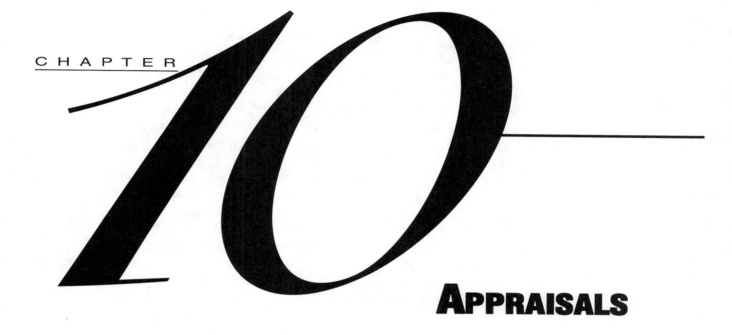

CHAPTER

10

APPRAISALS

Focus

- **Definition of appraisal**

- **Fair market value**

- **Price, cost and value**

- **Four elements of value**

- **Forces influencing value**

- **Principles of valuation**

- **Appraisal process**

- **Requirements for appraiser's license**

- **Professional appraisal organizations**

Pre-Test

The following is a self test to determine how much you know about appraisal before reading this chapter. Take it without studying, then read the material presented in the text. At the end of the chapter you will find a repeat of this exam. Test your knowledge by answering the questions again, then check your improvement. (The answers are found at the end of this chapter.) Good luck!

1. The most appropriate use of the income approach is for:
   a. new residences
   b. old residences
   c. rental property
   d. church

2. The most thorough and complete appraisal report is:
   a. a short form report
   b. a long form report
   c. a narrative report
   d. an oral report

3. In estimating the value of land, what is the least important element?
   a. size
   b. sales price of comparable land
   c. cost to build on it
   d. price asked

4. Granite Elvis statues on the front of an apartment building are considered a type of:
   a. functional obsolescence
   b. social obsolescence
   c. economic obsolescence
   d. physical deterioration

5. The first thing to do in the appraisal process is:
   a. arrange the data
   b. make beginning appraisal plan
   c. define the appraisal problem
   d. separate the data

6. Which of the following indicates a professional appraiser?
   a. National Association of Realtors (NAR)
   b. California Association of Realtors (CAR)
   c. Member Appraisal Institute (MAI)
   d. Certified Property Manager (CPM)

7. The term "highest and best use" means:
   a. highest net return
   b. greatest population density
   c. highest gross return
   d. highest elevation

8. Which of the following reflects the price paid?
   a. book value
   b. appraised value
   c. accrued value
   d. market value

9. All of the following are elements of value except:
   a. scarcity
   b. demand
   c. utility
   d. plottage

10. Which of the following is needed to use the capitalization approach?
   a. adjusted cost
   b. sales price
   c. net income
   d. gross income

Terms

The following terms are the keys to your success in learning about real estate. Refer to them as you study this chapter for greater understanding of subjects presented here.

Accrued

Accumulated over a period of time

Accrued Depreciation

The difference between the cost to replace the property and property's current appraised value

Actual Age

The real age of a building

Actual Depreciation

That depreciation occurring as a result of physical, functional or economic forces, causing loss in value to a building

Appraisal

An estimate or opinion of value supported by factual information as of a certain date

Appraisal Report

A written report stating an appraiser's estimate of a subject property's value

Appreciation

An increase in value

Book Depreciation

An accounting concept which refers to an allowance taken to provide for recovery of invested capital

Book Value

The initial cost of the property plus capital improvements minus the total accrued depreciation

Cap Rate

A term sometimes used when referring to capitalization rate

Capital Improvements

Any permanent improvement made to real estate for the purpose of increasing the useful life of the property or increasing the property's value

Capitalization

The process of calculating the present worth of a property on the basis of its capacity to continue to produce an income stream

Comps

A term used by real estate agents and appraisers to mean comparable properties

Contract Rent

The actual rent being paid by tenants

Corner Lot

A lot found at the intersection of two streets

Cost

Represents expenses in money, labor, material or sacrifices in acquiring or producing something

Cul-De-Sac Lot

A lot found on a dead-end street

Deferred Maintenance

Negligent care of a building; ordinary care and maintenance the owner fails to perform

Depreciation

Loss in value from any cause

Economic Life

The number of years of probable usefulness of a building

Effective Age

The years or age shown by the condition and utility of a structure, rather than its actual or chronological age

Fair Market Value

The price the property would bring if freely offered on the open market with both a willing buyer and a willing seller

Flag Lot

Looks like a flag on a pole, which represents the access to the site; usually located to the rear of another lot fronting a main street

Front Footage

The width of a property along a street

Gross Rent

Income (figured annually) received from rental units before any expenses are deducted

Improvements

Any buildings or structures on a lot

Interior Lot

One that is surrounded by other lots, with a frontage on the street; the most common type lot, which may or may not be desirable—depending on other factors

Key Lot

So named because it resembles a key fitting into a lock; one that is surrounded by the backyards of other lots, therefore is the least desirable because of the lack of privacy

Market Rent

The rent a property should bring in the open market

Net Income

Sometimes known as net operating income; the remaining income after operating expenses have been subtracted from the gross income of a property

Plottage or Assemblage

Putting several smaller, less valuable parcels together under one ownership to increase value of total property

Price

What is paid for something

Reconciliation

Sometimes called correlation, this is the adjustment process of weighing results of all three appraisal methods to arrive at a final estimate of the subject property's market value

Replacement Cost

The cost of replacing improvements with modern materials and techniques

Reproduction Cost

The current cost of building a replica of the subject structure, using similar quality materials

Site

The position, situation or location of a piece of land in a neighborhood

T-Intersection Lot

A lot that is fronted head-on by a street; noise and glare from headlights may be detractors from this type of lot

Utility Value

The usefulness of the property

Vacancy Factor

Loss of income because of a vacant unit

Value

The power of goods or services to command other goods in exchange for the present worth of future benefits arising from property ownership

Introduction

http://www.dre.ca.gov
Reference Book, Ch. 17

http://www.appraisalinstitute.org

http://www.orea.ca.gov
(California Office of Real Estate Appraisers)

Probably the most asked question in real estate is, "How much do you think it's worth?" Every day a client or customer will ask about the fair price or fair rental for a property, and an agent must be prepared to answer knowledgeably. Some of the most important services a listing agent can provide is to be familiar with how the worth of property is determined, and to be able to explain it to the client.

Most homeowners know, within a range, the value of their homes. They probably are not aware they have used some of the same techniques the listing agent and the professional appraiser will use in determining the value of their home. For example, they may know the selling price of their neighbors' house, and the selling price of the house down the street. They have added to—or subtracted from—the value of their own house, depending on amenities, location and condition, to come up with a pretty accurate value, if they are being honest with themselves.

This chapter will examine the appraisal process and the methods used to determine property values so that you as an agent can answer when a client or customer asks the question, "How much do you think it's worth?"

Definition of Appraisal

An **Appraisal** is an unbiased estimate or opinion of the property value on a given date. **Value** is the present worth of rights to future benefits that come from property ownership. An appraiser gives his or her opinion of value in a written statement called an **Appraisal Report**. It is the conclusion of the appraiser's research and analysis of all relevant data regarding the subject property.

Most of the time, an objective, third-party opinion is needed to determine the value of real property. The professional appraiser, because of training, experience and ethics, is responsible for giving clients an objective opinion of value, reached without bias. An appraiser has a serious responsibility to be correct in evaluating data and not allow other factors to influence evaluation of a property. The appraiser must remember to be a neutral party, responding only to the forces affecting value, and not to any other special interests who might want to influence his or her judgment.

There are several different reasons for determining the value of a particular property.

Reasons For An Appraisal

- Transfer of property ownership

- Financing and credit

- Taxation

- Condemnation

- Insurance

The estimate of value given for each of the above listed reasons may be different, depending on the reason for ordering the appraisal. The condemnation value is going to be different from the taxation value, the insurance value or the market value. An appraiser must know what those differences are and how to estimate the value of a property based on the purpose for which it is being used.

Fair Market Value

Real estate includes both land and anything belonging to the land, as well as rights or interests in that land. The price a property would bring if freely offered on the open market, with both a willing buyer and a willing seller, is known as **Fair Market Value**—or market value.

A property that is offered for sale as a result of default, foreclosure, bankruptcy, divorce, death or any other unusual circumstances cannot be said to be freely and willingly offered on the open market, and the sale price of such properties would not represent fair market value. An appraiser would take into account that there were special circumstances in those sales and would not use the price paid as a comparable measure of value. The following can be assumed of all fair market sales.

Fair Market Sales

- Buyer and seller are operating in their own interest.

- Buyer and seller are knowledgeable about the transaction and make careful decisions.

- The property is available for a reasonable time on the open market.

- The sale is for cash or trade, or is specifically financed.

- Normal financing, available to qualified borrowers, is used.

Price, Cost and Value

Market price is what a property *actually* sold for, where market value, or fair market value as it is sometimes called, is the price that it *should* have sold for.

Sometimes, **Value** and **Price** or **Cost** are the same, but they aren't necessarily. Circumstances of one buyer and one seller may affect the sale of a specific property, giving it its own value, apart from some other similar parcel. The job of an appraiser is to determine the special factors of a sale and assign a value based on each individual transaction.

Pamela and John wanted to buy their first house. They looked at several with their real estate agent, and finally decided on one that was beyond their means. They made a hopeful, low offer. Unknown to them, the seller had lost his job and was desperate to sell. He accepted their offer, which was well below market value.

In the above case, the seller did not sell freely, for market value, and the sales price only reflected his desperate situation, not the real value of the house.

Price, Cost and Value

- Price is what is paid for something.

- Cost represents expenses in money, labor, material or sacrifices in acquiring or producing something.

- Value has to do with the present and future anticipated enjoyment, or profit of something.

Remember

- Cost is not an essential element of value.

The value of a parcel can be defined in many ways. There is **Utility Value**, or the usefulness of the property. This is the subjective value or the value given for personal reasons. For example, a swimming pool might be important to one family, but of little value to another. Other amenities fall into this category as well. Six bedrooms would not be useful or have utility value to a couple with no children, nor would a home deep in the woods to a city worker.

Market value represents the amount in money for which a property can be sold in current market conditions at a given time. This is sometimes called the objective value, since it may be determined by actual data.

Four Elements of Value

There are only four elements of value, all of which must be considered in estimating the worth of a property. These are demand, utility, scarcity and transferability.

Remember

memory

aid:

"DUST"

The Four Elements of Value

D emand: the desire to buy and the ability to pay

U tility: usefulness

S carcity: the fewer available, the more valuable

T ransferability: title must be marketable, unclouded

The appraiser must decide if there is a demand for a property, such as a high-rise residential building, or a low-cost housing project. Can it be used for the purpose it was intended, such as a family home, or residential complex? How many projects like this one are there in the area? The fewer there are, the more value the subject property has. Is the title clear and can the seller easily give ownership to a buyer? As you can see, all of these factors are important in assigning a value to a property. An appraiser must hold each one up to the property in question to arrive at a correct estimate of value.

Forces Influencing Value

The essence of life is change, and real estate is not excluded from that force. Value is created, maintained, modified and destroyed by the relationship of the following four forces.

Forces Influencing Value

1. Environmental and Physical Characteristics

This includes quality of conveniences, availability of schools, shopping, public transportation, churches, similarity of land use. Environmental forces may be climate, soil, topography, oceans and mountains.

2. Social Ideals and Standards

Population growth and decline, age, marriage, birth, divorce and death rates all combine to cause changes in social patterns.

3. Economic Influences

Some economic forces that influence value are natural resources, industrial and commercial trends, employment trends, wage levels, availability of money and credit, interest rates, price levels, tax loads, regional and community economic base, new development, and rental and price patterns.

4. Political or Government Regulations

Some political forces that can affect value are building codes, zoning laws, public health measures, fire regulations, rent controls, environmental legislation and community economic base.

The Four Main Forces Influencing Value

- Physical forces
- Social forces
- Economic forces
- Political forces

Other Factors Influencing Value

Directional growth: This is determined by how the area or city expands. Property in a growth area tends to increase in value.

Location: This may be the most important factor influencing value, as far as highest and best use.

Utility: The property's ability to be used for the purpose it was intended fulfills its utility. Building restrictions and zoning ordinances affect utility.

Size: The use of a property may be determined by the width and depth of the land.

Corner influence: Commercial properties benefit from more exposure, while residential parcels may lose privacy and incur higher maintenance costs from increased frontage.

Shape: Irregular-shaped lots are more difficult and expensive to develop.

Thoroughfare conditions: Width of streets, traffic congestion and condition of pavement affect the value of properties fronting on those streets.

Exposure: The south and west sides of business streets are usually preferred by shopkeepers, because customers will seek the shady side of the street, and window displays will not be damaged by the sun.

Business climate: The presence of shopping areas, offices and medical suites as well as financial, wholesale, industrial and other consumer-friendly businesses is important to establishing value.

Plottage or Assemblage: By putting several smaller, less valuable parcels together under one ownership (through **Plottage or Assemblage**), rather than being owned by separate people, the value of the parcels will be increased.

Topography and soil: Construction costs will be affected by the terrain and soil condition.

Obsolescence: This may be caused by external or economic changes, and decreases usefulness of property or causes deterioration.

Building restrictions and zones: These may increase or depress values.

Principles of Valuation

http://www.dre.ca.gov
Reference Book, Ch. 17
p. 316

A real estate agent or a professional appraiser must know the following basic principles of valuation before assigning value to any property.

Principle of Conformity

When land uses are compatible and homes are similar in design and size, the maximum value is realized.

Principle of Change

Cities and neighborhoods are always changing, and individual homes within those neighborhoods reflect that change. An appraiser must be aware of trends that affect the value of real estate. Economic, environmental, government and social forces are always dynamic, causing changing values in real property.

Principle of Substitution

The basis of the appraisal process, this principle is the foundation of estimating the value of real property. Explained simply, value is set by the cost of getting an equally desirable substitute. An owner cannot expect to sell for more than someone would ordinarily pay for a similar property, under similar conditions.

Principle of Supply and Demand

Increasing supply or decreasing demand will reduce the price in the market. Reducing supply or increasing demand will raise the price in the market. The less there is of something, the higher the cost; the more there is, the lower the cost.

Principle of Highest and Best Use

This principle is based on the reasonable use of real property, at the time of the appraisal, that is most likely to produce the greatest net return to the land and/or the building over a given period of time. Evaluating the highest and best use includes assessing buyers' reasons for buying, the existing use of the property, benefits of ownership, the market's behavior and community or environmental factors.

Principle of Progression

A lesser valued property will be worth more because of the presence of a greater valued property nearby.

Principle of Regression

A greater valued property will be worth less because of the presence of a lower valued property nearby.

Principle of Contribution

The worth of an improvement is what it adds to the entire property's market value, regardless of the actual cost of the improvement. A remodeled attic may not contribute its entire cost to the value of the property, but a new family room will increase the value of the house by more than the cost to build. This principle must be kept in mind by homeowners who want to change the character of their house in such a way that it no longer fits in the neighborhood. The cost of the improvement may not add to the value if the house is overbuilt for the area.

Principle of Anticipation

Probable future benefits to be derived from a property will increase the value. An appraiser estimates the present worth of future benefits when he or she assigns a value based on anticipated returns.

Principle of Competition

When considerable profits are being made, competition is created. When there is a profitable demand for homes, there will be competition among builders. The supply would then increase in relation to the demand, bringing lower selling prices and unprofitable competition, leading to more decline in supply.

Principle of Balance

When contrasting, opposing or interacting elements are in balance in a neighborhood or area, value is created. A careful mix of varying land use creates value also. Over-improvement or under-improvement will cause imbalance.

Principle of Three Stage Life Cycle

All neighborhoods change. They start out as young, dynamic areas, and eventually disintegrate in the process of passing years. All property goes through three distinct stages.

Three Stages Of Property Change

- Development

- Maturity

- Old age

Growth and decline is normal in all areas, and many times it can be reversed just as it reaches the last stages. For example, when a lovely neighborhood grows to be old and worn out, young families may choose to move in and completely restore the process of change by starting the life cycle of the neighborhood all over again with development.

The Appraisal Process

http://www.mortgagespot. com/appraisal.htm

At the end of an appraisal, an appraiser must be prepared to answer two questions: What is the highest and best use of the property, and what is this use worth?

Professional appraisers have developed an orderly systematic method—known as the appraisal process—to arrive at an estimate of value. Not every step is used on every property, but—whether you are an appraiser or a real estate agent—there is a check list to help you evaluate the worth of a property in a consistent orderly way.

The Appraisal Process is made up of Four Steps

1. State the problem.

2. Gather data (general and specific).

3. Decide on the appraisal method to be used.

4. Reconcile or correlate the data for final value estimate.

State the Problem

The appraiser must know why the appraisal is necessary. He or she must identify and describe the property to be evaluated, and indicate the purpose of the appraisal. Then the extent of ownership to be appraised must be identified.

Rights affect value because they set the limits within which the property may be used, and so the appraiser must know how the property is owned in order to determine the value of those rights. Is it a fee simple, are there restrictions on use, or possibly a life estate or co-ownership? The purpose of the appraisal will determine the types of information that will be gathered.

Purposes Of An Appraisal

- Market value for a sale

- Value for mortgage loan purposes

- Value for insurance purposes

- Value for condemnation proceedings

- Value for inheritance purposes

- Value for Internal Revenue Service purposes

- Value for property tax purposes

Once the appraiser knows the purpose for the property evaluation, it is possible to move on to the next step.

Gather the Data

A general, preliminary survey of the neighborhood and the **Site** must be made by the appraiser to determine the highest and best use of the property. The type of property will determine the kind of specific data that will be needed. An appraisal of a single-family residence will require information about similar owner-occupied properties, while a residential income (apartment) building will require data on income and expenses of similar properties. So first, general data is gathered, such as information on the region, the city and the neighborhood. Then specific data on the location, the particular lot and improvements is gathered.

Information Gathered For Appraisal

General Data

1. Region
2. City
3. Neighborhood

Specific Data

1. Location
2. Lot
3. Improvements (buildings)

Demand and purchasing power available will affect the value of a property. Data should be obtained on population trends, income level and employment opportunities.

Information Sources:

1. General data can be obtained from government publications, newspapers and magazines.

2. Regional data (metropolitan areas such as San Francisco Bay, Southern California or the Central Coast) can be gathered from monthly bank summaries, regional planning commissions and government agencies.

3. Community data (town or city) can be obtained from the Chamber of Commerce, City Planning Commission, city government agencies, banks and real estate boards.

4. Neighborhood data can be obtained from personal inspections, real estate agents or area builders. The appraiser notices the age and appearance of the neighborhood; any negative influences such as physical or social hazards (run-down buildings, evidence of criminal activity); evidence of future development; proximity to schools, business, recreation and transportation.

Market data must be collected and analyzed for sales and listing prices of property in the area. Sources for sales information are assessor's records and county recorder's office, title insurance companies, other property owners in the area, the appraiser's own data base. Age of the buildings and other information regarding improvements can be gathered from the tax assessor's office, city building department or personal inspection of the improvements.

Site Analysis

Appraisers rely on available market information such as listings, offers, leases and sales reports as the foundation of their appraisal methods.

Even though the location of the neighborhood and city must be considered in any analysis of a specific site, or a plot of ground, the exact spot of the site itself is the most important factor in determining value. Since most sites are different sizes and in different locations, some are more desirable than others and should be evaluated separate from the improvements for highest and best use.

Location and Types of Lots

1. *Cul-de-sac*

   A **Cul-de-sac** is sometimes known as a dead-end street. It is a street that has only one way in and the same way out. This may be desirable because of the privacy and quiet, but the lot may be oddly pie-shaped if it is on the turn-around section of the street.

2. *Corner lot*

   A **Corner Lot** is found at the intersection of two streets. It may be desirable because of its accessibility, but may also be noisy and expensive to maintain because of the increased frontage.

3. *Key lot*

   A **Key Lot**, so named because it resembles a key fitting into a lock, is surrounded by the back yards of other lots. It is the least desirable because of the lack of privacy.

4. *T-intersection lot*

   A **T-Intersection Lot** is one that is fronted head-on by a street. The noise and glare from headlights may be detractors from this type of lot.

5. *Interior lot*

   An **Interior Lot** is one that is surrounded by other lots, with a frontage on the street. It is the most common type lot and may be desirable or not, depending on other factors.

6. *Flag lot*

   A **Flag Lot** looks like a flag on a pole. The pole represents the access to the site, which is usually located to the rear of another lot fronting a main street.

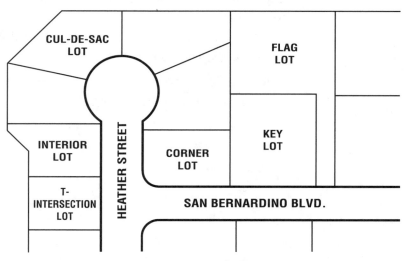

Appraiser Must Evaluate All Legal Data Connected With Site

- Legal description
- Taxes
- Zoning and general plan
- Restrictions and easements
- Determination of other interests in property

Physical Factors of Site for Appraiser to Consider

- Shape of the lot
- Topography and soil conditions
- Corner influence
- Relations of site to surroundings
- Availability of public utilities
- Encroachments
- Landscaping and subsurface land improvements

A depth table is one showing the value of lots that vary in depth from the street to the rear property line. Using the 4-3-2-1 rule, a depth table shows a percentage relationship between the depth of a lot being appraised and the value of a standard lot in the area. It is generally used to estimate the value of commercial property.

You can see from the following illustration that the highest value is located at the front of a lot, with values becoming lower as the lot gets deeper. The 4-3-2-1 rule states that the first one-fourth of the lot (fronting the street) gets 40% of the value, the second one-fourth of the lot gets 30% of the value, the third one-fourth of the lot gets 20% and the last one-fourth of the lot gets 10% of the value.

An appraiser will measure the square footage of the lot and apply this formula to estimate the lot's value.

Depth Table The "4-3-2-1" Rule

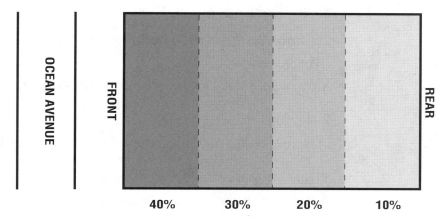

Remember

- Front Footage of a commercial property is usually the most valuable.

Buildings and Other Permanent Structures

When an appraiser considers **Improvements**, it means looking at any buildings or other permanent structures, such as fences, swimming pools, saunas or built-in jacuzzis. Real property is divided into land and improvements, as you recall from previous chapters, and each adds its own value to a site. We have discussed the desirable characteristics of land. Now let's look at the improvements—both on-site and off-site.

Improvements

- On-site improvements: structures permanently attached to the land, such as buildings, swimming pools and fences

- Off-site improvements: areas bordering site improved by the addition of street lights, sidewalks, greenbelts and curbs

Construction Basics: You will be asked certain construction questions on the California Real Estate License exam. It is important for you to learn the few basics presented here.

Common terms used in building (see following diagram):

1. Anchor Bolt

Attaches mud sill to foundation; embedded in concrete foundation

2. Bracing

Diagonal board nailed across wall framing to prevent sway

3. Building paper

Waterproof paper used between sheathing and roof covering

4. Closed sheathing

Foundation for exterior siding; boards nailed to studding

5. Crawl space

Area between floor and ground under the house

6. Cripple

Stud above or below a window opening or above a doorway

7. Eaves

Part of roof that hangs over the exterior walls

8. Fire stop

Boards nailed between studs to block the spread of fire in the walls

9. Flashing

Sheet metal that keeps the water out

10. Footing

Extended part of foundation

11. Foundation

Base of house; usually concrete

12. Header

The board over a doorway or window opening

13. Joists

Boards supporting floors or ceilings (A board supporting them is a girder.)

14. Mud sill

Redwood board that is fastened with bolts to the foundation

15. Open sheathing
Boards nailed to rafters to form foundation for roof

16. Rafters
Slanted boards that support the roof boards and shingles

17. Ridge board
Highest part of a frame building

18. Sill
Board along the bottom of window or door opening

19. Sole plate
Support for studs

20. Studs
Vertical 2"x 4" boards in the walls spaced 16" on center

Parts of a Building

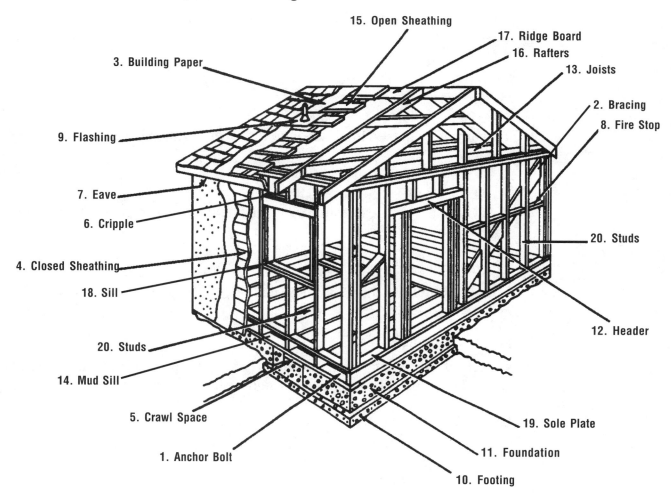

Other Terms

1. Backfill

Soil used to fill in holes or support a foundation

2. Bearing wall

A wall that supports a vertical load as well as its own weight

3. Board foot (144 cubic inches)

A measurement of lumber equal to the volume of a board 12"x12"x1"

4. BTU (British Thermal Unit)

A measurement that calculates heat; the amount of heat needed to raise one pound of water one degree Fahrenheit

5. Compaction

Extra soil matted down or compressed, which may be added to a lot to fill in the low areas or raise the level of the parcel; also used where the soil is unstable

6. Conduit

A flexible pipe in which electrical wiring is installed

7. Deciduous

Certain trees that lose their leaves seasonally

8. Drywall

Gypsum panels used in place of wet plaster to finish the inside of buildings

9. Elevation sheet

Shows front and side exterior views of finished buildings in the blueprint stage

10. Energy Efficient Ratio (EER)

A measurement of the efficiency of energy; used to determine the effectiveness of appliances

11. Hoskold Tables

A method used to value an annuity that is based on reinvesting capital immediately; used by appraiser to valuate income property

12. Insulation

Insulation's resistance to heat is measured by the R factor: When the R value is higher, the insulation is better

13. *Inwood Tables*

Means by which an income stream can be converted into present value; used by appraisers to valuate income property

14. *Kiosk*

A free-standing information booth, such as a flower or newspaper stand

15. *Minimum residential ceiling height*

7.5 feet

16. *Normal residential ceiling height*

8 feet

17. *Percolating water*

Underground water not flowing in a specific channel

18. *Percolation test*

A test used by builders to determine the ability of the land to absorb and drain water

19. *Potable*

Water that is safe to drink

20. *R-Value*

Used to calculate the heat resistance of insulation; the higher the better

21. *Setback*

A certain distance a building must be set back from the street; usually determined by local building code

22. *Shopping centers*

*Neighborhood shopping center (5,000-10,000 population required)
*Major shopping center or mall (50,000-100,000 population required)

23. *Wainscoting*

The bottom portion of a wall that is covered with wood siding; the top part is treated with another material

24. *Water table*

The natural level at which water will be found, either above or below the surface of the ground

25. *Water pressure*

Can be tested by turning on all faucets and flushing all toilets at the same time

Roof Types

Roof types are determined by the direction, steepness and number of roof planes. (See diagram for illustrations.)

Single Dormers

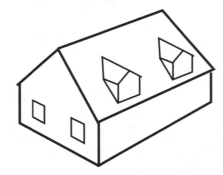

Gambrel

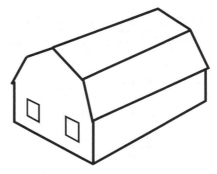

Mansard

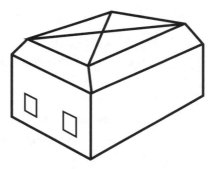

Pyramid

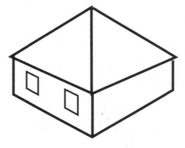

Roof Types (continued)

Dust Pan or Shed Dormer

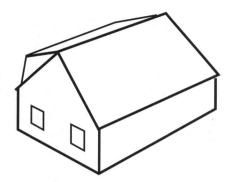

Gable

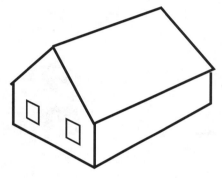

Hip

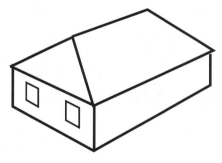

Flat

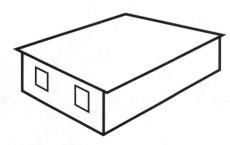

House Styles

Traditional House Styles used in building are interesting for their variety, and important for a real estate agent to know. (See diagram for illustrations.)

1. Cape Cod
2. Colonial
3. Contemporary
4. English Tudor
5. Mediterranean

6. Ranch
7. Split Level
8. Townhouse
9. Victorian

Cape Cod

http://www.charlestown.
ma.us/houses.html

Colonial

Contemporary

English Tudor

House Styles (continued)

Mediterranean

Ranch

Split Level

Townhouse

Victorian

Decide on Method of Appraising Property

http://www.dre.ca.gov
Reference Book, Ch. 17
p. 341

There are three main approaches to making a market value estimate.

Three Approaches To Appraising Property

Sales (or Market) Comparison Approach

- Recent sales and listings of similar properties in the area are evaluated to form an opinion of value.

Cost Approach

- This approach estimates the value of the land as if vacant, and adds that to the depreciated cost of new improvements to determine an estimate of value for the entire property.

Income Capitalization (or Income) Approach

- The potential net income of the property is considered and then capitalized into value.

Many times an appraiser will use all three methods to arrive at the market value of a property. In most appraisals, all three approaches will have something to add. Each method is used independently to reach an estimated value. Finally, by giving to each separate value a weight that is most compatible to the subject property, the appraiser will arrive at a value for the property. This process is called **Reconciliation** or Correlation.

Sales (or Market) Comparison Approach

This approach is the one most easily and commonly used by real estate agents. It is best for single family homes or condominiums and vacant lots because sales information is readily available and easily compared. Also, the process is relatively simple to learn and use.

Remember

- The market comparison approach uses the principle of substitution to compare similar properties.

As you recall, the principle of substitution says that a buyer will not pay more for a property than the cost of a similar one. The market comparison approach takes the current selling price of a similar property and adjusts it for any differences to arrive at the market value for the subject property.

The appraiser will collect data on comparable (called **Comps**) properties that are as "like-kind" to the property in question as possible, in certain categories.

Like-Kind Comparison

- Neighborhood location
- Size (comparable number of bedrooms/bathrooms as well as square footage)
- Age
- Architectural style
- Financing terms
- General price range

The market comparison approach is based on the idea that property is worth what it will sell for when there is no extra stress, if reasonable time is given to find a buyer. Because of this, the appraiser will research comparable sales to discover any special circumstances influencing those sales. Only those similar properties—sold on the open market, with approval of the seller, offered for a reasonable length of time—will be used for comparables. Also, if possible, only those properties that have sold within the past six months are selected. If the comparables are older than that, they are considered less reliable.

Features in either the property or the transaction itself are elements that can cause appraisals to vary.

Elements Causing Estimates of Value to Vary

- Financing terms
- Time of sale
- Sale conditions (arm's length)
- Location
- Physical features
- Income (if any) from the property

Thus, a price is found for each comparable property that should reflect its present value in the current market where the subject property is being sold. Those properties not as comparable are excluded, and greater weight is given to the comparable sales most like the property being appraised.

By using judgment to reconcile the comparables, the appraiser arrives at the final estimate of value for the subject property, using the compatible comparables to show the value and price to be asked for the subject property.

Advantages of Sales Comparison Approach

- Most easily understood method of valuation and most commonly used by real estate agents

- Easily applied for the sale of single family homes

Disadvantages of Sales Comparison Approach

- Finding enough recently sold similar properties to get comparable values

- Correctly adjusting amenities to make them comparable to the subject property

- Older sales unreliable with changing economic conditions

- Difficulty in confirming transaction details

The Procedure

1. Find similar properties, select and verify data.

2. Select appropriate elements of comparison, adjust sales price of each comparable. (Adjustment is always made to the comparable, not the subject property.)

3. Adjust sales prices of comparables by *subtracting* the adjustment if the subject property is inferior to the comparable and by *adding* the adjustment if the subject property is superior.

- The sales comparison approach is best for single family homes or condominiums and vacant lots.

Cost Approach

The cost approach looks at the value of the appraised parcel as the combination of two elements: the value of the land as if vacant, and the cost to rebuild the appraised building as new on the date of valuation, less the **Accrued** depreciation.

Formula for Determining Value Based on Cost Approach

	Value of the land
+	Cost to build structure new
-	Accrued depreciation
	Value of property

Using the principle of substitution, a person will not pay more for a substitute if he or she can get the subject property for less. In the cost approach, the substitute is the cost of reconstructing the present building new on vacant land. The cost approach tends to set the upper limit of value for a property. In other words, the most something would cost if it were built new.

The Procedure

1. Estimate the value of the land as if it were vacant, using comparable land sales. (Principle of Substitution)
2. Estimate the **Replacement** or **Reproduction** cost of the existing building as of the appraisal date.
3. Estimate the amount of **Accrued Depreciation** to the improvements.
4. Deduct the amount of the accrued depreciation from the replacement cost (new) to find the estimate of the depreciated value of the improvements.
5. Add the estimated present depreciated value for the improvements to the value of the land. The result is an estimate of value for the subject property.

The cost approach is used most often for appraising new buildings and special-purpose or unique structures. Depreciation on a new building is relatively easy to determine, whereas the cost approach is impractical with older buildings because of the difficulty in estimating depreciation. The cost approach is also used with buildings where it is difficult to find comparables because they are unique or one-of-a-kind, such as a church, fire station or hospital.

Occasionally, the cost approach is the only one an appraiser can use. If there have been no recent sales (such as during recession or when interest rates are too high), there will be no comparables for the market comparison approach. If the subject is not an income-producing property, the income method (to be discussed next) cannot be used. So the cost method is a reliable way for an appraiser or real estate agent to determine the value of a property when all else fails.

Remember

- The cost approach is used most often when appraising new or unique buildings.

To estimate the cost of building the structure new, an appraiser can use one of several methods.

Methods to Estimate the Cost of a New Building

Square-foot method

The square-foot method is the most common, used by appraisers and real estate agents to estimate the cost of construction. The size of the building in question is compared, by square foot, to other buildings with the same area. The building being appraised is compared with the most comparable standard building and its cost per square foot is used for the subject property. This is the fastest way to estimate value using the cost method.

Cubic-foot method

This is a lot like the square-foot method, except that it takes height as well as area into consideration. The cubic contents of buildings are compared instead of just the square footage.

Quantity survey method

This method is a detailed estimate of all labor and materials used in the components of a building. Items such as overhead, insurance and contractor's profit are added to direct costs of building. This method is time consuming but very accurate.

Unit-in-place cost method

Cost of units in the building as installed is computed and applied to the structure cost. The total costs of walls in place, heating units and roof are figured on a square-foot basis, including labor, overhead and profit. This is the most detailed method of estimating value.

Depreciation means loss in value from any cause. It is usually measured by estimating the difference between the current cost to replace new and the estimated value of the property as of the date of appraisal.

The opposite of depreciation is **Appreciation**, or an increase in value, usually as a result of inflation or some special supply and demand force relating to that specific property. Appreciation may balance the normal decrease of value due to depreciation.

All of the influences that reduce the value of a property below its cost new are included in the definition of depreciation.

Three Main Types of Depreciation

Physical Deterioration

This type of depreciation can come from wear and tear, negligent care (sometimes called **Deferred Maintenance**), damage by dry rot or termites or severe changes in temperature. This may or may not be curable.

Functional Obsolescence

Poor architectural design and style can contribute to functional obsolescence, as can lack of modern facilities, out-of-date equipment, changes in styles of construction or changes in utility demand. It may or may not be curable.

Economic Obsolescence

This type of depreciation occurs because of forces outside the property. Changes in the social or economic make-up of the neighborhood, zoning changes, over-supply of homes, under-supply of buyers, recession or legislative restrictions can cause economic obsolescence. It is almost always incurable.

Remember

Three Types of Depreciation

- Physical Deterioration

- Functional Obsolescence

- Economic Obsolescence

Depreciation for income tax purposes is **Book Depreciation**, or a mathematical calculation of steady depreciation or loss, from the owner's original purchase price (cost basis). This allows the owner to recover the cost of investment over the useful life of the building. It is mathematically accrued annually and taken as an income tax deduction from the owner's gross income.

Many times, this deduction makes gross income a negative amount on paper. The building seems to be losing value, giving the owner a "paper loss" that can be offset against other income. This "paper loss," or tax shelter, is why many people invest in income property.

Book Value is the current value (for accounting purposes) of a property, calculated as the original cost, plus **Capital Improvements**, minus accumulated or accrued depreciation. Remember, this is used as an accounting method, not to be confused with **Actual Depreciation** of a building. Depreciation is allowed on buildings only, not on land. The depreciation, for accounting—or tax—purposes, is only a mathematical wasting away of the improvements.

The book value of a property may be calculated by adding the depreciated value of the improvement (the building) to the assigned value of the land. It is important to remember that book value and book depreciation are used only to figure income tax, and are not particularly relevant to an appraiser.

Remember

	Original Cost
+	Improvements
-	Accrued Depreciation

Book Value

The book depreciation calculated by an accountant is not the depreciation considered by the appraiser, as we have seen. The appraiser doesn't look at the owner's original cost to purchase, but uses the cost to build new on the date of the appraisal as the basis for evaluation, using the cost method. An appraiser subtracts the estimate of accrued *actual* (not book) depreciation on the building from the cost to build new.

As you recall, in using the cost method, the value of the land and the value of the building (improvements) are determined separately, then added together to calculate the value of the entire property. So, the appraiser figures the actual depreciation on the building and subtracts it from the cost to construct the building new. The next step is to add that amount to the value given the land (using the principal of substitution from other land sales) to estimate the value of the whole parcel.

There are several ways to calculate accrued depreciation; however, for our purposes we will only discuss the straight-line (or age-life) method. It is the one most commonly used by real estate agents and appraisers because it is easy to calculate, is used by the Internal Revenue Service and is easily understood by the consumer.

Using the straight-line method to determine accrued depreciation, the appraiser assumes a building will decline in value the same amount each year, until nothing is left. For example, a property with an estimated effective age of 50 years would be said to depreciate at an equal rate of 2% per year (2% x 50 years equals 100% depreciation). In using this method of calculating accrued depreciation, the appraiser probably will not use the actual age of the building, rather the effective age, which is determined by its condition, not the number of years since it was built.

Actual Age is the real age of a building. **Effective Age** is not determined by the actual age of a building, but by its condition and usefulness. **Economic Life** is the estimated period over which a building may be profitably used. For example, if the subject property was really 25 years old, but was as well maintained and would sell for as much as nearby 20-year-old properties, it would be said to have an effective age of 20 years.

Remember

Effective Age

- Determined by the condition and usefulness of a property, not by actual age

Income Capitalization (or Income) Approach

http://www.dre.ca.gov
Reference Book, Ch. 12
p. 261

http://www.dre.ca.gov
Reference Book, Ch. 17
p. 355

The income approach estimates the present worth of future benefits from ownership of a property. The value of the property is based on its capacity to continue producing an income. This method is used to estimate the value of income-producing property (rentals), usually in combination with one or both of the other methods. The process of calculating a property's present worth on the basis of its capacity to continue producing an income stream is called **Capitalization**. This approach is based mainly on the appraisal principles of comparison, substitution and anticipation.

Remember

Using the Income Approach

- The value of the property is based on its capacity to continue producing an income.

Capitalization converts the future income stream into an indication of the property's present worth. The appraiser evaluates the expected future income and expenses of a property using the income approach to determine its present value.

Formula Used by an Appraiser to Estimate the Value of an Income Property

Net Income divided by the capitalization rate (**Cap Rate**) equals the value of the property

$$\frac{\text{Net Income}}{\text{Capitalization Rate}} = \text{Value of Property}$$

The appraiser must determine how much and how reliable the income is, and how long the income stream will last. There are <u>five basic steps</u> to do this.

1. Calculate the annual effective gross income.

The effective gross income is the total annual income from the property minus any vacancy or rental losses. That includes rental income plus any other income generated by the property such as laundry room income or parking fees. Loss of income because of a vacant unit is known as the **Vacancy Factor**. Current market rents are used to determine the loss from the vacancy factor. **Market Rent** is the rent the property should bring in the open market, while **Contract Rent** is the actual, or contracted, rent being paid by the tenants. The appraiser uses the market rent in his calculations.

Gross Scheduled Annual Income	$36,000
Annual Vacancy Factor/Rental loss	<u>-3,600</u>
Effective Gross Income	$32,400

2. Determine operating expenses.

Expenses are generally classified as being either fixed or variable.

<u>Fixed Expenses Include:</u>	<u>Variable Expenses Include:</u>
• Property Taxes	• Management
• Insurance	• Maintenance
	• Utilities

---

3. Calculate net *operating* income:

Taxes	$1920
Insurance	480
Management	2400
Maintenance	1000
Utilities	800
+ Reserves (roof, paint, carpets, water heaters, etc.)	800
Total Expenses	$7,400

To Calculate Net Income:

	T	Taxes
	I	Insurance
"Use study aid "TIMMUR"	**M**	Management
to remember how to	**M**	Maintenance
calculate net income	**U**	Utilities
	R +	Reserves
		Total Expenses

Do *not* include mortgage payments

	$32,400
Subtract total expenses from effective gross income	-7,400
Net operating income	$25,000

4. *Select a capitalization rate.*

The capitalization rate provides for the return of invested capital plus a return on the investment. The rate is dependent upon the return a buyer will demand before investing money in the property. The greater the risk of recapturing the investment price (making a profit), the higher the cap rate and the lower the price. The lower the risk, the lower the cap rate and the higher the price of the property.

Remember

About Cap Rates

- The greater the risk, the higher the cap rate and the lower the price.

- The lower the risk, the lower the cap rate and the higher the price.

Choosing a capitalization rate is the hardest part for appraisers using the income approach. Generally, a real estate agent will need further study and practice to use this approach to valuation. One way a capitalization rate can be determined is by a market analysis of similar income properties and using the same capitalization rate as have those recent sales. The net income is divided by the sales price to determine the cap rate used in each sale. There are other methods of calculating a capitalization rate which may be learned through more study of appraisal.

5. *Divide the net income by the chosen capitalization rate to determine market value.*

Net Income divided by Capitalization Rate = Market Value

Net Operating Income $25,000

Capitalization rate 8%

$$\frac{\$25,000}{.08} = \$312,500$$

Market value = $312,500

http://www.dre.ca.gov
Reference Book, Ch. 17
p. 364

The **Gross Rent Multiplier** is used by real estate agents and appraisers to quickly convert gross rent into market value. It is used for income producing properties and is an easy way to get a rough estimate of the value of rental units.

Gross Rent is income (may be figured annually or monthly) received before any expenses are deducted. A gross rent multiplier, when multiplied by the total annual rents, will give a rough estimate of a property value that can then be compared with other like properties. Generally, gross multipliers will be somewhere between x5 and x10, depending on the market, the condition and the location of the property.

In other words, a property with a gross annual income of $36,000, when multiplied by the current gross multiplier of 10, will be valued roughly at $360,000. So when you hear property values described as ten times gross, or five times gross, or seven times gross, it means the value is shown by whatever multiplier is used, times the gross income. This is only a quick estimate of value, as you can see, and is not meant to take the place of a professional appraisal.

The reverse process can be used to calculate the gross multiplier, rather than the market value. The reason you might want to do that is to compare properties to see if they are priced right, or are above or below market value. If you know that most rental properties are selling for around eight times the gross annual multiplier (eight times gross), simply divide the listed price by the gross income to arrive at the multiplier.

Listed price $360,000

Gross annual income .... $ 36,000

$$\frac{\$360,000}{\$ 36,000} = 10 \text{ (the gross multiplier is 10)}$$

The gross rent multipliers of several income properties may then be compared, using the market comparison method to estimate their value.

Remember

- A gross rent multiplier can be stated on either an annual or monthly basis.

Reconcile or Correlate

The final step in an appraisal, then, is to examine the values derived by the various approaches. Reconciliation or correlation of value occurs when the appraiser decides which of the values is the most appropriate for the subject property, and uses that figure to determine the final estimate for the property in question.

Remember

About Appraisal Approaches

- Single family homes: market comparison approach
- New or unusual buildings: cost approach
- Rental properties: income approach

The Appraisal Report

Each written appraisal report must be prepared in one of these three formats: Self-Contained Appraisal Report, Summary Appraisal Report, or Restricted Use Appraisal Report.

Three Types of Appraisal Reports

- Self-Contained Appraisal Report
- Summary Appraisal Report
- Restricted Use Appraisal Report

When the intended users of the report include parties other than the client, the report must be either a Self-Contained Appraisal Report or a Summary Appraisal Report. When the intended users do not include parties other than the client, the report can be a Restricted Use Appraisal Report. The difference among the options is in the content and level of information provided.

An appraiser must be careful in deciding which type of report to use. Appraisal standards set minimum requirements for the content and level of information in each type of report.

The Self-Contained Appraisal Report includes the indentity of the client and any intended users (by name or type), the intended use of the appraisal, the real estate involved, the real property interest appraised, the purpose of the appraisal, and dates of the appraisal and of the report. It also describes work used to develop the appraisal, the assumptions and limiting conditions, the information that was analyzed, the procedures followed, and the reasoning that supports the conclusions. The report states the current use of the real estate and the use reflected in the appraisal; the support for the appraiser's opinion of the highest and best use; and any departures from the standards. It includes a signed certification.

The Summary Appraisal Report covers the same categories as the Self-Contained Appraisal Report, but where the Self-Contained Appraisal Report includes descriptions, the Summary Appraisal Report contains summaries.

The Restricted Use Appraisal Report covers the came categories as the other two reports with several differences: only the client is named because there are no other users; the use of the report is limited to the client; and the report refers to the appraiser's work file as the source of necessary additional information about the appraisal.

Uniform Residential Appraisal Report (1 of 2)

	UNIFORM RESIDENTIAL APPRAISAL REPORT	File No.

Property Description

SUBJECT			
Property Address		City	State	Zip Code
Legal Description			County
Assessor's Parcel No.		Tax Year	R.E. Taxes $	Special Assessments $
Borrower	Current Owner		Occupant: ☐ Owner ☐ Tenant ☐ Vacant
Property rights appraised ☐ Fee Simple ☐ Leasehold	Project Type ☐ PUD ☐ Condominium (HUD/VA only)	HOA $ /Mo.
Neighborhood or Project Name	Map Reference	Census Tract
Sale Price $	Date of Sale	Description and $ amount of loan charges/concessions to be paid by seller
Lender/Client	Address	
Appraiser	Address	

NEIGHBORHOOD

Location	☐ Urban	☐ Suburban	☐ Rural	Predominant occupancy	Single family housing	Present land use %	Land use change
					PRICE $(000)	AGE (yrs)		
Built up	☐ Over 75%	☐ 25-75%	☐ Under 25%				One family	☐ Not likely ☐ Likely
Growth rate	☐ Rapid	☐ Stable	☐ Slow	☐ Owner	Low		2-4 family	☐ In process
Property values	☐ Increasing	☐ Stable	☐ Declining	☐ Tenant	High		Multi-family	To:
Demand/supply	☐ Shortage	☐ In balance	☐ Over supply	☐ Vacant (0-5%)	Predominant		Commercial	
Marketing time	☐ Under 3 mos.	☐ 3-6 mos.	☐ Over 6 mos.	☐ Vac.(over 5%)				

Note: Race and the racial composition of the neighborhood are not appraisal factors.

Neighborhood boundaries and characteristics:

Factors that affect the marketability of the properties in the neighborhood (proximity to employment and amenities, employment stability, appeal to market, etc.):

Market conditions in the subject neighborhood (including support for the above conclusions related to the trend of property values, demand/supply, and marketing time - - such as data on competitive properties for sale in the neighborhood, description of the prevalence of sales and financing concessions, etc.):

PUD

Project Information for PUDs (If applicable) - - Is the developer/builder in control of the Home Owners' Association (HOA)? ☐ Yes ☐ No

Approximate total number of units in the subject project _____ Approximate total number of units for sale in the subject project _____

Describe common elements and recreational facilities:

SITE

Dimensions		Topography	
Site area		Size	
Specific zoning classification and description	Corner Lot ☐ Yes ☐ No	Shape	
Zoning compliance ☐ Legal ☐ Legal nonconforming (Grandfathered use) ☐ Illegal ☐ No zoning	Drainage	
Highest & best use as improved: ☐ Present use ☐ Other use (explain)	View	

Utilities	Public	Other	Off-site Improvements	Type	Public	Private		
Electricity			Street				Landscaping	
Gas			Curb/gutter				Driveway Surface	
Water			Sidewalk				Apparent easements	
Sanitary sewer			Street lights				FEMA Special Flood Hazard Area ☐ Yes ☐ No	
Storm sewer			Alley				FEMA Zone ____ Map Date ____	
							FEMA Map No.	

Comments (apparent adverse easements, encroachments, special assessments, slide areas, illegal or legal nonconforming zoning use, etc.):

DESCRIPTION OF IMPROVEMENTS

GENERAL DESCRIPTION		EXTERIOR DESCRIPTION		FOUNDATION		BASEMENT		INSULATION	
No. of Units		Foundation		Slab		Area Sq. Ft.		Roof	
No. of Stories		Exterior Walls		Crawl Space		% Finished		Ceiling	
Type (Det./Att.)		Roof Surface		Basement		Ceiling		Walls	
Design (Style)		Gutters & Dwnspts.		Sump Pump		Walls		Floor	
Existing/Proposed		Window Type		Dampness		Floor		None	
Age (Yrs.)		Storm/Screens		Settlement		Outside Entry		Unknown	
Effective Age (Yrs.)		Manufactured House		Infestation					

ROOMS	Foyer	Living	Dining	Kitchen	Den	Family Rm.	Rec. Rm.	Bedrooms	# Baths	Laundry	Other	Area Sq. Ft.
Basement												
Level 1												
Level 2												

Finished area above grade contains: _____ Rooms: _____ Bedroom(s): _____ Bath(s): _____ Square Feet of Gross Living Area _____

INTERIOR	Materials/Condition	HEATING		KITCHEN EQUIP.		ATTIC		AMENITIES		CAR STORAGE:	
Floors		Type		Refrigerator		None		Fireplace(s) #		None	
Walls		Fuel		Range/Oven		Stairs		Patio		Garage	# of cars
Trim/Finish		Condition		Disposal		Drop Stair		Deck		Attached	
Bath Floor		COOLING		Dishwasher		Scuttle		Porch		Detached	
Bath Wainscot		Central		Fan/Hood		Floor		Fence		Built-in	
Doors		Other		Microwave		Heated		Pool		Carport	
		Condition		Washer/Dryer		Finished				Driveway	

Additional features (special energy efficient items, etc.):

COMMENTS

Condition of the improvements, depreciation (physical, functional, and external), repairs needed, quality of construction, remodeling/additions, etc.:

Adverse environmental conditions (such as, but not limited to, hazardous wastes, toxic substances, etc.) present in the improvements, on the site, or in the immediate vicinity of the subject property.:

Freddie Mac Form 70 6-93   "TOTAL" appraisal software by a la mode, inc. 1-800-ALAMODE   Fannie Mae Form 1004 6-93

PAGE 1 OF 2

Uniform Residential Appraisal Report (2 of 2)

UNIFORM RESIDENTIAL APPRAISAL REPORT   File No. _____

Valuation Section

COST APPROACH			
ESTIMATED SITE VALUE		= $ _____	
ESTIMATED REPRODUCTION COST-NEW-OF IMPROVEMENTS:			
Dwelling _____ Sq. Ft. @ $ _____	= $ _____		
_____ Sq. Ft. @ $ _____	= _____		
Garage/Carport _____ Sq. Ft. @ $ _____	= _____		
Total Estimated Cost New	= $ _____		
Less Physical Functional External			
Depreciation _____	= $ _____		
Depreciated Value of Improvements	= $ _____		
"As-Is" Value of Site Improvements	= $ _____		
INDICATED VALUE BY COST APPROACH	= $ _____		

Comments on Cost Approach (such as, source of cost estimate, site value, square foot calculation and for HUD, VA and FmHA, the estimated remaining economic life of the property): _____

ITEM	SUBJECT	COMPARABLE NO. 1	COMPARABLE NO. 2	COMPARABLE NO. 3
Address				
Proximity to Subject				
Sales Price	$	$	$	$
Price/Gross Liv. Area	$	$	$	$
Date and/or Verification Source				

VALUE ADJUSTMENTS	DESCRIPTION	DESCRIPTION	+ (-) $ Adjustment	DESCRIPTION	+ (-) $ Adjustment	DESCRIPTION	+ (-) $ Adjustment
Sales or Financing Concessions							
Date of Sale/Time							
Location							
Leasehold/Fee Simple							
Site							
View							
Design and Appeal							
Quality of Construction							
Age							
Condition							
Above Grade Total Bdrms Baths		Total Bdrms Baths		Total Bdrms Baths		Total Bdrms Baths	
Room Count							
Gross Living Area Sq. Ft.		Sq. Ft.		Sq. Ft.		Sq. Ft.	
Basement & Finished Rooms Below Grade							
Functional Utility							
Heating/Cooling							
Energy Efficient Items							
Garage/Carport							
Porch, Patio, Deck, Fireplace(s), etc.							
Fence, Pool, etc.							
Net Adj. (total)		+ - $		+ - $		+ - $	
Adjusted Sales Price of Comparable		$		$		$	

Comments on Sales Comparison (including the subject property's compatibility to the neighborhood, etc.): _____

ITEM	SUBJECT	COMPARABLE NO. 1	COMPARABLE NO. 2	COMPARABLE NO. 3
Date, Price and Data Source, for prior sales within year of appraisal				

Analysis of any current agreement of sale, option, or listing of the subject property and analysis of any prior sales of subject and comparables within one year of the date of appraisal: _____

INDICATED VALUE BY SALES COMPARISON APPROACH $ _____

INDICATED VALUE BY INCOME APPROACH (If Applicable) Estimated Market Rent $ _____ /Mo. x Gross Rent Multiplier _____ = $ _____

RECONCILIATION

This appraisal is made   ☐ "as is"   ☐ subject to the repairs, alterations, inspections or conditions listed below   ☐ subject to completion per plans and specifications.

Conditions of Appraisal: _____

Final Reconciliation: _____

The purpose of this appraisal is to estimate the market value of the real property that is the subject of this report, based on the above conditions and the certification, contingent and limiting conditions, and market value definition that are stated in the attached Freddie Mac Form 439/Fannie Mae Form 1004B (Revised _____).

I (WE) ESTIMATE THE MARKET VALUE, AS DEFINED, OF THE REAL PROPERTY THAT IS THE SUBJECT OF THIS REPORT, AS OF _____ (WHICH IS THE DATE OF INSPECTION AND THE EFFECTIVE DATE OF THIS REPORT) TO BE $ _____

APPRAISER:	SUPERVISORY APPRAISER (ONLY IF REQUIRED):	
Signature _____	Signature _____	☐ Did ☐ Did Not
Name _____	Name _____	Inspect Property
Date Report Signed _____	Date Report Signed _____	
State Certification # _____ State _____	State Certification # _____	State _____
Or State License # _____ State _____	Or State License # _____	State _____

Freddie Mac Form 70 6-93

"TOTAL" appraisal software by a la mode, inc. 1-800-ALAMODE
PAGE 2 OF 2

Fannie Mae Form 1004 6-93

Appraisal Licensing Standards

http://www.
appraisalfoundation.org

The Appraisal Foundation, a non-profit educational organization, was established in 1987 in response to the crisis in the savings and loan industry in the early 1980s. This crisis confirmed the importance of basing appraisals on established, recognized standards, free from outside pressures.

The Appraiser Qualifications Board was included in the Foundation structure to develop these standards. It created the Uniform Standards of Professional Appraisal Practice (USPAP) and established educational and experience requirements for the licensing of appraisers in all states. USPAP is recognized nationwide as the standard of professional appraisal practice, and all appraisers are required to abide by these standards.

In California, the Office of Real Estate Appraisers (OREA) was established in 1990 to license appraisers. OREA has licensed over 18,000 real estate appraisers.

Types of Appraisal Licenses

http://www.orea.ca.gov

There are four levels of real estate appraiser licensing in California:

- Trainee License
- Residential License
- Certified Residential License
- Certified General License

Each level requires a specific amount of education and experience, and each licensee must pass a state exam. Trainees must work under the supervision of a licensed appraiser. The type of structures that can be appraised are specified for each level. Continuing education is required to maintain the license.

Professional Appraisal Organizations

http://www.
appraisalinstitute.com

The major objective of these organizations is to make sure the members of the appraisal profession are knowledgeable and conform to a code of ethics and standards of professional appraisal practice.

The main professional organization is the Appraisal Institute (AI). Members may hold the title of Member Appraisal Institute (MAI), or Senior Residential Appraiser (SRA).

Appraisal Institute Designations

- Member Appraisal Institute (MAI)
- Senior Residential Appraiser (SRA)
- Senior Real Property Appraiser (SRPA)
- Senior Real Estate Analyst (SREA)
- Residential Member (RM)

Post Test

The following self test repeats the one you took at the beginning of this chapter. Now take the exam again—since you have read all the material—and check your knowledge of appraisals.

1. The most appropriate use of the income approach is for:
   - a. new residences
   - b. old residences
   - c. rental property
   - d. church

2. The most thorough and complete appraisal report is:
   - a. a short form report
   - b. a long form report
   - c. a narrative report
   - d. an oral report

3. In estimating the value of land, what is the least important element?
   - a. size
   - b. sales price of comparable land
   - c. cost to build on it
   - d. price asked

4. Granite Elvis statues on the front of an apartment building are considered a type of:
   - a. functional obsolescence
   - b. social obsolescence
   - c. economic obsolescence
   - d. physical deterioration

5. The first thing to do in the appraisal process is:
   - a. arrange the data
   - b. make beginning appraisal plan
   - c. define the appraisal problem
   - d. separate the data

6. Which of the following indicates a professional appraiser?
   - a. National Association of Realtors (NAR)
   - b. California Association of Realtors (CAR)
   - c. Member Appraisal Institute (MAI)
   - d. Certified Property Manager (CPM)

7. The term "highest and best use" means:
   - a. highest net return
   - b. greatest population density
   - c. highest gross return
   - d. highest elevation

8. Which of the following reflects the price paid?
   - a. book value
   - b. appraised value
   - c. accrued value
   - d. market value

9. All of the following are elements of value except:
   - a. scarcity
   - b. demand
   - c. utility
   - d. plottage

10. Which of the following is needed to use the capitalization approach?
    - a. adjusted cost
    - b. sales price
    - c. net income
    - d. gross income

Vocabulary

Read the definition, find the matching term and write the corresponding term number on the line provided.

Terms

1. Appraisal
2. Appraisal Report
3. Comps
4. Contract Rent
5. Corner Lot
6. Cul-de-sac Lot
7. Fair Market Value
8. Flag Lot
9. Front Footage
10. Improvements
11. Interior Lot
12. Market Rent
13. Plottage or Assemblage
14. Price
15. Reconciliation
16. Replacement Cost
17. T-Intersection Lot
18. Utility Value
19. Vacancy Factor
20. Value

Definitions

1. ___ The price the property would bring if freely offered on the open market with both a willing buyer and a willing seller

2. ___ An estimate or opinion of value supported by factual information as of a certain date

3. ___ The power of goods or services to command other goods in exchange for the present worth of future benefits arising from property ownership

4. ___ A written report stating an appraiser's estimate of subject property's value

5. ___ The usefulness of the property

6. ___ What is paid for something

7. ___ Putting several smaller, less valuable parcels together under one ownership to increase value of total property

8. ___ A lot found on a dead-end street

9. ___ A lot found at the intersection of two streets

10. ___ A lot that is fronted head-on by a street; noise and glare from headlights may be detractors from this type of lot

11. ___ A lot that is surrounded by other lots, with a frontage on the street; the most common type lot, which may or may not be desirable, depending on other factors

12. ___ A lot that looks like a flag on a pole, which represents the access to the site; usually located to the rear of another lot fronting a main street

13. ___ The width of a property along a street

14. ___ Any buildings or structures on a lot

15. ___ Sometimes called correlation, this is the adjustment process of weighing results of all three appraisal methods to arrive at a final estimate of the subject property's market value

16. ___ A term used by real estate agents and appraisers to mean comparable properties

17. ___ The cost of replacing improvements with modern materials and techniques

18. ___ Loss of income because of a vacant unit

19. ___ The rent a property should bring in the open market

20. ___ The actual, or contracted, rent being paid by tenants

Answers

Pre-Test/Post Test

1. c
2. c
3. d
4. a
5. c
6. c
7. a
8. a
9. d
10. c

Vocabulary

1. 7
2. 1
3. 20
4. 2
5. 18
6. 14
7. 13
8. 6
9. 5
10. 17
11. 11
12. 8
13. 9
14. 10
15. 15
16. 3
17. 16
18. 19
19. 12
20. 4

CHAPTER

11

REAL ESTATE TAXATION

Focus

- **Assessment and collection of taxes**
- **Real and personal property taxes**
- **Federal income taxes**
- **State income taxes**
- **Foreign Investment in Real Property Tax Act (FIRPTA)**
- **Documentary transfer tax**
- **Estate and inheritance taxes**
- **Gift taxes**

Pre-Test

The following is a self test to determine how much you know about taxation before reading this chapter. Take it without studying, then read the material presented in the text. At the end of the chapter you will find a repeat of this exam. Test your knowledge by answering the questions again, then check your improvement. (The answers are found at the end of this chapter.) Good luck!

1. Property taxes become a lien on property:
   a. January 1st
   b. November 1st
   c. February 1st
   d. July 1st

2. When local government levies a tax to finance underground utilities, it is called:
   a. an et ux tax
   b. an ad valorem tax
   c. property tax
   d. an assessment

3. Where does a taxpayer appeal a tax assessed bill that may not be correct?
   a. county tax collector
   b. assessment appeals board
   c. county tax assessor
   d. state tax assessor

4. Proposition 13 limits the amount that property assessed values can be raised annually:
   a. 2%
   b. 1%
   c. 3%
   d. 4%

5. When property is sold, the buyer's property tax is based on:
   a. 1% of full cash value
   b. 2% of full cash value
   c. 3% of full cash value
   d. 4% of full cash value

6. The law that allows someone over the age of 55 to transfer his or her present tax base to a new property is:
   a. Proposition 13
   b. Proposition 2
   c. Proposition 60
   d. Unruh Act

7. The fiscal year runs from:
   a. January 1 through December 31
   b. July 30 through July 29
   c. June 1 through May 30
   d. July 1 through June 30

8. The first installment of property taxes is due:
   a. December 10
   b. February 1
   c. November 1
   d. March 1

9. When a "tax delinquent property sale" takes place:
   a. the owner has five years to redeem the property
   b. the owner may not redeem the property
   c. the owner loses possession
   d. the state takes over the title and possession

10. What kind of deed does a buyer at a tax sale receive?
    a. grant deed
    b. gift deed
    c. trust deed
    d. tax deed

Terms

The following terms are the keys to your success in learning about real estate. Refer to them as you study this chapter for greater understanding of subjects presented here.

Adjusted Cost Basis

Original basis plus capital improvements and costs of the sale, less depreciation if income producing

Ad Valorem

A Latin prefix meaning "according to value." Local governments levy real property tax based on the assessed value; property taxes are known as ad valorem taxes

Assessment Roll or Tax Roll

A list of all taxable property showing the assessed value of each parcel; establishes the tax base

Book Sale

A sale of real property to the state, in name only, when a taxpayer is delinquent in paying property tax

Boot

Money or any "non-like" property put into a sale by an investor to balance the equities in a 1031 tax deferred exchange; cash or mortgage relief in an exchange

Calendar Year

Starts on January 1 and continues through December 31 of the same year

Capital Improvements

Physical improvements made to a property

Cost Basis

Usually the price paid for a property

Economic Life

The estimated period over which an improved property may be profitably used to yield a return

Fiscal Year

Starts on July 1 and runs through June 30 of the following year; used for real property tax purposes

Homeowner's Exemption

A $7,000 tax exemption on principal residence of the owner. Not available for vacation homes.

Tax Deed

A deed given to a successful bidder at a tax auction

Introduction

http://www.caltax.org/
taxhist.htm

Most people have questions about taxes in a real estate transaction. It may not be apparent, but taxation is an indirect—yet important—factor in affecting the value of property. In this chapter we will see how taxes impact buying and selling. As a student, use this chapter for general knowledge about real estate taxation; however, always refer your clients and customers to an expert for their own tax information as well as current tax laws.

Assessment and Collection of Taxes

http://www.dre.ca.gov
Reference Book, Ch. 18

> ### Real Estate Investments are Taxed at the Federal, State and Local Levels
>
> - Federal government: income tax, estate and gift tax
> - State government: income tax
> - Local government: **Ad Valorem** property taxes, special assessments and transfer taxes

AD VALOREM — "According to Value"

Real Property Taxes

Personal Property Taxes

People considering the purchase of real property must examine the tax benefits and burdens of their purchase. Many times, the tax implications will seriously affect a sale and cause a buyer or seller to realize that—because of the taxes—full value of ownership may not be possible. What might look like a good deal could turn into a losing proposition after tax considerations.

Taxes are imposed on real or personal property to raise money so the government can carry out its general duties. All property within the locality of the taxing authority, whether it is the federal, state or local government, will be taxed unless specifically exempt.

There are certain jobs that must be carried out during the process of assessing and collecting taxes. The following is a list of officials responsible for the correct taxation of real property.

Implementing the Job of Taxation

- County board of supervisors: determines the tax rate (limited to 1% of fair market value) plus any county bond debt or other assessments

- City councils: sets property tax rates for cities

- City or county auditor: maintains tax rolls (public records identifying parcels of land to be taxed, the owner and the assessed value)

- City or county assessor: assesses the value of all taxable property in the county yearly to establish the tax base; sends out the tax bills. The annual assessments appear in the **Assessment Roll** or **Tax Roll**, a public record. Real property is assessed at 100% of fair market value. The tax bill identifies a property by an assessor's parcel number, which is not a legal description but is used for taxation purposes only.

- City or county tax collector: decides how much tax is to be paid by each property owner, depending on individual assessments. Land and improvements are assessed separately, but taxed at one rate.

- Assessment appeals board: appeals board for taxpayers' complaints about unfair taxation

Real and Personal Property Taxes

http://www.calproptax.com

The idea of land taxation began with the Domesday or Doomsday book, in 1086, in England. Taxation was based on the notion that taxes should be assessed according to an owner's ability to pay. At that time, such an ability was reliably determined by how much and how good the owner's agricultural holdings were—since most people's income came almost entirely from products of their land. Therefore, land became the basis for determining the amount of tax imposed.

Proposition 13

As of June 1978, Proposition 13 became the measure to use in assessing property in California. If there had been no change in ownership since March 1, 1975, the value of the property at that time was used as a starting point to assess the property (the initial full cash value). Under the new law, the maximum annual tax was limited to 1% of full cash value (market value). After that, a maximum increase of no more than 2% per year was allowed. Since June 1978, whenever property transfers to a new owner, it is re-assessed at 1% of the new sales price. Commonly, local taxes may be added to the 1% assessment.

Transfer of Ownership

Upon a change in ownership of real property unless the change is between spouses, a new assessment is made, based on 1% of the new purchase price. For example, if the sale price is $350,000, the new property tax would be $3,500. Any person buying real property is required to file a change-in-ownership statement with the county recorder or assessor. The change-in-ownership statement must be filed within 45 days of the change date. Failure to report a change results in a $100 penalty. A supplementary tax bill will be sent to the new owner, reflecting the change in taxes as of the date of transfer.

Proposition 60

http://www.caltitle.com/prop6090.htm

Homeowners who are at least 55 years of age may sell their homes and transfer their present base year property tax value to another home of equal or less value. The new home must be in the same county, or in a county that allows Proposition 60 to be used. The base-year property value is whatever the value of the home was on March 1, 1975, or in the year they purchased the property after that time. Thus, they are allowed to continue with the original figure as their tax base, adding a maximum of 2% every year, to arrive at their tax bill, rather than be required to step up to 1% of the value of their new purchase.

Maggie and Marvin bought their home in 1976 for $80,000. Now that the kids were grown and the house was too big for them, they decided to sell and move to a smaller home in the same town. Over the years, their *property had appreciated greatly, and now sold for $250,000. The tax assessment on their original home was $102,400 at the time of the sale, and they were allowed to carry that to the new property because of Proposition 60. Instead of being taxed at 1% of the price of the new house ($250,000), their new tax bill was based on the assessed value of the one they sold.*

Comparison of Maggie and Marvin's Tax Bills

- $250,000 x 1%= $2,500 tax bill

- $102,400 x 1%= $1,024 tax bill

Important Tax Dates to Remember

A **Fiscal Year**, or tax year, is used for tax purposes as compared to a **Calendar Year**. The fiscal year starts on July 1 and goes through June 30 of the following year.

Remember

- Tax year goes from July 1 through June 30

On January 1, preceding the tax year, property taxes become a lien on real property. Then on November 1 the first installment is due and is delinquent on December 10. The second installment is due February 1 and is delinquent on April 10.

Remember

Taxes are Due

memory aid	
No	November 1 (1st installment due)
Darn	December 10 (1st installment delinquent)
Fooling	February 1 (2nd installment due)
Around	April 10 (2nd installment delinquent)

(helps you remember these important tax dates)

If a property owner does not pay the tax when it is due, the property is then listed as a delinquent account by the tax collector and a **Book Sale,** or tax delinquent property sale, to the state takes place on June 30 of the same year. The taxpayer doesn't actually lose title, keeps possession and has five years to pay the delinquent taxes. If the taxes are not paid within that five-year period a tax sale takes place, and the property may be sold at public auction to the highest bidder for cash. The buyer receives a **Tax Deed**.

Remember

Taxation Time Line

Jan. 1	July 1	Nov. 1	Dec. 10	Feb. 1	Apr. 10	June 30
taxes become a lien (precedes tax year)	tax year starts	1st due	delinquent	2nd due	delinquent	tax year ends

Tax Sale

- June 8 Delinquent Tax List Published
- June 30 Property "Sold" to State
- Five-Year Redemption Period
- Unredeemed Property Deeded to State
- Tax Collector Publishes Notice of Intent to Sell
- Public Auction Tax Sale
- Tax Deed

Tax Exemptions

A property owner may claim a **Homeowner's Exemption** in California on a residence that is both owned and occupied at 12:01 a.m. on January 1. Claims must be filed by February 15 following the change of ownership. If the prior owner claimed the Homeowner's Exemption, claim forms are mailed in the beginning of January for filing by February 15. The exemption reduces the assessed value by $7,000 and reduces the tax bill by at least $70.

It is the homeowner's responsibility to apply for the exemption. To receive the full exemption, the claim must be filed with the Assessor's office between January 1 and February 15, or within 30 days of a Notice of Supplemental Assessment. (A late filing is accepted from February 16 to December 10 for 80 percent of the exemption.) Your exemption automatically continues each year as long as you continue to own and occupy the property as your primary residence. It is the homeowner's responsibility to terminate the exemption when no longer eligible.

<u>**Homeowner's Exemption**</u>

$350,000	(assessed value)
-<u>7,000</u>	(homeowner's exemption, must be filed by Feb. 15)
$343,000	(taxable amount)

Another exemption available to some homeowners is the **Veteran's Exemption**. A resident of California who has been in the military during wartime is eligible to take a $4,000 tax exemption. If the resident takes the regular homeowner's exemption, the veteran's exemption may not be taken on the same dwelling, but may be used for another property owned by the veteran.

Other tax exemptions are available for a variety of property owners. Certain senior citizens may qualify for tax relief. So may churches; non-profit organizations; and owners of timberlands, young orchards or grape-vines less than three years old.

Special Assessments

Street Improvement Act of 1911

When specific improvements that benefit a certain area are needed—such as underground utilities, sewers or streets—special assessments are lev-ied to pay for them. Special assessment liens are placed on the properties involved and usually paid at the same time as property taxes. One of the laws that empowers cities and counties to levy a special assessment to repair streets is the Street Improvement Act of 1911. The difference be-tween a special assessment and property taxes is that the latter are used to operate the government in general, where as special assessments are used for specific local purposes.

Mello-Roos Community Facilities Act

http://www.dre.ca.gov
Reference Book, Ch.18
p. 391

Public services such as roads, sewers, parks, schools and fire stations in new developments may be financed under this law. A Mello-Roos lien is placed on each parcel in a new development by the developer to pay off municipal bonds issued to fund off-site improvements for the develop-ment. The developer must make the payments on the bond until the homes are sold, and then the new owners are responsible. Mello-Roos liens are a way a developer can make improvements and have each homeowner pay for them, without charging the improvements to property taxes.

http://www.irs.ustreas.gov

As we have seen, taxes are limited by Proposition 13 to a maximum of 1% of the assessed value of the property. The city, through the sale of municipal bonds, can include the cost and maintenance of infrastructure items in the property tax bill as a special assessment, exempt from the limitations of Proposition 13.

http://www.1040.com

New buyers must be told by real estate agents that a project is subject to a Mello-Roos special assessment because their tax bill will be higher than if they only paid property taxes without the special assessment.

An agent may be disciplined by the Real Estate Commissioner for failure to provide a Mello-Roos disclosure. Failure to give notice to a buyer or lessee (if more than five years) before signing a sales contract or lease allows the buyer or lessee a three-day right to cancel after receiving the disclosure.

Federal Income Taxes

http://www.dre.ca.gov
Reference Book, Ch. 18
p. 391

The federal government taxes individuals based on their earning by means of a progressive income tax. The important consideration of a progressive tax is that the tax rate on which the taxpayers obligation increases rises with additional levels of income ("brackets"). One of the major reasons for buying real estate is to get relief from taxes.

The tax benefits of home ownership may differ from those available to owners of investment property. The legal reduction of tax liability, otherwise known as tax shelter, is available to all owners of a primary residence as well as to a taxpayer owning investment property. Different rules apply to each type of property, however, and must be followed carefully to earn the desired tax shelter.

Personal Residence

Individuals are generally permitted to exclude from taxable income up to $250,000 ($500,000 for married couples) of gain on the sale of their principal residence. To qualify, the taxpayer must have owned and used the property as a principal residence for at least two years during the five years prior to the sale or exchange. The exclusion is generally allowed no more often than once every two years. Taxpayers who fail to meet either if these two-year requirements because of an employment change, health problems, or other unforeseen circumstances may be eligible for a partial exclusion, scaled back to the amount of time they did occupy the residence compared to the two-year requirement.

This exclusion replaces the "rollover" rules that have allowed taxpayers to defer all or part of the gain on a sale or exchange of a principal residence that is replaced with a new principal residence within a four-year period. The once-in-a-lifetime $125,000 exclusion on a sale of a principal residence for taxpayers age 55 and over is also replaced.

The new exclusion rules are effective for sales or exchanges of a principal residence occurring after May 6, 1997. However, in certain circumstances taxpayers may elect to apply the old rules (i.e., the rollover, or the $125,000 exclusion)

Deductions are another way a homeowner can limit tax liability. Certain expenses are deductible to homeowners, such as interest and property taxes on first and second homes. Deducting maintenance expenses and depreciation are not allowed. New tax laws may or may not allow a deduction for the loss on the sale of a personal residence.

The cost of **Capital Improvements** or physical improvements made to the property such as the cosmetic addition of a new roof, swimming pool or driveway may not be deducted yearly, but may be added to the **Cost Basis** of the property when it is sold. The cost basis is usually the original cost to buy the property.

Limiting Tax Liability

Deductible

- Interest
- Property taxes

Non-Deductible

- Maintenance
- Depreciation
- Capital improvements

To calculate the gain on the sale of a primary residence, as you recall, the cost basis usually is determined by the original purchase price. The taxable gain generally is the difference between the purchase price plus capital improvements and the price when sold. Closing costs on the sale also may be added to the cost basis. When capital improvements plus costs of the sale are added to the original cost basis, the **Adjusted Cost Basis** is the result.

To Calculate Capital Gain

Purchase price	$250,000
Improvements plus costs of sale	+ 50,000
Adjusted cost basis	$300,000
Selling price	$400,000
Adjusted cost basis	-300,000
Taxable gain	$100,000

The gain, or profit, after the $250,000 ($500,000) exclusion from the sale of a personal residence is then taxed according to current capital gains tax law.

Income Property

The tax laws reward an investor for the financial risk taken and benefit the economy from the investment by allowing the taxpayer to reduce tax liability in numerous ways. As long as an investment is income producing, such as apartment buildings or commercial property, certain reductions in tax liability are allowed.

One of the most important tax benefits of income property ownership is the depreciation allowance. While a homeowner can exclude a certain amount of profit from being taxed, the owner of income property may not. However, the investor may claim depreciation and other deductions to reduce the tax bill beyond that which is allowed a homeowner.

Depreciation for tax purposes is not based on actual deterioration, but on the calculated useful life of the property. The theory is that improvements, not land, deteriorate and lose their value. A building is thought to have a certain number of years where it can generate an income and after that is no longer a practical investment. The investor is compensated for the loss by being allowed to deduct a certain dollar amount each year based on the useful life of the property until, on paper at least, the property no longer has any value as an investment.

However, tax laws regarding depreciation change so often, it is advisable for the reader to check current Internal Revenue Service (IRS) rules for calculating depreciation.

One common method that may be used to determine the dollar amount per year that may be deducted is straight line, where the same amount is deducted every year over the depreciable life of a property. When using the straight line method to calculate depreciation, the value of the improvements is divided by the depreciable life of the property, to arrive at the annual depreciation that can be taken. Here is how it works.

<hr>

To Calculate Depreciation

- Determine what the IRS allowance for the depreciable life of a residential income property is by checking current tax law. For our purposes let's assume it is 27 1/2 years.

- Subtract the value of the land from the value of the property to determine the value of the building.

Value of property	$400,000
Value of land	-160,000
Value of building	$240,000

- $240,000 divided by 27 1/2 years = $8,727 annual depreciation allowance.

http://www.divorceinfo.com/
realpropertyinformation.htm

Jorge and Catalina bought a four-plex at the beach. They paid $600,000 for the property. The land was valued at 40% of the total investment, leaving 60% for the value of the improvements. How much depreciation could they claim each year when filing their income tax if they were allowed to depreciate the property over 27 1/2 years?

Step #1

Calculate the dollar amount for the value of the improvements.
$600,000 x 60% (.60) = $360,000

Step #2

Divide the dollar amount of the improvements by the allowed depreciable life.
$360,000 divided by 27 1/2 years =
$13,091 allowable annual depreciation.

When Jorge and Catalina sell the property, the amount depreciated over the years will be subtracted from their cost basis to determine their capital gain.

Also, when the property is sold, the new owner is allowed to begin depreciating the building as if the building were new, based on the new sales price.

Other Investor Tax Benefits

Mortgage interest, property taxes, insurance, management, maintenance and utilities may be deducted.

Loss on the sale of income property may be deducted.

The gain on an income-producing property is calculated much like that for a personal residence, except any depreciation that has been claimed over the years must be subtracted from the adjusted cost basis. This means the dollar amount that has been deducted for depreciation over the time of property ownership must be subtracted from the cost basis to arrive at the adjusted cost basis. The amount of taxable gain is then calculated by subtracting the adjusted cost basis from the selling price.

To Calculate Amount of Capital Gain on Income Property

Purchase price (cost basis)	$600,000
Improvements	+100,000
	700,000
Depreciation claimed	-75,000
Adjusted cost basis	$625,000
Selling price	$700,000
Expenses of sale (commission, etc.)	-42,000
Adjusted selling price	$ 658,000
Adjusted cost basis	-625,000
Capital gain (or loss)	$ 33,000

Unlike a primary residence where a certain amount of gain may be excluded from being taxed, taxes are owed on any profit made whenever income producing property is sold. However, there are ways an investor may legally defer the gain to a later time.

Installment Sale

An installment sale is one where payments are made, by the buyer, to the seller, over a period of more than one year. This is one way capital gain and the tax payments owed can be spread out over a period of time. Part of the tax liability can be deferred by the seller taking back a note and trust deed, or an All Inclusive Trust Deed (AITD) or contract of sale, with monthly payments. Only the amount of the gain that is collected in the tax year is taxable income and the tax due on the rest can be deferred until collected. Once again, the reader should check current tax laws about installment sales.

Tax-Deferred Exchanges (1031 Exchange)

http://www.arizonarealtor.
com/1031tax.htm

Sometimes called a "tax-free" exchange, this method of deferring tax liability allows an investor to exchange a property for a "like" property, and defer the gain until the property is sold. It is not really a tax-free exchange. The taxes are simply put off until a later date.

Most real property qualifies as "like" property, as long as it is held as an investment. It may be an apartment building, a commercial building, a business or raw land. However, a personal residence would not qualify as a "like" property in an exchange with investment property.

If equities are not equal in two properties being exchanged, money or anything of value (cars, boats, stocks, furniture) other than like-kind property, may be put in by the investor who is "trading up" to balance the equities. This extra cash or non-like property put into an exchange is known as **Boot**.

Property A
Value	$400,000
Encumbrances	-50,000
Equity	$350,000

Property B
Value	$600,000
Encumbrances	-200,000
Equity	$400,000

To qualify for a tax-deferred exchange, Investor A needs to add $50,000 (boot) to the sale to make the equities match. Investor A would have no tax liability on the sale and Investor B would be taxed on the amount of the boot received in the year of the sale (if he realized a gain from the sale). If the amount of the boot exceeds the amount of the gain, tax liability is limited to the amount of the gain.

In calculating the gain on each property, the cost basis of the property being exchanged becomes the cost basis of the property being acquired, if no boot is given or received, and the cost basis follows the taxpayer through subsequent exchanges or sales. The profit or taxable gain is determined by subtracting the adjusted cost basis from the exchange value of the property.

Tax-deferred exchanges can become very complicated. An accountant should be consulted before entering into the sale of a tax-deferred property. In this text, our discussion is mainly an overview of the subject. We recommend that you study the topic further if you find it of interest.

As a real estate agent, never give tax advice. Always recommend that your clients and customers see a tax specialist for their special needs before making any decisions to purchase or sell property.

Remember

- A personal residence does not qualify for a tax-deferred exchange.

State Income Tax

California state income tax brackets are different from the federal requirements. A taxpayer is required to file both a federal and state income tax return.

Foreign Investment in Real Property Tax Act (FIRPTA)

Both federal and state tax laws are affected by the Foreign Investment in Real Property Tax Act (FIRPTA). In both cases the buyer is responsible for making sure either the proper disclosures have been made and/or the proper funds have been set aside. Generally, the broker and escrow agent make sure this is done. All documents must be kept by the broker and the buyer for five years.

Federal Income Tax FIRPTA Requirements

10% of the sales price of property sold by a foreigner (either a non-citizen of the U.S. or a non-resident alien) must be withheld to make sure any capital gain tax is paid. Residential property under the sales price of $300,000 is exempt from FIRPTA disclosure requirements.

The seller must sign a Seller's Affidavit of Nonforeign Status, stating that he or she is not a foreigner.

The buyer must sign a Buyer's Affidavit of Residency, stating whether he or she is a resident or citizen, that the sales price of the property does not exceed $300,000, and that the property will be used as a residence.

If the above requirements have been fulfilled, the buyer is exempt from the withholding requirement.

California State Income Tax FIRPTA Requirements

3$^{1/2}$% of the sales price of property sold by a non-citizen of the U.S. or a resident of another state must be withheld for the Franchise Tax Board (state tax), unless:

- *the price is $100,000 or less*
- *the home is the seller's principal residence*
- *the seller signs the Seller's Affidavit of Nonforeign Status and the Buyer's Affidavit of Residency for California.*

Remember, the buyer and the agent are responsible for making sure this law is observed. The paperwork is usually completed through escrow.

Buyer's Affidavit

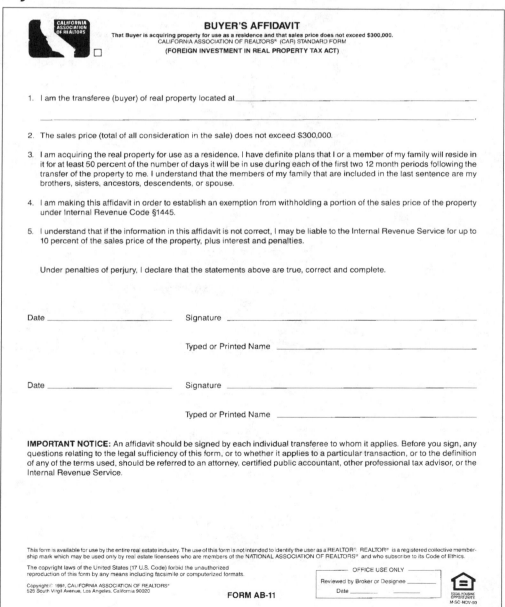

BUYER'S AFFIDAVIT

That Buyer is acquiring property for use as a residence and that sales price does not exceed $300,000.
CALIFORNIA ASSOCIATION OF REALTORS® (CAR) STANDARD FORM

(FOREIGN INVESTMENT IN REAL PROPERTY TAX ACT)

1. I am the transferee (buyer) of real property located at _____

2. The sales price (total of all consideration in the sale) does not exceed $300,000.

3. I am acquiring the real property for use as a residence. I have definite plans that I or a member of my family will reside in it for at least 50 percent of the number of days it will be in use during each of the first two 12 month periods following the transfer of the property to me. I understand that the members of my family that are included in the last sentence are my brothers, sisters, ancestors, descendents, or spouse.

4. I am making this affidavit in order to establish an exemption from withholding a portion of the sales price of the property under Internal Revenue Code §1445.

5. I understand that if the information in this affidavit is not correct, I may be liable to the Internal Revenue Service for up to 10 percent of the sales price of the property, plus interest and penalties.

Under penalties of perjury, I declare that the statements above are true, correct and complete.

Date _____ Signature _____

Typed or Printed Name _____

Date _____ Signature _____

Typed or Printed Name _____

IMPORTANT NOTICE: An affidavit should be signed by each individual transferee to whom it applies. Before you sign, any questions relating to the legal sufficiency of this form, or to whether it applies to a particular transaction, or to the definition of any of the terms used, should be referred to an attorney, certified public accountant, other professional tax advisor, or the Internal Revenue Service.

This form is available for use by the entire real estate industry. The use of this form is not intended to identify the user as a REALTOR®. REALTOR® is a registered collective membership mark which may be used only by real estate licensees who are members of the NATIONAL ASSOCIATION OF REALTORS® and who subscribe to its Code of Ethics.

The copyright laws of the United States (17 U.S. Code) forbid the unauthorized reproduction of this form by any means including facsimile or computerized formats.

Copyright© 1991, CALIFORNIA ASSOCIATION OF REALTORS®
525 South Virgil Avenue, Los Angeles, California 90020

FORM AB-11

OFFICE USE ONLY

Reviewed by Broker or Designee _____

Date _____

M-SC-NOV-93

Seller's Affidavit of Nonforeign Status

SELLER'S AFFIDAVIT OF NONFOREIGN STATUS AND/OR CALIFORNIA RESIDENCY
CALIFORNIA ASSOCIATION OF REALTORS® (CAR) STANDARD FORM
(FOREIGN INVESTMENT IN REAL PROPERTY TAX ACT
AND CALIFORNIA OUT-OF-STATE SELLER WITHHOLDING LAW)

Section 1445 of the Internal Revenue Code provides that a transferee of a U.S. real property interest must withhold tax if the transferor is a "foreign person." Section 18805 of the California Revenue and Taxation Code provides that a transferee of a California real property interest must withhold tax if the transferor's proceeds will be disbursed to a financial intermediary of the transferor or to the transferor with a last known street address outside of California. Section 26131 of the California Revenue and Taxation Code includes additional provisions for corporations.

I understand that this certification may be disclosed to the Internal Revenue Service and to the California Franchise Tax Board by the transferee and that any false statement I have made herein (if an entity transferor, on behalf of the transferor) could be punished by fine, imprisonment, or both. To inform the transferee that withholding of tax is not required upon the disposition of a U.S. and/or California real property interest located at _____

I hereby declare, under penalty of perjury, the following (if an entity transferor, on behalf of the transferor):

FEDERAL LAW (FIRPTA)

THIS SECTION FOR INDIVIDUAL TRANSFEROR:
1. I am not a nonresident alien for purposes of U.S. income taxation;
2. My U.S. taxpayer identifying number (Social Security number) is _____ ; and
3. My home address is _____

THIS SECTION FOR CORPORATION, PARTNERSHIP, TRUST, OR ESTATE TRANSFEROR:
1. _____ [name of transferor] ("Transferor") is not a foreign corporation, foreign partnership, foreign trust, or foreign estate (as those terms are defined in the Internal Revenue Code and Income Tax Regulations);
2. Transferor's U.S. employer identification number is _____
3. Transferor's office address is _____ ; and
4. I, the undersigned individual, declare that I have authority to sign this document on behalf of the Transferor.

Date _____   Signature _____

Telephone _____   Typed or Printed Name _____

Title [if signed on behalf
of an entity transferor] _____

CALIFORNIA LAW

THIS SECTION FOR INDIVIDUAL TRANSFEROR:
1. I am a ☐ married, ☐ single resident of California and reside at _____ ; or the California real property located at _____ was my principal residence within the meaning of IRC §1034; and
2. My U.S. taxpayer identifying number (Social Security number) is _____

THIS SECTION FOR CORPORATION TRANSFEROR:
1. _____ [name of transferor] ("Transferor") is a corporation qualified to do business in California or has a permanent place of business in California at the address shown below;
2. Transferor's California Corporation number issued by the Secretary of State is _____
3. Transferor's office address is _____ ; and
4. I, the undersigned individual, declare that I have authority to sign this document on behalf of the Transferor.

Date _____   Signature _____

Telephone _____   Typed or Printed Name _____

Title [if signed on behalf
of an entity transferor] _____

IMPORTANT NOTICE: An affidavit should be signed by each individual or entity transferor to whom or to which it applies. Before you sign, any questions relating to the legal sufficiency of this form, or to whether it applies to a particular transaction, or to the definition of any of the terms used, should be referred to an attorney, certified public accountant, other professional tax advisor, the Internal Revenue Service, or the California Franchise Tax Board.

OFFICE USE ONLY

Reviewed by Broker or Designee

Date ___

FORM AS-14

Documentary Transfer Tax

This tax is required whenever real property is transferred from one owner to another. In most cases, it is based on $.55 per $500 of purchase price, or $1.10 per $1,000 of purchase price. The money goes to local government, either city or county.

The full price of the property is taxed at the above rate if the sale is all cash, or if a new loan is involved, where the seller gets all cash. The tax is levied only on the equity transferred (or consideration) if the buyer assumes an existing loan. For example, if a buyer purchased a home for $l00,000, assuming an existing loan of $50,000, the tax would be based on the $50,000 the buyer paid as a down payment, or the new money put into the transaction. The tax is usually paid through escrow or at the time the deed is recorded.

> ### Documentary Transfer Tax
> $50,000 x $1.10 per $1,000 = $55.00 tax

The county recorder places stamps on the recorded grant deed to indicate the amount of the documentary transfer tax paid. These are sometimes call "doc stamps."

Remember

> ### Documentary Transfer Tax
> • Based on consideration (selling price less existing loans assumed by the buyer)

Estate and Inheritance Taxes

http://familyhaven.com/
retirement/inheritance.html

Federal estate taxes may be due on estates greater than $600,000. However there is no limit to the amount of property that can be left to a spouse. There are no inheritance taxes in California.

Gift Taxes

Federal tax laws allow a donor to give $10,000 per year to any number of donees with no gift tax due. There are no gift taxes in California.

Post Test

The following self test repeats the one you took at the beginning of this chapter. Now take the exam again—since you have read all the material—and check your knowledge of taxation.

1. Property taxes become a lien on property:
   a. January 1st
   b. November 1st
   c. February 1st
   d. July 1st

2. When local government levies a tax to finance underground utilities, it is called:
   a. an et ux tax
   b. an ad valorem tax
   c. property tax
   d. an assessment

3. Where does a taxpayer appeal a tax assessed bill that may not be correct?
   a. county tax collector
   b. assessment appeals board
   c. county tax assessor
   d. state tax assessor

4. Proposition 13 limits the amount that property assessed values can be raised annually:
   a. 2%
   b. 1%
   c. 3%
   d. 4%

5. When property is sold, the buyer's property tax is based on:
   a. 1% of full cash value
   b. 2% of full cash value
   c. 3% of full cash value
   d. 4% of full cash value

6. The law that allows someone over the age of 55 to transfer his or her present tax base to a new property is:
   a. Proposition 13
   b. Proposition 2
   c. Proposition 60
   d. Unruh Act

7. The fiscal year runs from:
   a. January 1 through December 31
   b. July 30 through July 29
   c. June 1 through May 30
   d. July 1 through June 30

8. The first installment of property taxes is due:
   a. December 10
   b. February 1
   c. November 1
   d. March 1

9. When a "tax delinquent property sale" takes place:
   a. the owner has five years to redeem the property
   b. the owner may not redeem the property
   c. the owner loses possession
   d. the state takes over the title and possession

10. What kind of deed does a buyer at a tax sale receive?
   a. grant deed
   b. gift deed
   c. trust deed
   d. tax deed

Vocabulary

Read the definition, find the matching term and write the corresponding term number on the line provided.

Terms

1. Adjusted Cost Basis
2. Ad Valorem
3. Assessment Roll or Tax Roll
4. Tax Delinquent Property
5. Boot
6. Calendar Year
7. Capital Improvements
8. Cost Basis
9. Useful Life
10. Fiscal Year
11. Homeowner's Exemption
12. Tax Deed

Definitions

1. ___ A Latin prefix meaning "according to value." Local governments levy real property tax based on the assessed value

2. ___ Starts on July 1 and runs through June 30 of the following year; used for real property tax purposes

3. ___ Starts on January 1 and continues through December 31 of the same year

4. ___ A sale of real property to the state, in name only, when a taxpayer is delinquent in paying property tax

5. ___ Deed given to a successful bidder at a tax auction

6. ___ A $7,000 tax exemption available to all owner-occupied dwellings

7. ___ The estimated period over which an improved property may be profitably used to yield a return

8. ___ Original basis plus capital improvements and costs of the sale, less depreciation if income producing

9. ___ Physical improvements made to a property

10. ___ Money or any "non-like" property put into a sale by an investor to balance the equities in a 1031 tax deferred exchange

11. ___ Usually the price paid for a property

12. ___ A list of all taxable property showing the assessed value of each parcel; establishes the tax base

Answers

Pre-Test/Post Test

1. a
2. d
3. b
4. a
5. a
6. c
7. d
8. c
9. a
10. d

Vocabulary

1. <u>2</u>
2. <u>10</u>
3. <u>6</u>
4. <u>4</u>
5. <u>12</u>
6. <u>11</u>
7. <u>9</u>
8. <u>1</u>
9. <u>7</u>
10. <u>5</u>
11. <u>8</u>
12. <u>3</u>

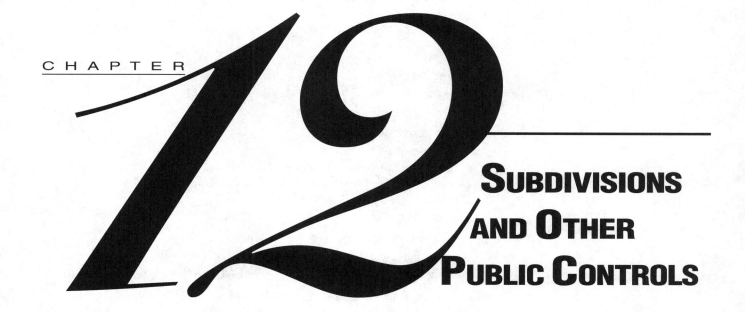

CHAPTER

12
SUBDIVISIONS AND OTHER PUBLIC CONTROLS

Focus

- Definition of subdivision

- Basic subdivision laws

- Compliance and governmental consultation

- Fair housing

Pre-Test

The following is a self test to determine how much you know about subdivisions and public controls before reading this chapter. Take it without studying, then read the material presented in the text. At the end of the chapter you will find a repeat of this exam. Test your knowledge by answering the questions again, then check your improvement. (The answers are found at the end of this chapter.) Good luck!

1. The main purpose of zoning laws is to:
    a. regulate the sale of private property
    b. control county and city law enforcement
    c. regulate the use of land and types of structures
    d. control traffic

2. Complaints about discrimination in housing in California should be taken to the:
    a. Department of Fair Employment and Housing
    b. Department of Housing and Urban Development (HUD)
    c. California Housing Council
    d. California Association of Realtors (CAR)

3. The California Fair Housing Act is also known as:
    a. Rumford Act
    b. Civil Rights Law
    c. Unruh Act
    d. Fair Practice Law

4. In which of the following is the Federal Fair Housing Law found?
    a. Civil Rights Act of 1964
    b. Civil Rights Act of 1960
    c. Civil Rights Act of 1968
    d. Jones v. Mayer

5. Which zoning symbol is used for multiple family dwellings?
    a. A-4
    b. M-4
    c. C-4
    d. R-4

6. According to the Alquist-Priolo Act, a special permit may be required for subdivisions lying within:
    a. a special studies zone
    b. city limits
    c. flood plains
    d. unincorporated territory

7. As specified in the Civil Rights Act of 1968, discrimination should be reported in which of the following ways?
    a. file a complaint in superior court
    b. go to the county civil rights office
    c. file a complaint with HUD
    d. file criminal charges

8. A zoning law allows a certain use of a property, but there is a restriction in the deed limiting the use of the property. In such a case, what is used as a measure?
    a. deed restrictions
    b. planning restrictions
    c. county building code
    d. zoning law

9. Restrictions on lots in a new subdivision would probably be found in the:
    a. original deed held by the developer
    b. recorded declaration of restrictions
    c. zoning regulations
    d. association by-laws

10. An important U.S. Supreme Court case about discrimination in housing was:
    a. Hope v. Charity
    b. Jones v. Mayer
    c. Roe v. Wade
    d. Rumford v. Unruh

Terms

The following terms are the keys to your success in learning about real estate. Refer to them as you study this chapter for greater understanding of subjects presented here.

Block Busting

Causing panic selling by telling people that values in a neighborhood will decline because of a specific event, such as the purchase of homes by minorities

Condemnation

A common name for eminent domain, or the right of the government to take private property from an owner for the public good, paying fair market value

Eminent Domain

The right of the government to take private property from an owner, for the public good, paying fair market value

Environmental Impact Report (EIR)

A study of how a development will affect the ecology of its surroundings

Land Projects

Subdivisions located in sparsely populated areas of California, made up of 50 parcels or more

Manufactured Housing

Another name for a mobile home

Police Power

The right of the state to regulate for the purpose of promoting health, safety, welfare and morality

Redlining

The use of a property's location to deny financing

Steering

Illegal practice of only showing clients property in certain areas

Subdivided Lands Act

A state law protecting purchasers of property in new subdivisions from fraud, misrepresentation or deceit in the marketing of subdivided property; concerned with financial aspects of a development

Subdivision Map Act

Outlines rules for filing subdivision maps to create subdivisions; concerned with physical aspects of a development

Subdivision

The division of land into five or more lots for the purpose of sale, lease or financing

Variance

An exception granted to existing zoning regulations for special reasons

Introduction

http://www.dre.cahwnet.
gov/submenu.htm

http://www.dre.ca.gov
Reference Book, Ch. 19

Because of the rapid and continuing growth of cities, and the movement of people into once quiet rural areas, government has found itself in the real estate business.

Such population changes have created problems which seem to demand government involvement. The range of problems is wide and varied: preventing fraud and misrepresentation selling subdivided real property; regulating lot design and physical improvements for orderly and proper development of communities; constructing streets, highways and parking areas; regulating airways over the land; providing a water supply; protecting life and property by police and firemen; maintaining clean air; mandating noise abatement; providing sewage and waste disposal and utility services.

When cities grow rapidly without design or control, problems are made worse and the need for planning is greater. Through state laws regulating subdivision, and by use of planning commissions, master plans, zoning laws and building codes, communities try to make sure that individuals and families have a quality place to live. The real estate agent often contributes to the success of such efforts by furnishing ideas and support.

Definition of Subdivision

A **Subdivision** is the division of land into five or more lots for the purpose of sale, lease or financing. Practically every place where people live has been subdivided at some time. All developments started as a large parcel of land that was divided up and sold to separate individuals. Sometimes the parcels were large enough to be subdivided again and again, creating a need for some control to make sure a desirable quality of life was protected.

Basic Subdivision Laws

The background and purpose of the two basic laws under which subdivisions are controlled in California—the Subdivision Map Act and the Subdivided Lands Act—are discussed in this chapter. To understand these two laws, it is important to know they were enacted for separate purposes. Different meanings of a subdivision were adopted in each law to achieve each of their objectives. Both were created for the protection of the consumer, however.

The Two Laws that **Control Subdivisions are:**   • Subdivision Map Act   • Subdivided Lands Act

Subdivision Map Act

The main objective of the **Subdivision Map Act** is to define the rules and procedures for filing maps to create subdivisions. It is directly controlled by local authorities (city and county) and is concerned with the physical aspects of a subdivision—such as building design, streets and environmental impact.

As a result of the Subdivision Map Act, the direct control of the kind and type of subdivisions to be allowed in each community and the physical improvements to be installed are left to local jurisdictions (city and county) within certain general limits specified in the act.

Subdivision Map Act has Two Major Objectives: 1. To coordinate the subdivision plans and planning, including lot design, street patterns, right-of-way for drainage and sewers, etc., with the community pattern and plan, as laid out by the local planning authorities   2. To ensure initial proper improvement of areas dedicated for public purposes by filing subdivision maps, including public streets and other public areas, by the subdivider so that these necessities will not become an undue burden in the future for taxpayers in the community

The Subdivision Map Act requires every city and county to adopt a subdivision law to regulate subdivisions for which a tentative and final map (for five or more lots), or a parcel map (for two to four lots), is required. Also, the act allows cities and counties to adopt laws for subdivisions for which no map is required. The following is a diagram showing typical steps in subdivision procedure under the act:

Basic Outline of Final Map Preparation and Approval

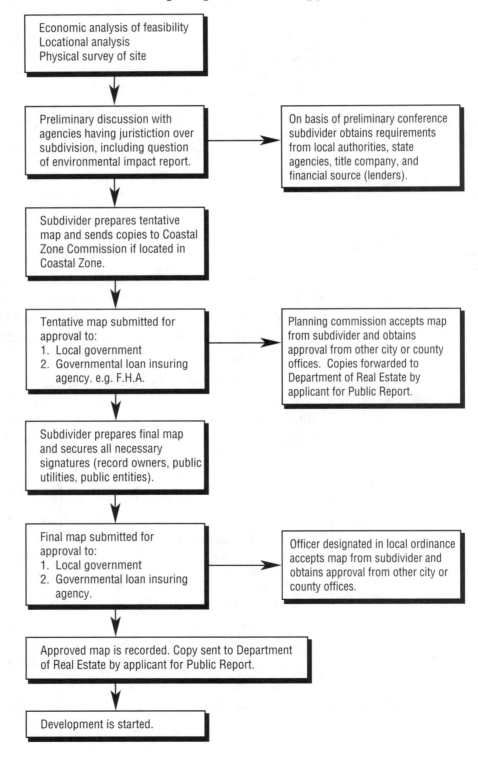

Economic analysis of feasibility
Locational analysis
Physical survey of site

↓

Preliminary discussion with agencies having juristiction over subdivision, including question of environmental impact report. → On basis of preliminary conference subdivider obtains requirements from local authorities, state agencies, title company, and financial source (lenders).

↓

Subdivider prepares tentative map and sends copies to Coastal Zone Commission if located in Coastal Zone.

↓

Tentative map submitted for approval to:
1. Local government
2. Governmental loan insuring agency. e.g. F.H.A. → Planning commission accepts map from subdivider and obtains approval from other city or county offices. Copies forwarded to Department of Real Estate by applicant for Public Report.

↓

Subdivider prepares final map and secures all necessary signatures (record owners, public utilities, public entities).

↓

Final map submitted for approval to:
1. Local government
2. Governmental loan insuring agency. → Officer designated in local ordinance accepts map from subdivider and obtains approval from other city or county offices.

↓

Approved map is recorded. Copy sent to Department of Real Estate by applicant for Public Report.

↓

Development is started.

> **Remember**
>
> ## Subdivision Map Act
>
> - Controlled by city or county authorities
> - Concerned with physical aspects of a subdivision

Subdivided Lands Act

The **Subdivided Lands Act** is directly administered by the Real Estate Commissioner. Its objective is to protect buyers of property in new subdivisions from fraud, misrepresentation or deceit in the marketing of subdivided lots, parcels, units and undivided interests.

The Real Estate Commissioner must issue a subdivision public report before any subdivision can be offered for sale in California. This even applies to lands outside the state, if they are being marketed in California. The public report is a document disclosing all important facts about the marketing and financing of the subdivision.

The public report must show that the subdivider (developer) can complete and maintain all improvements and that the lots or parcels can be used for the purpose for which they are being sold.

Before a developer can sell each lot in the project, he or she must give a copy of the commissioner's final report to the buyer for approval. The buyer signs a receipt for the report stating it has been read. The seller (developer) must keep a copy of the statement for three years.

Receipt for Public Report

RECEIPT FOR PUBLIC REPORT

The Laws and Regulations of the Real Estate Commissioner require that you as a prospective purchaser or lessee be afforded an opportunity to read the public report for this subdivision before you make any written offer to purchase or lease a subdivision interest or before any money or other consideration toward purchase or lease of a subdivision interest is accepted from you.

In the case of a preliminary subdivision public report you must be afforded an opportunity to read the report before a written reservation or any deposit in connection therewith is accepted from you.

In the case of a conditional subdivision public report, delivery of legal title or other interest contracted for will not take place until issuance of a final subdivision public report. Provision is made in the sales agreement and escrow instructions for the return to you of the entire sum of money paid or advanced by you if you are dissatisfied with the final public report because of a material change. (See Business and Professions Code §11012.)

DO NOT SIGN THIS RECEIPT UNTIL YOU HAVE RECEIVED A COPY OF THE REPORT AND HAVE READ IT.

I read the Commissioner's public report on _____
                                                [File Number]

_____.
                     [Tract Number or Name]

I understand the report is not a recommendation or endorsement of the subdivision, but is for information only.

The issue date of the public report which I received and read is: _____.

_____   _____
Signature   *Date*

_____
Address

The public report is valid for five years, with any material changes in the development reported to the commissioner, who then can issue an amendment to the original report.

It can take many months for a developer to get project approval, once all the proper paperwork is submitted to the commissioner. During that time, the developer may want to begin marketing the project while waiting for the final report. By submitting a minimum application filing package the developer can get a preliminary public report which allows taking reservations for the project, but not accepting any non-refundable money or entering into any binding contracts until receiving the final report from the commissioner.

Reservation Instrument

State of California   Department of Real Estate

RESERVATION INSTRUMENT

RE 612 (Rev. 12/86)

THIS IS NOT A CONTRACT NOR AN OFFER TO PURCHASE OR SELL

_____ (hereinafter "Subdivider")

acknowledges receipt from _____

(hereinafter "Potential Buyer") of _____
                                        (Address)

of the sum of $ _____ for the reservation of _____
                                                          (Lot or Unit Number)

in _____ ,
                     (Name of Subdivision)

County of _____ , State of California.

Subdivider hereby reserves the above-identified lot or unit for Potential Buyer and represents that he will immediately place the deposit and a signed copy of this document in the following neutral escrow depository:

FIRM NAME		STREET ADDRESS (Do not list Post Office box)	
CITY	STATE	ZIP CODE	TELEPHONE NUMBER ( )

1. *This instrument does not create a contractual obligation to buy or sell on the part of either Subdivider or Potential Buyer. Either party may, at any time, cancel this reservation instrument without incurring liability to the other. In the event of cancellation by either party, the deposit shall be immediately returned to Potential Buyer without any deduction except as provided in (2) below.*

2. If Potential Buyer so requests by completing appropriate instructions below, subdivider will make arrangements with the escrow depository for the earning of interest on Potential Buyer's deposit. $ _____ will be deducted by escrow depository from interest earned on the deposit as a charge for providing the service to Potential Buyer. The balance of the interest earned will be paid to Potential Buyer or credited to his/her account.

3. By initialing here _____, Potential Buyer agrees to the payment of charges as set forth above and requests that the deposit be placed into an interest bearing account as follows:

NAME AS ACCOUNT IS TO BE HELD	TAXPAYER IDENTIFICATION NO. (Social Security No.)

4. CAVEAT: If the deposit is to be placed into an interest bearing account:

    (a) Escrow depository will not deposit funds into the account on Potential Buyer's behalf -- and therefore interest will not accrue -- until escrow depository has been notified that Potential Buyer's check has cleared.
    (b) There may be a delay in returning the deposit to Potential Buyer on his request.
    (c) There may be an interest penalty in the case of an early withdrawal from the account.
    (d) If after Potential Buyer has received a Final Subdivision Public Report for this subdivision, he enters into a contract with Subdivider to purchase the reserved subdivision interest, the deposit plus interest earned on the deposit, if any, may be applied toward purchase of the subdivision interest with the express authorization of Potential Buyer.

5. The price and other terms of purchase of the subdivision interest will be those set forth in a purchase contract if Potential Buyer enters into one after receiving a copy of the Final Subdivision Public Report.

NAME OF SUBDIVIDER	POTENTIAL BUYER(S)	DATE
BY (Authorized Agent)	DATE	DATE

Remember

Subdivided Lands Act

- Administered by Real Estate Commissioner
- Concerned with protecting the public from fraud

As a student of real estate, sometimes it is difficult to sort out the differences between two very like sounding laws. The following list comparing the Subdivision Map Act and the Subdivided Lands Act will help you compare the two laws.

Comparison Of Subdivision Laws

Subdivision Map Act

- Two or more lots or parcels
- Lots must be adjacent to each other
- No exemption for 160 acre and larger parcels
- Administered by local authorities
- No public report needed

Subdivided Lands Act

- Five or more lots or parcels
- Parcels need not be adjacent
- 160 acres and selected larger parcels are exempt
- Administered by Real Estate Commissioner
- Requires a final public report

Compliance and Governmental Consultation

Complete compliance with all provisions of both subdivision laws is required in any subdivided development. Developers and their professional consultants must be thoroughly familiar not only with the provisions of state laws, but also with specific provisions in local subdivision control ordinance in the community where the subdivision is being developed. In various local subdivision ordinances there are many differences because of the great diversity in types of communities and conditions throughout California.

Land developers and subdividers should always consult the Department of Real Estate at an early planning stage in any subdivision development. A developer should be fully aware of the Real Estate Commissioner's current requirements for the subdivision qualification under consideration.

The role of the federal government is important in financing home building through its mortgage insurance program. It is critical in a subdivision where there is FHA or VA participation that the developer consult with those and any other appropriate agencies.

Laws Regulating Subdivisions Differ

The Real Estate Commissioner regulates conditions surrounding the sale or lease of subdivided real property while the city or county regulates the lot design and physical improvements. The commissioner is concerned with preventing fraud and misrepresentation in selling; the city or county is concerned with the orderly and proper development of the community.

Commonly, we think of a subdivision as a partition of a large piece of property into units designed for sale or lease for specific purposes. Usually, this is the case. The majority of subdivisions might be designated as lot and residential subdivisions. The parcels created are meant to be sold to private individuals who plan to build homes on them, or to speculators who will build houses for sale, or— in many cases—to the developer who will build houses and sell the dwelling and lot as one package.

Manufactured Housing

Because manufactured homes offer permanent housing, they have become an important factor in the housing industry. The sale and certain leases of five or more lots in a mobile home park are under the jurisdiction of the commissioner and the provisions of the Subdivided Lands Act.

The state Department of Housing and Community Development oversees the rental of lots in a mobile-home park. A mobile-home park is any area or tract of land where two or more mobile-home lots are rented or leased or held out for rent or lease to accommodate manufactured homes or mobile homes used for human habitation. Local authorities may enforce the Health and Safety Code if they assume the responsibility.

Resort Properties

Resort type subdivisions involve such properties as lots or interests created with the intention of selling them to people who want to build a retirement home or second vacation home, or have an interest in a time-share project.

Common Interest Subdivisions

Due to the scarcity of land suitable for subdividing, the subdivision process has become more sophisticated, often resulting in higher land prices and new types of subdivisions. The legislature recognized this trend and has enacted laws to regulate such developments, including planned neighborhoods, community apartment houses, condominiums, limited-equity housing cooperatives and undivided interest subdivisions. These projects do not follow the traditional subdivision model as being the simple division of a large piece of land into smaller parcels for the construction of individual homes. Restrictions on lots in a new subdivision would be found in a recorded declaration of restrictions.

Classification of Subdivisions

Standard

A land division with no common or mutual rights of either ownership or use among the owners of the parcels created by the division is considered a standard subdivision.

Common Interest

Individuals own a separate lot or unit, or an interest therein, together with an undivided interest or membership interest in the common areas of the entire project. Those common areas are usually governed by a homeowners association. These subdivisions vary both in physical design and legal form. Condominiums, planned developments, stock cooperatives and community apartment projects are examples, as are time-sharing projects.

Undivided Interests

The buyer receives an undivided interest in a parcel of land as a tenant in common with all the other owners. All owners have the nonexclusive right to the use and occupancy of the property. A recreational vehicle park with campground and other leisure-time amenities is an example.

Land Project

Subdivisions located in sparsely populated areas (fewer than 1,500 registered voters within the subdivision or within two miles of its boundaries), made up of 50 parcels or more, are known as **Land Projects**. In the past, it appeared that these projects had been sold more on the intense promotion of alleged benefits than on the actual value of the project. There was a need for legislation to regulate these sales.

The Real Estate Commissioner was given the authority to oversee sales in land projects to make sure the consumer was protected. The law now allows a buyer 14 days after signing a contract to purchase property in a land project to rescind the offer, with a full refund of any money paid. This gives the buyer time to investigate the project and decide, unpressured, whether he or she still wants to go through with the purchase, and whether it was represented accurately or not.

Remember

A Land Project is a Subdivision of:

- 50 parcels or more

- In a sparsely populated area

Functions in Land Subdivision

Title Company

Title companies can help a developer greatly in creating a subdivision. After the land to be subdivided has been acquired, the title company will issue a preliminary guaranty showing the names of the persons required to sign the subdivision map as specified by the Map Act. The title company also provides the preliminary title report required by the Department of Real Estate when application for a public report is filed by the subdivider.

Interstate Land Sales Full-Disclosure Act

http://www.dre.cahwnet.
gov/2regs97.htm

This federal law regulates land sales when there are two or more states involved. Subdividers must conform to this law if they have 50 or more lots in one state and want to sell them in another state. A public report from HUD must be given to each prospective buyer as a protection from less-than-truthful advertising in far-away places.

Types of Subdivisions

The following Common Interest Developments (CIDs) are all considered subdivisions and under the control of the subdivision laws.

Condominiums

A **Condominium** consists of a separate fee interest in a particular specific space (the unit), plus an undivided interest in all common or public areas of the development. Each unit owner has a deed, separate financing and pays the property taxes for their unit.

Condominiums

- Fee simple ownership to living unit

- Undivided interest in land and common areas

- Separate property tax bill, deed, deed of trust

- Operations Controlled by elected governing board

Remember

An Undivided Interest

- Allows all owners of a fee interest condominium to use entire common area. Each owner has an ownership interest in all of the common area, with the right to use any part of it.

Planned Unit Developments (PUDs)

Planned Unit Developments (PUDs) are similar to condominiums, except the owner has title to the land under the unit, as well as the air space within, and an undivided interest in the common area.

Stock Cooperatives

A corporation formed for the purpose of owning property is known as a stock cooperative. Each stockholder is given the use of a living unit, with the building being owned by the corporation.

Community Apartments

When two or more people join together to buy an apartment complex, with each person having the right to live in a particular unit, it is known as a community apartment. Each person has an undivided interest in the whole building, with the right to sell his or her share. A buyer then occupies the seller's particular apartment.

Upon Sale of an Existing Common Interest Development, a Buyer must be Provided with:

- A copy of the Conditions, Covenants and Restrictions (CC&Rs), articles of incorporation, association by-laws, governing documents and a current financial statement on the homeowners' association

- Written notification of any known pending special assessments, claims or lawsuits against the seller or the homeowners association

- A statement showing whether the seller's account with the homeowners association is paid up-to-date

Time Share Ownership

Time sharing is a favorite way to have an interest in a building, with the right to occupy limited to a specific time period. This type of ownership is popular in resorts and other desirable areas where people like to vacation once or twice a year, but do not need the right of possession the rest of the time.

Other Government Controls

Environmental Impact Report (EIR)

An **Environmental Impact Report (EIR)** is a study of how a development will affect the ecology of its surroundings. An EIR may be required by authorities before issuing a building permit to developers and private parties building for themselves.

Residential Lead-Based Paint Hazard Reduction Act

A lead-hazard information brochure and disclosure form must be provided to a buyer or lessee by a seller or landlord. Also, the presence of any known lead-based paint must be disclosed.

A lead-warning statement is included in the deposit receipt, with a statement (to be signed by the buyer) that it has been read by the buyer. Some real estate companies require an extra disclosure form to be signed by the buyer and seller.

Notice to Purchasers of Housing Constructed Before 1978 (page 1 of 2)

U. S. Department of Housing and Urban Development

NOTICE TO PURCHASERS OF HOUSING CONSTRUCTED BEFORE 1978

WATCH OUT FOR LEAD-BASED PAINT POISONING!

If the home you intend to purchase was built before 1978, it may contain lead-based paint. About three out of every four pre-1978 buildings have lead-based paint.

YOU NEED TO READ THIS NOTICE ABOUT LEAD

What Is Lead Poisoning?

Lead poisoning means having high concentrations of lead in the body.
LEAD CAN:

- Cause major health problems, especially in children under 7 years old.
- Damage a child's brain, nervous system, kidneys, hearing, or coordination.
- Affect learning.
- Cause behavior problems, blindness, and even death.
- Cause problems in pregnancy and affect a baby's normal development.

Who Gets Lead Poisoning?

Anyone can get it, but children under 7 are at the greatest risk, because their bodies are not fully grown and are easily damaged. The risk is worse if the child:

- Lives in an older home (built/constructed before 1978, and even more so before 1960).
- Does not eat regular meals (an empty stomach accepts lead more easily).
- Does not eat enough foods with iron or calcium.
- Has parents who work in lead-related jobs.
- Has played in the same places as brothers, sisters, and friends who have been lead poisoned, (lead poison cannot be spread from person to person. It comes from contact with lead).

Women of childbearing age are also at risk, because lead poisoning can cause miscarriages, premature births, and the poison can be passed onto their unborn babies.

Where Does it Come From?

The lead hazards that children most often touch are lead dust, leaded soil, loose chips and chewable surfaces painted with lead-based paint. A child may be harmed when it puts into its mouth toys, pacifiers, or hands that have leaded soil or lead dust on them. Lead also comes from:

- Moving parts of windows, and doors that can make lead dust and chips.
- Lead-based paint on windows, doors, wood trim, walls and cabinets in kitchens and bathrooms, on porches, stairs, railings, fire escapes and lamp posts.
- Soil next to exterior of buildings that have been painted with lead-based paint and leaded gasoline dust in soil near busy streets.
- Drinking water, (pipes and solder)
- Parents who may bring lead dust home from work on skin, clothes, and hair.
- Colored newsprint and car batteries.
- Highly glazed pottery and cookware from other countries.
- Removing old paint when refinishing furniture.

In recent years some uses of lead in products that could cause lead poisoning have been reduced or banned. This is true for lead in gasoline, lead in solder used in water pipes, and lead in paint. Still, a great deal of lead remains in and around older homes, and lead-based paint an accompanying lead dust are seen as the major sources.

Page 1 of 2 pages

Notice to Purchasers of Housing Constructed Before 1978 (page 2 of 2)

How Do I Know if My Child Is Affected?

Is your child:

- cranky?
- vomiting?
- tired?
- unwilling to eat or play?

- complaining of stomach aches or headaches?
- unable to concentrate?
- hyperactive?
- playing with children who have these symptoms?

These can be signs of lead poisoning. However, your children might not show these signs and yet be poisoned; only your clinic or Doctor can test for sure.

What Can I Do About It?

Your child should first be tested for lead in the blood between six months and one year old. Ask the clinic or your doctor to do it during a regular checkup. Your doctor will tell you how often you should have your child tested after that. A small amount of lead in the blood may not make your child seem very sick, but it can affect how well he or she can learn. If you child does have high amounts of lead in the blood, you should seek treatment and have your home tested for lead-based paint and lead dust.

How Do I Know if My Home Has Lead-Based Paint?

The HUD inspection does not determine whether a home actually has lead-based paint. It only identifies where there is defective paint in a home that might have lead-based paint. Therefore, the only way you can know for sure is to have the home tested by a qualified firm or laboratory. Both the interior and exterior should be tested. You should contact your local health or environmental office for help.

What Do I Do if My Home Does Have Lead?

Do not try to get rid of lead-based paint yourself, you could make things worse for you and your family. If your home contains lead-based paint, contact a company that specializes in lead -based paint abatement. Have professionals do the job correctly and safely. This may cost thousands of dollars, depending on the amount of lead-based paint and lead dust found in your home, but it will also protect you and your children from the effects of lead poisoning. In the meantime, there are things you can do immediately to protect your child:

- Keep your child away from paint chips and dust.
- Wet-mop floors and wipe down surfaces often, especially where the floors and walls meet. Be sure to clean the space where the window sash rests on the sill. Keeping the floor clear of paint chips, dust and dirt is easy and very important. Do not sweep or vacuum lead-based paint chips or lead dust with an ordinary vacuum cleaner. Lead dust is so fine it will pass through a vacuum cleaner bag and spread into the air you breathe.
- Make sure your children wash their hand frequently and always before eating.
- Wash toys, teething rings, and pacifiers frequently.

Will HUD Insure a Mortgage Loan on a Home with Lead-Based Paint?

Hud will insure a mortgage on a house even if it has lead-based paint. If you purchase a property with lead-based paint, HUD will not remove it. You will have to pay for the cost of removal yourself.

Acknowledgment

I acknowledge that I have received and read a copy of this Notice before signing the sales contract to purchase my property.

Date: _____   Signature(s): _____

Page 2 of 2 pages

PROFESSIONAL PUBLISHING

Alquist-Priolo Special Studies Zone Act

Special earthquake zones have been identified and studied by the California Division of Mines and Geology. Any prospective property buyer in an identified zone must be made aware of the facts by the seller or the real estate agent. The Alquist-Priolo Special Studies Zone Act is a law requiring geological reports for project approval within one quarter mile of hazardous earthquake faults. A disclosure of earthquake fault activity is included in the deposit receipt.

Geologic, Seismic and Flood Hazard Disclosure

GEOLOGIC, SEISMIC AND FLOOD HAZARD DISCLOSURE
CALIFORNIA ASSOCIATION OF REALTORS® STANDARD FORM

The paragraph(s) below, when initialled by both Buyer and Seller, are hereby incorporated in and made a part of the ☐ Real Estate Purchase Contract and Receipt for Deposit, ☐ Investment Purchase Contract and Receipt for Deposit, ☐ Commercial Real Estate Purchase Contract and Receipt for Deposit, ☐ Business Purchase Contract and Receipt for Deposit, ☐ Lots and Land Purchase Contract and Receipt for Deposit, ☐ Mobile Home Purchase Contract and Receipt for Deposit, ☐ Other _____

dated _____ 19___, on property known as _____
in which _____ is referred to as Buyer
and _____ is referred to as Seller.

Buyer's Initials   Seller's Initials
____ / ____   ____ / ____   **1. FLOOD HAZARD AREA DISCLOSURE:** Buyer is informed that the Property is situated in a "Special Flood Hazard Area" designated by the Federal Emergency Management Agency (FEMA) in a "Flood Insurance Rate Map" (FIRM) or "Flood Hazard Boundary Map" (FHBM). The law provides that as a condition of obtaining financing on most structures located in a Special Flood Hazard Area, lender(s) may require flood insurance where the Property or its attachments are security for a loan.
    The extent of coverage and the cost may vary. For further information consult the lenders or insurance agents. No representation or recommendation is made by the Seller and the Broker(s) in this transaction as to the legal effect or economic consequences of the National Flood Insurance Program and related legislation.

Buyer's Initials   Seller's Initials
____ / ____   ____ / ____   **2. GEOLOGIC, SEISMIC HAZARD DISCLOSURE:**
(a) Buyer is informed that the Property is situated in the zone(s)/area(s) designated below:
    ☐ Special Studies Zone (SSZ) designated under Public Resources Code §§2621-2625.
    ☐ Seismic Hazards Zone (SHZ) designated under Public Resources Code §§2690-2699.6.
    ☐ Locally designated zone(s)/area(s) where disclosure is required by local ordinance:
    ☐ _____
    ☐ _____
    ☐ _____

    ☐ Local ordinance additionally requires disclosure of the following information:
    _____
    _____

(b) The construction or development of any structure for human occupancy located within one of these zone(s)/area(s) may be subject to the findings of a geologic report prepared by a geologist registered in the State of California unless such report is waived by the City or County under the terms of those statute(s)/ordinance(s). Disclosure of SSZs or SHZs are required only where the respective maps, or information contained in the maps, are "reasonably available."

3. **This paragraph applies only if the above referenced contract DOES NOT CONTAIN a provision for Buyer's disapproval or approval of the applicable flood, geologic or seismic hazards information:**
(a) Buyer is allowed _____ calendar days after receipt of the above disclosure(s) to make further inquiries at appropriate governmental agencies, lenders, insurance agents, or other appropriate entities concerning use of the Property under local building, zoning, fire, health and safety codes as may be applicable under the Special Studies Zone Act, Seismic Hazards Mapping Act, local geologic ordinances, or National Flood Insurance Program. Buyer shall provide written notice to Seller of any items disapproved within this time period.
(b) If Buyer gives written notice of disapproval of items under the above paragraph(s), Seller shall respond in writing within _____ calendar days after receipt of such notice. If Seller is unwilling or unable to correct items reasonably disapproved by Buyer, then Buyer may cancel this Agreement by giving written notice of cancellation to Seller within _____ calendar days (after receipt of Seller's response, or after expiration of the time for Seller's response, whichever occurs first), in which case Buyer's deposit shall be returned to Buyer. BUYER'S FAILURE TO GIVE WRITTEN NOTICE OF DISAPPROVAL OF ITEMS OR CANCELLATION OF THIS AGREEMENT WITHIN THE SPECIFIED TIME PERIODS SHALL CONCLUSIVELY BE DEEMED BUYER'S ELECTION TO PROCEED WITH THE TRANSACTION WITHOUT CORRECTION OF ANY REMAINING DISAPPROVED ITEMS WHICH SELLER HAS NOT AGREED TO CORRECT. Buyer and Seller may agree in writing to extend these time periods.

The undersigned acknowledge receipt of a copy.

Date _____   Date _____

Buyer _____   Seller _____

Buyer _____   Seller _____

THIS STANDARD DOCUMENT HAS BEEN APPROVED BY THE CALIFORNIA ASSOCIATION OF REALTORS® IN FORM ONLY. NO REPRESENTATION IS MADE AS TO THE LEGAL VALIDITY OF ANY PROVISION OR THE ADEQUACY OF ANY PROVISION IN ANY SPECIFIC TRANSACTION.

A REAL ESTATE BROKER IS THE PERSON QUALIFIED TO ADVISE ON REAL ESTATE TRANSACTIONS. IF YOU DESIRE LEGAL OR TAX ADVICE, CONSULT AN APPROPRIATE PROFESSIONAL.

This form is available for use by the entire real estate industry. The use of this form is not intended to identify the user as a REALTOR®. REALTOR® is a registered collective membership mark which may be used only by real estate licensees who are members of the NATIONAL ASSOCIATION OF REALTORS® and who subscribe to its Code of Ethics.

The copyright laws of the United States (17 U.S. Code) forbid the unauthorized reproduction of this form by any means including facsimile or computerized formats.
Copyright © 1991, CALIFORNIA ASSOCIATION OF REALTORS®
525 South Virgil Avenue, Los Angeles, California 90020

OFFICE USE ONLY
Reviewed by Broker or Designee _____
Date _____

FORM GFD-14

M-SC-SEP-93

Zoning

The regulation of structures and uses of property within selected districts is known as zoning. The regulation of the use of land, lot sizes, types of structures permitted, building heights, setbacks and density are affected by zoning laws.

Zoning laws are exercises of a city's or county's **Police Power**, and are upheld as long as they reasonably protect the public health, safety and general welfare of an area. When the state uses police power, it is not required to compensate a property owner for any loss in property values as a result of the regulation, as it must do under the power of eminent domain.

The right of the government to take private property from an owner, for the public good, paying fair market value, is known as **Eminent Domain**, or commonly, **Condemnation**. This is not an example of police power, as is zoning.

Government May Control Land Use Through:

Police Power
> Building Codes
>
> Health Codes
>
> Subdivision Regulations
>
> Zoning

Eminent Domain

Acquiring Land After Payment of Just Compensation

Symbols used to show Different Zoning Areas

- A—Agricultural
- C—Commercial
- M—Manufacturing
- P—Parking lots and parks
- R—Homes, other residences
- R1—Single family home
- R2—Duplex
- R3—Multiple dwelling or triplex
- R4—Fourplex or higher density dwellings

A city or county may allow a **Variance**, or an exception to existing zoning regulations for special reasons.

Mobile Homes

A mobile home is a manufactured unit constructed on a chassis and wheels and designed for permanent or semi-attachment to land. Another name for a mobile home is **Manufactured Housing**. A real estate agent may sell mobile homes that have been converted to real property by the removal of wheels, have been placed on a foundation and have a building permit. The mobile home must be in place on a lot rented or leased for human habitation in an established mobile home park.

Fair Housing Laws

California Laws

Unruh Civil Rights Act

This law covers discrimination in business. It is against the law for anyone to deny a person the right to business products and services. The Unruh Act applies to a real estate brokerage because it is a business and may not discriminate against clients or customers. It is particularly important for the real estate licensee to be aware of **Steering**, or the illegal practice of only showing clients property in certain areas, and **Redlining**, or the use of a property's location to deny financing. **Block Busting**, or causing panic selling by telling people that values in a neighborhood will decline because of a specific event, such as the purchase of homes by minorities, is also prohibited by this law.

California Fair Employment and Housing Act (formerly the Rumford Act)

Discrimination in the sale, rental or financing of practically all types of housing is illegal. Violations are reported to the state Department of Fair Employment and Housing.

Housing Financial Discrimination Act (Holden Act)

This law prohibits all financial institutions from discriminating in real estate loan approvals based on the geographic location, the neighborhood or any other characteristic of the property. In particular, redlining—the practice of disapproving real estate loans in economically or physically blighted areas—is forbidden unless it can be proved to be based on sound business practice.

Violations may be reported to the state Secretary for Business and Transportation, who must act on the complaint within 30 days.

California Civil Code (Section 54-55.1)

This section of the Civil Code prohibits discrimination in the rental, leasing or sale of housing accommodations to the blind, visually handicapped, deaf or otherwise physically disabled. It also precludes restrictions on seeing eye dogs and signal dogs from "no pet" clauses.

Federal Laws

1866 Civil Rights Act

This federal law prohibits discrimination based on race in all property transactions. However, it was basically ignored until 1968.

http://www.fairhousing.com

U.S. Supreme Court Case of Jones vs. Mayer of 1968

Jones vs. Mayer prohibits discrimination based on race by upholding the 1866 Civil Rights Act and the 13th Amendment to the U.S. Constitution prohibiting slavery.

Civil Rights Act of 1968 and 1988 Amendments

In leasing or selling residential property, the Civil Rights Act of 1968 expands the definition of discrimination to include not only race, but national origin, color, and religion. The Fair Housing Amendments Act of 1988 (effective March 12,1989) further broadens the definition to include age, sex and handicapped status. Under these laws, real estate offices are required to display fair housing posters. Any complaints must be filed with HUD.

Fair Housing Act

The Fair Housing Amendments Act of 1988 and Title VIII of the Civil Rights Act of 1968, taken together, constitute the Fair Housing Act. Specifically, the Fair Housing Act provides protection against the following discriminatory housing practices if they are based on race, sex, religion, color, handicap, familial status or national origin:

Acts Prohibited by Fair Housing Act

- Refusing to rent housing
- Refusing to sell housing
- Treating applicants differently for housing
- Treating residents differently in connection with terms and conditions
- Advertising a discriminatory housing preference or limitation
- Providing false information about the availability of housing
- Harassing, coercing or intimidating people from enjoying or exercising their rights under the act
- "Blockbusting" for profit; persuading an owner to sell or rent housing by saying people of a particular race, religion, etc. are moving into the neighborhood
- Imposing different loan terms for purchasing, constructing, improving, repairing or maintaining a residence
- Denying use of or participation in real estate services, such as brokers' organizations or multiple listing services

Enforcement of the Fair Housing Act

The Fair Housing Act gives HUD the authority to hold administrative hearings unless one of the parties elects to have the case heard in U.S. District Court and to issue subpoenas. The Administrative Law Judge in these proceedings can issue an order for relief, including actual damages, injunctive or other equitable relief and penalties.

http://www.hud.gov/ hotline.html

The penalties range from up to $10,000, for a first violation, to up to $50,000, for the third violation and those thereafter. The penalties are paid to the federal government. The damage payments go to the proven victims.

The act adds criminal penalties of a $100,000 maximum fine and imprisonment as sanctions against people who willfully fail to give information and evidence or who willfully give false information in a fair housing investigation or proceeding.

Protection for People with Disabilities

> ### The Act Defines a Handicap as:
>
> - Physical or mental impairment which substantially limits one or more major life activities
> - Having a record of such an impairment
> - Being regarded as having such an impairment

Handicap includes mental illness, AIDS, blindness, hearing impairment, mental retardation, mobility impairment.

Housing For Older Persons

In response to the concerns of senior citizens residing in elderly or retirement communities, Congress provided an exemption for housing for older persons which meets certain criteria.

> ### Senior Citizen Housing is Exempt from the Prohibition Based on Familial Status when:
>
> - The housing is provided under a state or federal program specifically designed and operated to assist the elderly
> - The housing is intended for, and solely occupied by, people 62 years or older
> - The housing is intended and operated for occupancy by at least one person 55 years of age or older in each unit
> - The housing has significant facilities and services to meet the physical or social needs of older persons
> - 80% of the units are occupied by at least one person 55 years old or older
> - The policies and procedures demonstrate the intent to provide housing for persons 55 years or older

Federal Policy on Real Estate Advertising

Section 804 of the Federal Fair Housing Law states in part "...it shall be unlawful to make, print, or publish, or cause to be made, printed, or published any notice, statement, or advertisement, with respect to the sale or rental of a dwelling that indicates any preference, limitation, or discrimination based on race, color, religion, sex, handicap, familial status, or national origin, or any intention to make any such preference, limitation or discrimination."

As the federal official named by Congress with the authority and responsibility to administer the Federal Fair Housing Law, the Secretary of HUD published in 1989 fair housing advertising regulations which provide specific instructions for complying with provisions of Section 804.

All advertising media, advertising agencies and other persons who use advertising with respect to the sale, rental or financing of dwellings are required to take care that their words, phrases, symbols and visual aids do not signal a prohibited preference or limitation.

All residential real estate advertising should contain the equal housing opportunity logotype and slogan. The logotype should be sufficiently large or visible to be noticed and understood. When the size of the logotype is so small that the facial features (ethnicities) of the people are not *clearly* distinguishable, then *it is too small*.

The logotype should be a clear sign or symbol of welcome to all potentially qualified buyers or renters regardless of race, color, etc.

Human models in photographs, drawings or other graphic techniques may not be used to indicate exclusiveness because of race, color, religion, sex, handicap, familial status or national origin. If models are used in display advertising campaigns, they should be clearly definable as reasonable representation of majority and minority groups in the metropolitan area, both sexes and—when appropriate—families with children. Models, if used, should portray persons in an equal social setting and indicate to the general public that the housing is open to all without regard to race, color, religion, sex, handicap, familial status or national origin, and is not for the exclusive use of one such group.

Use of the HUD advertising criteria will be considered by the HUD General Counsel in deciding if there is reasonable cause to believe that the Fair Housing Act has been violated.

Use of Words

Real estate ads should not have words that state or imply a preference or limitation with regard to race, color, religion, handicap, sex or familial status. Some words are clearly objectionable. Other words or phrases are marginal and—depending on a wider context—convey a wrong signal, particularly to those who have been victims of discrimination in the past.

Advertisers should avoid offensive and marginal expressions. The following words and phrases typify those most often used in real estate ads to convey discriminatory preferences or limitations.

Offensive, Marginal and Acceptable Advertising

Clearly Offensive:
Adult Building
Hispanic Area
Near Synagogue
Ideal for Physically Fit
Prefer Bright, Healthy Person
Restrictive
Catholic Church Nearby
Chinese Businesses in Area
Male or Female Only
Singles Only
No Children
Integrated Neighborhood Racially

Marginally Offensive:
Exclusive
Private Community
For Mature Adults
For Active Adults

Acceptable Words:
Gated
Parks Nearby
Houses of Worship Nearby
Quiet Residential Area

Important Court Cases

There have not been a large number of court cases or formal complaints to illustrate clearly and specifically those ads or practices found to be offensive. Since 1987, however, unfair advertising complaints have been filed with increasing frequency. Most noteworthy have been the following:

Ragin v. the New York Times: This lawsuit challenges a 20-year practice on the part of the New York Times of publishing real estate advertisements that feature virtually all-white models.

In a decision dated December 18, 1989, Judge Charles Haight of the U.S. District Court of the Southern District of New York denied the Time's motion to dismiss the case. The decision is being appealed at this writing. This decision can be significant, if sustained, because it recognizes that:

An ad picturing all-white models may communicate the same illegal racist message as the words "White Only."

The Fair Housing Act applies to newspapers, entitling them to no greater First Amendment protection than a real estate owner, an advertiser or any other person.

The First Amendment does not shield illegal commercial speech such as racist pictures used to sell or rent real estate.

This case could illustrate the meaning of "fair representation" versus "tokenism" in the use of models of different races.

Saunders v. General Services Corporation: On May 13, 1987, U.S. District Judge Robert Merhige, Jr. ruled that General Services Corporation, a large real estate holding company in Richmond, Virginia, violated the Fair Housing Act by almost exclusively using white models in the company's advertising brochures. The court awarded $12,800 to the plaintiffs. It was the first time a judge had ever ruled on the merits of an unfair advertising claim.

Spann v. the Avenel Corporation: In September of 1989, the Avenel Corporation of Potomac, Maryland, a real estate development firm, agreed to pay $325,000 for excluding African Americans from their promotional campaign for a new luxury homes project in Maryland. It was the largest settlement of its kind.

Post Test

The following self test repeats the one you took at the beginning of this chapter. Now take the exam again—since you have read all the material—and check your knowledge of subdivisions and public controls.

1. The main purpose of zoning laws is to:
   a. regulate the sale of private property
   b. control county and city law enforcement
   c. regulate the use of land and types of structures
   d. control traffic

2. Complaints about discrimination in housing in California should be taken to the:
   a. Department of Fair Employment and Housing
   b. Department of Housing and Urban Development (HUD)
   c. California Housing Council
   d. California Association of Realtors (CAR)

3. The California Fair Housing Act is also known as:
   a. Rumford Act   c. Unruh Act
   b. Civil Rights Law   d. Fair Practice Law

4. In which of the following is the Federal Fair Housing Law found?
   a. Civil Rights Act of 1964   c. Civil Rights Act of 1968
   b. Civil Rights Act of 1960   d. Jones v. Mayer

5. Which zoning symbol is used for multiple family dwellings?
   a. A-4   c. C-4
   b. M-4   d. R-4

6. According to the Alquist-Priolo Act, a special permit may be required for subdivisions lying within:
   a. a special studies zone   c. flood plains
   b. city limits   d. unincorporated territory

7. As specified in the Civil Rights Act of 1968, discrimination should be reported in which of the following ways?
   a. file a complaint in superior court   c. file a complaint with HUD
   b. go to the county civil rights office d. file criminal charges

8. A zoning law allows a certain use of a property, but there is a restriction in the deed limiting the use of the property. In such a case, what is used as a measure?
   a. deed restrictions   c. county building code
   b. planning restrictions   d. zoning law

9. Restrictions on lots in a new subdivision would probably be found in the:
   a. original deed held by the developer   c. zoning regulations
   b. recorded declaration of restrictions d. association by-laws

10. An important U.S. Supreme Court case about discrimination in housing was:
    a. Hope v. Charity   c. Roe v. Wade
    b. Jones v. Mayer   d. Rumford v. Unruh

Vocabulary

Read the definition, find the matching term and write the corresponding term number on the line provided.

Terms

1. Block Busting
2. Condemnation
3. Eminent Domain
4. Environmental Impact Report (EIR)
5. Manufactured Housing
6. Police Power
7. Redlining
8. Steering
9. Subdivided Lands Act
10. Subdivision Map Act
11. Subdivision
12. Variance
13. Land Project

Definitions

1. ___ The division of land into five or more lots for the purpose of sale, lease or financing

2. ___ Outlines rules for filing subdivision maps to create subdivisions; concerned with physical aspects of land use

3. ___ Subdivisions located in sparsely populated areas of California, made up of 50 parcels or more

4. ___ A study of how a development will affect the ecology of its surroundings

5. ___ The right of the state to regulate for the purpose of promoting health, safety, welfare and morality

6. ___ The right of the government to take private property from an owner, for the public good, paying fair market value

7. ___ A common name for eminent domain, or the right of the government to take private property from an owner for the public good, paying fair market value

8. ___ An exception granted to existing zoning regulations for special reasons

9. ___ Another name for a mobile home

10. ___ Illegal practice of only showing clients property in certain areas

11. ___ The use of a property's location to deny financing

12. ___ Causing panic selling by telling people that values in a neighborhood will decline because of a specific event, such as the purchase of homes by minorities

13. ___ A state law protecting purchasers of property in new subdivisions from fraud, misrepresentation or deceit in the marketing of subdivided property; concerned with financial aspects of a development

Answers

Pre-Test/Post Test

1. c
2. a
3. a
4. c
5. d
6. a
7. c
8. a
9. b
10. b

Vocabulary

1. 11
2. 10
3. 13
4. 4
5. 6
6. 3
7. 2
8. 12
9. 5
10. 8
11. 7
12. 1
13. 9

REAL ESTATE PRACTICE

13
REAL ESTATE BROKERAGE AND ETHICS

Focus

- **Definition of brokerage**
- **Operations of a real estate brokerage**
- **Requirements of a real estate transaction**
- **Specific disclosures required in a real estate transaction**
- **Professionalism and ethics**
- **Regulations of the Commissioner**
- **Code of Ethics**
- **Trust funds**

Pre-Test

The following is a self test to determine how much you know about real estate brokerage and ethics before reading this chapter. Take it without studying, then read the material presented in the text. At the end of the chapter you will find a repeat of this exam. Test your knowledge by answering the questions again, then check your improvement. (The answers are found at the end of this chapter.) Good luck!

1. A listing belongs to:
   a. the seller
   b. the buyer
   c. the listing agent
   d. the listing broker

2. Which of the following are not operations of a real estate brokerage?
   a. securing listings
   b. finding buyers
   c. paying non-licensees for assisting in sale of real property
   d. arranging financing

3. Real estate salespersons usually are paid:
   a. on a commission basis
   b. a straight salary
   c. on a sliding, pre-determined scale
   d. by the seller

4. Who sets the amount of real estate commission in a sale?
   a. the broker
   b. the seller
   c. it is negotiable between broker and seller
   d. the buyer

5. Commonly, what is the commission split for a new agent?
   a. 50-50
   b. 60-40
   c. 30-70
   d. 20-80

6. When an agent receives funds on behalf of someone else, the funds are called:
   a. trust funds
   b. escrow funds
   c. commission
   d. up-front fees

7. Trust funds must be deposited not later than:
   a. one week following the acceptance of the offer
   b. two days following the acceptance of the offer
   c. the next business day following receipt of the funds
   d. three business days following receipt of the funds

8. The offeree in a typical real estate sale is:
   a. the broker
   b. the buyer
   c. the seller
   d. the selling agent

9. Before the acceptance of an offer, trust funds from the buyer belong to:
   a. the buyer
   b. the seller
   c. the broker
   d. a neutral depository

10. How much personal money may a broker keep in a trust account?
    a. up to $200
    b. up to $300
    c. up to $100
    d. up to $50

Terms

The following terms are the keys to your success in learning about real estate. Refer to them as you study this chapter for greater understanding of subjects presented here.

Brokerage

The occupation of a broker; the business of selling real estate through a broker who negotiates the sale for a commission

Commingling

The mixing of a broker's private funds over $200 with other people's money such as trust funds

Commission Split

The previously agreed upon division of money between a broker and sales-associate when the brokerage has been paid a commission from a sale made by the associate

Neutral Depository

An escrow business conducted by someone who is a licensed escrow holder

Trust Funds

Money received by real estate brokers or salespersons on behalf of others

Introduction

As you have journeyed through this book, you have studied the regulation of real estate and the legal, financial, economic and political aspects of real estate practice. Now you have reached the chapter where you will see how a real estate brokerage works. This section examines the business and practical aspects of a brokerage and the real estate business in general.

Definition of Brokerage

The term **Brokerage** generally means an activity involving the sale of something through an intermediary who negotiates the transaction for payment. In the case of a real estate brokerage, what is sold is real property, with the broker as negotiator and agent of the principal, expecting a commission at the end of the negotiation.

Let's review the definition of an agent, a broker and a salesperson. An agent is someone who represents a principal in negotiating with a third party. Both a broker and salesperson (or sales associate, as they are sometimes called) are agents. However, a salesperson must be in the employ of—and supervised by—a broker who is ultimately responsible for the actions of those operating under his or her broker license. Many times the term broker will be used loosely by the public, or even by a licensee, to mean a real estate agent. The important thing to remember is that a brokerage is operated by a licensed broker who employs licensed salespersons who help conduct the business, and who all earn commissions for selling real estate.

Types of Licensees

Real Estate Agent
Someone licensed by the Department of Real Estate, holding either a broker or salesperson license, who negotiates sales for other people

Real Estate Broker
Someone holding a broker license and permitted by law to employ those holding a salesperson license, who may negotiate sales for other people

Real Estate Salesperson
Someone holding a salesperson license and employed by a real estate broker, for pay, to perform any of the activities of a real estate broker

---

Also, as you recall, since a salesperson represents his or her broker in all operations, listings belong to the brokerage, not to the salesperson. When a salesperson leaves the employ of a particular broker, any listings he or she has will remain at the brokerage. The reason is that the seller's listing contract is with the brokerage, not the listing agent (unless the broker happens to be the listing agent). This is a common source of confusion and sometimes disagreement between listing agents—who want to take their listings with them to a new broker—and the former broker who owns the listings. However, the law says the listings stay with the original broker.

Operations of a Real Estate Brokerage

The operations of a brokerage are varied. They can be divided into five separate areas: securing listings, finding buyers, negotiating transactions, arranging financing and closing transactions.

Brokerage Operations

- Listing
- Selling
- Negotiating
- Arranging financing
- Closing sales

All of these activities are conducted in a competitive and mostly cooperative way. Agents in a single real estate office and agents from different offices all compete for listings and buyers, yet usually cooperate to sell each other's listings. Generally, a spirit of friendly competition prevails.

Even though selling is the main activity of a real estate brokerage, there also is a major amount of paperwork. Filling out forms; keeping track of listings, open escrows and closings; completing loan applications; ordering special reports; and keeping records of prospects are all essential to the practice of real estate. The agent who does not keep adequate records or complete paperwork will not be in the business for long.

Choosing a Brokerage

Imagine your first day as a real estate agent. You haven't a clue about what to do with your time or how to get started. You pray the telephone doesn't ring, because you might have to commit yourself to some action that may or may not result in approval by your broker or the prospective client.

Hopefully you have selected your brokerage with great care and for the right reasons. The new broker should be available to give guidance and problem-solving advice, and should be trained, confident, informed and up-to-date on developments in the real estate industry. The broker's professional advice should come from knowledge and experience. Also, the sales associates in the office should be full-time professionals. They too should be trained, confident, informed and up-to-date. Most importantly, they should be honest and straightforward with clients, co-brokers, business contacts and each other.

You should look for a company with a big inventory of in-house listings in all price ranges. If you have selected your new office carefully, the brokerage will have a great deal of referral business, which will be passed on to the sales staff, who will be people-oriented, fair, cooperative, dependable and loyal.

Training

Training is something else to look for in selecting a brokerage for which to work. A new salesperson may get good, indifferent or no training, depending on the company. Firms who are more selective of their salespersons tend to judge their potential and think of them as valuable additions to their staff, to be trained and treated with respect.

Most real estate companies do provide extensive sales training, as well as on the job training, with the broker accompanying new agents to their first appointments. Remember, the broker is responsible for everything a salesperson does, and does not want anyone making costly mistakes—in money and or reputation.

Commissions

More than likely, you will be paid on a commission basis. Commissions are based on a certain percentage of the sales price of a property. The amount is not set by law, and must be decided between the broker (or the agent) and each new agent. You, as a salesperson, will receive your share of the commission from your broker when a transaction for which you are responsible closes. It will be based on the **Commission Split** agreement you have with your broker. Your split will be a certain percentage of the commission that comes to the brokerage from your sales.

Usually, a new agent can count on a 50-50 split at first. That means the broker gets 50% and you get 50% of the commission on any sale you make. For example, if the agreed upon commission split is 50-50, and the commission paid to the brokerage on one of your sales was $6,000, the broker gets $3,000, and you get $3,000.

Commissions are disbursed at the close of escrow, by the escrow agent, according to instructions. The commission paid to your brokerage is probably one-half the total commission paid if there is an agent from another brokerage involved. That is the normal split between a selling broker and listing broker. (Only the brokers are issued funds, which they then disburse to the deserving agent.)

A home sold for $200,000, with a 6% commission paid by the seller. ReMax real estate company was the listing broker, and Grubb and Ellis was the selling broker. Individual agents for each company were on a 50-50 split with their brokers.

How Commission is Paid

$200,000	-	Selling price
x .06	-	6% commission
$12,000		Total commission paid by seller
$12,000	÷ 2 =	$6,000 to each broker
$6,000	÷ 2 =	$3,000 to broker (50-50 split)
		$3,000 to agent

Requirements of a Real Estate Transaction

A real estate transaction usually starts at the time a broker obtains a listing from a property owner. The most common type of listing is an Exclusive Authorization and Right to Sell. As you recall, with this type of listing, the seller must pay a commission no matter who sells the property—even if the owner makes the sale. The agent promises to use due diligence to find a ready, willing and able buyer under the exact terms of the listing contract, and the seller promises to pay a commission when the agent fulfills the contract.

At some point, either the listing agent or an agent from another brokerage will find a buyer and write an offer. There are certain items the agent must consider carefully when preparing the offer to purchase (also known as a deposit receipt or purchase contract). The following list of items that must be included in the offer apply only to the most common aspects of a residential purchase. Commercial, industrial, vacant land, farm or ranch development and other types of properties require different treatment by a real estate agent.

Specifically, offers to purchase residential property must address more than two-dozen important items.

1. Date and place the contract is signed by the buyer

2. Correct name and address of the buyer

3. Form of the buyer's deposit: cash, check, cashier's check, promissory note, money order or other

4. Designee to hold the deposit: broker, seller or escrow

5. Purchase price of the property

6. Terms under which the property will be purchased: all cash, refinance, loan assumption or taking title "subject to" the existing loan. Do any of the existing loans contain acceleration clauses or prepayment penalties? If so, has the buyer approved the terms?

7. Amount of time to be allowed for the seller to consider the buyer's offer to purchase, and to complete the transaction. Is time of the essence?

8. Definite termination date stated in the contract

9. Covenants, Conditions and Restrictions; easements; rights or other conditions of record that affect the property: Are they acceptable to the buyer?

10. Deed of conveyance: Is it to be executed by the seller to contain any exceptions or reservations? Has the buyer approved of this?

11. Are there any stipulations or agreements regarding any tenancies or rights of persons in possession of the property?

12. Roof and electrical wiring inspections: Who pays for inspections and work, and who orders reports?

13. Are there any stipulations or agreements regarding facts a survey would reveal, such as the existence of a common wall, other encroachments or easements?

14. Are there any special or unusual costs or charges to be adjusted through escrow? Who will pay for the title policy, escrow services and other customary charges? Who pays for any unusual charges?

15. Who will select the escrow holder? The parties should reach a mutual agreement on this.

16. Are there any special documents to be drawn in the transaction, and if so, who will prepare them?

17. If prorations are not to be made as of the date escrow closes, what date is to be used?

18. If possession is granted prior to the close of escrow, what type of agreement must be prepared to cover this occupancy and who will prepare it?

19. If structural pest control inspection report and certification are to be furnished, who will pay the cost? Who will pay for any required work? Will multiple reports be required?

20. Are other brokers involved in this transaction? What are their names, addresses and telephone numbers?

21. What is the negotiated sales commission? How and when is it to be paid? If the deposit receipt initially establishes that a commission will be paid, it must contain the commission negotiability statement, which declares that by law all commissions are negotiable. (Business and Professions Code Section 10147.5)

22. Make sure all parties sign the contract. Check for signatures of all buyers, all sellers and the agents.

23. Every purchase contract prepared or signed by a real estate salesperson must be reviewed, initialed and dated by the salesperson's broker within five working days after preparation or signing by the salesperson or before the close of escrow, whichever occurs first. The broker may delegate this responsibility and authority under certain conditions.

24. If the transaction is a residential sale of four-or-fewer units and involves seller-assisted financing, and a licensee is the arranger of such credit, a financing disclosure statement must be prepared and provided to both buyer and seller.

25. A specific written disclosure must be made to prospective buyers of one-to-four dwelling units with facts about the particular piece of property that could materially affect the property's value and desirability.

26. Licensees acting as listing and selling brokers in certain residential real estate transactions must make informational written and oral disclosures concerning who is representing whom.

27. A real estate licensee who acts as the agent for either the buyer or the seller in the sale or transfer of real property, including manufactured housing, must disclose to both parties the form, amount and source of any compensation received or expected to be received from a lender involved in financing related to the transaction.

As soon as possible following the opening of escrow the seller should furnish escrow with the following specifics. (This is usually authorized in the escrow instructions by the seller.)

1. Escrow instructions signed by all of the sellers

2. The latest available tax and assessment bills and any other statements or bills which are to be prorated through escrow

3. Seller's loan payment books and records

4. Seller's fire, liability and other insurance policies, if they are to be assigned to the buyer

5. A beneficiary statement, demand, certificate or offset statement from the holder of any mortgage or trust deed of record on the property; the items that show the amount due on any loan of record; the payment date; the date to which interest is paid; and other important information. Consent to the transfer from lenders of record must be given.

6. Any subordination or other agreement required by the purchase contract, to be approved by the parties through escrow

7. Certificates or releases showing satisfaction of mechanic's liens, security agreements (chattel mortgages), judgments or mortgages which are to be paid off through escrow

8. List of tenants' names and the apartments they occupy, together with the amount of rent paid and unpaid, the dates when rents are due, and—if required—an assignment to the buyer of any unpaid rent, as well as details on advance security deposits, if any

9. Assignment to buyer of all leases affecting the property

10. Letters from the seller to tenants instructing them to pay all subsequent rent to the buyer and reaffirming the conditions of the tenancy, including notice of the transfer of the security deposit, if any, to the buyer

11. The seller's executed and acknowledged deed of conveyance to the buyer or a valid authority to execute the deed of the seller by the seller's attorney-in-fact if the seller is acting through an agent

12. An executed bill of sale covering any personal property to be conveyed to the buyer, together with an inventory of the items for the buyer's approval

13. A security agreement (chattel mortgage) for execution by the buyer covering any personal property included in the purchase price but not paid for by the buyer in cash

14. The deed by which the seller acquired title to the property and the seller's policy of title insurance

15. Any unrecorded instruments affecting the title

16. Any other documents or instruments which the seller is to prepare or deliver

17. Any approvals required for documents the seller is to receive at closing

18. Information required to be disclosed to the buyer under the seller financing disclosure, if necessary

As soon as possible after the opening of escrow, the buyer should furnish the escrow holder with certain documents and information, and should review or inspect personally all of the following items.

1. Review escrow instructions signed by all purchasers.

2. Review the preliminary title report for the subject property to make sure that there are no items of record affecting the property which have not already been approved by the buyer.

3. Review any Conditions, Covenants and Restrictions affecting the property, whether of record or not.

4. Confirm the terms of any mortgages or deeds of trust to be assumed by the buyer or which will remain an encumbrance on the property.

5. Examine any beneficiary statements, fire insurance or liability policies if they are to be assigned to the buyer.

6. Examine offset statements on loans to be assumed, or those under which the buyer is taking title to the property "subject to" existing loan terms; verify the unpaid principal balances owed, the interest rates, dates to which interest is paid and other vital information.

7. Review and approve structural pest control and other reports to be delivered through escrow.

8. Carefully review all new loan documents prior to signing.

9. Compare the terms of the purchase contract, escrow instructions, title report and deed to make sure there are no discrepancies in the transaction documents.

10. If tenancies are involved, review the names, addresses and telephone numbers of tenants; the rent amounts, rent due dates, copies of rent agreements or leases, letters from the seller to the tenants verifying

the terms of occupancy and notifying the tenants of change of ownership, the assignments of any unpaid rent and leases, details on security deposits if any.

11.   Examine the bill of sale and inventory covering the items of personal property to be conveyed to the purchaser.

12.   Review copies of any bills to be prorated in escrow.

13.   Verify all amounts and prorations on the estimated escrow settlement sheet.

14.   Reinspect the property to determine that it is in the same condition as it was when the buyer made the purchase offer. Recheck for any undisclosed items which might affect the use of the property, such as: party walls, access roads to other properties, irrigation canals or ditches, common drives or persons in occupancy or possession of the property, which the county records would not disclose.

15.   Deposit sufficient cash or clear funds to cover any balance owed on the purchase contract plus buyer's closing costs and expenses, and approvals as required.

The parties should always keep copies of any documents and instruments they sign, deliver to or receive from any party in the real estate transaction.

Specific Disclosures Required for a Real Estate Transaction

http://www.stargroup. com/walkthru.html

http://www.norcalrealty. com/review.htm

As the business of buying and selling real estate gets more complex, so do the required disclosures. What used to be a matter of a buyer's or seller's word and honesty is now elevated (or reduced, depending on your point of view) to multiple sworn copies of those same statements, with serious penalties for untruth.

As a real estate agent, you will be required to guide all parties through the minefield of disclosure. The following list of disclosures that must be made during a real estate transaction includes some that have been mentioned in prior chapters in this book—but are important enough to emphasize again.

Real Estate Transfer Disclosure Statement (TDS)

Many facts about a residential property could materially affect its value and desirability. In the Real Estate Transfer Disclosure Statement, the seller reveals any information that would be important to the buyer regarding condition of the property, and states that—to the seller's knowledge—everything pertinent has been disclosed. Here are material facts of interest to a buyer, that must be included in the TDS.

<u>**Required Disclosures**</u>

- Age, condition and any defects or malfunctions of the structural components and/or plumbing, electrical, heating or other mechanical systems
- Easements, common driveways or fences
- Room additions, structural alterations, repairs, replacements or other changes, especially those made without required building permits
- Flooding, drainage or soils problems on, near or in any way affecting the property
- Zoning violations, such as nonconforming uses or insufficient setbacks
- Homeowners' association obligations and deed restrictions or common area problems
- Citations against the property, or lawsuits against the owner or affecting the property
- Location of the property within a known earthquake zone
- Major damage to the property from fire, earthquake or landslide

California law requires that a seller of one-to-four dwellings deliver to prospective buyers a certain written disclosure statement about the condition of the property. This requirement extends to any transfer: by sale, exchange, installment land sale contract, lease with an option to purchase, any other option to purchase, or ground lease coupled with improvements.

<u>**Exempt from the Obligation to Deliver the Statement are Various Transfers such as:**</u>

- A foreclosure sale
- A court-ordered transfer by a fiduciary in the administration of a probate estate or a testamentary trust
- To a spouse or another related person resulting from a judgment of dissolution of marriage or of legal separation or from a property settlement agreement incidental to such a judgment
- From one co-owner to another
- By the state controller for unclaimed property
- Result from the failure to pay taxes
- From or to any governmental entity
- The first sale of a residential property within a subdivision where a copy of a public report is delivered to the purchaser or where such a report is not required

The required disclosure must be made to the prospective buyer as soon as practicable before transfer of title, or in the case of a lease option, sales contract, or ground lease coupled with improvements, before the execution of the contract. Should any disclosure or amended disclosure be delivered after the required date, the buyer/transferee has three days after delivery in person or five days after delivery by deposit in the U.S. mail to terminate the offer or agreement to purchase. A written notice of termination is the instrument that must reach the seller/transferor or the seller's agent for that purpose.

The obligation to prepare and deliver disclosures is imposed on the seller and the seller's agent and any agent acting in cooperation with them. Should more than one real estate agent be involved in the transaction (unless otherwise instructed by the seller), the agent obtaining the offer is required to deliver the disclosures to the prospective buyer.

Delivery to the prospective buyer of a report or an opinion prepared by a licensed engineer, land surveyor, geologist, structural pest control operator, contractor or other expert (with a specific professional license or expertise) may limit the liability of the seller and the real estate agents when making required disclosures. The overall intention is to provide meaningful disclosures about the condition of the property being transferred. A violation of the law does not invalidate a transfer; however, the seller may be liable for any actual damages suffered by the buyer.

For information about the neighborhood or community, a city or county may require use of a Local Option Transfer Disclosure Statement disclosing special local facts.

Mello-Roos Disclosure

http://www.mello-roos.com

The Mello-Roos Community Facilities Act of 1982 authorizes the formation of community facilities districts, the issuance of bonds and the levying of special taxes which will finance designated public facilities and services. Effective July 1, 1993, the seller of a property consisting of one-to-four dwelling units subject to the lien of a Mello-Roos community facilities district must make a good faith effort to obtain from the district a disclosure notice concerning the special tax and give the notice to a prospective buyer. Exempt from this requirement are the various transfers listed earlier for the Transfer Disclosure Statement.

Smoke Detector Statement of Compliance

http://www.realtychek.
com/ncs-mell.htm

Whenever a sale or exchange of a single-family dwelling occurs, the seller must provide the buyer with a written statement representing that the property is in compliance with California law regarding smoke detectors. The state building code mandates that all existing dwelling units must have a smoke detector installed in a central location outside each sleeping area. In a two-story home with bedrooms on both floors, at least two smoke detectors would be required.

New construction, or any additions, alterations or repairs exceeding $1,000 and for which a permit is required, must include a smoke detector installed in each bedroom and also at a point centrally located in a corridor or area outside the bedrooms. This standard applies for the addition of one or more bedrooms, no matter what the cost.

In new home construction, the smoke detector must be hard-wired, with a battery backup. In existing dwellings, the detector may be only battery operated.

Disclosure Regarding Lead-Based Paint Hazards

The Residential Lead-Based Paint Hazard Reduction Act of 1992 (Title X) became effective on September 6, 1996 for owners of property with four or fewer units. This requires that certain conditions be met with regard to disclosures of lead -based paint and lead-based paint hazards in a transaction for a sale or lease of pre-1978 housing (including mobile homes).

The seller, landlord and real estate agent involved in the sale or rental of pre- 1978 housing each have certain obligations under the new law.

http://www.car.org

http://www.nolo.com/
chunkRE/disclosures.html

Seller/Landlord Obligations

- Give buyers/tenants a pamphlet entitled "Protect Your Family From Lead in Your Home".
- Disclose all known lead-based paint and lead-based paint hazards in the dwelling and provide /buyer/tenants with any available reports.
- Include standard warning language as an attachment to the contract or lease.
- Complete and sign statements verifying completion of requirements.
- Retain the signed acknowledgment for 3 years.
- For sale transactions only, sellers must give buyers a 10-day opportunity to test for lead.

Agent Responsibilities

Agents must ensure that:

- Seller/landlords are aware of their obligations.
- Seller/landlords disclose the proper information to buyers and tenants.
- Leases and sales contracts include proper disclosure language and signatures.
- Sellers give buyers the opportunity to conduct an inspection for 10 days or another mutually-agreed upon time period.

Agents must comply with the law if the seller or landlord fail to do so. However, the agent is not responsible if an owner conceals information or fails to disclose information.

Disclosures Regarding State Responsibility Areas

The Department of Forestry and Fire Protection has produced maps identifying rural lands classified as state responsibility areas. In such an area, the state (as opposed to a local or federal agency) has the primary financial responsibility for the prevention and extinguishing of fires. Maps of these state responsibility areas and any changes (including new maps to be produced every five years) are to be provided to assessors in the affected counties.

Should the seller know his or her real property is located in a state responsibility area, or if the property is included on a map given by the department to the county assessor, the seller must disclose the possibility of substantial fire risk in such wild land area and that the land is subject to certain preventative requirements.

With the department's agreement, and by ordinance, a county may assume responsibility for all fires, including those occurring in state responsibility areas. If there is such an ordinance, the seller of property located in the area must disclose to the buyer that the state is not obligated to provide fire protection services for any building or structure unless such protection is required by a cooperative agreement with a county, city or district.

Delivery of Structural Pest Control Inspection and Certification Reports

The law does not require that a structural pest control inspection be performed on real property prior to transfer. Should an inspection report and certification be required as a condition of transfer or obtaining financing, however, it must be done as soon as possible. Before transfer of title or before executing a real property sales contract, the selling agent must deliver to the buyer a copy of the report. There must also be written certification attesting to the presence or absence of wood-destroying termites in the visible and accessible areas of the property. Such an inspection report and written certification must be prepared and issued by a registered structural pest-control company.

Upon request from the party ordering such a report, the company issuing same must divide it into two categories: one part to identify the portions of the property where existing damage, infection or infestation are noted; and the other to point out areas that may have impending damage, infection or infestation. Generally, there is more than one real estate agent in the transaction, the agent who obtained the offer is responsible for delivering the report unless the seller has given written directions regarding delivery to another agent involved in the transaction. Delivery of the required documents may be in person or by mail to the buyer. The real estate agent responsible for delivery must retain for three years a complete record of the actions taken to effect delivery.

Disclosure of Geological Hazards and Special Studies Zones

Geologists describe the surface of the earth as always changing. Some of these geological changes are relatively unimportant—not requiring a disclosure. Other changes are apparent by casual inspection—of a nature that a potential buyer should be able to judge the impact of the existing geological condition on the intended property's use.

In some cases, disclosure of a geological condition must be made. This is true of potential hazards from earthquakes, flooding, landslides, erosion and expansive soils. One condition requiring such disclosure is "fault creep," caused by stress and/or earthquake shaking.

Geology in the context of the required disclosures refers to the type of soil and how that soil will respond to earthquakes. Soft sediments tend to amplify shaking, whereas bedrock soils tend to lessen the shaking. Generally, the closer in location to the fault, the more intense the shaking will be. However, soil types and conditions may be more important than distance from the epicenter.

The state geologist is in the process of identifying areas of the state susceptible to "fault creep," to be shown on maps prepared by the State Division of Mines and Geology. These maps also identify known historic landslides. The seller or the seller's agent and any agent acting in cooperation with such agent may usually rely on the identification of the special studies zones by the state geologist for disclosure purposes.

In some instances, additional investigation may be required. Construction on real property of any structure for human occupancy may be subject to the findings and recommendations of a geologic report prepared by a geologist or soils engineer registered in or licensed by the state of California.

A seller of real property situated in a special studies zone, or the agent of the seller and any agent acting in cooperation with such agent, must disclose to the buyer that the property is or may be situated in such a zone as designated under the Alquist-Priolo Special Studies Zones Act. This disclosure must be made on either the Real Estate Transfer Disclosure Statement, the Local Option Real Estate Transfer Disclosure Statement or in the purchase agreement.

Excluded from Requirements of the Special Studies Zones Act:

- Structures in existence prior to May 4, 1975
- Single family wood-frame or steel-frame dwellings for which geologic reports have been approved, to be built in subdivisions authorized by the Subdivision Map Act
- Single family wood-frame or steel dwellings not over two stories, provided the dwelling is not part of a development of four or more dwellings (includes mobile homes over eight-feet wide)
- Conversions of existing apartments into condominiums, except it must be disclosed that the property is located within a delineated special-studies zone
- Alterations under 50% of the value of the structure

The cities of Berkeley or Oakland may apply to the state geologist for an exemption regarding any structure within their jurisdiction which was damaged by the fires between October 20th and October 23rd, 1991. Granting such an exemption does not relieve a seller of real property or the seller's agent of the obligation to disclose to a prospective purchaser that the property is located within a special studies zone.

In addition, under the California Legislature's authorization, the Seismic Safety Commission developed a *Homeowner's Guide to Earthquake Safety* for distribution to real estate licensees and the general public. The guide includes information on geologic and seismic hazards for all areas, explanations of related structural and nonstructural hazards, and recommendations for mitigating the hazards of an earthquake. The guide states that safety or damage prevention cannot be guaranteed with respect to a major earthquake and that only precautions such as retrofitting can be undertaken to reduce the risk of various types of damage.

Should a buyer of real property receive a copy of the Homeowner's Guide, neither the seller nor the agent are required to provide additional information regarding geologic and seismic hazards. Sellers and real estate agents must disclose that the property is in a special studies zone, however, and that there are known hazards affecting the real property being transferred.

Delivery of the Homeowner's Guide to Earthquake Safety is Required in the following Transactions:

- Transfer of any real property with a residential dwelling built prior to January 1, 1960 and consisting of one-to-four units any of which are of conventional light-frame construction
- Transfer of any masonry building with wood-frame floors or roofs built before January 1, 1975

In a transfer subject to the first item above, the following structural deficiencies and any corrective measures taken that are within the transferor's actual knowledge, are to be disclosed to prospective buyers.

Certain exemptions apply to the obligation to deliver the booklet when transferring either a dwelling of one-to-four units or a reinforced masonry building. These exemptions are essentially the same as those that apply to delivery of the Real Estate Transfer Disclosure Statement described earlier in this section.

The buyer and/or agent may be responsible for making further inquiries of appropriate governmental agencies. The obligation of the buyer and/or agent to make further inquiry does not eliminate the duty of the seller's agent to make a diligent inquiry to identify the location of the real property in relationship to a defined special studies zone— and to determine whether the property is subject to any local ordinance regarding geological and soils conditions. Full and complete disclosure is required of all material facts regarding a special studies zone, local ordinances or known structural deficiencies affecting the property.

Natural Hazard Disclosure Statement

California took an important step to standardize natural hazard disclosure requirements in real property transactions with the passage of the Natural Hazard Disclosure Law (AB1195) in 1998. This state law requires all sellers and their real estate agents to determine and disclose to prospective purchasers if a parcel is in certain officially mapped natural hazard zones (geologic, flood and fire). Sellers and real estate agents must consult information sources to determine whether the property in question is in one of the mapped hazard zones and advise the buyer accordingly.

The new law requires six specific disclosures, but does not lessen the basic disclosure obligation a seller or agent has in telling prospective buyers of any other hazards of which they have actual knowledge.

Four of the six disclosures in the Natural Hazard Disclosure Statement (NHD) are already required by law. Those four deal with whether the property is located in an earthquake fault zone, a seismic hazard zone, a flood hazard area or a state-responsibility fire area. The two new disclosures inform whether the property is located in an area subject to flooding in a dam failure or a very high fire hazard severity zone.

The disclosure must be made as soon as practicable before the transfer of title, unless the purchase contract provides for an earlier deadline. It is in the seller's and listing agent's interest to disclose early because the buyer can rescind the purchase contract during a certain period after getting the information. The rescission period is three days if the disclosures are hand-delivered or five days if the disclosures are sent by mail.

Disclosures may be made on a Natural Hazard Disclosure Statement (NHDS) or the Transfer Disclosure Statement.

Secured Water Heater Law

Water heaters are the cause of many common problems in an earthquake. If they are not secured, they can fall and break gas or electrical lines, cause a fire as well as extensive water damage.

The seller of any residential property must certify, in writing, to the buyer that all water heaters have been braced, anchored or strapped in accordance with local requirements to resist falling in an earthquake. A recommended disclosure form is included in *The Homeowner's Guide to Earthquake Safety.*

Disclosure of Ordnance Location

Federal and state agencies have identified certain areas once used for military training and which may contain live ammunition as part of the ordnance—or military supplies—from past activity. A seller of residential property located within one mile of such a hazard must give the buyer written notice as soon as practicable before transfer of title. This obligation depends upon the seller having actual knowledge of the hazard.

Environmental Hazard Disclosures

Numerous federal, state and local laws have been enacted to address the problems created by environmental hazards. Responsible parties, or persons deemed responsible, for the improper disposal of hazardous waste and owners of contaminated property may be held liable for contamination cleanup.

Several disclosure laws relating to the transfer of land affected by hazardous waste contamination have also been enacted. The California Real Estate Transfer Disclosure Statement now requires sellers to disclose whether they are aware of the presence of hazardous substances, materials or products including—but not limited to—asbestos, formaldehyde, radon gas, lead-based paint, fuel or chemical storage tanks, contaminated soil, water, or mold.

Any owner of nonresidential property who knows or suspects that there has been a release of a hazardous substance or that it may occur on or beneath the property must notify a buyer, lessee or renter of that condition prior to the sale, lease, or rental of that property. Failure to give written notice may subject the owner to actual damages and/or civil penalties.

Under Proposition 65, certain businesses may not knowingly and intentionally expose any individual to a cancer-causing chemical or reproductive toxin without first giving clear, reasonable warning to such individuals. Recently, the law has also imposed extensive asbestos disclosure requirements on owners of commercial buildings constructed prior to January 1, 1979.

The Department of Real Estate and Office of Environmental Health Hazard Assessment have developed a booklet to help educate and inform consumers about environmental hazards that may affect real property. The booklet identifies common environmental hazards, describes the risks involved with each, discusses mitigation techniques and provides lists of publications and sources from which consumers can obtain more detailed information.

Hazards Discussed in the Environmental Hazard Booklet

- Asbestos
- Radon
- Lead
- Formaldehyde

Once the booklet is provided to a prospective buyer of real property, neither the seller nor a real estate agent involved in the sale has a duty to provide further information on such hazards. If the seller or agent has actual knowledge of environmental hazards on or affecting the subject property, that information must be disclosed.

Energy Conservation Retrofit and Thermal Insulation Disclosure

State law prescribes a minimum energy conservation standard for all new construction, without which a building permit may not be issued. Local governments also have ordinances that impose additional energy conservation measures on new and/or existing homes. Some local ordinances impose energy retrofitting as a condition of selling an existing home. The requirements of the various ordinances, as well as who is responsible for compliance, may vary among local jurisdictions. The existence and basic requirements of local energy ordinances should be disclosed to a prospective buyer by the seller and/or the seller's agent and any agent cooperating in the deal.

Federal law requires a "new home" seller to disclose in every sales contract the type, thickness and R-value of the insulation which has been or will be installed in each part of the house, including the ceiling and interior and exterior walls. This law also applies to developers of "new home" subdivisions.

Special Flood Hazard Area Disclosure and Responsibilities of the Federal Emergency Management Agency (FEMA)

Flood Hazard Boundary Maps identify the general flood hazards within a community. They are also used in flood plain management and for flood insurance purposes. These maps, developed by the Federal Emergency Management Agency (FEMA) in conjunction with communities participating in the National Flood Insurance Program (NFIP) show areas within 100-year flood boundary, termed "special flood zone areas." Also identified are areas between 100 and 500-year levels termed "areas of moderate flood hazards" and the remaining areas above the 500-year level termed "areas of minimal risk."

A seller of property located in a special flood hazard area, or the seller's agent and/or any agent cooperating in the deal, must disclose that fact to the buyer and that federal law requires flood insurance as a condition of obtaining financing on most structures located in a special flood hazard area. Since the cost and extent of flood insurance coverage may vary, the buyer should contact an insurance carrier or the intended lender for further information.

Local Requirements Resulting from City and County Ordinances

Residential properties in cities and counties throughout California are typically subject to specific local ordinances on occupancy, zoning and use, building code compliance, fire, health and safety code regulations and land subdivision descriptions. The various requirements for compliance as well as who and what is affected thereby should be disclosed to the prospective buyer of the property by the seller or the seller's agent and any agent acting in cooperation with such agent.

Foreign Investment in Real Property Tax Act

Federal law requires that a buyer of real property must withhold and send to the Internal Revenue Service (IRS) 10% of the gross sales price if the seller of the real property is a foreign person.

Primary Grounds for Exemption from this Requirement are:

- Seller's nonforeign affidavit and U.S. taxpayer I.D. number
- A qualifying statement obtained through the IRS saying arrangements have been made for the collection of or exemption from the tax
- Sales price does not exceed $300,000
- Buyer intends to reside on the property

Because of the number of exemptions and other requirements relating to this law, it is recommended that the IRS be consulted for more detailed information. Sellers and buyers and the real estate agents involved who desire further advice should consult an attorney, CPA or other qualified tax advisor.

Notice and Disclosure to Buyer of State Tax Withholding on Disposition of California Real Property

In certain California real estate sale transactions, the buyer must withhold $3\,^{1/3}\%$ of the total sale price as state income tax and deliver the sum withheld to the state Franchise Tax Board. The escrow holder, in applicable transactions, is required by law to notify the buyer of this responsibility.

A buyer's failure to withhold and deliver the required sum may result in penalties. Should the escrow holder fail to notify the buyer, penalties may be levied against the escrow holder.

Transactions Subject to the Law*

- The seller shows an out-of-state address, or sale proceeds are to be disbursed to the seller's financial intermediary
- The sales price exceeds $100,000
- The seller does not certify that he or she is a California resident, or that the property being conveyed is his or her personal residence

*For further information, contact the Franchise Tax Board

Furnishing Controlling Documents and a Financial Statement

The owner (other than a subdivider) of a separate legal share in a common interest development (community apartment project, condominium project, planned development or stock cooperative) must provide a prospective buyer with the following:

Required Disclosures:

- A copy of the governing documents of the development
- Should there be an age restriction not consistent with the law, a statement that the age restriction is only enforceable to the extent permitted by law; and applicable provisions of the law
- A copy of the homeowners association's most recent financial statement
- A written statement from the association specifying the amount of current regular and special assessments as well as any unpaid assessment, late charges, interest and costs of collection which are or may become a lien against the property
- Information on any approved change in the assessments or fees not yet due and payable as of the disclosure date

---

Notice Regarding the Advisability of Title Insurance

In an escrow for a sale (or exchange) of real property where no title insurance is to be issued, the buyer (or both parties to an exchange) must receive and sign the following notice as a separate document in the escrow:

> **Important:** In a purchase or exchange of real property, it may be advisable to obtain title insurance in connection with the close of escrow where there may be prior recorded liens and encumbrances which affect your interest in the property being acquired. A new policy of title insurance should be obtained in order to ensure your interest in the property that you are acquiring.

While the law does not expressly assign the duty, it is reasonable to assume that the escrow holder is obligated to deliver the notice. A real estate agent conducting an escrow also would be responsible for delivering the notice.

Professionalism and Ethics

Staying informed is probably the most important task left to the real estate agent. Those who make continuing efforts to learn and stay current on the real estate industry will be the ones to successfully compete in the future.

One of the most critical responsibilities imposed on real estate licensees is the duty of full disclosure. Your broker will provide you with the proper forms, but it is your responsibility to make sure you have complied with the law for each disclosure required. Most of the required disclosures will be set forth in the deposit receipt, however, and it is your job to explain each one to your clients and customers.

http://www.leginfo.ca.gov
(California Bills and Statutes)

Real estate agents must be prepared to meet the duties and obligations required by law. If they do not comply, they may be subject to civil, criminal and/or Department of Real Estate action and penalties. All around the country, courts and legislatures are continuing to hold real estate agents accountable for their activities. Increasingly, agents must know what and how to disclose—as well as when, where, why, by and to whom. The uninformed real estate agent is highly vulnerable to court action in our consumer-oriented society.

The Real Estate Commissioner is empowered to adopt regulations to enforce the Real Estate Law. Duly adopted regulations become part of the California Code of Regulations and, in effect, have the force and authority of the law itself. Real Estate Law is found in the Business and Professions Code.

Therefore, all licensees and prospective licensees should be thoroughly familiar with the Real Estate Commissioner's regulations. They should be considered in conjunction with the law, as they specifically outline procedure directed and authorized by the statutes. The following is a partial listing of "Regulations of the Commissioner" of the sections that are of utmost importance to those who practice real estate. Also included is the "Commissioner's Code of Ethics and Professional Conduct" and the "Code of Ethics and Standards of Practice" of the National Association of Realtors (NAR).

Regulations of the Commissioner (articles 10 and 11)

Article 10. Discrimination and Panic Selling

2780. Discriminatory Conduct as the Basis for Disciplinary Action.
Prohibited discriminatory conduct by a real estate licensee based upon race, color, sex, religion, ancestry, physical handicap, marital status or national origin includes, but is not limited to, the following:

(a) Refusing to negotiate for the sale, rental or financing of the purchase of real property or otherwise making unavailable or denying real property to any person because of such person's race, color, sex, religion, ancestry, physical handicap, marital status or national origin.

(b) Refusing or failing to show, rent, sell or finance the purchase of real property to any person or refusing or failing to provide or volunteer information to any person about real property, or channeling or steering any person away from real property, because of that person's race, color, sex, religion, ancestry, physical handicap, marital status or national origin or because of the racial, religious, or ethnic composition of any occupants of the area in which the real property is located.

It shall not constitute discrimination under this subdivision for a real estate licensee to refuse or fail to show, rent, sell or finance the purchase of real property to any person having a physical handicap because of the presence of hazardous conditions or architectural barriers to the physically handicapped which conform to applicable state or local building codes and regulations.

(c) Discriminating because of race, color, sex, religion, ancestry, physical handicap, marital status or national origin against any person in the sale or purchase or negotiation or solicitation of the sale or purchase or the collection of payment or the performance of services in connection with contracts for the sale of real property or in connection with loans secured directly or collaterally by liens on real property or on a business opportunity.

Prohibited discriminatory conduct by a real estate licensee under this subdivision does not include acts based on a person's marital status which are reasonably taken in recognition of the community property laws of this state as to the acquiring, financing, holding or transferring of real property.

(d) Discriminating because of race, color, sex, religion, ancestry, physical handicap, marital status or national origin against any person in the terms, conditions or privileges of sale, rental or financing of the purchase of real property.

This subdivision does not prohibit the sale price, rent or terms of a housing accommodation containing facilities for the physically

Regulations of the Commissioner (articles 10 and 11)
(continued)

handicapped to differ reasonably from a housing accommodation not containing such facilities.

(e) Discriminating because of race, color, sex, religion, ancestry, physical handicap, marital status or national origin against any person in providing services or facilities in connection with the sale, rental or financing of the purchase of real property, including but not limited to: processing applications differently, referring prospects to other licensees because of the prospects' race, color, sex, religion, ancestry, physical handicap, marital status or national origin, using with discriminatory intent or effect, codes or other means of identifying minority prospects, or assigning real estate licensees on the basis of a prospective client's race, color, sex, religion, ancestry, physical handicap, marital status or national origin.

Prohibited discriminatory conduct by a real estate licensee under this subdivision does not include acts based on a person's marital status which are reasonably taken in recognition of the community property laws of this state as to the acquiring, financing, holding or transferring of real property.

(f) Representing to any person because of his or her race, color, sex, religion, ancestry, physical handicap, marital status or national origin that real property is not available for inspection, sale or rental when such real property is in fact available.

(g) Processing an application more slowly or otherwise acting to delay, hinder or avoid the sale, rental or financing of the purchase of real property on account of the race, color, sex, religion, ancestry, physical handicap, marital status or national origin of a potential owner or occupant.

(h) Making any effort to encourage discrimination against persons because of their race, color, sex, religion, ancestry, physical handicap, marital status or national origin in the showing, sale, lease or financing of the purchase of real property.

(i) Refusing or failing to cooperate with or refusing or failing to assist another real estate licensee in negotiating the sale, rental or financing of the purchase of real property because of the race, color, sex, religion, ancestry, physical handicap, marital status or national origin of any prospective purchaser or tenant.

(j) Making any effort to obstruct, retard or discourage the purchase, lease or financing of the purchase of real property by persons whose race, color, sex, religion, ancestry, physical handicap, marital status or national origin differs from that of the majority of persons presently residing in a structural improvement to real property or in an area in which the real property is located.

Regulations of the Commissioner (articles 10 and 11)

(continued)

REGULATIONS

(k) Performing any acts, making any notation, asking any questions or making or circulating any written or oral statement which when taken in context, expresses or implies a limitation, preference or discrimination based upon race, color, sex, religion, ancestry, physical handicap, marital status or national origin; provided, however, that nothing herein shall limit the administering of forms or the making of a notation required by a federal, state or local agency for data collection or civil rights enforcement purposes; or in the case of a physically handicapped person, making notation, asking questions or circulating any written or oral statement in order to serve the needs of such a person.

(l) Making any effort to coerce, intimidate, threaten or interfere with any person in the exercise or enjoyment of, or on account of such person's having exercised or enjoyed, or on account of such person's having aided or encouraged any other person in the exercise or enjoyment of any right granted or protected by a federal or state law, including but not limited to: assisting in any effort to coerce any person because of his or her race, color, sex, religion, ancestry, physical handicap, marital status or national origin to move from, or to not move into, a particular area; punishing or penalizing real estate licensees for their refusal to discriminate in the sale or rental of housing because of the race, color, sex, religion, ancestry, physical handicap, marital status or national origin of a prospective purchaser or lessee; or evicting or taking other retaliatory action against any person for having filed a fair housing complaint or for having undertaken other lawful efforts to promote fair housing.

(m) Soliciting of sales, rentals or listings of real estate from any person, but not from another person within the same area because of differences in the race, color, sex, religion, ancestry, physical handicap, marital status or national origin of such persons.

(n) Discriminating because of race, color, sex, religion, ancestry, physical handicap, marital status or national origin in informing persons of the existence of waiting lists or other procedures with respect to the future availability of real property for purchase or lease.

(o) Making any effort to discourage or prevent the rental, sale or financing of the purchase of real property because of the presence or absence of occupants of a particular race, color, sex, religion, ancestry, physical handicap, marital status or national origin, or on the basis of the future presence or absence of a particular race, color, sex, religion, ancestry, physical handicap, marital status or national origin, whether actual, alleged or implied.

(p) Making any effort to discourage or prevent any person from renting, purchasing or financing the purchase of real property through any representations of actual or alleged community opposition based upon race, color, sex, religion, ancestry, physical handicap, marital status or national origin.

Regulations of the Commissioner (articles 10 and 11)
(continued)

(q) Providing information or advice to any person concerning the desirability of particular real property or a particular residential area(s) which is different from information or advice given to any other person with respect to the same property or area because of differences in the race, color, sex, religion, ancestry, physical handicap, marital status or national origin of such persons.

This subdivision does not limit the giving of information or advice to physically handicapped persons for the purpose of calling to the attention of such persons the existence or absence of housing accommodation services or housing accommodations for the physically handicapped.

(r) Refusing to accept a rental or sales listing or application for financing of the purchase of real property because of the owner's race, color, sex, religion, ancestry, physical handicap, marital status or national origin or because of the race, color, sex, religion, ancestry, physical handicap, marital status or national origin of any of the occupants in the area in which the real property is located.

(s) Entering into an agreement, or carrying out any instructions of another, explicit or understood, not to show, lease, sell or finance the purchase of real property because of race, color, sex, religion, ancestry, physical handicap, marital status or national origin.

(t) Making, printing or publishing, or causing to be made, printed or published, any notice, statement or advertisement concerning the sale, rental or financing of the purchase of real property that indicates any preference, limitation or discrimination because of race, color, sex, religion, ancestry, physical handicap, marital status or national origin, or any intention to make such preference, limitation or discrimination.

This subdivision does not prohibit advertising directed to physically handicapped persons for the purpose of calling to the attention of such persons the existence or absence of housing accommodation services or housing accommodations for the physically handicapped.

(u) Using any words, phrases, sentences, descriptions or visual aids in any notice, statement or advertisement describing real property or the area in which real property is located which indicates any preference, limitation or discrimination because of race, color, sex, religion, ancestry, physical handicap, marital status or national origin.

This subdivision does not prohibit advertising directed to physically handicapped persons for the purpose of calling to the attention of such persons the existence or absence of housing accommodation services or housing accommodations for the physically handicapped.

(v) Selectively using, placing or designing any notice, statement or advertisement having to do with the sale, rental or financing of the

Regulations of the Commissioner (articles 10 and 11)
(continued)

purchase of real property in such a manner as to cause or increase discrimination by restricting or enhancing the exposure or appeal to persons of a particular race, color, sex, ancestry, physical handicap, marital status or national origin.

This subdivision does not limit in any way the use of an affirmative marketing program designed to attract persons of a particular race, color, sex, religion, ancestry, physical handicap, marital status or national origin who would not otherwise be attracted to the real property or to the area.

(w) Quoting or charging a price, rent or cleaning or security deposit for a particular real property to any person which is different from the price, rent or security deposit quoted or charged to any other person because of differences in the race, color, sex, religion, ancestry, physical handicap, marital status or national origin of such persons.

This subdivision does not prohibit the quoting or charging of a price, rent or cleaning or security deposit for a housing accommodation containing facilities for the physically handicapped to differ reasonably from a housing accommodation not containing such facilities.

(x) Discriminating against any person because of race, color, sex, religion, ancestry, physical handicap, marital status or national origin in performing any acts in connection with the making of any determination of financial ability or in the processing of any application for the financing or refinancing of real property.

Nothing herein shall limit the administering of forms or the making of a notation required by a federal, state or local agency for data collection or civil rights enforcement purposes. In any evaluation or determination as to whether, and under what terms and conditions, a particular lender or lenders would be likely to grant a loan, licensees shall proceed as though the lender or lenders are in compliance with Sections 35800 through 35833 of the California Health and Safety Code (The Housing Financial Discrimination Act of 1977).

Prohibited discriminatory conduct by a real estate licensee under this subdivision does not include acts based on a person's marital status which are reasonably taken in recognition of the community property laws of this state as to the acquiring, financing, holding or transferring of real property.

(y) Advising a person of the price or value of real property on the basis of factors related to the race, color, sex, religion, ancestry, physical handicap, marital status or national origin of residents of an area or of residents or potential residents of the area in which the property is located.

Regulations of the Commissioner (articles 10 and 11)
(continued)

(z) Discriminating in the treatment of, or services provided to, occupants of any real property in the course of providing management services for the real property because of the race, color, sex, religion, ancestry, physical handicap, marital status or national origin of said occupants.

This subdivision does not prohibit differing treatment or services to a physically handicapped person because of the physical handicap in the course of providing management services for a housing accommodation.

(aa) Discriminating against the owners or occupants of real property because of the race, color, sex, religion, ancestry, physical, handicap, marital status or national origin of their guests, visitors or invitees.

(bb) Making any effort to instruct or encourage, expressly or impliedly, by either words or acts, licensees or their employees or other agents to engage in any discriminatory act in violation of a federal or state fair housing law.

(cc) Establishing or implementing rules that have the effect of limiting the opportunity for any person because of his or her race, color, sex, religion, ancestry, physical handicap, marital status or national origin to secure real property through a multiple listing or other real estate service.

(dd) Assisting or aiding in any way, any person in the sale, rental or financing of the purchase of real property where there are reasonable grounds to believe that such person intends to discriminate because of race, color, sex, religion, ancestry, physical handicap, marital status or national origin.

2781. Panic Selling as the Basis for Disciplinary Action.
Prohibited discriminatory conduct includes, but is not limited to, soliciting sales or rental listings, making written or oral statements creating fear or alarm, transmitting written or oral warnings or threats, or acting in any other manner so as to induce or attempt to induce the sale or lease of real property through any representation, express or implied, regarding the present or prospective entry of one or more persons of another race, color, sex, religion, ancestry, marital status or national origin into an area or neighborhood.

2782. Duty to Supervise.
A broker licensee shall take reasonable steps to become aware of and to be familiar with and to familiarize his or her salespersons with the requirements of federal and state laws and regulations relating to the prohibition of discrimination in the sale, rental or financing of the purchase of real property. Such laws and regulations include but are not limited to the current provisions and any amendments thereto of:

Regulations of the Commissioner (articles 10 and 11)
(continued)

(a) Sections 12900 through 12996 of the California Government Code.

(b) Sections 51 and 52 of the California Civil Code (Unruh Civil Rights Act).

(c) Title VIII and IX of the United States Civil Rights Act of 1968 (Fair Housing).

(d) Sections 35800 through 35833 of the California Health and Safety Code (The Housing Financial Discrimination Act of 1977).

(e) Sections 54 through 55.1 of the Civil Code (Blind and Other Physically Disabled Persons).

Article 11. Code of Ethics and Professional Conduct

2785. Professional Conduct.
In order to enhance the professionalism of the California real estate industry, and maximize protection for members of the public dealing with real estate licensees, whatever their area of practice, the following standards of professional conduct and business practices are adopted.

(a) Unlawful Conduct in Sale, Lease and Exchange Transactions. Licensees when performing acts within the meaning of Section 10131(a) of the Business and Professions Code shall not engage in conduct which would subject the licensee to adverse action, penalty or discipline under Sections 10176 and 10177 of the Business and Professions Code including, but not limited to, the following acts and omissions:

(1) Knowingly making a substantial misrepresentation of the likely value of real property to:

(A) Its owner either for the purpose of securing a listing or for the purpose of acquiring an interest in the property for the licensee's own account.

(B) A prospective buyer for the purpose of inducing the buyer to make an offer to purchase the real property.

(2) Representing to an owner of real property when seeking a listing that the licensee has obtained a bona fide written offer to purchase the property, unless at the time of the representation the licensee has possession of a bona fide written offer to purchase.

(3) Stating or implying to an owner of real property during listing negotiations that the licensee is precluded by law, by regulation, or by the rules of any organization, other than the broker firm seeking

Regulations of the Commissioner (articles 10 and 11)
(continued)

the listing, from charging less than the commission or fee quoted to the owner by the licensee.

(4) Knowingly making substantial misrepresentations regarding the licensee's relationship with an individual broker, corporate broker, or franchised brokerage company or that entity's/person's responsibility for the licensee's activities.

(5) Knowingly underestimating the probable closing costs in a communication to the prospective buyer or seller of real property in order to induce that person to make or to accept an offer to purchase the property.

(6) Knowingly making a false or misleading representation to the seller of real property as to the form, amount and/or treatment of a deposit toward the purchase of the property made by an offeror.

(7) Knowingly making a false or misleading representation to a seller of real property, who has agreed to finance all or part of a purchase price by carrying back a loan, about a buyer's ability to repay the loan in accordance with its terms and conditions.

(8) Making an addition to or modification of the terms of an instrument previously signed or initialed by a party to a transaction without the knowledge and consent of the party.

(9) A representation made as a principal or agent to a prospective purchaser of a promissory note secured by real property about the market value of the securing property without a reasonable basis for believing the truth and accuracy of the representation.

(10) Knowingly making a false or misleading representation or representing, without a reasonable basis for believing its truth, the nature and/or condition of the interior or exterior features of a property when soliciting an offer.

(11) Knowingly making a false or misleading representation or representing, without a reasonable basis for believing its truth, the size of a parcel, square footage of improvements or the location of the boundary lines of real property being offered for sale, lease or exchange.

(12) Knowingly making a false or misleading representation or representing to a prospective buyer or lessee of real property, without a reasonable basis to believe its truth, that the property can be used for certain purposes with the intent of inducing the prospective buyer or lessee to acquire an interest in the real property.

Regulations of the Commissioner (articles 10 and 11)
(continued)

(13) When acting in the capacity of an agent in a transaction for the sale, lease or exchange of real property, failing to disclose to a prospective purchaser or lessee facts known to the licensee materially affecting the value or desirability of the property, when the licensee has reason to believe that such facts are not known to nor readily observable by a prospective purchaser or lessee.

(14) Willfully failing, when acting as a listing agent, to present or cause to be presented to the owner of the property any written offer to purchase received prior to the closing of a sale, unless expressly instructed by the owner not to present such an offer, or unless the offer is patently frivolous.

(15) When acting as the listing agent, presenting competing written offers to purchase real property to the owner in such a manner as to induce the owner to accept the offer which will provide the greatest compensation to the listing broker without regard to the benefits, advantages and/or disadvantages to the owner.

(16) Failing to explain to the parties or prospective parties to a real estate transaction for whom the licensee is acting as an agent the meaning and probable significance of a contingency in an offer or contract that the licensee knows or reasonably believes may affect the closing date of the transaction, or the timing of the vacating of the property by the seller or its occupancy by the buyer.

(17) Failing to disclose to the seller of real property in a transaction in which the licensee is an agent for the seller the nature and extent of any direct or indirect interest that the licensee expects to acquire as a result of the sale. The prospective purchase of the property by a person related to the licensee by blood or marriage, purchase by an entity in which the licensee has an ownership interest, or purchase by any other person with whom the licensee occupies a special relationship where there is a reasonable probability that the licensee could be indirectly acquiring an interest in the property shall be disclosed to the seller.

(18) Failing to disclose to the buyer of real property in a transaction in which the licensee is an agent for the buyer the nature and extent of a licensee's direct or indirect ownership interest in such real property. The direct or indirect ownership interest in the property by a person related to the licensee by blood or marriage, by an entity in which the licensee has an ownership interest, or by any other person with whom the licensee occupies a special relationship shall be disclosed to the buyer.

(19) Failing to disclose to a principal for whom the licensee is acting as an agent any significant interest the licensee has in a particular entity when the licensee recommends the use of the services or products of such entity.

Regulations of the Commissioner (articles 10 and 11)
(continued)

(20)   The refunding by a licensee, when acting as an agent for seller, all or part of an offeror's purchase money deposit in a real estate sales transaction after the seller has accepted the offer to purchase, unless the licensee has the express permission of the seller to make the refund.

(b) Unlawful Conduct When Soliciting, Negotiating or Arranging a Loan Secured by Real Property or the Sale of a Promissory Note Secured by Real Property. Licensees when performing acts within the meaning of subdivision (d) or (e) of Section 10131 of the Business and Professions Code shall not violate any of the applicable provisions of subdivision (a), or act in a manner which would subject the licensee to adverse action, penalty or discipline under Sections 10176 and 10177 of the Business and Professions Code including, but not limited to, the following acts and omissions:

(1)   Knowingly misrepresenting to a prospective borrower of a loan to be secured by real property or to an assignor/endorser of a promissory note secured by real property that there is an existing lender willing to make the loan or that there is a purchaser for the note, for the purpose of inducing the borrower or assignor/endorser to utilize the services of the licensee.

(2) (A) Knowingly making a false or misleading representation to a prospective lender or purchaser of a loan secured directly or collaterally by real property about a borrower's ability to repay the loan in accordance with its terms and conditions;

(B) Failing to disclose to a prospective lender or note purchaser information about the prospective borrower's identity, occupation, employment, income and credit data as represented to the broker by the prospective borrower;

(C) Failing to disclose information known to the broker relative to the ability of the borrower to meet his or her potential or existing contractual obligations under the note or contract including information known about the borrower's payment history on an existing note, whether the note is in default or the borrower in bankruptcy.

(3) Knowingly underestimating the probable closing costs in a communication to a prospective borrower or lender of a loan to be secured by a lien on real property for the purpose of inducing the borrower or lender to enter into the loan transaction.

(4) When soliciting a prospective lender to make a loan to be secured by real property, falsely representing or representing without a reasonable basis to believe its truth, the priority of the security, as a lien against the real property securing the loan, i.e., a first, second or third deed of trust.

Regulations of the Commissioner (articles 10 and 11)
(continued)

(5) Knowingly misrepresenting in any transaction that a specific service is free when the licensee knows or has a reasonable basis to know that it is covered by a fee to be charged as part of the transaction.

(6) Knowingly making a false or misleading representation to a lender or assignee/endorsee of a lender of a loan secured directly or collaterally by a lien on real property about the amount and treatment of loan payments, including loan payoffs, and the failure to account to the lender or assignee/endorsee of a lender as to the disposition of such payments.

(7) When acting as a licensee in a transaction for the purpose of obtaining a loan, and in receipt of an "advance fee" from the borrower for this purpose, the failure to account to the borrower for the disposition of the "advance fee".

(8) Knowingly making false or misleading representation about the terms and conditions of a loan to be secured by a lien on real property when soliciting a borrower or negotiating the loan.

(9) Knowingly making a false or misleading representation or representing, without a reasonable basis for believing its truth, where soliciting a lender or negotiating a loan to be secured by a lien on real property about the market value of the securing real property, the nature and/or condition of the interior or exterior features of the securing real property, its size or the square footage of any improvements on the securing real property.

NOTE: The Real Estate Commissioner has issued Suggestions for Professional Conduct in Sale, Lease and Exchange Transactions and Suggestions for Professional Conduct When Negotiating or Arranging Loans Secured by Real Property or Sale of a Promissory Note Secured by Real Property.

The purpose of the Suggestions is to encourage real estate licensees to maintain a high level of ethics and professionalism in their business practices when performing acts for which a real estate license is required.

The Suggestions are not intended as statements of duties imposed by law nor as grounds for disciplinary action by the Department of Real Estate, but as suggestions for elevating the professionalism of real estate licensees.

Copies of the Suggestions may be obtained from the Department of Real Estate.

The following are the Suggestions:

Regulations of the Commissioner (articles 10 and 11)
(continued)

(a) Suggestions for Professional Conduct in Sale, Lease and Exchange Transactions. In order to maintain a high level of ethics and professionalism in their business practices, real estate licensees are encouraged to adhere to the following suggestions in conducting their business activities:

(1) Aspire to give a high level of competent, ethical and quality service to buyers and sellers in real estate transactions.

(2) Stay in close communication with clients or customers to ensure that questions are promptly answered and all significant events or problems in a transaction are conveyed in a timely manner.

(3) Cooperate with the California Department of Real Estate's enforcement of, and report to that Department evident violations of, the Real Estate Law.

(4) Use care in the preparation of any advertisement to present an accurate picture or message to the reader, viewer or listener.

(5) Submit all written offers in a prompt and timely manner.

(6) Keep oneself informed and current on factors affecting the real estate market in which the licensee operates as an agent.

(7) Make a full, open and sincere effort to cooperate with other licensees, unless the principal has instructed the licensee to the contrary.

(8) Attempt to settle disputes with other licensees through mediation or arbitration.

(9) Advertise or claim to be an expert in an area of specialization in real estate brokerage activity, e.g., appraisal, property management, industrial siting, mortgage loan, etc., only if the licensee has had special training, preparation or experience in such area.

(10) Strive to provide equal opportunity for quality housing and a high level of service to all persons regardless of race, color, sex, religion, ancestry, physical handicap, marital status or national origin.

(11) Base opinions of value, whether for the purpose of advertising or promoting real estate brokerage business, upon documented objective data.

(12) Make every attempt to comply with these Suggestions for Professional Conduct and the Code of Ethics of any organized real estate industry group of which the licensee is a member.

Regulations of the Commissioner (articles 10 and 11)
(continued)

(b) Suggestions for Professional Conduct When Negotiating or Arranging Loans Secured by Real Property or Sale of a Promissory Note Secured by Real Property. In order to maintain a high level of ethics and professionalism in their business practices when performing acts within the meaning of subdivisions (d) and (e) of Section 10131 and Sections 10131.1 and 10131.2 of the Business and Professions Code, real estate licensees are encouraged to adhere to the following suggestions, in addition to any applicable provisions of subdivision (a), in conducting their business activities:

(1) Aspire to give a high level of competent, ethical and quality service to borrowers and lenders in loan transactions secured by real estate.

(2) Stay in close communication with borrowers and lenders to ensure that reasonable questions are promptly answered and all significant events or problems in a loan transaction are conveyed in a timely manner.

(3) Keep oneself informed and current on factors affecting the real estate loan market in which the licensee acts as an agent.

(4) Advertise or claim to be an expert in an area of specialization in real estate mortgage loan transactions only if the licensee has had special training, preparation or experience in such area.

(5) Strive to provide equal opportunity for quality mortgage loan services and a high level of service to all borrowers or lenders regardless of race, color, sex, religion, ancestry, physical handicap, marital status or national origin.

(6) Base opinions of value in a loan transaction, whether for the purpose of advertising or promoting real estate mortgage loan brokerage business, on documented objective data.

(7) Respond to reasonable inquiries of a principal as to the status or extent of efforts to negotiate the sale of an existing loan.

(8) Respond to reasonable inquiries of a borrower regarding the net proceeds available from a loan arranged by the licensee.

(9) Make every attempt to comply with the standards of professional conduct and the code of ethics of any organized mortgage loan industry group of which the licensee is a member.

The conduct suggestions set forth in subsections (a) and (b) are not intended as statements of duties imposed by law nor as grounds for disciplinary action by the Department of Real Estate, but as guidelines for elevating the professionalism of real estate licensees.

Code of Ethics and Standards of Practice

Code of Ethics and Standards of Practice
of the
NATIONAL ASSOCIATION OF REALTORS®

Effective January 1, 1995

Where the word REALTORS® is used in this Code and Preamble, it shall be deemed to include REALTOR-ASSOCIATE®s.

While the Code of Ethics establishes obligations that may be higher than those mandated by law, in any instance where the Code of Ethics and the law conflict, the obligations of the law must take precedence.

Preamble...

Under all is the land. Upon its wise utilization and widely allocated ownership depend the survival and growth of free institutions and of our civilization. REALTORS® should recognize that the interests of the nation and its citizens require the highest and best use of the land and the widest distribution of land ownership. They require the creation of adequate housing, the building of functioning cities, the development of productive industries and farms, and the preservation of a healthful environment.

Such interests impose obligations beyond those of ordinary commerce. They impose grave social responsibility and a patriotic duty to which REALTORS® should dedicate themselves, and for which they should be diligent in preparing themselves. REALTORS®, therefore, are zealous to maintain and improve the standards of their calling and share with their fellow REALTORS® a common responsibility for its integrity and honor.

In recognition and appreciation of their obligations to clients, customers, the public, and each other, REALTORS® continuously strive to become and remain informed on issues affecting real estate and, as knowledgeable professionals, they willingly share the fruit of their experience and study with others. They identify and take steps, through enforcement of this Code of Ethics and by assisting appropriate regulatory bodies, to eliminate practices which may damage the public or which might discredit or bring dishonor to the real estate profession.

Realizing that cooperation with other real estate professionals promotes the best interests of those who utilize their services, REALTORS® urge exclusive representation of clients; do not attempt to gain any unfair advantage over their competitors; and they refrain from making unsolicited comments about other practitioners. In instances where their opinion is sought, or where REALTORS® believe that comment is necessary, their opinion is offered in an objective, professional manner, uninfluenced by any personal motivation or potential advantage or gain.

NATIONAL ASSOCIATION
OF REALTORS®
430 North Michigan Avenue
Chicago, Illinois 60611-4087

The term REALTOR® has come to connote competency, fairness, and high integrity resulting from adherence to a lofty ideal of moral conduct in business relations. No inducement of profit and no instruction from clients ever can justify departure from this ideal.

In the interpretation of this obligation, REALTORS® can take no safer guide than that which has been handed down through the centuries, embodied in the Golden Rule, "Whatsoever ye would that others should do to you, do ye even so to them."

Accepting this standard as their own, REALTORS® pledge to observe its spirit in all of their activities and to conduct their business in accordance with the tenets set forth below.

Duties to Clients and Customers

Article 1

When representing a buyer, seller, landlord, tenant, or other client as an agent, REALTORS® pledge themselves to protect and promote the interests of their client. This obligation of absolute fidelity to the client's interests is primary, but it does not relieve REALTORS® of their obligation to treat all parties honestly. When serving a buyer, seller, landlord, tenant or other party in a non-agency capacity, REALTORS® remain obligated to treat all parties honestly. *(Amended 1/93)*

- **Standard of Practice 1-1**
  REALTORS®, when acting as principals in a real estate transaction, remain obligated by the duties imposed by the Code of Ethics. *(Amended 1/93)*

- **Standard of Practice 1-2**
  The duties the Code of Ethics imposes on agents/representatives are applicable to REALTORS® acting as agents, transaction brokers, facilitators, or in any other recognized capacity except for any duty specifically exempted by law or regulation. *(Adopted 1/95)*

- **Standard of Practice 1-3**
  REALTORS®, in attempting to secure a listing, shall not deliberately mislead the owner as to market value.

- **Standard of Practice 1-4**
  REALTORS®, when seeking to become a buyer/tenant representative, shall not mislead buyers or tenants as to savings or other benefits that might be realized through use of the REALTOR®'s services. *(Amended 1/93)*

- **Standard of Practice 1-5**
  REALTORS® may represent the seller/landlord and buyer/tenant in the same transaction only after full disclosure to and with informed consent of both parties. *(Adopted 1/93)*

- **Standard of Practice 1-6**
  REALTORS® shall submit offers and counter-offers objectively and as quickly as possible. *(Adopted 1/93, Amended 1/95)*

- **Standard of Practice 1-7**
  When acting as listing brokers, REALTORS® shall continue to submit to the seller/landlord all offers and counter-offers until closing or execution of a lease unless the seller/landlord has waived this obligation in writing. REALTORS® shall not be obligated to continue to market the property after an offer

Code of Ethics and Standards of Practice *(continued)*

has been accepted by the seller/landlord. REALTORS® shall recommend that sellers/landlords obtain the advice of legal counsel prior to acceptance of a subsequent offer except where the acceptance is contingent on the termination of the pre-existing purchase contract or lease. *(Amended 1/93)*

Standard of Practice 1-8
REALTORS® acting as agents of buyers/tenants shall submit to buyers/tenants all offers and counter-offers until acceptance but have no obligation to continue to show properties to their clients after an offer has been accepted unless otherwise agreed in writing. REALTORS® acting as agents of buyers/tenants shall recommend that buyers/tenants obtain the advice of legal counsel if there is a question as to whether a pre-existing contract has been terminated. *(Adopted 1/93)*

Standard of Practice 1-9
The obligation of REALTORS® to preserve confidential information provided by their clients continues after the termination of the agency relationship. REALTORS® shall not knowingly, during or following the termination of a professional relationship with their client:
1) reveal confidential information of the client; or
2) use confidential information of the client to the disadvantage of the client; or
3) use confidential information of the client for the REALTOR®'s advantage or the advantage of a third party unless the client consents after full disclosure except where the REALTOR® is:
   a) required by court order; or
   b) it is the intention of the client to commit a crime and the information is necessary to prevent the crime; or
   c) necessary to defend the REALTOR® or the REALTOR®'s employees or associates against an accusation of wrongful conduct. *(Adopted 1/93, Amended 1/95)*

Standard of Practice 1-10
REALTORS® shall, consistent with the terms and conditions of their property management agreement, competently manage the property of clients with due regard for the rights, responsibilities, benefits, safety and health of tenants and others lawfully on the premises. *(Adopted 1/95)*

Standard of Practice 1-11
REALTORS® who are employed to maintain or manage a client's property shall exercise due diligence and make reasonable efforts to protect it against reasonably foreseeable contingencies and losses. *(Adopted 1/95)*

Article 2
REALTORS® shall avoid exaggeration, misrepresentation, or concealment of pertinent facts relating to the property or the transaction. REALTORS® shall not, however, be obligated to discover latent defects in the property, to advise on matters outside the scope of their real estate license, or to disclose facts which are confidential under the scope of agency duties owed to their clients. *(Amended 1/93)*

Standard of Practice 2-1
REALTORS® shall be obligated to discover and disclose adverse factors reasonably apparent to someone with expertise in only those areas required by their real estate licensing authority.

Article 2 does not impose upon the REALTOR® the obligation of expertise in other professional or technical disciplines. *(Amended 11/86)*

Standard of Practice 2-2
When entering into listing contracts, REALTORS® must advise sellers/landlords of:
1) the REALTOR®'s general company policies regarding cooperation with subagents, buyer/tenant agents, or both;
2) the fact that buyer/tenant agents, even if compensated by the listing broker, or by the seller/landlord will represent the interests of buyers/tenants; and
3) any potential for the listing broker to act as a disclosed dual agent, e.g. buyer/tenant agent. *(Adopted 1/93)*

Standard of Practice 2-3
When entering into contracts to represent buyers/tenants, REALTORS® must advise potential clients of:
1) the REALTOR®'s general company policies regarding cooperation with other firms; and
2) any potential for the buyer/tenant representative to act as a disclosed dual agent, e.g. listing broker, subagent, landlord's agent, etc. *(Adopted 1/93)*

Standard of Practice 2-4
REALTORS® shall not be parties to the naming of a false consideration in any document, unless it be the naming of an obviously nominal consideration.

Standard of Practice 2-5
Factors defined as "non-material" by law or regulation or which are expressly referenced in law or regulation as not being subject to disclosure are considered not "perinent" for purposes of Article 2. *(Adopted 1/93)*

Article 3
REALTORS® shall cooperate with other brokers except when cooperation is not in the client's best interest. The obligation to cooperate does not include the obligation to share commissions, fees, or to otherwise compensate another broker. *(Amended 1/95)*

Standard of Practice 3-1
REALTORS®, acting as exclusive agents of sellers/landlords, establish the terms and conditions of offers to cooperate. Unless expressly indicated in offers to cooperate, cooperating brokers may not assume that the offer of cooperation includes an offer of compensation. Terms of compensation, if any, shall be ascertained by cooperating brokers before beginning efforts to accept the offer of cooperation. *(Amended 1/94)*

Standard of Practice 3-2
REALTORS® shall, with respect to offers of compensation to another REALTOR®, timely communicate any change of compensation for cooperative services to the other REALTOR® prior to the time such REALTOR® produces an offer to purchase/lease the property. *(Amended 1/94)*

Standard of Practice 3-3
Standard of Practice 3-2 does not preclude the listing broker and cooperating broker from entering into an agreement to change cooperative compensation. *(Adopted 1/94)*

Code of Ethics and Standards of Practice *(continued)*

- **Standard of Practice 3-4**

  REALTORS®, acting as listing brokers; have an affirmative obligation to disclose the existence of dual or variable rate commission arrangements (i.e., listings where one amount of commission is payable if the listing broker's firm is the procuring cause of sale/lease and a different amount of commission is payable if the sale/lease results through the efforts of the seller/landlord or a cooperating broker). The listing broker shall, as soon as practical, disclose the existence of such arrangements to potential cooperating brokers and shall, in response to inquiries from cooperating brokers, disclose the differential that would result in a cooperative transaction or in a sale/lease that results through the efforts of the seller/landlord. If the cooperating broker is a buyer/tenant representative, the buyer/tenant representative must disclose such information to their client. *(Amended 1/94)*

- **Standard of Practice 3-5**

  It is the obligation of subagents to promptly disclose all pertinent facts to the principal's agent prior to as well as after a purchase or lease agreement is executed. *(Amended 1/93)*

- **Standard of Practice 3-6**

  REALTORS® shall disclose the existence of an accepted offer to any broker seeking cooperation. *(Adopted 5/86)*

- **Standard of Practice 3-7**

  When seeking information from another REALTOR® concerning property under a management or listing agreement, REALTORS® shall disclose their REALTOR® status and whether their interest is personal or on behalf of a client and, if on behalf of a client, their representational status. *(Amended 1/95)*

- **Standard of Practice 3-8**

  REALTORS® shall not misrepresent the availability of access to show or inspect a listed property. *(Amended 11/87)*

Article 4

REALTORS® shall not acquire an interest in or buy or present offers from themselves, any member of their immediate families, their firms or any member thereof, or any entities in which they have any ownership interest, any real property without making their true position known to the owner or the owner's agent. In selling property they own, or in which they have any interest, REALTORS® shall reveal their ownership or interest in writing to the purchaser or the purchaser's representative. *(Amended 1/91)*

- **Standard of Practice 4-1**

  For the protection of all parties, the disclosures required by Article 4 shall be in writing and provided by REALTORS® prior to the signing of any contract. *(Adopted 2/86)*

Article 5

REALTORS® shall not undertake to provide professional services concerning a property or its value where they have a present or contemplated interest unless such interest is specifically disclosed to all affected parties.

Article 6

When acting as agents, REALTORS® shall not accept any commission, rebate, or profit on expenditures made for their principal, without the principal's knowledge and consent. *(Amended 1/92)*

- **Standard of Practice 6-1**

  REALTORS® shall not recommend or suggest to a client or a customer the use of services of another organization or business entity in which they have a direct interest without disclosing such interest at the time of the recommendation or suggestion. *(Amended 5/88)*

- **Standard of Practice 6-2**

  When acting as agents or subagents, REALTORS® shall disclose to a client or customer if there is any financial benefit or fee the REALTOR® or the REALTOR®'s firm may receive as a direct result of having recommended real estate products or services (e.g., homeowner's insurance, warranty programs, mortgage financing, title insurance, etc.) other than real estate referral fees. *(Adopted 5/88)*

Article 7

In a transaction, REALTORS® shall not accept compensation from more than one party, even if permitted by law, without disclosure to all parties and the informed consent of the REALTOR®'s client or clients. *(Amended 1/93)*

Article 8

REALTORS® shall keep in a special account in an appropriate financial institution, separated from their own funds, monies coming into their possession in trust for other persons, such as escrows, trust funds, clients' monies, and other like items.

Article 9

REALTORS®, for the protection of all parties, shall assure whenever possible that agreements shall be in writing, and shall be in clear and understandable language expressing the specific terms, conditions, obligations and commitments of the parties. A copy of each agreement shall be furnished to each party upon their signing or initialing. *(Amended 1/95)*

- **Standard of Practice 9-1**

  For the protection of all parties, REALTORS® shall use reasonable care to ensure that documents pertaining to the purchase, sale, or lease of real estate are kept current through the use of written extensions or amendments. *(Amended 1/93)*

Duties to the Public

Article 10

REALTORS® shall not deny equal professional services to any person for reasons of race, color, religion, sex, handicap, familial status, or national origin. REALTORS® shall not be parties to any plan or agreement to discriminate against a person or persons on the basis of race, color, religion, sex, handicap, familial status, or national origin. *(Amended 1/90)*

- **Standard of Practice 10-1**

  REALTORS® shall not volunteer information regarding the racial, religious or ethnic composition of any neighborhood and shall not engage in any activity which may result in panic selling. REALTORS® shall not print, display or circulate any statement or advertisement with respect to the selling or renting of a property that indicates any preference, limitations or discrimination based on race, color, religion, sex, handicap, familial status or national origin. *(Adopted 1/94)*

Code of Ethics and Standards of Practice *(continued)*

Article 11

The services which REALTORS® provide to their clients and customers shall conform to the standards of practice and competence which are reasonably expected in the specific real estate disciplines in which they engage; specifically, residential real estate brokerage, real property management, commercial and industrial real estate brokerage, real estate appraisal, real estate counseling, real estate syndication, real estate auction, and international real estate.

REALTORS® shall not undertake to provide specialized professional services concerning a type of property or service that is outside their field of competence unless they engage the assistance of one who is competent on such types of property or service, or unless the facts are fully disclosed to the client. Any persons engaged to provide such assistance shall be so identified to the client and their contribution to the assignment should be set forth. *(Amended 1/95)*

- ### Standard of Practice 11-1
  The obligations of the Code of Ethics shall be supplemented by and construed in a manner consistent with the Uniform Standards of Professional Appraisal Practice (USPAP) promulgated by the Appraisal Standards Board of the Appraisal Foundation. *(Adopted 1/95)*

- ### Standard of Practice 11-2
  The obligations of the Code of Ethics in respect of real estate disciplines other than appraisal shall be interpreted and applied in accordance with the standards of competence and practice which clients and the public reasonably require to protect their rights and interests considering the complexity of the transaction, the availability of expert assistance, and, where the REALTOR® is an agent or subagent, the obligations of a fiduciary. *(Adopted 1/95)*

Article 12

REALTORS® shall be careful at all times to present a true picture in their advertising and representations to the public. REALTORS® shall also ensure that their professional status (e.g., broker, appraiser, property manager, etc.) or status as REALTORS® is clearly identifiable in any such advertising. *(Amended 1/93)*

- ### Standard of Practice 12-1
  REALTORS® shall not offer a service described as "free of charge" when the rendering of a service is contingent on the obtaining of a benefit such as a listing or commission.

- ### Standard of Practice 12-2
  REALTORS® shall not represent that their services are free or without cost if they expect to receive compensation from any source other than their client. *(Adopted 1/95)*

- ### Standard of Practice 12-3
  The offering of premiums, prizes, merchandise discounts or other inducements to list, sell, purchase, or lease is not, in itself, unethical even if receipt of the benefit is contingent on listing, selling, purchasing, or leasing through the REALTOR® making the offer. However, REALTORS® must exercise care and candor in any such advertising or other public or private representations so that any party interested in receiving or otherwise benefiting from the REALTOR®'s offer will have clear, thorough, advance understanding of all the terms and conditions of the offer. The offering of any inducements to do business is subject to the limitations and restrictions of state law and the ethical obligations established by any applicable Standard of Practice. *(Amended 1/95)*

- ### Standard of Practice 12-4
  REALTORS® shall not offer for sale/lease or advertise property without authority. When acting as listing brokers or as subagents, REALTORS® shall not quote a price different from that agreed upon with the seller/landlord. *(Amended 1/93)*

- ### Standard of Practice 12-5
  REALTORS® shall not advertise nor permit any person employed by or affiliated with them to advertise listed property without disclosing the name of the firm. *(Adopted 11/86)*

- ### Standard of Practice 12-6
  REALTORS®, when advertising unlisted real property for sale/lease in which they have an ownership interest, shall disclose their status as both owners/landlords and as REALTORS® or real estate licensees. *(Amended 1/93)*

- ### Standard of Practice 12-7
  Only REALTORS® as listing brokers, may claim to have "sold" the property, even when the sale resulted through the cooperative efforts of another broker. However, after transactions have closed, listing brokers may not prohibit successful cooperating brokers from advertising their "cooperation," "participation," or "assistance" in the transaction, or from making similar representations.

  Only listing brokers are entitled to use the term "sold" on signs, in advertisements, and in other public representations. *(Amended 1/90)*

Article 13

REALTORS® shall not engage in activities that constitute the unauthorized practice of law and shall recommend that legal counsel be obtained when the interest of any party to the transaction requires it.

Article 14

If charged with unethical practice or asked to present evidence or to cooperate in any other way, in any disciplinary proceeding or investigation, REALTORS® shall place all pertinent facts before the proper tribunals of the Member Board or affiliated institute, society, or council in which membership is held and shall take no action to disrupt or obstruct such processes. *(Amended 1/90)*

- ### Standard of Practice 14-1
  REALTORS® shall not be subject to disciplinary proceedings in more than one Board of REALTORS® or affiliated institute, society or council in which they hold membership with respect to alleged violations of the Code of Ethics relating to the same transaction or event. *(Amended 1/95)*

- ### Standard of Practice 14-2
  REALTORS® shall not make any unauthorized disclosure or dissemination of the allegations, findings, or decision developed in connection with an ethics hearing or appeal or in connection with an arbitration hearing or procedural review. *(Amended 1/92)*

Code of Ethics and Standards of Practice *(continued)*

- **Standard of Practice 14-3**

  REALTORS® shall not obstruct the Board's investigative or disciplinary proceedings by instituting or threatening to institute actions for libel, slander or defamation against any party to a professional standards proceeding or their witnesses. *(Adopted 11/87)*

- **Standard of Practice 14-4**

  REALTORS® shall not intentionally impede the Board's investigative or disciplinary proceedings by filing multiple ethics complaints based on the same event or transaction. *(Adopted 11/88)*

Duties to REALTORS®

Article 15

REALTORS® shall not knowingly or recklessly make false or misleading statements about competitors, their businesses, or their business practices. *(Amended 1/92)*

Article 16

REALTORS® shall not engage in any practice or take any action inconsistent with the agency of other REALTORS®.

- **Standard of Practice 16-1**

  Article 16 is not intended to prohibit aggressive or innovative business practices which are otherwise ethical and does not prohibit disagreements with other REALTORS® involving commission, fees, compensation or other forms of payment or expenses. *(Adopted 1/93, Amended 1/95)*

- **Standard of Practice 16-2**

  Article 16 does not preclude REALTORS® from making general announcements to prospective clients describing their services and the terms of their availability even though some recipients may have entered into agency agreements with another REALTOR®. A general telephone canvass, general mailing or distribution addressed to all prospective clients in a given geographical area or in a given profession, business, club, or organization, or other classification or group is deemed "general" for purposes of this standard.

  Article 16 is intended to recognize as unethical two basic types of solicitations:

  First, telephone or personal solicitations of property owners who have been identified by a real estate sign, multiple listing compilation, or other information service as having exclusively listed their property with another REALTOR®; and

  Second, mail or other forms of written solicitations of prospective clients whose properties are exclusively listed with another REALTOR® when such solicitations are not part of a general mailing but are directed specifically to property owners identified through compilations of current listings, "for sale" or "for rent" signs, or other sources of information required by Article 3 and Multiple Listing Service rules to be made available to other REALTORS® under offers of subagency or cooperation. *(Amended 1/93)*

- **Standard of Practice 16-3**

  Article 16 does not preclude REALTORS® from contacting the client of another broker for the purpose of offering to provide, or entering into a contract to provide, a different type of real estate service unrelated to the type of service currently being provided (e.g., property management as opposed to brokerage). However, information received through a Multiple Listing Service or any other offer of cooperation may not be used to target clients of other REALTORS® to whom such offers to provide services may be made. *(Amended 1/93)*

- **Standard of Practice 16-4**

  REALTORS® shall not solicit a listing which is currently listed exclusively with another broker. However, if the listing broker, when asked by the REALTOR®, refuses to disclose the expiration date and nature of such listing; i.e., an exclusive right to sell, an exclusive agency, open listing, or other form of contractual agreement between the listing broker and the client, the REALTOR® may contact the owner to secure such information and may discuss the terms upon which the REALTOR® might take a future listing or, alternatively, may take a listing to become effective upon expiration of any existing exclusive listing. *(Amended 1/94)*

- **Standard of Practice 16-5**

  REALTORS® shall not solicit buyer/tenant agency agreements from buyers/tenants who are subject to exclusive buyer/tenant agency agreements. However, if a buyer/tenant agent, when asked by a REALTOR®, refuses to disclose the expiration date of the exclusive buyer/tenant agency agreement, the REALTOR® may contact the buyer/tenant to secure such information and may discuss the terms upon which the REALTOR® might enter into a future buyer/tenant agency agreement or, alternatively, may enter into a buyer/tenant agency agreement to become effective upon the expiration of any existing exclusive buyer/tenant agency agreement. *(Adopted 1/94)*

- **Standard of Practice 16-6**

  When REALTORS® are contacted by the client of another REALTOR® regarding the creation of an agency relationship to provide the same type of service, and REALTORS® have not directly or indirectly initiated such discussions, they may discuss the terms upon which they might enter into a future agency agreement or, alternatively, may enter into an agency agreement which becomes effective upon expiration of any existing exclusive agreement. *(Amended 1/93)*

- **Standard of Practice 16-7**

  The fact that a client has retained a REALTOR® as an agent in one or more past transactions does not preclude other REALTORS® from seeking such former client's future business. *(Amended 1/93)*

- **Standard of Practice 16-8**

  The fact that an agency agreement has been entered into with a REALTOR® shall not preclude or inhibit any other REALTOR® from entering into a similar agreement after the expiration of the prior agreement. *(Amended 1/93)*

- **Standard of Practice 16-9**

  REALTORS®, prior to entering into an agency agreement, have an affirmative obligation to make reasonable efforts to determine whether the client is subject to a current, valid exclusive agreement to provide the same type of real estate service. *(Amended 1/93)*

Code of Ethics and Standards of Practice *(continued)*

- **Standard of Practice 16-10**

  REALTORS®, acting as agents of buyers or tenants, shall disclose that relationship to the seller/landlord's agent at first contact and shall provide written confirmation of that disclosure to the seller/landlord's agent not later than execution of a purchase agreement or lease. *(Amended 1/93)*

- **Standard of Practice 16-11**

  On unlisted property, REALTORS® acting as buyer/tenant agents shall disclose that relationship to the seller/landlord at first contact for that client and shall provide written confirmation of such disclosure to the seller/landlord not later than execution of any purchase or lease agreement.

  REALTORS® shall make any request for anticipated compensation from the seller/landlord at first contact. *(Amended 1/93)*

- **Standard of Practice 16-12**

  REALTORS®, acting as agents of sellers/landlords or as subagents of listing brokers, shall disclose that relationship to buyers/tenants as soon as practicable and shall provide written confirmation of such disclosure to buyers/tenants not later than execution of any purchase or lease agreement. *(Amended 1/93)*

- **Standard of Practice 16-13**

  All dealings concerning property exclusively listed, or with buyer/tenants who are exclusively represented shall be carried on with the client's agent, and not with the client, except with the consent of the client's agent. *(Adopted 1/93)*

- **Standard of Practice 16-14**

  REALTORS® are free to enter into contractual relationships or to negotiate with sellers/landlords, buyers/tenants or others who are not represented by an exclusive agent but shall not knowingly obligate them to pay more than one commission except with their informed consent. *(Amended 1/94)*

- **Standard of Practice 16-15**

  In cooperative transactions REALTORS® shall compensate cooperating REALTORS® (principal brokers) and shall not compensate nor offer to compensate, directly or indirectly, any of the sales licensees employed by or affiliated with other REALTORS® without the prior express knowledge and consent of the cooperating broker.

- **Standard of Practice 16-16**

  REALTORS®, acting as subagents or buyer/tenant agents, shall not use the terms of an offer to purchase/lease to attempt to modify the listing broker's offer of compensation to subagents or buyer's agents nor make the submission of an executed offer to purchase/lease contingent on the listing broker's agreement to modify the offer of compensation. *(Amended 1/93)*

- **Standard of Practice 16-17**

  REALTORS® acting as subagents or as buyer/tenant agents, shall not attempt to extend a listing broker's offer of cooperation and/or compensation to other brokers without the consent of the listing broker. *(Amended 1/93)*

- **Standard of Practice 16-18**

  REALTORS® shall not use information obtained by them from the listing broker, through offers to cooperate received through Multiple Listing Services or other sources authorized by the listing broker, for the purpose of creating a referral prospect to a third broker, or for creating a buyer/tenant prospect unless such use is authorized by the listing broker. *(Amended 1/93)*

- **Standard of Practice 16-19**

  Signs giving notice of property for sale, rent, lease, or exchange shall not be placed on property without consent of the seller/landlord. *(Amended 1/93)*

Article 17

In the event of a contractual dispute between REALTORS® associated with different firms, arising out of their relationship as REALTORS®, the REALTORS® shall submit the dispute to arbitration in accordance with the regulations of their Board or Boards rather than litigate the matter.

In the event clients of REALTORS® wish to arbitrate contractual disputes arising out of real estate transactions, REALTORS® shall arbitrate those disputes in accordance with the regulations of their Board, provided the clients agree to be bound by the decision. *(Amended 1/94)*

- **Standard of Practice 17-1**

  The filing of litigation and refusal to withdraw from it by REALTORS® in an arbitrable matter constitutes a refusal to arbitrate. *(Adopted 2/86)*

- **Standard of Practice 17-2**

  Article 17 does not require REALTORS® to arbitrate in those circumstances when all parties to the dispute advise the Board in writing that they choose not to arbitrate before the Board. *(Amended 1/93)*

The Code of Ethics was adopted in 1913. Amended at the Annual Convention in 1924, 1928, 1950, 1951, 1952, 1955, 1956, 1961, 1962, 1974, 1982, 1986, 1987, 1989, 1990, 1991, 1992, 1993 and 1994.

EXPLANATORY NOTES

The reader should be aware of the following policies which have been approved by the Board of Directors of the National Association:

In filing a charge of an alleged violation of the Code of Ethics by a REALTOR®, the charge must read as an alleged violation of one or more Articles of the Code. Standards of Practice may be cited in support of the charge.

The Standards of Practice serve to clarify the ethical obligations imposed by the various Articles and supplement, and do not substitute for, the Case Interpretations in **Interpretations of the Code of Ethics**.

Modifications to existing Standards of Practice and additional new Standards of Practice are approved from time to time. Readers are cautioned to ensure that the most recent publications are utilized.

NATIONAL ASSOCIATION OF REALTORS®
430 North Michigan Avenue
Chicago, Illinois 60611-4087

NOTES

NOTES

Because real estate agents are licensed, they are expected to have a certain degree of knowledge about the business. If you feel comfortable with your knowledge—after reading the following list—you may be assured of a successful career in the real estate business. (This also is a good list to use in preparing for your state licensing exam.)

An Agent should be Knowledgeable about

- **Property Ownership**
  Classes of property
  Land characteristics
  Encumbrances
  Types of ownership
  Descriptions of property
- **Land Use Controls and Regulations**
  Government rights in land
  Public controls
  Private controls
  Water rights
- **Valuation and Market Analysis**
  Value
  Methods of estimating value/appraisal process
  Competitive market analysis
- **Financing**
  General concepts
  Types of loans
  Sources of funds
  Government programs
  Deeds of trust
  Financing/credit laws
- **Laws of Agency/Disclosures**
  Law, definition and nature of agency relationships, types of agencies and agents
  Creation of agency and agency agreements
  Responsibilities of agent to principal
  Responsibilities to buyer and third parties
  Disclosure of agency
  Disclosure of acting as principal or other interest
  Termination of agency
  Commission and fees
- **Contracts**
  General
  Listing agreements
  Buyer/broker agreements
  Offers/purchase agreements
  Counteroffers/multiple counteroffers
  Leases as contracts
  Options
  Rescission and cancellation agreements
  Broker/salesperson agreements
- **Transfer of Property**
  Title insurance
  Deeds
  Escrow
  Special reports
  Tax aspects
  Probate
- **Practice of Real Estate**
  Commercial property/income property
  Trust accounts
  Fair housing laws
  Advertising
  Maintaining transaction files
  Disciplinary actions
  Specialty areas

In addition to understanding the basics of the real estate business, an agent must know how to apply those basics in transactions. The following is a list of activities a licensee must be able to perform in the course of pursuing a career in real estate.

Agent's Activities

- Locating and listing property
- Marketing property
- Negotiating sales contracts
- Arranging financing
- Assisting with transfer of property
- Managing property/other special areas
- Keeping informed about changes in the industry
- Managing brokerage

Trust Funds

Real estate brokers and salespersons, in their capacity as agents, receive money from people, usually in the form of a check, to be used in a real estate transaction. The law is very clear about how these funds, called **Trust Funds**, should be handled. When an agent receives funds on behalf of someone else, a fiduciary duty is created to the owner of the funds. Agents must handle, control and account for these trust funds according to specific legal guidelines. Non-compliance with the law can result in unfavorable business consequences. A license can be suspended or revoked for improper handling of trust funds, and an agent held financially responsible for damages occurring because of inept, negligent or criminal actions regarding trust funds.

First of all, a licensee must be able to identify trust funds and distinguish them from non-trust funds. Trust funds are money or anything of value received by an agent on behalf of a principal or any other person, held for someone's benefit in the performance of any acts for which a real estate license is required. Examples of items that fall into the trust fund definition are: cash, a check used as a deposit for a purchase or a personal note made payable to the seller. Don't confuse other moneys such as commissions, general operating funds and rents and deposits from broker-owned real estate with trust funds. Because these funds belong to someone else, not the broker, they require a certain amount of trust, and must be accounted for separately.

The licensee has a fiduciary responsibility to the owners of the funds entrusted to his or her care. The funds can only be used for purposes authorized by the funds' owners and the licensee must maintain accurate, complete, lawful and up-to-date records.

When a broker or salesperson receives trust funds from a principal in connection with the purchase or lease of real property, the transaction begins. Trust funds must be placed into the hands of the owner of the funds, into a neutral escrow depository or into a lawful trust account not later than three business days following receipt of the funds by the broker or the broker's salesperson.

The only exception is when a check is received from an offeror in connection with an offer to purchase or lease real property. A deposit check may be held uncashed by the broker until acceptance of the offer, if the following conditions are met.

A Broker may hold a Deposit Check Uncashed if:

- The check is not made out to the broker, or if the offeror (buyer) has given written instructions that the check may not be deposited or cashed until acceptance of the offer.

- The offeree (seller) is informed, before or at the time the offer is presented for acceptance, that the check is being held uncashed.

Remember

- Offeror = buyer
- Offeree = seller

Once the offer is accepted, the broker or salesperson may continue to hold the check undeposited only with written authorization from the offeree (seller). It is most important to remember that after acceptance of the offer, unless otherwise directed, the check must be placed not later than three business days into a neutral escrow depository, into the broker's trust fund bank account or into the hands of the offeree, if expressly authorized in writing by both the offeror and offeree. A **Neutral Depository** is an escrow business conducted by someone who is a licensed escrow holder.

Before the seller accepts an offer, the buyer owns the funds, and they must be handled according to the buyer's instructions. *After* the seller accepts the offer, the funds must be handled according to instructions from both the buyer and seller.

Trust Funds must be Handled as Instructed

- An offeror's check held uncashed by the broker before an offer is accepted may be held uncashed after acceptance only upon written authorization from the offeree.

- The offeror's check may be given to the offeree only if both expressly authorize it in writing.

- All or part of an offeror's deposit may not be refunded by an agent or subagent of the seller without the express written permission of the offeree to make the refund.

Trust Fund Bank Accounts

A Broker's Trust Fund Account must meet these Requirements:

- It must be designated as a trust account in the name of the broker as trustee.

- It must be maintained with a bank or recognized depository located in California.

- It may not be an interest-bearing account for which prior written notice can be required for withdrawal of funds, except for certain instances.

- Withdrawals from a trust account may be made upon the signature of one or more specified persons.

Who can Withdraw Funds from a Trust Account?

1. The broker in whose name the account is maintained

2. The designated broker-officer if the account is in the name of a corporate broker

3. An individual specifically authorized in writing by the broker or a salesperson licensed to the broker

4. An unlicensed employee of the broker, if specifically authorized in writing by the broker, covered by a fidelity bond at least equal to the maximum amount of the trust fund to which the employee has access at any time

---

Commingling

Trust funds may not be mixed with funds belonging to the broker. **Commingling** is strictly prohibited by the Real Estate Law and may be punished by revocation or suspension of a real estate license.

Commingling Occurs When

- Personal or company funds are deposited into the trust fund bank account. This violates the law even if separate records are kept.

- Trust funds are deposited into the licensee's general or personal bank account rather than into the trust fund account.

- Commissions, fees or other income earned by the broker and collected from the trust account are left in the trust account for more than 30 days from the date they were earned.

A broker may keep up to $200 of personal funds in the trust fund account to pay for bank charges or service fees related to the trust account. When receiving commissions or other earned payment from the trust fund account, the broker may not use those moneys to pay bills or other expenses directly from the trust account. Rather, a check to the broker must be written first, and deposited in a personal account for personal use.

Remember

- A broker can keep up to $200 of personal money in a trust account.

In this chapter we have examined how the business of real estate is conducted. We also have discussed how licensees must conduct themselves, according to the law. Know this well, for it could mean the difference between a successful real estate career and none at all.

Post Test

The following self test repeats the one you took at the beginning of this chapter. Now take the exam again—since you have read all the material—and check your knowledge of real estate brokerage and ethics.

1. A listing belongs to:
    a. the seller
    b. the buyer
    c. the listing agent
    d. the listing broker

2. Which of the following are not operations of a real estate brokerage?
    a. securing listings
    b. finding buyers
    c. paying non-licensees for assisting in sale of real property
    d. arranging financing

3. Real estate salespersons are usually paid:
    a. on a commission basis
    b. a straight salary
    c. on a sliding, pre-determined scale
    d. by the seller

4. Who sets the amount of real estate commission in a sale?
    a. the broker
    b. the seller
    c. it is negotiable between broker and seller
    d. the buyer

5. Commonly, what is the commission split for a new agent?
    a. 50-50
    b. 60-40
    c. 30-70
    d. 20-80

6. When an agent receives funds on behalf of someone else, the funds are called:
    a. trust funds
    b. escrow funds
    c. commission
    d. up-front fees

7. Trust funds must be deposited not later than:
    a. one week following the acceptance of the offer
    b. two days following the acceptance of the offer
    c. the next business day following receipt of the funds
    d. three business days following receipt of the funds

8. The offeree in a typical real estate sale is:
    a. the broker
    b. the buyer
    c. the seller
    d. the selling agent

9. Before the acceptance of an offer, trust funds from the buyer belong to:
    a. the buyer
    b. the seller
    c. the broker
    d. a neutral depository

10. How much personal money may a broker keep in a trust account?
    a. up to $200
    b. up to $300
    c. up to $100
    d. up to $50

Vocabulary

Read the definition, find the matching term and write the corresponding term number on the line provided.

Terms

1. Brokerage
2. Commingling
3. Commission Split
4. Neutral Depository
5. Trust Funds

Definitions

1. ___ The occupation of a broker; the business of selling real estate through a broker who negotiates the sale for a commission

2. ___ The previously agreed upon division of money between a broker and sales-associate when the brokerage has been paid a commission from a sale made by the associate

3. ___ An escrow business conducted by someone who is a licensed escrow holder

4. ___ Money received by real estate brokers or salespersons on behalf of others

5. ___ The mixing of a broker's private funds with trust funds

Answers

Pre-Test/Post Test

1. d
2. c
3. a
4. c
5. a
6. a
7. d
8. c
9. a
10. a

Vocabulary

1.   1
2.   3
3.   4
4.   5
5.   2

SECTION SIX

SPECIALIZATION

CHAPTER

14

SPECIALIZED FIELDS OF REAL ESTATE

Focus

- **Mobile home brokerage**
- **Business opportunity brokerage**
- **Probate sales**

Pre-Test

The following is a self test to determine how much you know about specialized fields of real estate before reading this chapter. Take it without studying, then read the material presented in the text. At the end of the chapter you will find a repeat of this exam. Test your knowledge by answering the questions again, then check your improvement. (The answers are found at the end of this chapter.) Good luck!

1. Another name for a mobile home is:
   - a. commercial housing
   - b. manufactured housing
   - c. residential housing
   - d. factory-built housing

2. Which of the following is not a requirement for a mobile home to become real property?
   - a. a building permit
   - b. a permanent foundation
   - c. a certificate of completion
   - d. a certificate of occupancy

3. Prior to becoming real property, a mobile home was registered with the:
   - a. Uniform Commercial Code (UCC)
   - b. Department of Motor Vehicles (DMV)
   - c. County Assessor
   - d. Department of Alcoholic Beverage Control (ABC)

4. What agency must be notified if an owner wants to move a mobile home from a permanent foundation?
   - a. Department of Housing and Urban Development (HUD)
   - b. Uniform Commercial Code (UCC)
   - c. State Board of Equalization
   - d. Department of Housing and Community Development (HCD)

5. The sale of a mobile home by a real estate agent must be reported within how many days?
   - a. 30
   - b. 45
   - c. 10
   - d. 5

6. If a real estate agent is involved in a probate sale, the amount of commission is set by the:
   - a. probate court
   - b. heirs
   - c. Real Estate Commissioner
   - d. buyer

7. Who licenses mobile homes?
   - a. Department of Motor Vehicles (DMV)
   - b. Uniform Commercial Code (UCC)
   - c. Department of Housing and Community Development (HCD)
   - d. Department of Housing and Urban Development (HUD)

8. An expectation of continued patronage is otherwise known as:
   - a. wishful thinking
   - b. a business plan
   - c. goodwill
   - d. consideration

9. Chattel is:
   - a. a building
   - b. inventory
   - c. a fixture
   - d. emblements

10. Bulk transfer laws affect which of the following:
   - a. the sale of a business
   - b. the sale of a residence
   - c. the sale of a commercial building
   - d. the sale of an apartment building

Terms

The following terms are the keys to your success in learning about real estate. Refer to them as you study this chapter for greater understanding of subjects presented here.

Bill of Sale

Transfers ownership of personal property

Bulk Transfer Law

The law concerning transfer in bulk (not a sale in the ordinary course of the seller's business)

Business Opportunity

Any type of business that is for lease or sale

Financing Statement

A written notice filed with the county recorder by a creditor who has extended credit for the purchase of personal property; establishes the creditor's interests in the personal property which is security for the debt

Goodwill

An intangible, salable asset arising from the reputation of a business; the expectation of continued public patronage

Manufactured Housing

A housing unit primarily constructed in a factory and moved to a permanent site; another name for a mobile home

Mobile Home

A manufactured unit constructed on a chassis and wheels, designed for permanent or semi-attachment to land

Probate Sale

A court-approved sale of the property of a deceased person

Sales Tax

Collected as a percentage of the retail sales of a product, by a retailer, and forwarded to the State Board of Equalization

Seller's Permit

Allows a retailer to buy the product at wholesale prices without paying sales tax. The retailer must then collect the proper sales tax from customers and pay it to the State Board of Equalization

Introduction

Easily, the majority of real estate selling is done in the residential market. Most licensees start out in a real estate office that specializes in selling homes, spending most of their time prospecting for listings on homes and buyers to buy them. After a time, the licensee may decide to specialize and become an expert in only one particular area of real estate, such as appraisal, property management, mortgage brokerage, commercial real estate, mobile home brokerage or business opportunities.

We have discussed most of the above real estate specialty areas in other parts of this book. This chapter examines the detailed special knowledge and capability required in mobile home sales and business opportunity brokerage. Probate sales, another specialty area, also is discussed in this chapter.

Mobile Home Brokerage

A **Mobile Home** is a manufactured unit constructed on a chassis and wheels and designed for permanent or semi-attachment to land. In the past, mobile homes were known as trailers, and were used mainly as a second, traveling home.

http://www.apolloproperties.
com/archive.htm

Because of the increased need for affordable housing and the relative low cost to build, however, mobile homes have become a major source of the residential housing supply. Today a majority of mobile homes are attached to a permanent foundation, and are considered real property. Sometimes known as **Manufactured Housing**, they are primarily constructed in a factory, then transported to a lot where they are permanently set.

http://www.wma.org

Once mobile homes are moved from the factory to a permanent lot, very few are ever moved again. They are built in 8, 10 and 12-foot widths, and up to 60 feet in length, making them expensive and difficult to move once they are put in place. When two units are put together side by side, an extra-large, double-width residence results. After being secured to a foundation, the mobile home is as practical and useful as homes constructed in the traditional way, for a fraction of the cost.

Mobile Homes as Real Property

A mobile home becomes real property when the following four requirements are met:

Requirements for a Mobile Home

1. A building permit is acquired.
2. The mobile home is set on a permanent foundation.
3. A certificate of occupancy is obtained.
4. A recorded document is filed stating that the mobile home has been placed on a foundation.

> ## After Meeting the Requirements, the Mobile Home is:
> 1. Taxable as real property
> 2. No longer required to be registered with the Department of Motor Vehicles (DMV)
> 3. Registered with the county recorder as real property

If an owner wants to move a mobile home after it has become real property, anyone who has an interest in it must approve, and 30 days before moving it the owner must notify the Department of Housing and Community Development (HCD) as well as the local tax assessor. The mobile home becomes personal property once again and returns to the unsecured property tax rolls after the owner obtains a new registration or transportation permit from the HCD or DMV.

Mobile Home Sales by Real Estate Agents

As we have seen, mobile homes have become part of the residential home supply, providing a source of employment for real estate agents involved in their purchase and sale.

Real estate agents can only sell mobile homes which are considered real property and are located in established mobile home parks. All sales must be reported within 10 calendar days to the HCD. Only licensed mobile home dealers can sell new or used dwellings which are still on chassis and movable.

There are many laws and regulations involved in the practice of mobile home brokerage. It is a relatively new speciality area for real estate licensees, with limitations on the actions of agents. The following is a summary of approved activities for licensees involved in the sale of mobile homes.

> ## Approved Activities for Licensees
> 1. A real estate agent may sell any mobile home that has been classified as real property. It may be listed and sold in the same manner as any other residence.
> 2. A real estate agent may sell used mobile homes which are not real property, but have been licensed for at least a year and are a minimum of 8 feet wide and 30 feet long.
> 3. Sales of new mobile homes are restricted to specially licensed dealers.
> 4. All sales must be reported by the licensee to the Department of Housing and Community Development (HCD) within 10 days.

Transfer of Title

The HCD registers and licenses mobile homes, and must be notified by anyone acquiring or releasing an interest in same within 20 days after a sale. A copy of the registration will then be provided to all lien holders. Both the buyer and seller must sign a certificate of title. If the mobile home is real property, a clearance of tax liability must be signed by the county tax collector.

Mobile Home Financing

Financing of mobile homes is available from the same sources as for fixed-foundation residences. Loans are available through government participation programs such as the FHA, VA and Cal-Vet.

Mobile Home Parks

Failure on the part of a real estate agent to become familiar with the rules and regulations of a mobile home park could result in a cancelled sale, bad feelings or even a lawsuit. The mobile home's desirability to a buyer may be affected by the rules of the park. The real estate agent must disclose all known facts.

For example, many parks have a minimum age requirement that at least one of the buyers must be 55 years or over. There may be strict rules about animals, where they may be kept and how they must be supervised when outside. Most mobile home parks require buyers to sign a copy of the rules and agree to comply with them. At the time the licensee accepts the mobile home listing, a copy of the park's rules and regulations should be obtained.

When a buyer takes title to a mobile home, a new rental agreement must be negotiated with the owner of the mobile home park. The new tenant (mobile home owner) of the park must be approved by the owner, and must agree to all terms of the park's rules and regulations.

Business Opportunity Brokerage

http://www.census.gov
(U.S. Census Bureau)

http://www.sbaonline.sba.gov

A **Business Opportunity** is any type of business that is for lease or sale, including the **Goodwill**, or expectation of continued patronage, of an existing business. The sale of a business is considered to be the sale of personal property, and the rules about the transfer of chattels are applied. A real estate broker, as well as both buyer and seller, should be aware of the application of the **Bulk Transfer Laws** on the sale of a business.

A licensee, in the course of the usual business opportunity sale, may become involved in the sale of shoe stores, bars, hotels and book stores. Stock, fixtures and goodwill almost always will be included in the sale of a business. A licensee must be aware of certain legal demands, however, that might not be required in the sale of other types of nonbusiness properties. The sale of a business opportunity may be negotiated by anyone holding a real estate license.

In dealing with the sale of a business, a real estate agent usually will be dealing with three elements: the real property or a lease, the personal property or the inventory and equipment, and the goodwill or the reputation enjoyed by the business. Each of the three elements in the sale is worth value and must be considered when listing a business opportunity.

Elements of the Sale of a Business

- Lease

- Inventory

- Goodwill

The sale of a business requires special knowledge and experience by a real estate agent, and the steps involved in the sale can be complicated. All sales do not include the same order of events, but the following is a general outline of the normal course of a business opportunity sale.

1. The business is listed.

2. A special business opportunity deposit receipt is completed when a buyer is found.

3. The offer is presented to the seller by the broker for approval.

4. Escrow is opened if offer is acceptable.

5. Creditors are notified of the sale and a notice of intended bulk sale is published, according to the requirements of the Bulk Sales Act.

6. A **Financing Statement** (a written notice of a creditor's interests in personal property) is filed with the secretary of state and/or the recorder's office, according to the requirements of the Uniform Commercial Code (UCC).

7. If a liquor license is part of the sale, the required forms are filed with the Department of Alcoholic Beverage Control (ABC).

8. Arrangements for the assignment or transfer of the lease are made with the landlord.

9. Copies of the seller's permit and a clearance receipt are obtained from the Board of Equalization, according to the Sales and Use Tax Law. The buyer then is protected from liability from any unpaid sales tax that the seller might owe.

10. Information about employee's salaries, benefits and unemployment insurance tax is noted.

11. An inventory is taken of stock, fixtures and any other personal property that will be transferred by the sale, and the seller executes a **Bill of Sale** which transfers ownership of all personal property belonging to the business.

12. At the close of escrow, buyer and seller receive closing statements.

Rules and Regulations for the Sale of a Business Opportunity

There are certain legal requirements that must be met in the sale of a business. In order to complete the transaction, a real estate agent must understand the requirements of the UCC, the Bulk Transfer Act, California sales and use tax regulations and the Alcoholic Beverage Control Act.

Uniform Commercial Code (UCC)

http://www.ss.ca.gov/business/ucc/ucc.htm

Whenever money has been borrowed for the sale of a business opportunity, someone has a security interest in the personal property belonging to the business. Division 9 of the UCC sets out the requirements for regulating security transactions in personal property. A financing statement must be filed with the secretary of state or in the county recorder's office giving public notice of the security interest created by the debt.

When money is borrowed, a promissory note is signed, just as in the financing of nonbusiness property. The note is the evidence of the debt. At the same time, the borrower executes a security agreement, which gives the lender an interest in the personal property, and the financing statement, which is recorded. By recording the financing statement, public notice of the security interest is given, and all parties are made aware of any interests in the property, much as a recorded trust deed gives public notice of a debt against a nonbusiness property.

Bulk Transfer Act

Bulk sales, or the sale of a substantial part of the inventory of a business, are regulated by Division 6 of the UCC. The purpose of the Bulk Transfer Act is to protect the creditors of a person who sells a business. When a business is sold and most or all of the inventory, supplies and other materials are transferred with the sale, public notice must be given.

> ## Public Notice Must Be Given When a Business Is Sold
>
> - Twelve business days before the transfer, notice of the sale must be filed with the county recorder.
>
> - Twelve business days before the transfer, notice must be published in a local newspaper in the county where the business is located.
>
> - Twelve business days before the transfer, notice must be delivered to the county tax collector.

The above requirements give fair warning of the business inventory's sale to possible creditors. Any bulk sale that takes place without complying with the requirements of the bulk transfer law are considered valid between the buyer and seller, but fraudulent and void against creditors. That means creditors have recourse against the debtor (the seller) because he or she sold the security for the debt without notifying them.

California Sales and Use Tax

The Sales and Use Tax Law protects a buyer from liability for unpaid sales tax, owed by the seller. **Sales Tax** is collected as a percentage of the retail sales of a product, by a retailer. The owner of a retail business may obtain a **Seller's Permit**, which allows him to buy his product at wholesale prices without paying sales tax. The retailer must then collect the proper sales tax from customers and pay it to the State Board of Equalization, usually quarterly. A copy of the seller's permit and a clearance receipt, stating that the business is current on sales taxes, from the State Board of Equalization, should be requested by a buyer before assuming the ownership of a business.

Alcohol Beverage Control Act

http://www.abc.ca.gov
(Alcoholic Beverage Control)

Whenever transfer of a liquor license is involved in a business opportunity sale, a buyer must not assume an automatic transfer of the license. The Department of Alcoholic Beverage Control (ABC) issues liquor licenses and must approve a buyer who requests transfer of a liquor license. A buyer must apply for the license, and may be turned down for various reasons. The maximum price for a new general liquor license is $12,000, but after two years from the issue date of the original license the price is negotiable between buyer and seller.

Codes and Laws Involved in the Sale of a Business

- Uniform Commercial Code
- Bulk Transfer Act
- California Sales and Use Tax Law
- Alcoholic Beverage Control Act

Remember

- Maximum price for a new liquor license: $6,000

Probate Sales

A **Probate Sale** is a court-approved sale of the property of a person who is deceased. Ownership of property that is inherited may be subject to the approval of the probate court. In California, any estate over $60,000 must be approved by the probate court.

The purpose of a probate court is to discover any creditors of the deceased and pay them out of the estate of the person who died. After all debts are paid, anything of value that remains is distributed to the proper heirs, either according to a will or to the law of succession.

Even though it is called the probate court, the section where probate action occurs is not a separate court, but a department of the Superior Court. When there is a probate sale of real property, certain procedures must be followed. Here is a short review of those procedures, first discussed in Chapter 5.

Summary of Probate Court Procedures

1. An offer to purchase must be for at least 90% of the appraised value.
2. The buyer, or a representative, must petition the court to approve the sale. When the court has set a hearing, others may bid at that time.
3. To open the bidding, there must be an increase of at least 10% of the first $10,000 of the original bid, and 5% of anything over that amount.
4. The court decides which bid is the best obtainable and confirms the sale.
5. At the time the sale is confirmed, the court will set the amount of commission to be paid if there is a real estate agent involved.

After court confirmation of a sale, usually normal escrow procedures are used to complete the transaction on the terms and conditions approved by the court.

About Commissions

- The probate court sets the amount of commission when there is a real estate agent involved in the sale.

Post Test

The following self test repeats the one you took at the beginning of this chapter. Now take the exam again—since you have read all the material— and check your knowledge of specialized fields of real estate.

1. Another name for a mobile home is:
   a. commercial housing
   b. manufactured housing
   c. residential housing
   d. factory-built housing

2. Which of the following is not a requirement for a mobile home to become real property?
   a. a building permit
   b. a permanent foundation
   c. a certificate of completion
   d. a certificate of occupancy

3. Prior to becoming real property, a mobile home was registered with the:
   a. Uniform Commercial Code (UCC)
   b. Department of Motor Vehicles (DMV)
   c. County Assessor
   d. Department of Alcoholic Beverage Control (ABC)

4 What agency must be notified if an owner wants to move a mobile home from a permanent foundation?
   a. Department of Housing and Urban Development (HUD)
   b. Uniform Commercial Code (UCC)
   c. State Board of Equalization
   d. Department of Housing and Community Development (HCD)

5. The sale of a mobile home by a real estate agent must be reported within how many days?
   a. 30
   b. 45
   c. 10
   d. 5

6. If a real estate agent is involved in a probate sale, the amount of commission is set by the:
   a. probate court
   b. heirs
   c. Real Estate Commissioner
   d. buyer

7. Who licenses mobile homes?
   a. Department of Motor Vehicles (DMV)
   b. Uniform Commercial Code (UCC)
   c. Department of Housing and Community Development (HCD)
   d. Department of Housing and Urban Development (HUD)

8. An expectation of continued patronage is otherwise known as:
   a. wishful thinking
   b. a business plan
   c. goodwill
   d. consideration

9. Chattel is:
   a. a building
   b. inventory
   c. a fixture
   d. emblements

10. Bulk transfer laws affect which of the following:
   a. the sale of a business
   b. the sale of a residence
   c. the sale of a commercial building
   d. the sale of an apartment building

Vocabulary

Read the definition, find the matching term and write the corresponding term number on the line provided.

Terms

1. Bill of Sale
2. Bulk Transfer Law
3. Business Opportunity
4. Financing Statement
5. Goodwill
6. Manufactured Housing
7. Mobile Home
8. Probate Sale
9. Sales Tax
10. Seller's Permit

Definitions

1. ___ A manufactured unit constructed on a chassis and wheels, designed for permanent or semi-attachment to land

2. ___ A housing unit primarily constructed in a factory and moved to a permanent site; another name for mobile home

3. ___ Any type of business that is for lease or sale

4. ___ An intangible, salable asset arising from the reputation of a business; the expectation of continued public patronage

5. ___ The law concerning transfer in bulk (not a sale in the ordinary course of the seller's business)

6. ___ A written notice filed with the county recorder by a creditor who has extended credit for the purchase of personal property; establishes the creditor's interests in the personal property which is security for the debt

7. ___ Transfers ownership of personal property

8. ___ Collected as a percentage of the retail sales of a product, by a retailer, and forwarded to the State Board of Equalization

9. ___ Allows a retailer to buy the product at wholesale prices without paying sales tax. The retailer must then collect the proper sales tax from customers and pay it to the State Board of Equalization

10. ___ A court-approved sale of the property of a person who is deceased

Answers

Pre-Test/Post Test

1. b
2. c
3. b
4. d
5. c
6. a
7. c
8. c
9. b
10. a

Vocabulary

1. 7
2. 6
3. 3
4. 5
5. 2
6. 4
7. 1
8. 9
9. 10
10. 8

CHAPTER

15

REAL ESTATE MATH

Focus

- **Basic math principles**
- **Three variables**
- **Investments**
- **Discounting notes**
- **Capitalization problems**
- **Commission problems**
- **Interest and loan problems**
- **Cost and selling price problems**
- **Square footage problems**
- **Proration**
- **Documentary transfer tax**

Pre-Test

The following is a self test to determine how much you know about real estate math before reading this chapter. Take it without studying, then read the material presented in the text. At the end of the chapter you will find a repeat of this exam. Test your knowledge by answering the questions again, then check your improvement. (The answers are found at the end of this chapter.) Good luck!

1. The charge for the use of money is called:
   - a. interest
   - b. usury
   - c. principal
   - d. proration

2. The original amount of money borrowed is known as:
   - a. interest
   - b. principal
   - c. capitalized loan amount
   - d. compounded loan amount

3. The mark that sets apart a whole number from a fractional part of that number is called:
   - a. fraction
   - b. decimal point
   - c. percentage
   - d. period

4. What is the first position to the right of the decimal point called?
   - a. 100th
   - b. 1,000th
   - c. 10th
   - d. units

5. What numbers are found to the left of a decimal point?
   - a. fractions
   - b. decimals
   - c. percentages
   - d. whole numbers

6. A building with six-inch thick walls has interior dimensions of 25 feet by 29 feet. The building covers a land area of how many square feet?
   - a. 1,054
   - b. 780
   - c. 720
   - d. 540

7. The maximum number of 50-foot x 110-foot lots that could be obtained from an acre of land would be:
   - a. 10 lots
   - b. 8 lots
   - c. 7 lots
   - d. 5 lots

8. A property produced a 9% gross return on a $20,000 purchase price for a one-year period. The owner's only expense was an 8% annual interest rate on a $15,000 loan. What is the percentage return on the owner's equity?
   - a. 9%
   - b. 11%
   - c. 12%
   - d. 13%

9. A percentage lease calls for 2% of gross sales or a guaranteed minimum base of $1,200 per month. If the annual sales are $700,000, what is the monthly rent?
   - a. $1,167
   - b. $1,200
   - c. $1,363
   - d. $1,500

10. What percent of a section is 1/60th of a township?
    - a. 40%
    - b. 50%
    - c. 60%
    - d. 70%

Terms

The following terms are the keys to your success in learning about real estate. Refer to them as you study this chapter for greater understanding of subjects presented here.

Decimal Point

The period that sets apart a whole number from a fractional part of that number

Divisor

A number by which another number is divided

Dividend

A number to be divided by another number

Interest

The charge for the use of money

Principal

The amount of money borrowed

Proration

The process of making a fair distribution of expenses, through escrow, at the close of the sale

Rate

The percentage of interest charged on the principal

Time

Duration of loan

Introduction

This chapter will explain the basic mathematical procedures you will need to be successful in your new real estate career. Many people are intimidated by the word "math," but in this case the concepts presented for your understanding are mainly a review of information you already possess—and probably use in your daily life. An understanding of the principles and formulas explained in this chapter will help you as a licensee in solving math problems you will meet everyday.

Basic Math Principles

It will be beneficial to review the concept of decimals here before starting our study of how to solve various real estate problems. The period that sets apart a whole number from a fractional part of that number is called a **Decimal Point**. The value of the number is determined by the position of the decimal point.

Any numerals to the right of the decimal point are less than one. The "10th" position is the first position to the right of the decimal point, the "100th" position is the second to the right of the decimal point, the "1,000th" position is the third to the right of the decimal point, and so forth.

The whole numerals are to the left of the decimal point. The "units" are in the first position to the left of the decimal point, the "10s" in the second position to the left of the decimal point, the "100s" in the third position to the left of the decimal point, the "1,000s" in the fourth position to the left of the decimal point, and so forth.

Equivalent Amounts:

Percentage	Decimal	Fraction
4$^{1/2}$%	0.045	45/1000
6$^{2/3}$%	0.0667	1/15
10%	0.10	1/10
12$^{1/2}$%	0.125	1/8
16$^{2/3}$%	0.1667	1/6
25%	0.25	1/4
33$^{1/3}$%	0.333	1/3
50%	0.50	1/2
66$^{2/3}$%	0.6667	2/3
75%	0.75	3/4
100%	1.00	1/1

Converting Percentages to Decimals

Looking at a number expressed as a percentage, such as 10% or 20%, the decimal point is assumed to be on the right side of the number. Move the decimal point two places to the left to remove the percentage sign. Thus 6% becomes .06, 30% becomes .30, 2.3% becomes .023, 210% becomes 2.10.

Converting Decimals to Percentages

Reverse the above process to convert a number expressed as a decimal to a percentage; in other words, move the decimal point two places to the right. Thus .02 becomes 2%, .57 becomes 57%, .058 becomes 5.8%, and 9.02 becomes 902%.

Addition of Decimal Numbers

All numbers must be in a vertical column when adding numbers with decimals. Always be sure to line up the decimals vertically.

$$
\begin{array}{r}
902.36 \\
2.053 \\
+\ 387.1 \\
\hline
1,291.513
\end{array}
$$

Subtraction of Decimal Numbers

In subtracting numbers with decimals, the same process is used, making sure to line up the decimals vertically.

$$
\begin{array}{r}
43,267.23 \\
-\ 235.10 \\
\hline
43,032.13
\end{array}
$$

Multiplication of Decimal Numbers

After multiplying the numbers just as you would in a non-decimal problem, count the total number of decimal places in the numbers being multiplied and place the decimal point in the answer that many places from the right.

$$
\begin{array}{r}
4.327 \\
\times\quad 82.2 \\
\hline
355.6794
\end{array}
$$

Division of Decimal Numbers

The decimal point must be removed before solving the problem when there is a decimal in the **Divisor**. Move the decimal point in the divisor to the right, then move the decimal point in the **Dividend** the same number of places to the right. Add zeros to the dividend if it has fewer numerals than are needed to carry out this procedure. Put the decimal point in the answer directly above the new decimal point in the dividend.

Quotient

Divisor .021) 40000. / 840.000

Dividend

When there is no decimal point in the divisor, put the decimal point in the answer directly above the decimal point in the dividend.

94) .19 / 18.43

The following problem-solving techniques are explained for the beginning or remedial math student. By remedial, we mean someone who has not used math techniques for quite some time and just needs a little practice to become proficient.

There are several ways any of the following examples may be solved, and we have attempted to be consistent in our explanations for the beginner. Some students will recognize the algebraic solutions presented, and will use their own techniques for solving the problems.

The math problems presented here are the same types you will find on the state exam.

Three Variables

There are usually only three variables in any real estate problem—two things that are known and one that is not known. One way to solve these types of problems is to imagine a circle divided into three sections. One-third is labeled *Made*, one-third is labeled *Paid* and the last third is labeled *Rate or Percentage*.

As you can see from the next figure:

"Paid" times "Rate" will give you "Made."

"Made" divided by "Rate" will give you "Paid," and

"Made" divided by "Paid" will give you "Rate."

Stop and think about this simple way to solve most real estate math problems and look carefully at the circle until you grasp this easy concept.

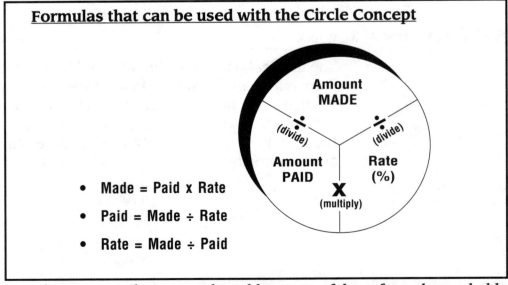

Formulas that can be used with the Circle Concept

- **Made = Paid x Rate**
- **Paid = Made ÷ Rate**
- **Rate = Made ÷ Paid**

Whenever you have a math problem, one of these formulas probably can be used. You will always know two of the quantities and will be asked to find the third. From the information given in the problem, you must decide whether to multiply or divide the two numbers that you know in order to find the third.

Most of your calculations probably will be done on a calculator which will place the decimal point correctly for you, but it is important that you understand the concepts.

Some math problems will have a two-step solution. In other words, some process (add, subtract, multiply) will have to be performed either before or after the above formula can be applied. Use the circle concept as an easy way to solve the math problems included here. Once you know into which section of the circle your information fits, simply perform the math function indicated.

Investments

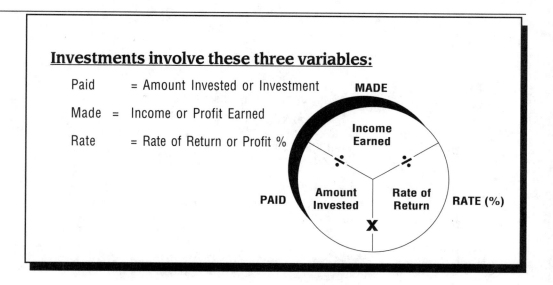

Investments involve these three variables:

Paid = Amount Invested or Investment

Made = Income or Profit Earned

Rate = Rate of Return or Profit %

Here are several guidelines for you to follow to answer some of the most basic math questions you will need to solve. To find the dollar amount to be invested when the income and rate of return are given:

$$\text{Amount Invested (Paid)} = \frac{\text{Income Earned (Made)}}{\text{Rate of Return (Rate)}}$$

To find the rate(%) of return when the income and the dollar amount invested are given:

$$\text{Rate of Return (Rate)} = \frac{\text{Income Earned (Made)}}{\text{Amount Invested (Paid)}}$$

To find the income when the amount of money invested and the rate (%) are given:

$$\text{Income Earned (Made)} = \text{Amount Invested (Paid)} \times \text{Rate Return (Rate)}$$

When you see or are asked to find an amount resulting from an interest rate, it will almost always be an annual number. Make sure you annualize, or convert any monthly figures to annual or yearly figures by multiplying the monthly figures by 12.

Practice Problem #1

Steve has a savings account and wants to earn $100 per month in interest. If the account pays 4% interest, how much should Steve keep in the account?

The variables are:

Made = $1,200 per year ($100 x 12 months)
Rate = 4%
Paid = ?

The amount of the investment is what we don't know. Using the formula, we get:

$$\text{Amount Invested} = \frac{\text{Income}}{\text{Rate of Return}}$$

$$= \frac{\$1,200}{.04}$$

$$= \$30,000$$

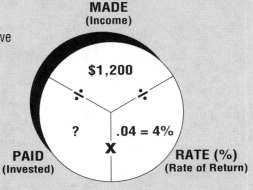

Practice Problem #2

Mitch bought a house for $145,000. The house was later sold for $165,000. What is the rate (%) of profit Mitch made on this sale?

The variables are:

Paid = $145,000
Made = $20,000 ($165,000 − $145,000)
Rate = ?

The rate of profit is not known. Using the formula, we get:

$$\text{Profit \%} = \frac{\text{Profit}}{\text{Investment}}$$

$$= \frac{\$20,000}{\$145,000}$$

$$= 13.8\%$$

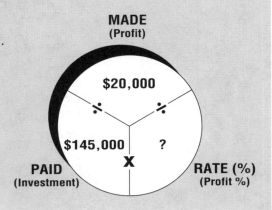

Discounting Notes

As you recall, when someone buys a note at a discount, it means the buyer pays less than the dollar amount shown on the note, and the profit is the difference between what the buyer paid and the amount paid when the note is due. In other words, a certain amount is paid for the note, but a greater amount is received when the note is paid off.

Discounting notes involve these three variables:

Paid = Investment = Principal – Discount
   (Original note amount less the discount amount)

Made = Profit = Interest + Discount
   (Total interest payment plus the
   discount amount)

Rate = Rate of Return on Investment

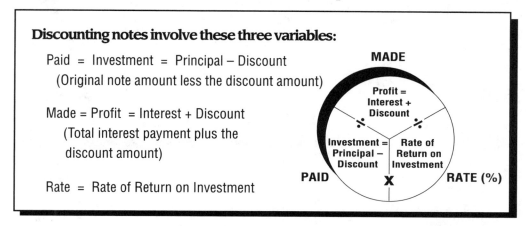

Before the rate of return can be determined, the dollar amount of profit made by the investor must be known. Using the circle concept, Made = Paid x Rate.

Practice Problem #3

Tex signed a note for $3,000, in favor of (or owed to) a private lender, which is to be paid off in 12 months. He owes the $3,000 plus 9% interest when the note is due. An investor buys the note at a 20% discount. What is the rate of return on the amount invested by the investor?

The variables are:

Made	=	Interest+Discount
	=	$3,000 x .09 = $270 (interest due on due date)
	+	$3,000 x .20 = $600 (20% discount allowed investor)
		$870
Paid	=	Principal – Discount
	=	$3,000 – (.20 x $3,000)
	=	$2,400
Rate	=	?

What we don't know is the rate (%).
Using the formula, we get:

$$\text{Rate of Return} = \frac{\text{Profit}}{\text{Investment}}$$

$$= \frac{\$870}{\$2,400}$$

$$= 36.25\%$$

MADE
(Profit)

$870

$2,400   ?

PAID   **X**   **RATE (%)**
(Investment)   **(Rate of Return)**

Capitalization Problems

Capitalization Problems involve these three variables:

Paid = Value of Property

Made = Annual Net Income or Loss

Rate = Capitalization Rate

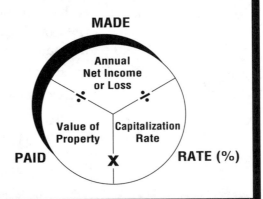

Net Income or Loss = Value of Property x Capitalization Rate

$$\text{Value of Property} = \frac{\text{Net Income or Loss}}{\text{Capitalization Rate}}$$

$$\text{Capitalization Rate} = \frac{\text{Net Income or Loss}}{\text{Value of Property}}$$

Practice Problem #4

A duplex brings in $600 per month per unit. Gail and Kevin are interested in buying the property as an investment, and need an investment rate (capitalization rate, or cap rate) of a 10% return. What should Gail and Kevin pay for the duplex?

The variables are:

Made = $600 per unit x 2 units = $1,200 net income per month
$1,200 x 12 months = $14,400 annual net income
$14,400

Rate = 10%

Paid = ?

What we don't know is what should be paid. Using the formula:

$$\text{Value of Property} = \frac{\text{Net Income}}{\text{Capitalization Rate}}$$

$$= \frac{\$14,400}{.10}$$

$$= \$144,000$$

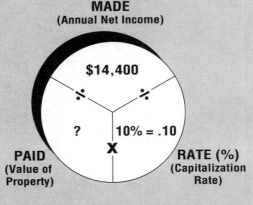

Gail and Kevin should pay no more than $144,000.

Practice Problem #5

Shirley paid $900,000 for a eight-unit apartment building. The gross income is $800 per month per unit, with expenses of $4,000 annually. What capitalization rate (%) will Shirley make on her investment?

As you recall, *net income* rather than gross income is used to calculate a capitalization rate. So, the first step is to subtract the expenses from the gross income.

Gross Income   = $800/month x 8 units = $6,400/month

                 $6,400/month x 12 months = $76,800/year

             = $76,800

Exenses   = $4,000

The variables are:

      Made = Net Income

            = Gross Income – Expenses

            = $76,800 – $4,000

            = $72,800

     Paid   = $900,000

     Rate   = ?

What we don't know is the capitalization rate. Using the formula:

Capitalization Rate   = $\dfrac{\text{Net Income}}{\text{Value of Property}}$

                = $\dfrac{\$72,800}{\$900,000}$

Capitalization Rate   = 8.1%

MADE
(Annual Net Income)

$72,800

÷   ÷

$900,000   ?

X

PAID
(Value of Property)

RATE (%)
(Capitalization Rate)

Commission Problems

Commission Problems involve these three variables:

Paid = Selling Price of Property

Made = Amount of Commission

Rate = Commission Rate

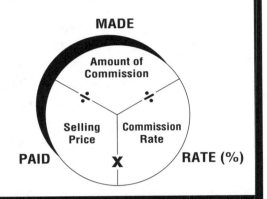

Amount of Commission	=	Selling Price x Commission Rate
Commission Rate	=	$\dfrac{\text{Amount of Commission}}{\text{Selling Price}}$
Selling Price	=	$\dfrac{\text{Amount of Commission}}{\text{Commission Rate}}$

Practice Problem #6

Effie, a real estate salesperson, found a buyer for a $600,000 house. The seller agreed to pay a 6% commission on the sale to Effie's broker. Effie is on a 50-50 split with her broker. What is the amount of her commission?

First, the total commission paid must be calculated.

The variables are:

Paid = $600,000
Rate = 6%
Made = ?

What we don't know is the dollar amount of the commission paid to the broker. Using the formula:

Total Amount
of Commission = Selling Price
x Commission Rate
= $600,000 x .06
= $36,000

Effie's
Commission = Total Commission ÷ 2
= $36,000 ÷ 2
= $18,000

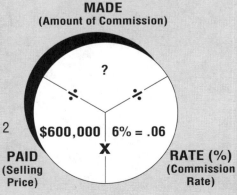

Practice Problem #7

Paul, a real estate broker, listed a parcel of land for $500,000, with a commission of 10%. A few days later he presented an offer which was 5% less than the listed price. The seller agreed to accept the price if the broker would reduce his commission by 15%. If Paul agrees to the seller's proposal, how much will his commission be?

The variables are:

    Paid = $500,000 less 5% ($25,000) = $475,000
    Rate = 10% less 15% [.10 − (.15 x .10)] = .085
          = 8.5%
    Made = ?

What we don't know is the dollar amount of the commission. Using the formula:

Amount of
Commission = Selling Price
               x Commission Rate
            = $475,000 x .085
            = $40,375

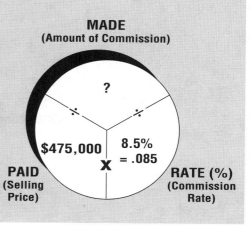

MADE
(Amount of Commission)

?

$475,000 | 8.5% = .085

X

PAID
(Selling Price)

RATE (%)
(Commission Rate)

Interest and Loan Problems

The charge for the use of money is called interest. The rate of interest that is charged will determine the total dollar amount of the payments. When money is borrowed, both the principal and interest must be paid back according to the agreement between the borrower and lender.

Useful Terms for Calculating Interest and Loan Problems

Interest (I): the charge for the use of money

Principal (P): the dollar amount of money borrowed

Rate (R): the percentage of interest charged

Time (T): duration of loan

When Solving Interest and Loan Problems, Adapt the Circle Formula to:

I	=	Made	= Dollar Amount of Interest
P	=	Paid	= Amount of Loan (Principal)
R	=	Rate	= Annual Interest Rate
T	=	Time	= Number of Years

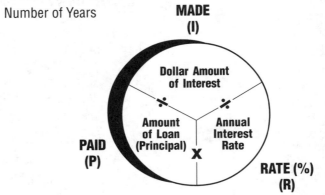

Amount of Loan (Principal) = $\dfrac{\text{Amount of Interest}}{\text{Annual Interest Rate x Number of Years}}$

$$P = \dfrac{I}{R \times T}$$

Annual Interest Rate = $\dfrac{\text{Amount of Interest}}{\text{Amount of Loan (Principal) x Number of Years}}$

$$R = \dfrac{I}{P \times T}$$

Amount of Interest = Amount of Loan (Principal)
x Annual Interest Rate
x Number of Years

$$I = P \times R \times T$$

Practice Problem #8

Andrea borrowed $6,000 for one year and paid $520 interest. What was the interest rate she paid?

The variables are:

    P = Paid = $6,000
    I = Made = $520
    T = Time = 1 year
    R = Rate = ?

What we don't know is the interest rate Andrea paid. Using the formula:

$$R = \frac{I}{P \times T}$$

$$= \frac{\$520}{\$6,000 \times 1}$$

Interest Rate = 8.67%

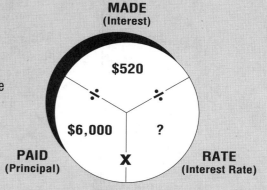

Practice Problem #9

If one month's interest is $50 on a five-year, straight interest-only note, and the interest rate on the note is 10% per year, what is the amount of the loan?

The variables are:

    R = Rate = 10%
    I = Made = $50/month x 12 months = $600/year
    T = Time = 1 year
    P = Paid = ?

What we don't know is the amount paid. Using the formula, we get:

    P   =

            =

Loan Amount = $6,000

Cost and Selling Price Problems

This type of problem is easy to identify. Whenever you are given a selling price and are asked to calculate the amount of profit or the cost before a profit, use the following formulas:

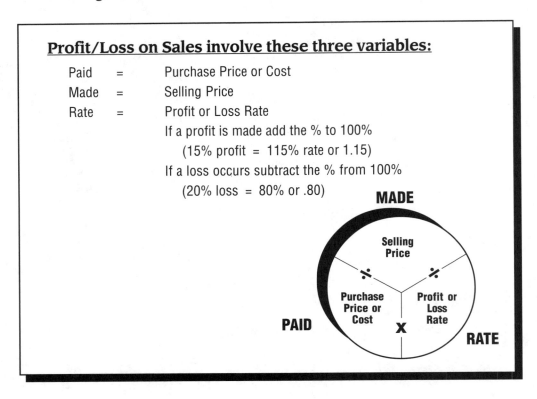

Profit/Loss on Sales involve these three variables:

Paid	=	Purchase Price or Cost
Made	=	Selling Price
Rate	=	Profit or Loss Rate

If a profit is made add the % to 100%
    (15% profit = 115% rate or 1.15)
If a loss occurs subtract the % from 100%
    (20% loss = 80% or .80)

Selling Price = Purchase Price x Profit/Loss Rate

$$\text{Purchase Price} = \frac{\text{Selling Price}}{\text{Profit/Loss Rate}}$$

$$\text{Profit/Loss Rate} = \frac{\text{Selling Price}}{\text{Purchase Price}}$$

Practice Problem #10

Maureen sold a rural cabin for $30,000, which allowed her to make a 20% profit. What did she pay for the property?

The variables are:

      Made = $30,000
      Rate   = 100% + 20% = 120% = 1.20
      Paid   = ?

Purchase Price = $\dfrac{\text{Selling Price}}{\text{Profit Rate}}$

             = $\dfrac{\$30,000}{1.20}$

             = $25,000

MADE
(Selling Price)
$30,000 ÷ ÷ ? 120% or 1.20 X
PAID (Purchase Price)   **RATE** (Profit Rate)

You may be asked to find the selling price or amount of a loan when the seller receives a net amount.

Practice Problem #11

A farmer put his land on the market, wanting to net a certain amount. The real estate agent who found a buyer gave the farmer a check for $90,000, after deducting a 10% commission. What was the selling price of the farm?

The variables are:

      Made = $90,000
      Rate   = 100% − 10% = 90%
      Paid   = ?

Selling Price = $\dfrac{\text{Seller's Net}}{\text{Commission Rate}}$

            = $\dfrac{\$90,000}{.90}$

            = $100,000

MADE (Selling Price)
$90,000 ÷ ÷ ? 90% or .90 X
PAID (Seller's Net)   **RATE** (Commission Rate)

Square Footage and Area Calculations

On the state exam, you may be asked to solve problems about square footage. Also, in actual practice, you may have to use the cost method of appraising property occasionally. Square footage problems are fairly simple and can be solved easily using these simple formulas.

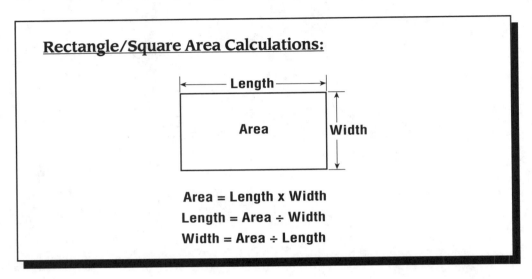

Rectangle/Square Area Calculations:

Area = Length x Width
Length = Area ÷ Width
Width = Area ÷ Length

As you recall, the way to determine the value of a building using the cost method is to measure the square footage (buildings are measured on the outside). Then check with a contractor to determine the standard cost to build per square foot. Multiply that cost by the square footage of the building to derive the cost to build new, or the upper limit of value.

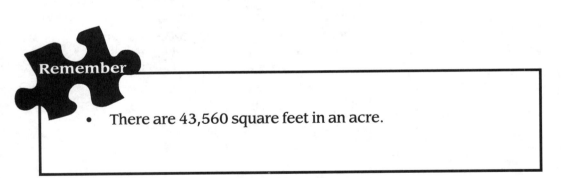

Remember

- There are 43,560 square feet in an acre.

Practice Problem #12

Felix owned four acres of land with a front footage of 500 feet along the street. What is the depth of the land?

First, convert the acres to square feet

> 43,560 sq. ft./acre x 4 acres = 174,240 square feet.

The variables are:

> Area = 174,240 sq. ft.
> Width = 500 feet
> Length = ?

What we don't know is the length (depth) of the parcel. Using the formula:

$$\text{Length} = \frac{\text{Area}}{\text{Width}}$$

$$= \frac{174,240}{500}$$

Length = 348.48 feet

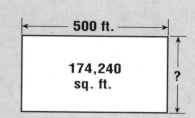

All buildings are not square or rectangular and therefore may be irregular in shape. Always reduce the building to squares, rectangles and triangles, for which you know the formula to determine the square footage.

Remember

Basic Formulas

- The Area of a Square = Length x Width
- The Area of a Rectangle = Length x Width
- The Area of a Triangle = Altitude x Base ÷ 2

Practice Problem #13

Lydia and Cliff bought a lot, with the intention of building a house on it. First they needed to determine the square footage of the lot, and second—how much it would cost them to build the house. They were told by contractors the cost to build was $40 per square foot for a garage and $80 per square foot for a home.

To find the square footage of the lot, divide the diagram into an imaginary square and triangle:

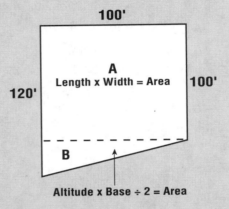

Then calculate the area (square footage) of each figure:

Square A	= 100 x 100 = 10,000 square feet
Triangle B	= 20 x 100 ÷ 2 = 1,000 square feet
Total lot size	= 10,000 + 1,000 = 11,000 square feet

After figuring the square footage of the lot, Lydia and Cliff had plans drawn for the house. They used the total square footage of the house and garage to figure the cost to build.

To find the square footage of the house, divide the diagram into imaginary rectangles:

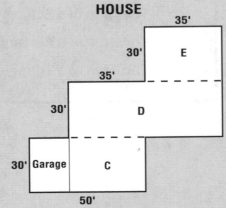

Then calculate the area of each rectangle:

Rectangle C	= 35 x 30 = 1,050 square feet
Rectangle D	= 70 x 30 = 2,100 square feet
Rectangle E	= 30 x 35 = 1,050 square feet
Area of house	= 4,200 square feet
Garage	= 15 x 30 = 450 square feet
Total	= 4,200 square feet + 450 square feet = 4,650 square feet in house and garage

To calculate the cost of the building:

4,200 square feet x $80 per square foot = $336,000

450 square feet x $40 per square foot = $18,000

Cost of house at $336,000 + cost of garage at $18,000 = Total cost to build house and garage at $354,000

Proration

When property is bought and sold, there are certain expenses that are charged to each party. It is one of the jobs of escrow to credit and debit the buyer and seller correctly as of the closing date of escrow. **Proration** is the process of making a fair distribution of expenses, through escrow, at the close of the sale.

Remember

- For purposes of proration, there are 30 days in a month and 360 days in a year.

The Process Of Proration Includes:

- Determining the number of days to be prorated
- Calculating the cost per day
- Multiplying the number of days by the cost per day
- Deciding whether the item should be a credit or a debit to the seller or to the buyer

Common Expenses that are Usually Prorated:

- Property taxes
- Interest on assumed loans
- Fire and hazard insurance
- Rents

Practice Problem #14

Lynn sold her home on September 1, 1998. She has an existing loan of $200,000 on the house. The interest on the loan is 8%. Terry took over Lynn's loan with interest paid to August 15, l998. Terry also assumed an existing three-year fire insurance policy for $360 per year, paid by Lynn until November 15, 1999. Lynn also owes property taxes of $1,900 for the year.

Calculate the following:

 Interest proration, and who is credited or debited

 Insurance proration, and who is credited or debited

 Tax proration, and who is credited or debited

To calculate the interest proration:

 August 15 to September 1 = 15 days

 $200,000 x 8% = $16,000 annual interest

 $16,000 ÷ 360 days in year = $44.44 per day

 15 days x $44.44 per day = $666.60 interest

 Credit the buyer and debit the seller.

To calculate the insurance proration:

 September 1, 1998, through November 15, 1999 = 435 days

 $360 ÷ 360 = $1.00 per day

 435 days x $1.00 = $435

 Credit the seller and debit the buyer.

To calculate the tax proration:

 July 1 to September 1 = 60 days

 $1,900 ÷ 360 = $5.27 per day

 60 days x $5.27 = $316.66

 Debit the seller and credit the buyer.

About proration

- Expenses that have been paid to some time after escrow closes, credit the seller and debit the buyer.

- Expenses that will be due after the close of escrow, debit the seller and credit the buyer.

Documentary Transfer Tax

http://www.dre.ca.gov
Reference Book, Ch. 18
p. 393

Each county, upon the transfer of property, may charge a documentary transfer tax. As you recall, the amount of the transfer tax is stamped in the upper right-hand corner of a recorded deed. The amount of the tax is based on $1.10 per $1,000 or $.55 per $500 of transferred value.

How to Calculate Documentary Transfer Tax

- When a sale is all cash, or a new loan is obtained by the buyer, the tax is calculated on the entire sales price.

- When an existing loan is assumed by a buyer, the tax is calculated on the difference between the assumed loan and the sales price.

Practice Problem #15

Denise sold her home for $250,000, with the buyer obtaining a new loan. What is the amount of the documentary tax?

250 x $1.10 = $275.00

The questions presented in this chapter are similar to those you will encounter on the state exam. The situations they represent are those you will experience in real life. Learn to recognize the type of problem, and the math solution it requires, and you will be proficient in your real estate career.

Post Test

The following self test repeats the one you took at the beginning of this chapter. Now take the exam again—since you have read all the material— and check your knowledge of real estate math.

1. The charge for the use of money is called:
   a. interest
   b. usury
   c. principal
   d. proration

2. The original amount of money borrowed is known as:
   a. interest
   b. principal
   c. capitalized loan amount
   d. compounded loan amount

3. The mark that sets apart a whole number from a fractional part of that number is called:
   a. fraction
   b. decimal point
   c. percentage
   d. period

4. What is the first position to the right of the decimal point called?
   a. 100th
   b. 1,000th
   c. 10th
   d. units

5. What numbers are found to the left of a decimal point?
   a. fractions
   b. decimals
   c. percentages
   d. whole numbers

6. A building with six-inch thick walls has interior dimensions of 25 feet by 29 feet. The building covers a land area of how many square feet?
   a. 1,054
   b. 780
   c. 720
   d. 540

7. The maximum number of 50-foot x 110-foot lots that could be obtained from an acre of land would be:
   a. 10 lots
   b. 8 lots
   c. 7 lots
   d. 5 lots

8. A property produced a 9% gross return on a $20,000 purchase price for a one-year period. The owner's only expense was an 8% annual interest rate on a $15,000 loan. What is the percentage return on the owner's equity?
   a. 9%
   b. 11%
   c. 12%
   d. 13%

9. A percentage lease calls for 2% of gross sales or a guaranteed minimum base of $1,200 per month. If the annual sales are $700,000, what is the monthly rent?
   a. $1,167
   b. $1,200
   c. $1,363
   d. $1,500

10. What percent of a section is 1/60th of a township?
    a. 40%
    b. 50%
    c. 60%
    d. 70%

Vocabulary

Read the definition, find the matching term and write the corresponding term number on the line provided.

Terms

1. Decimal
2. Divisor
3. Dividend
4. Interest
5. Principal
6. Proration
7. Rate

Definitions

1. ___ A number to be divided by another number

2. ___ The charge for the use of money

3. ___ The percentage of interest charged on the principal

4. ___ The process of making a fair distribution of expenses, through escrow, at the close of the sale

5. ___ The period that sets apart a whole number from a fractional part of that number

6. ___ The amount of money borrowed

7. ___ A number by which another number is divided

Answers

Pre-Test/Post Test

1. a
2. b
3. b
4. c
5. d
6. b **Square footage problem**

    25 feet + 6" west wall + 6" east wall = 26 feet
    29 feet + 6" north wall + 6" south wall = 30 feet

    26 feet x 30 feet = 780 sq. ft.

7. c **Lots per acre problem**

    50' x 110' = 5,500 sq. ft. per lot

    $$\frac{43,560 \text{ sq. ft. acre}}{5,500 \text{ sq. ft. per lot}} = 7.92 \text{ lots}$$

    Maximum number would be 7, as you cannot round to get 8th lot.

8. c **Return on equity problem**

    $20,000 price x 9% gross return = $1,800
    less interest expense = $15,000 loan x 8%   1,200
    net return $600

    $20,000 price
    -15,000 loan
     $5,000 equity

    $$\frac{\$600 \quad \text{Net return}}{\$5,000 \text{ equity}} = 12\% \text{ return in equity}$$

9. b **Percentage lease problem**

    $700,000 x 2% = $14,000
                    12 mos. = $1,167

    However, $1,200 minimum is greater

10. c **Township problem**

    36 sections in a township

    $$\frac{1}{60} \times \frac{36}{1} = \frac{36}{60} = \frac{36}{60} = 60\%$$

Vocabulary

1.	3	4.	6	7.	2
2.	4	5.	1		
3.	7	6.	5		

$\mathcal{G}$LOSSARY

http://www.dre.ca.gov
Reference Book, Ch. 29
Glossary

http://www.chanrobles.com/
realestate.htm

http://www.matisse.net/files/
glossary.html

A

A.L.T.A.
American Land Title Association

A.L.T.A. Owner's Policy
American Land Title Association policy of extended title insurance

Abstract of Title
A full summary of all consecutive grants, conveyances, wills, records and judicial proceedings affecting title to a specific parcel of real estate

Abstractor
A person who, historically, searches out anything affecting the title to real property and summarizes the information in the findings

Acceleration Clause
A clause in a loan document describing certain events that would cause the entire loan to be due

Acceptance
An unqualified agreement to the terms of an offer

Accession
The acquisition of title to additional land or to improvements as a result of annexing fixtures or as a result of natural causes such as alluvial deposits along the banks of streams by accretion

Accretion
A buildup of soil by natural causes on property bordering a river, lake or ocean

Accrued
Accumulated over a period of time

Accrued Depreciation
The difference between the cost to replace the property and property's current appraised value

Acknowledgment
A signed statement, made before a notary public, by a named person confirming the signature on a document and that it was made of free will

Action
A lawsuit brought to court

Actual Age
The real age of a building

Actual Depreciation
That depreciation occurring as a result of physical, functional or economic forces, causing loss in value to a building

Actual Notice
Knowledge gained based on an actual observance, as opposed to Constructive Notice

Ad Valorem
A Latin prefix meaning "according to value." Local governments levy real property tax based on the assessed value; property taxes are known as ad valorem taxes

Adjustable Rate Mortgage (ARM)
A loan which allows for the interest rate to adjust periodically in relationship to a predetermined index based on the maintenance of a pre-established margin

Adjusted Cost Basis
Original basis plus capital improvements and costs of the sale, less depreciation if income producing

Administrator/Administratrix

A person appointed by the court to handle the affairs of a deceased person when there is no one mentioned in a will to do so

Adverse Possession

Acquiring title to property by continued possession and payment of taxes

After Acquired Title

Any benefits that come to a property after a sale must follow the sale and accrue to the new owner

Agency

A relationship in which one party (principal) authorizes another party (agent) to act as the principal's representative in dealing with third parties

Agent

A person who acts for and in the place of another, called a principal, for the purpose of affecting the principal's legal relationship with third persons

Agreement of Sale

A contract for the sale of real property where the seller gives up possession, but retains the title until the purchase price is paid in full

Alienate

Transfer ownership or sell

Alienation Clause

A clause in a loan document that would allow the lender to call the entire loan due upon the sale of the property

All-Inclusive Trust Deed

A purchase money deed of trust subordinate to—but still including—the original loan

Alluvial Deposit

Sand or mud, carried by water and deposited on land

Alluvium

Soil that builds up as a result of accretion

Annual Percentage Rate (APR)

The relationship of the total finance charge to the total amount to be financed as required under the Truth-in-Lending Act

Appraisal

An estimate or opinion of value supported by factual information as of a certain date

Appraisal Report

A written report stating an appraiser's estimate of a subject property's value

Appreciation

An increase in value

Appurtenance

Those rights, privileges and improvements that belong to and pass with the transfer of real property but are not necessarily a part of the actual property

Arm's Length Transaction

A transaction, such as a sale of property, in which all parties involved are acting in their own self-interest and are under no undue influence or pressure from the other parties

Assessment Roll or Tax Roll

A list of all taxable property showing the assessed value of each parcel; establishes the tax base

Assignee

The person to whom a claim, benefit or right in property is made

Assignment

The transfer of a claim, benefit or right in property from one person to another

Assignment of Rents

An agreement between a property owner and the holder of a trust deed or mortgage by which the holder receives, as security, the right to collect rents from tenants of the property in the event of default by the borrower

Assignor

The person transferring a claim, benefit or right in property to another

Assumption Clause

A buyer takes over the existing loan and agrees to be liable for the repayment of the loan

Attorney in Fact

A competent and disinterested person who is authorized by another person to act in his or her place in legal matters

Avulsion

The sudden washing or tearing away of land by the action of water

B

Balloon Payment
Under an installment loan, a final payment that is substantially larger than any other payment and repays the debt in full

Base Line
A survey line running east and west, used as a reference when mapping land

Beneficiary
The lender under a deed of trust

Beneficiary Statement
A statement of the unpaid balance of a loan and the condition of the debt, as it relates to a deed of trust

Bequest
A gift of personal property by will; see legacy

Bilateral Contract
A contract in which each party to the contract promises to perform some act or duty in exchange for the promise of the other party

Bill of Sale
A written agreement used to transfer ownership in personal property

Blanket Loan
A loan secured by several properties

Block Busting
Causing panic selling by telling people that values in a neighborhood will decline because of a specific event, such as the purchase of homes by minorities

Book Depreciation
An accounting concept which refers to an allowance taken to provide for recovery of invested capital

Book Sale
A sale of real property to the state, in name only, when a taxpayer is delinquent in paying property tax

Book Value
The initial cost of the property plus capital improvements minus the total accrued depreciation

Boot
Money or any "non-like" property put into a sale by an investor to balance the equities in a 1031 tax deferred exchange; cash or mortgage relief in an exchange

Breach of Contract
A failure to perform on part or all of the terms and conditions of a contract

Brokerage
The occupation of a broker; the business of selling real estate through a broker who negotiates the sale for a commission

Bulk Transfer Law
The law concerning transfer in bulk (not a sale in the ordinary course of the seller's business)

Bundle of Rights
An ownership concept describing all the legal rights that attach to the ownership of real property

Business Opportunity
Any type of business that is for lease or sale

C

C.L.T.A.
California Land Title Association

Calendar Year
Starts on January 1 and continues through December 31 of the same year

California Land Title Association
A trade organization of the state's title companies

Cap Rate
A term sometimes used when referring to capitalization rate

Capital Improvements
Any permanent improvement made to real estate for the purpose of increasing the useful life of the property or increasing the property's value

Capitalization
The process of calculating the present worth of a property on the basis of its capacity to continue to produce an income stream

Chain of Title
A chronological history of property's ownership

Chattel
Personal property

Chattel Real

An item of personal property which is connected to real estate; for example, a lease

Client

The person who employs an agent to perform a service for a fee

Codicil

A change in a will before the maker's death

Collateral

Something of value given as security for a debt

Commingling

To deposit client funds in the broker's personal account

Commission Split

The previously agreed upon division of money between a broker and sales-associate when the brokerage has been paid a commission from a sale made by the associate

Comps

A term used by real estate agents and appraisers to mean comparable properties

Condemnation

A common name for eminent domain, or the right of the government to take private property from an owner for the public good, paying fair market value

Condition Precedent

A condition which requires something to occur before a transaction becomes absolute and enforceable; for example, a sale that is contingent on the buyer obtaining financing

Condition Subsequent

A condition which, if it occurs at some point in the future, can cause a property to revert to the grantor; for example, a requirement in a grant deed that a buyer must never use the property for anything other than a private residence

Consideration

Something of value—such as money, a promise, property or personal services

Constructive Notice

Recordation of deed or possession of property

Contract of Sale

A contract for the sale of real property where the seller gives up possession but retains title until the total of the purchase price is paid off

Contract Rent

The amount of rental income due from the tenant as agreed in the lease agreement

Contractual Intent

Intention to be bound by an agreement, thus preventing jokes and jests from becoming valid contracts

Conversion

The appropriation of property belonging to another

Convey

To transfer ownership or title

Conveyance

The transfer of title to land from one person to another by use of a written instrument

Corner Lot

A lot found at the intersection of two streets

Cost

Represents expenses in money, labor, material or sacrifices in acquiring or producing something

Cost Basis

Usually the price paid for a property

Counteroffer

The rejection of an original offer that becomes a new offer

Cul-De-Sac Lot

A lot found on a dead-end street

Customer

A prospective buyer of real estate

D

Decimal Point

The period that sets apart a whole number from a fractional part of that number

Declaration of Homestead

The recorded document that protects a homeowner from foreclosure by certain judgment creditors

Default
Failure to pay a debt or on a contract

Deferred Maintenance
Negligent care of a building

Deficiency Judgment
A judgment against a borrower for the balance of a debt owed when the security for the loan is not sufficient enough to pay the debt

Definite and Certain
Precise acts to be performed are to be clearly stated

Demise
A conveyance of an estate in real property to someone for a certain length of time, as in a lease; to let

Deposit Receipt
Also known as a sales contract; the primary document used to present an offer on real property

Depreciation
Loss in value from any cause

Deregulation
A process where financial institutions that formerly had been restrained in their lending activities by the law are allowed to compete freely for profits in the marketplace

Devise
A gift of real property by will

Disintermediation
The process of depositors removing funds from savings

Dividend
A number to be divided by another number

Divisor
A number by which another number is divided

Doctrine of Correlative User
Owner may use only a reasonable amount of the total underground water supply for his or her beneficial use

Dominant Tenement
The property that benefits from an easement

Dual Agent
An agent who represents both parties in a transaction

Duress
The use of force to get agreement in accepting a contract

E

Easement
The right to use another's land for a specified purpose, sometimes known as a right-of-way

Easement in Gross
An easement that is not appurtenant to any one parcel; for example, public utilities

Economic Life
The estimated period over which an improved property may be profitably used to yield a return

Economic Rent
What a leased property would be expected to rent for under current market conditions if the property were vacant and available for rent

Effective Age
The years or age shown by the condition and utility of a structure, rather than its actual or chronological age

Emancipated Minor
Someone who is legally set free from parental control/ supervision

Emblements
Annual crops produced for sale

Eminent Domain
The right of the government to take private property from an owner, for the public good, paying fair market value

Encroachment
The placement of permanent improvements on adjacent property owned by another

Environmental Impact Report (EIR)
A study of how a development will affect the ecology of its surroundings

Equal Credit Opportunity Act
A federal law that requires lenders to assure that credit is available with fairness, impartiality and without discrimination

Equitable Title
The interest held by the trustor or vendee

Equity

The value remaining in a property after payment of all liens

Equity of Redemption

Also known as the right of redemption; the right of a debtor, before a foreclosure sale, to reclaim property that had been given up due to mortgage default

Erosion

The gradual wearing away of land by natural processes

Escrow

The deposit of funds or documents with a neutral third party who is instructed to carry out the provisions of an agreement

Escrow Holder

An independent third party legally bound to carry out the written provisions of an escrow agreement; a neutral, bonded third party who is a dual agent for the principals; sometimes called an escrow agent

Escrow Instructions

Written directions, signed by a buyer and seller, detailing the procedures necessary to close a transaction and directing the escrow agent how to proceed

Estate

A legal interest in land; defines the nature, degree, extent and duration of a person's ownership in land

Estate at Sufferance

A tenancy created when one is in wrongful possession of real estate even though the original possession may have been legal

Estate at Will

The tenancy may be ended by the unilateral decision of either party; no agreed upon termination date, however, and either party must give 30 days notice before ending the tenancy

Estate for Years

A leasehold estate with a definite end date; must be renegotiated; commonly used for commercial leases

Estate from Period to Period

A leasehold estate that is automatically renewed for the same term; a conveyance for an indefinite period of time; does not need to be renegotiated upon each renewal; commonly a month to month rental

Estate in Fee

The most complete form of ownership of real property; a freehold estate that can be passed by descent or by will after the owner's death; also known as estate of inheritance or fee simple estate

Estate of Inheritance

See estate in fee

Estoppel

A legal doctrine which prevents a person from denying something to be true or a fact which is contrary to previous statements made by that same person

Ethics

A set of principles or values by which an individual guides his or her own behavior and judges that of others

Eviction

The legal process of removing a tenant from the premises for some breach of the lease

Execute

To perform or complete; to sign

Executed Contract

A contract in which the obligations have been performed on both sides of the contract and nothing is left to be completed

Execution

Completion of an act or process, such as an escrow

Executor/Executrix

A person named in a will to handle the affairs of a deceased person

Executory Contract

A contract in which obligation to perform exists on one or both sides of the contract

Expedientes

Land grants recorded by the Mexican government in California

Express Contract

The parties declare the terms and put their intentions in words, either oral or written

Extended Policy

An extended title insurance policy

F

Fair Market Value

The price the property would bring if freely offered on the open market with both a willing buyer and a willing seller

Fee

See estate in fee or fee simple absolute

Fee Simple Absolute

The largest, most complete ownership recognized by law; an estate in fee with no restrictions on its use

Fee Simple Defeasible

Also known as fee simple qualified

Fee Simple Estate

See estate in fee

Fee Simple Qualified

An estate in which the holder has a fee simple title, subject to return to the grantor if a specified condition occurs

Fiduciary

A relationship that implies a position of trust or confidence

Financial Intermediary

An organization that obtains funds through deposits and then lends those funds to earn a return—such as savings banks, commercial banks, credit unions and mutual savings banks

Financing Statement

A written notice filed with the county recorder by a creditor who has extended credit for the purchase of personal property; establishes the creditor's interests in the personal property which is security for the debt

Fiscal Year

Starts on July 1 and runs through June 30 of the following year; used for real property tax purposes

Fixture

Personal property that has become affixed to real estate

Flag Lot

Looks like a flag on a pole, which represents the access to the site; usually located to the rear of another lot fronting a main street

Forbearance

Refraining from action by a creditor against the debt owed by a borrower after the debt has become due

Foreclosure

A legal procedure by which mortgaged property in which there has been default on the part of the borrower is sold to satisfy the debt

Foreclosure Sale

A sale where property is sold to satisfy a debt

Fraud

An act meant to deceive in order to get someone to part with something of value

Freehold Estate

An estate in real property which continues for an indefinite period of time

Front Footage

The width of a property along a street

Fully Amortized Note

A note that is fully repaid at maturity by periodic reduction of the principal

G

Gift Deed

Used to make a gift of property to a grantee, usually a close friend or relative

Good Consideration

Gifts such as real property based solely on love and affection

Goodwill

An intangible, salable asset arising from the reputation of a business; the expectation of continued public patronage

Grace Period

An agreed-upon time after the payment of a debt is past due, during which a party can perform without being considered in default

Graduated Lease

A lease calling for periodic increases in the rental payments; sometimes called a stair-step lease

Graduated Payment Adjustable Mortgage (GPAM)

A loan in which the monthly payment graduates by a certain percentage each year for a specific number of years, then levels off for the remaining term of the loan

Grant Deed

A type of deed in which the grantor warrants that he or she has not previously conveyed the property being granted, has not encumbered the property except as disclosed, and will convey to the grantee any title to the property acquired later

Grantee

The person receiving the property, or the one to whom it is being conveyed

Grantor

The person conveying, or transferring, the property

Gross Lease

Landlord pays for most of the operating expenses, including property taxes, maintenance and repairs

Gross Rent

Income (figured annually) received from rental units before any expenses are deducted

Guarantee of Title

An assurance of clear title

H

Hard Money Loan

The evidence of a debt that is given in exchange for cash

Holder

The party to whom a promissory note is made payable

Holder in Due Course

A person who has obtained a negotiable instrument (promissory note, check) in the ordinary course of business before it is due, in good faith and for value, without knowledge that it has been previously dishonored

Holographic Will

Written in the maker's own handwriting, dated and signed by the maker

Home Equity Loan

A cash loan made against the equity in the borrower's home

Homeowner's Exemption

A $7,000 tax exemption available to all owner-occupied dwellings

I

Implied Contract

Agreement is shown by acts and conduct rather than words

Improvements

Any buildings or structures on a lot

Instrument

A written legal document setting forth the rights and liabilities of the parties involved

Interest

The charge for the use of money

Interior Lot

One that is surrounded by other lots, with a frontage on the street; the most common type lot, which may or may not be desirable—depending on other factors

Intermediation

The process of transfer capital from those who invest funds to those who wish to borrow

Intestate

Dying without leaving a will

J

Judgment

The final legal decision of a judge in a court of law regarding the legal rights of parties to disputes

Judicial Foreclosure

Foreclosure by court action

Junior Trust Deed

Any trust deed that is recorded after a first trust deed, whose priority is less than that first trust deed

K

Key Lot

So named because it resembles a key fitting into a lock; one that is surrounded by the backyards of other lots, therefore is the least desirable because of the lack of privacy

L

Land Contract

A contract for the sale of real property where the seller gives up possession, but retains the title until the purchase price is paid in full; also known as a contract of sale or agreement of sale

Land Projects

Subdivisions located in sparsely populated areas of California, made up of 50 parcels or more

Landlord

Lessor; property owner

Leasehold or Lease

An agreement, written or unwritten, transferring the right to exclusive possession and use of real estate for a definite period of time

Legacy

A gift of personal property by will

Legal Title

Title that is complete and perfect regarding right of ownership; may be held by a trustee under a deed of trust

Less-Than-Freehold Estate

A leasehold estate, considered to exist for a definite period of time or successive periods of time until termination

Lessee

Tenant; renter

Lessor

Landlord; property owner

License

Permission to use a property, which may be revoked at any time

Lien

A claim on the property of another for the payment of a debt

Life Estate

An estate that is limited in duration to the life of its owner or the life of some other chosen person

Linear Foot

A measurement meaning one foot or 12 inches in length as contrasted to a square foot or a cubic foot

Liquidated Damages

Sets in advance a specified amount of money as a penalty in the event of a breach of contract

Lis Pendens

A recorded notice that indicates pending litigation affecting title on a property, preventing a conveyance or any other transfer of ownership until the lawsuit is settled and the lis pendens removed

Listing

A contract by which a principal employs an agent to do certain things for the principal

Littoral

Land bordering a lake, ocean or sea—as opposed to land bordering a stream or river (running water)

Love and Affection

Consideration used in a gift deed

M

Maker

The borrower who executes a promissory note and becomes primarily liable for payment to the lender

Manufactured Housing

A housing unit primarily constructed in a factory and moved to a permanent site; another name for a mobile home

Market Rent

The rent a property should bring in the open market

Marketable Title

Good or clear saleable title reasonably free from risk of litigation over possible defects

Menace

Using threat of violence to get agreement in accepting a contract

Meridian

A survey line running north and south, used as a reference when mapping land

Metes and Bounds

A method of land description in which the dimensions of the property are measured by distance and direction

Minor

Someone under 18 years of age

Misrepresentation

An innocent or negligent misstatement of a material fact causing someone loss or harm

Mistake

An error or misunderstanding

Mobile Home

A manufactured unit constructed on a chassis and wheels, designed for permanent or semi-attachment to land

Monument

A fixed landmark used in a metes and bounds land description

Mortgage

A legal document used as security for a debt

Mortgage Loan Disclosure Statement

A statement that informs the buyer of all charges and expenses related to a particular loan

Mortgagee

The lender under a mortgage

Mortgagor

The borrower under a mortgage

Mutual Consent

Agreement to the provisions of a contract by the parties involved; a mutual willingness to enter into a contract

N

Naked Legal Title

Title lacking the rights and privileges commonly associated with ownership

Negotiable Instrument

Any written instrument that may be transferred by endorsement or delivery

Net Income

Sometimes known as net operating income; the remaining income after operating expenses have been subtracted from the gross income of a property

Net Lease

A lease where the tenant pays such costs as taxes, insurance and repairs, as well as a set amount for rent; a triple net lease is one where the tenant pays all expenses of operating the property as well as a set amount of rent

Neutral Depository

An escrow business conducted by someone who is a licensed escrow holder

Notice of Default

A notice to a defaulting party that there has been a nonpayment of a debt

Notice of Trustee's Sale

Notice given, and published, that a trustee's sale will be held to sell a property to satisfy a debt

Novation

The substitution by agreement of a new obligation for an existing one

O

Offer

A presentation or proposal for acceptance to form a contract

Offeree

The party receiving an offer

Offeror

The party making an offer

Open End Loan

A loan where the borrower is given a limit up to which may be borrowed, with each advance secured by the same trust deed

Option

A right—given for consideration—to a party (optionee) by a property owner (optionor)

"Or More" Clause

A clause in a promissory note that allows a borrower to pay it off early with no penalty

P

Package Loan

A loan on real property that can be secured by land, structure, fixtures and other personal property

Parole Evidence

Oral or written negotiations made prior to a dispute about an executed contract

Partially Amortized Installment Note

A promissory note with a repayment schedule that is not sufficient to amortize the loan over its term

Partition Action

A court action to divide a property held by co-owners

Patent Deed

A deed given by the government to a private individual as evidence of title transfer from the government to the private person

Percentage Lease

A lease where the landlord receives a percentage of the gross sales as part or all of the rental payment

Personal Property

Anything movable that is not real property

Plat Map

A map of a town or subdivision showing the location and boundaries of individual properties, used in the recorded tract system to describe land

Pledge

The transfer of property to a lender to be held as security for repayment of a debt; lender takes possession of property

Plottage or Assemblage

Putting several smaller, less valuable parcels together under one ownership to increase value of total property

Police Power

The power of the state to pass laws, within lawful limits, that promote the order, safety, health, morals and general welfare of its citizens

Power of Attorney

A written instrument giving a person legal authority to act on behalf of another person

Power of Sale

A clause in a trust deed or mortgage that gives the holder the right to sell the property in the event of default by the borrower

Preliminary Title Report

An examination of the public land records to determine the extent to which someone has legal interest in a parcel; a report on the quality of the title that searches for encumbrances and liens or any other items of record that might effect ownership; used as a basis for title insurance

Prepayment Clause

A clause in a trust deed that allows a lender to collect a certain percentage of a loan as a penalty for an early payoff

Price

What is paid for something

Principal

Someone who directs or authorizes another to act in his or her place regarding relations with third persons; buyer or seller; the amount of money borrowed; the original amount borrowed

Private Grant

The granting of private property to other private persons

Probate Sale

A court-approved sale of the property of a deceased person

Promissory Note

A written promise or order to pay, evidence of a debt

Property

The rights or interests which an owner has in something owned

Proration

The division and distribution of expenses and/or income between the buyer and seller of property as of the date of closing or settlement

Public Dedication

When private property is intended for public use, it may be acquired in this manner

Public Grant

The transfer of title by the government to a private individual

Puffing
Exaggerated comments or opinions not made as representations of fact, thus not grounds for misrepresentation

Purchase Money Loan
A trust deed created as evidence of a debt at the time of the sale of real property

Q

Quitclaim Deed
Transfers any interest the grantor may have at the time the deed is signed with no warranties of clear title

R

Range
A land description used in the U.S. government survey system consisting of a strip of land located every six miles east and west of each principal meridian

Rate
The percentage of interest charged on the principal

Ratification
The approval of a previously authorized act, performed on behalf of a person, which makes the act valid and legally binding

Ratified
Approved

Real Estate Agent
Someone licensed by the Department of Real Estate, holding either a broker or salesperson license, who negotiates sales for other people

Real Estate Broker
Someone holding a broker license and permitted by law to employ those holding a salesperson license, who may negotiate sales for other people

Real Estate Investment Trust (REIT)
A way investors with a small amount of capital can pool their resources to buy real estate

Real Estate Law
The law that affects the licensing and conduct of real estate agents

Real Estate Sales Associate
The same as a real estate salesperson, holding a salesperson license, employed by a broker

Real Estate Salesperson
Someone holding a salesperson license and employed by a real estate broker, for pay, to perform any of the activities of a real estate salesperson

Real Property
Land, anything affixed to the land, anything appurtenant to the land, anything immovable by law

Reconciliation
Sometimes called correlation, this is the adjustment process of weighing results of all three appraisal methods to arrive at a final estimate of the subject property's market value

Reconveyance Deed
Conveys title to property from a trustee back to the borrower (trustor) upon payment in full of the debt secured by the trust deed

Red Flag
Something that would warn a reasonably observant person of a potential problem, thus requiring further investigation

Redlining
The use of a property's location to deny financing

Reinstate
Bring current and restore

Release Clause
A provision found in many blanket loans enabling the borrower to obtain partial release from the loan of specific parcels

Reliction
Occurs when land that has been covered by water is exposed by receding water

Rent
Consideration paid for the use of a property

Replacement Cost
The cost of replacing improvements with modern materials and techniques

Reproduction Cost
The current cost of building a replica of the subject structure, using similar quality materials

Request for Notice

A notice that is sent, upon request, to any parties interested in a trust deed, informing them of a default

Rescission

Legal action taken to repeal a contract either by mutual consent of the parties or by one party when the other party has breached a contract

Residential Rental Property

Property from which 80 percent or more of the gross rental income is from dwelling units

Retaliatory Eviction

An act whereby a landlord evicts a tenant in response to some complaint made by the tenant

Reverse Annuity Mortgage

A loan that enables elderly homeowners to borrow against the equity in their homes by receiving monthly payments from a lender, that are needed to help meet living costs

Reversionary Right

The lessor (landlord) grants the right of possession to the lessee (tenant), but retains the right to retake possession after the lease's term has expired

Revocation

The cancelling of an offer to contract by the person making the original offer

Revoke

Recall and make void

Riparian Rights

The rights of a landowner whose land is next to a natural watercourse to reasonable use of whatever water flows past the property

Rollover Mortgage

A loan that allows the rewriting of a new loan at the termination of a prior loan

S

Sandwich Lease

A lease agreement created when a tenant sublets the property to another person, thus creating a sublessor-sublessee relationship. The person in the "sandwich" is a lessee to the owner and a lessor to the sub-lessee

Second Trust Deed

The evidence of a debt that is recorded after a first trust deed; a junior trust deed

Section

An area of land, as used in the government survey method of land description; a land area of one square mile or 640 acres; 1/36 of a township

Security

Evidence of obligations to pay money

Security Agreement

The device commonly used to secure a loan on personal property

Seller's Permit

Allows a retailer to buy the product at wholesale prices without paying sales tax. The retailer must then collect the proper sales tax from customers and pay it to the State Board of Equalization

Servient Tenement

The property that is burdened by an easement

Severalty

Ownership of real property by one person or entity

Shared Appreciation Mortgage (SAM)

Lender and borrower agree to share a certain percentage of the appreciation in market value of the property

Sheriff's Deed

A deed given to a buyer when property is sold through court action in order to satisfy a judgment for money or foreclosure of a mortgage

Site

The position, situation or location of a piece of land in a neighborhood

Soldier's and Sailor's Relief Act

A federal law designed to protect persons in the military service from loss of property when their ability to make the payment has been affected by their entering military service

Specific Performance

An action brought in a court to compel a party to carry out the terms of a contract

Sales Tax
Collected as a percentage of the retailing sales of a product, by a retailer, and forwarded to the State Board of Equalization

Standard Policy
A policy of title insurance covering only matters of record

Statutory
Regarding laws created by the enactment of legislation as opposed to law created by court decisions

Steering
Illegal practice of only showing clients property in certain areas

Straight Note
A promissory note in which payments of interest only are made periodically during the term of the note, with the principal payment due in one lump sum upon maturity; may also be a note with no payments on either principal or interest until the entire sum is due

Subagent
An agent of a person who is already acting as an agent for a principal

Subdivided Lands Act
A state law protecting purchasers of property in new subdivisions from fraud, misrepresentation or deceit in the marketing of subdivided property; concerned with financial aspects of a development

Subdivision
The division of land into five or more lots for the purpose of sale, lease or financing

Subdivision Map Act
Outlines rules for filing subdivision maps to create subdivisions; concerned with physical aspects of a development

"Subject-To" Clause
A buyer takes over the existing loan payments, but assumes no personal liability for the loan

Sublease
Transfers less than the entire leasehold, with the original lessee being primarily liable for the rental agreement

Subordination Clause
A clause in which the holder of a trust deed permits a subsequent loan to take priority

Succession
The legal transfer of a person's interest in real and personal property under the laws of descent

Surrender
The giving up of a lease, voluntarily

Suspend
Temporarily make ineffective

Swing Loan
A short-term loan used to enable the purchaser of a new property to buy that property on the strength of the equity from the property the purchaser is now selling

T

T-Intersection Lot
A lot that is fronted head-on by a street; noise and glare from headlights may be detractors from this type of lot

Tax Deed
A deed given to a successful bidder at a tax auction

Tenant
A renter

Tender
An offer by one of the parties to a contract to carry out his or her part of the contract

Testator/Testatrix
A person who has made a will

Third Party
A person who may be affected by the terms of an agreement but who is not a party to the agreement

Tight Money
An economic situation in which the supply of money is limited, and the demand for money is high, as evidenced by high interest rates

Time
Duration of loan

Timely Manner
An act must be performed within certain time limits described in a contract

Title
Evidence of land ownership

Title Insurance
An insurance policy that protects the named insured against loss or damage due to defect in the property's title

Title Plant
The storage facility of a title company in which it has accumulated complete title records of properties in its area

Tort
A negligent or intentional wrongful act arising from breach of duty created by law and not contract

Township
A land description used in the U.S. government survey system consisting of a six-by-six mile area containing 36 sections, each one mile square

Trade Association
A voluntary nonprofit organization of independent and competing business units engaged in the same industry or trade, formed to help solve industry problems, promote progress and enhance service Trade Fixture

Trade Fixture
An article of personal property affixed to leased property by the tenant as a necessary part of business; may be removed by tenant as personal property upon termination of the lease

Treaty of Guadalupe Hidalgo
Ended the war with Mexico in 1848, and California became a possession of the United States

Trust Deed
A document where title to property is transferred to a third party trustee as security for a debt owed by the trustor (borrower) to the beneficiary (lender)

Trust Funds
Money received by real estate brokers or salespersons on behalf of others

Trustee
Holds naked legal title to property as a neutral third party where there is a deed of trust

Trustee's Deed
A deed given to a buyer of real property at a trustee's sale

Trustee's Sale
The forced sale of real property, by a lender, to satisfy a debt

Trustor
The borrower under a deed of trust

Truth in Lending Act (Regulation Z)
A law that requires borrowers to be informed about the cost of borrowing money

U

Undivided Interest
That interest a co-owner has in property, which carries with it the right to possession and use of the whole property, along with the co-owners

Undue Influence
Using unfair advantage to get agreement in accepting a contract

Unenforceable
A contract that was valid when made but either cannot be proved or will not be enforced by a court

Unilateral Contract
An agreement in which one party promises to pay consideration or to do something in return for the performance of an act by another party; the party making the promise is not legally obligated to act unless the other party performs (a promise for an act)

Unilateral Rescission
Legal action taken to repeal a contract by one party when the other party has breached a contract

Unlawful Detainer Action
A lawsuit filed with the court against a tenant who remains in unlawful possession of rental property after breaching the terms of a lawful lease

Usury
The act of charging a rate of interest in excess of that permitted by law

Utility Value
The usefulness of the property

V

Vacancy Factor
Loss of income because of a vacant unit

Valid
Legally binding

Valuable Consideration
Each party to a contract must give up something to make the agreement binding

Value
The power of goods or services to command other goods in exchange for the present worth of future benefits arising from property ownership

Variable Rate Mortgage (VRM)
A mortgage where the interest rate varies according to an agreed-upon index, thus resulting in a change in the borrower's monthly payments

Variance
An exception granted to existing zoning regulations for special reasons

Vendee
The buyer under a contract of sale (land contract)

Vendor
The seller under a contract of sale (land contract)

Vested
Owned by

Void
An agreement which is totally absent of legal effect

Voidable
An agreement which is valid and enforceable on its face, but may be rejected by one or more of the parties

W

Warehousing
The process of assembling into one package a number of mortgage loans, prior to selling them to an investor

Warranty Deed
No longer used in California; a deed used to transfer title to property, guaranteeing that the title is clear and the grantor has the right to transfer it

Will
A written instrument whereby a person makes a disposition of his property to take effect after his death

Witnessed Will
Will usually prepared by an attorney and signed by the maker and two witnesses

Wrap-Around Loan
A method of financing where a new loan is placed in a secondary position; the new loan includes both the unpaid principal balance of the first loan and whatever sums are loaned by the lender; sometimes called an All-Inclusive Trust Deed (AITD)

Writ of Possession
A court order directing the sheriff to remove the tenant and his or her possessions within five days

INDEX

Property Address: _____   Date: _____

18. DISPUTE RESOLUTION:

    A. **MEDIATION:** Seller and Broker agree to mediate any dispute or claim arising between them out of this agreement, or any resulting transaction, before resorting to arbitration or court action, subject to paragraph 18C below. Mediation fees, if any, shall be divided equally among the parties involved. If any party commences an action based on a dispute or claim to which this paragraph applies, without first attempting to resolve the matter through mediation, then that party shall not be entitled to recover attorney's fees, even if they would otherwise be available to that party in any such action. THIS MEDIATION PROVISION APPLIES WHETHER OR NOT THE ARBITRATION PROVISION IS INITIALED.

    B. **ARBITRATION OF DISPUTES:** Seller and Broker agree that any dispute or claim in Law or equity arising between them regarding the obligation to pay compensation under this agreement, which is not settled through mediation, shall be decided by neutral, binding arbitration, subject to paragraph 18C below. The arbitrator shall be a retired judge or justice, or an attorney with at least five years of residential real estate law experience, unless the parties mutually agree to a different arbitrator, who shall render an award in accordance with substantive California Law. In all other respects, the arbitration shall be conducted in accordance with Part III, Title 9 of the California Code of Civil Procedure. Judgment upon the award of the arbitrator(s) may be entered in any court having jurisdiction. The parties shall have the right to discovery in accordance with Code of Civil Procedure §1283.05.

        "NOTICE: BY INITIALING IN THE SPACE BELOW YOU ARE AGREEING TO HAVE ANY DISPUTE ARISING OUT OF THE MATTERS INCLUDED IN THE 'ARBITRATION OF DISPUTES' PROVISION DECIDED BY NEUTRAL ARBITRATION AS PROVIDED BY CALIFORNIA LAW AND YOU ARE GIVING UP ANY RIGHTS YOU MIGHT POSSESS TO HAVE THE DISPUTE LITIGATED IN A COURT OR JURY TRIAL. BY INITIALING IN THE SPACE BELOW YOU ARE GIVING UP YOUR JUDICIAL RIGHTS TO DISCOVERY AND APPEAL, UNLESS THOSE RIGHTS ARE SPECIFICALLY INCLUDED IN THE 'ARBITRATION OF DISPUTES' PROVISION. IF YOU REFUSE TO SUBMIT TO ARBITRATION AFTER AGREEING TO THIS PROVISION, YOU MAY BE COMPELLED TO ARBITRATE UNDER THE AUTHORITY OF THE CALIFORNIA CODE OF CIVIL PROCEDURE. YOUR AGREEMENT TO THIS ARBITRATION PROVISION IS VOLUNTARY."

        "WE HAVE READ AND UNDERSTAND THE FOREGOING AND AGREE TO SUBMIT DISPUTES ARISING OUT OF THE MATTERS INCLUDED IN THE 'ARBITRATION OF DISPUTES' PROVISION TO NEUTRAL ARBITRATION."   Seller's Initials _____/_____   Broker's Initials _____/_____

    C. **EXCLUSIONS FROM MEDIATION AND ARBITRATION:** The following matters are excluded from Mediation and Arbitration hereunder: (a) A judicial or non-judicial foreclosure or other action or proceeding to enforce a deed of trust, mortgage, or installment land sale contract as defined in Civil Code §2985; (b) An unlawful detainer action; (c) The filing or enforcement of a mechanic's lien; (d) Any matter which is within the jurisdiction of a probate, small claims, or bankruptcy court; and (e) An action for bodily injury or wrongful death, or for any right of action to which Code of Civil Procedure §337.1 or §337.15 applies. The filing of a court action to enable the recording of a notice of pending action, for order of attachment, receivership, injunction, or other provisional remedies, shall not constitute a violation of the mediation and arbitration provisions.

19. ENTIRE CONTRACT: All prior discussions, negotiations, and agreements between the parties concerning the subject matter of this agreement are superseded by this agreement, which constitutes the entire contract and a complete and exclusive expression of their agreement, and may not be contradicted by evidence of any prior agreement or contemporaneous oral agreement. This agreement and any supplement, addendum, or modification, including any photocopy or facsimile, may be executed in counterparts.

Seller acknowledges that Seller has read and understands this Agreement, and has received a copy.

Seller _____   Date _____
Address _____ City _____ State _____ Zip _____
Telephone _____ Fax _____ E-mail _____

Seller _____   Date _____
Address _____ City _____ State _____ Zip _____
Telephone _____ Fax _____ E-mail _____

Real Estate Broker (Firm) _____ By (Agent) _____ Date _____
Address _____ City _____ State _____ Zip _____
Telephone _____ Fax _____ E-mail _____

Published and Distributed by:
REAL ESTATE BUSINESS SERVICES, INC.
a subsidiary of the CALIFORNIA ASSOCIATION OF REALTORS®
525 South Virgil Avenue, Los Angeles, California 90020

REVISION DATE 4/2000

Reviewed by _____
Broker or Designee _____ Date _____

BROKER'S COPY

RESIDENTIAL LISTING AGREEMENT-EXCLUSIVE (LA-11 PAGE 3 OF 3)

FORM BIA

CALIFORNIA
ASSOCIATION
OF REALTORS®

BUYER'S INSPECTION ADVISORY
(C.A.R. Form BIA, Revised 10/02)

Property Address: _____ ("Property").

A. IMPORTANCE OF PROPERTY INVESTIGATION: The physical condition of the land and improvements being purchased is not guaranteed by either Seller or Brokers. For this reason, you should conduct thorough investigations of the Property personally and with professionals who should provide written reports of their investigations. A general physical inspection typically does not cover all aspects of the Property nor items affecting the Property that are not physically located on the Property. If the professionals recommend further investigations, including a recommendation by a pest control operator to inspect inaccessible areas of the Property, you should contact qualified experts to conduct such additional investigations.

B. BUYER RIGHTS AND DUTIES: You have an affirmative duty to exercise reasonable care to protect yourself, including discovery of the legal, practical and technical implications of disclosed facts, and the investigation and verification of information and facts that you know or that are within your diligent attention and observation. The purchase agreement gives you the right to investigate the Property. If you exercise this right, and you should, you must do so in accordance with the terms of that agreement. This is the best way for you to protect yourself. It is extremely important for you to read all written reports provided by professionals and to discuss the results of inspections with the professional who conducted the inspection. You have the right to request that Seller make repairs, corrections or take other action based upon items discovered in your investigations or disclosed by Seller. If Seller is unwilling or unable to satisfy your requests, or you do not want to purchase the Property in its disclosed and discovered condition, you have the right to cancel the agreement if you act within specific time periods. If you do not cancel the agreement in a timely and proper manner, you may be in breach of contract.

C. SELLER RIGHTS AND DUTIES: Seller is required to disclose to you material facts known to him/her that affect the value or desirability of the Property. However, Seller may not be aware of some Property defects or conditions. Seller does not have an obligation to inspect the Property for your benefit nor is Seller obligated to repair, correct or otherwise cure known defects that are disclosed to you or previously unknown defects that are discovered by you or your inspectors during escrow. The purchase agreement obligates Seller to make the Property available to you for investigations.

D. BROKER OBLIGATIONS: Brokers do not have expertise in all areas and therefore cannot advise you on many items, such as soil stability, geologic or environmental conditions, hazardous or illegal controlled substances, structural conditions of the foundation or other improvements, or the condition of the roof, plumbing, heating, air conditioning, electrical, sewer, septic, waste disposal, or other system. The only way to accurately determine the condition of the Property is through an inspection by an appropriate professional selected by you. If Broker gives you referrals to such professionals, Broker does not guarantee their performance. You may select any professional of your choosing. In sales involving residential dwellings with no more than four units, Brokers have a duty to make a diligent visual inspection of the accessible areas of the Property and to disclose the results of that inspection. However, as some Property defects or conditions may not be discoverable from a visual inspection, it is possible Brokers are not aware of them. If you have entered into a written agreement with a Broker, the specific terms of that agreement will determine the nature and extent of that Broker's duty to you. **YOU ARE STRONGLY ADVISED TO INVESTIGATE THE CONDITION AND SUITABILITY OF ALL ASPECTS OF THE PROPERTY. IF YOU DO NOT DO SO, YOU ARE ACTING AGAINST THE ADVICE OF BROKERS.**

E. YOU ARE ADVISED TO CONDUCT INVESTIGATIONS OF THE ENTIRE PROPERTY, INCLUDING, BUT NOT LIMITED TO THE FOLLOWING:
  1. **GENERAL CONDITION OF THE PROPERTY, ITS SYSTEMS AND COMPONENTS:** Foundation, roof, plumbing, heating, air conditioning, electrical, mechanical, security, pool/spa, other structural and non-structural systems and components, fixtures, built-in appliances, any personal property included in the sale, and energy efficiency of the Property. (Structural engineers are best suited to determine possible design or construction defects, and whether improvements are structurally sound.)
  2. **SQUARE FOOTAGE, AGE, BOUNDARIES:** Square footage, room dimensions, lot size, age of improvements and boundaries. Any numerical statements regarding these items are APPROXIMATIONS ONLY and have not been verified by Seller and cannot be verified by Brokers. Fences, hedges, walls, retaining walls and other natural or constructed barriers or markers do not necessarily identify true Property boundaries. (Professionals such as appraisers, architects, surveyors and civil engineers are best suited to determine square footage, dimensions and boundaries of the Property.)
  3. **WOOD DESTROYING PESTS:** Presence of, or conditions likely to lead to the presence of wood destroying pests and organisms and other infestation or infection. Inspection reports covering these items can be separated into two sections: Section 1 identifies areas where infestation or infection is evident. Section 2 identifies areas where there are conditions likely to lead to infestation or infection. A registered structural pest control company is best suited to perform these inspections.

BIA REVISED 10/02 (PAGE 1 OF 2) Print Date BDC Oct 02

Buyer's Initials (_____)(_____)
Seller's Initials (_____)(_____)

Reviewed by _____ Date _____

EQUAL HOUSING
OPPORTUNITY

MASTER COPY

Buyer's Inspection Advisory (2 of 2)

Property Address: _____ Date: _____

4. **SOIL STABILITY:** Existence of fill or compacted soil, expansive or contracting soil, susceptibility to slippage, settling or movement, and the adequacy of drainage. (Geotechnical engineers are best suited to determine such conditions, causes and remedies.)
5. **ROOF:** Present condition, age, leaks, and remaining useful life. (Roofing contractors are best suited to determine these conditions.)
6. **POOL/SPA:** Cracks, leaks or operational problems. (Pool contractors are best suited to determine these conditions.)
7. **WASTE DISPOSAL:** Type, size, adequacy, capacity and condition of sewer and septic systems and components, connection to sewer, and applicable fees.
8. **WATER AND UTILITIES; WELL SYSTEMS AND COMPONENTS:** Water and utility availability, use restrictions and costs. Water quality, adequacy, condition, and performance of well systems and components.
9. **ENVIRONMENTAL HAZARDS:** Potential environmental hazards, including, but not limited to, asbestos, lead-based paint and other lead contamination, radon, methane, other gases, fuel oil or chemical storage tanks, contaminated soil or water, hazardous waste, waste disposal sites, electromagnetic fields, nuclear sources, and other substances, materials, products, or conditions (including mold (airborne, toxic or otherwise), fungus or similar contaminants). (For more in formation on these items, you may consult an appropriate professional or read the booklets "Environmental Hazards: A Guide for Homeowners ,Buyers, Landlords and Tenants," "Protect Your Family From Lead in Your Home" or both.)
10. **EARTHQUAKES AND FLOODING:** Susceptibility of the Property to earthquake/seismic hazards and propensity of the Property to flood. (A Geologist or Geotechnical Engineer is best suited to provide information on these conditions.)
11. **FIRE, HAZARD AND OTHER INSURANCE:** The availability and cost of necessary or desired insurance may vary. The location of the Property in a seismic, flood or fire hazard zone, and other conditions, such as the age of the Property and the claims history of the Property and Buyer, may affect the availability and need for certain types of insurance. Buyer should explore insurance options early as this information may affect other decisions, including the removal of loan and inspection contingencies. (An insurance agent is best suited to provide information on these conditions.)
12. **BUILDING PERMITS, ZONING AND GOVERNMENTAL REQUIREMENTS:** Permits, inspections, certificates, zoning, other governmental limitations, restrictions, and requirements affecting the current or future use of the Property, its development or size. (Such information is available from appropriate governmental agencies and private information providers. Brokers are not qualified to review or interpret any such information.)
13. **RENTAL PROPERTY RESTRICTIONS:** Some cities and counties impose restrictions that limit the amount of rent that can be charged, the maximum number of occupants; and the right of a landlord to terminate a tenancy. Deadbolt or other locks and security systems for doors and windows, including window bars, should be examined to determine whether they satisfy legal requirements. (Government agencies can provide information about these restrictions and other requirements.)
14. **SECURITY AND SAFETY:** State and local Law may require the installation of barriers, access alarms, self-latching mechanisms and/or other measures to decrease the risk to children and other persons of existing swimming pools and hot tubs, as well as various fire safety and other measures concerning other features of the Property. Compliance requirements differ from city to city and county to county. Unless specifically agreed, the Property may not be in compliance with these requirements. (Local government agencies can provide information about these restrictions and other requirements.)
15. **NEIGHBORHOOD, AREA, SUBDIVISION CONDITIONS; PERSONAL FACTORS:** Neighborhood or area conditions, including schools, proximity and adequacy of law enforcement, crime statistics, the proximity of registered felons or offenders, fire protection, other government services, availability, adequacy and cost of any speed-wired, wireless internet connections or other telecommunications or other technology services and installations, proximity to commercial, industrial or agricultural activities, existing and proposed transportation, construction and development that may affect noise, view, or traffic, airport noise, noise or odor from any source, wild and domestic animals, other nuisances, hazards, or circumstances, protected species, wetland properties, botanical diseases, historic or other governmentally protected sites or improvements, cemeteries, facilities and condition of common areas of common interest subdivisions, and possible lack of compliance with any governing documents or Homeowners' Association requirements, conditions and influences of significance to certain cultures and/or religions, and personal needs, requirements and preferences of Buyer.

Buyer and Seller acknowledge and agree that Broker: **(i)** Does not decide what price Buyer should pay or Seller should accept; **(ii)** Does not guarantee the condition of the Property; **(iii)** Does not guarantee the performance, adequacy or completeness of inspections, services, products or repairs provided or made by Seller or others; **(iv)** Shall not be responsible for identifying defects that are not known to Broker and **(a)** are not visually observable in reasonably accessible areas of the Property; **(b)** are in common areas; or **(c)** are off the site of the Property; **(v)** Shall not be responsible for inspecting public records or permits concerning the title or use of Property; **(vi)** Shall not be responsible for identifying the location of boundary lines or other items affecting title; **(vii)** Shall not be responsible for verifying square footage, representations of others or information contained in Investigation reports, Multiple Listing Service, advertisements, flyers or other promotional material; **(viii)** Shall not be responsible for providing legal or tax advice regarding any aspect of a transaction entered into by Buyer or Seller; and **(ix)** Shall not be responsible for providing other advice or information that exceeds the knowledge, education and experience required to perform real estate licensed activity. Buyer and Seller agree to seek legal, tax, insurance, title and other desired assistance from appropriate professionals.

By signing below, Buyer and Seller each acknowledge that they have read, understand, accept and have received a Copy of this Advisory. Buyer is encouraged to read it carefully.

Buyer Signature _____ Date _____   Buyer Signature _____ Date _____

Seller Signature _____ Date _____   Seller Signature _____ Date _____

THIS FORM HAS BEEN APPROVED BY THE CALIFORNIA ASSOCIATION OF REALTORS® (C.A.R.). NO REPRESENTATION IS MADE AS TO THE LEGAL VALIDITY OR ADEQUACY OF ANY PROVISION IN ANY SPECIFIC TRANSACTION. A REAL ESTATE BROKER IS THE PERSON QUALIFIED TO ADVISE ON REAL ESTATE TRANSACTIONS. IF YOU DESIRE LEGAL OR TAX ADVICE, CONSULT AN APPROPRIATE PROFESSIONAL.

This form is available for use by the entire real estate industry. It is not intended to identify the user as a REALTOR®. REALTOR® is a registered collective membership mark which may be used only by members of the NATIONAL ASSOCIATION OF REALTORS® who subscribe to its Code of Ethics.

SURE TRAC
The System for Success™
Published by the
California Association of REALTORS®

Reviewed by _____ Date _____

EQUAL HOUSING OPPORTUNITY

BIA REVISED 10/02 (PAGE 2 OF 2)   MASTER COPY

BUYER'S INSPECTION ADVISORY (BIA PAGE 2 OF 2)

Property Address: _____ Date: _____

18. **PRORATIONS OF PROPERTY TAXES AND OTHER ITEMS:** Unless otherwise agreed in writing, the following items shall be PAID CURRENT and prorated between Buyer and Seller as of Close Of Escrow: real property taxes and assessments, interest, rents, HOA regular, special, and emergency dues and assessments imposed prior to Close Of Escrow, premiums on insurance assumed by Buyer, payments on bonds and assessments assumed by Buyer, and payments on Mello-Roos and other Special Assessment District bonds and assessments that are now a lien. The following items shall be assumed by Buyer WITHOUT CREDIT toward the purchase price: prorated payments on Mello-Roos and other Special Assessment District bonds and assessments and HOA special assessments that are now a lien but not yet due. Property will be reassessed upon change of ownership. Any supplemental tax bills shall be paid as follows: **(i)** for periods after Close Of Escrow, by Buyer; and **(ii)** for periods prior to Close Of Escrow, by Seller. TAX BILLS ISSUED AFTER CLOSE OF ESCROW SHALL BE HANDLED DIRECTLY BETWEEN BUYER AND SELLER. Prorations shall be made based on a 30-day month.

19. **WITHHOLDING TAXES:** Seller and Buyer agree to execute any instrument, affidavit, statement or instruction reasonably necessary to comply with federal (FIRPTA) and California withholding Law, if required (C.A.R. Forms AS and AB).

20. **MULTIPLE LISTING SERVICE ("MLS"):** Brokers are authorized to report to the MLS a pending sale and, upon Close Of Escrow, the terms of this transaction to be published and disseminated to persons and entities authorized to use the information on terms approved by the MLS.

21. **EQUAL HOUSING OPPORTUNITY:** The Property is sold in compliance with federal, state and local anti-discrimination Laws.

22. **ATTORNEY FEES:** In any action, proceeding, or arbitration between Buyer and Seller arising out of this Agreement, the prevailing Buyer or Seller shall be entitled to reasonable attorney fees and costs from the non-prevailing Buyer or Seller, except as provided in paragraph 17A.

23. **SELECTION OF SERVICE PROVIDERS:** If Brokers refer Buyer or Seller to persons, vendors, or service or product providers ("Providers"), Brokers do not guarantee the performance of any Providers. Buyer and Seller may select ANY Providers of their own choosing.

24. **TIME OF ESSENCE; ENTIRE CONTRACT; CHANGES:** Time is of the essence. All understandings between the parties are incorporated in this Agreement. Its terms are intended by the parties as a final, complete and exclusive expression of their Agreement with respect to its subject matter, and may not be contradicted by evidence of any prior agreement or contemporaneous oral agreement. If any provision of this Agreement is held to be ineffective or invalid, the remaining provisions will nevertheless be given full force and effect. **Neither this Agreement nor any provision in it may be extended, amended, modified, altered or changed, except in writing Signed by Buyer and Seller.**

25. **OTHER TERMS AND CONDITIONS,** including attached supplements:
    A. ☑ Buyer's Inspection Advisory (C.A.R. Form BIA) _____
    B. ☐ Purchase Agreement Addendum (C.A.R. Form PAA paragraph numbers: _____) _____
    C. _____
    _____
    _____

26. **DEFINITIONS:** As used in this Agreement:
    A. **"Acceptance"** means the time the offer or final counter offer is accepted in writing by a party and is delivered to and personally received by the other party or that party's authorized agent in accordance with the terms of this offer or a final counter offer.
    B. **"Agreement"** means the terms and conditions of this accepted California Residential Purchase Agreement and any accepted counter offers and addenda.
    C. **"C.A.R. Form"** means the specific form referenced or another comparable form agreed to by the parties.
    D. **"Close Of Escrow"** means the date the grant deed, or other evidence of transfer of title, is recorded. If the scheduled close of escrow falls on a Saturday, Sunday or legal holiday, then close of escrow shall be the next business day after the scheduled close of escrow date.
    E. **"Copy"** means copy by any means including photocopy, NCR, facsimile and electronic.
    F. **"Days"** means calendar days, unless otherwise required by Law.
    G. **"Days After"** means the specified number of calendar days after the occurrence of the event specified, not counting the calendar date on which the specified event occurs, and ending at 11:59PM on the final day.
    H. **"Days Prior"** means the specified number of calendar days before the occurrence of the event specified, not counting the calendar date on which the specified event is scheduled to occur.
    I. **"Electronic Copy"** or **"Electronic Signature"** means, as applicable, an electronic copy or signature complying with California Law. Buyer and Seller agree that electronic means will not be used by either party to modify or alter the content or integrity of this Agreement without the knowledge and consent of the other.
    J. **"Law"** means any law, code, statute, ordinance, regulation, rule or order, which is adopted by a controlling city, county, state or federal legislative, judicial or executive body or agency.
    K. **"Notice to Buyer to Perform"** means a document (C.A.R. Form NBP), which shall be in writing and Signed by Seller and shall give Buyer at least 24 hours **(or as otherwise specified in paragraph 14C(4))** to remove a contingency or perform as applicable.
    L. **"Repairs"** means any repairs (including pest control), alterations, replacements, modifications or retrofitting of the Property provided for under this Agreement.
    M. **"Signed"** means either a handwritten or electronic signature on an original document, Copy or any counterpart.
    N. **Singular and Plural** terms each include the other, when appropriate.

Buyer's Initials (_____)(_____)
Seller's Initials (_____)(_____)

RPA-CA REVISED 10/02 (PAGE 6 OF 8)

Reviewed by _____ Date _____

EQUAL HOUSING OPPORTUNITY

MASTER COPY

CALIFORNIA RESIDENTIAL PURCHASE AGREEMENT (RPA-CA PAGE 6 OF 8)

Property Address: _____ Date: _____

27. AGENCY:

A. DISCLOSURE: Buyer and Seller each acknowledge prior receipt of C.A.R. Form AD "Disclosure Regarding Real Estate Agency Relationships."

B. POTENTIALLY COMPETING BUYERS AND SELLERS: Buyer and Seller each acknowledge receipt of a disclosure of the possibility of multiple representation by the Broker representing that principal. This disclosure may be part of a listing agreement, buyer-broker agreement or separate document (C.A.R. Form DA). Buyer understands that Broker representing Buyer may also represent other potential buyers, who may consider, make offers on or ultimately acquire the Property. Seller understands that Broker representing Seller may also represent other sellers with competing properties of interest to this Buyer.

C. CONFIRMATION: The following agency relationships are hereby confirmed for this transaction:
Listing Agent _____ (Print Firm Name) is the agent of (check one): ☐ the Seller exclusively; or ☐ both the Buyer and Seller.
Selling Agent _____ (Print Firm Name) (if not same as Listing Agent) is the agent of (check one): ☐ the Buyer exclusively; or ☐ the Seller exclusively; or ☐ both the Buyer and Seller. Real Estate Brokers are not parties to the Agreement between Buyer and Seller.

28. JOINT ESCROW INSTRUCTIONS TO ESCROW HOLDER:

A. **The following paragraphs, or applicable portions thereof, of this Agreement constitute the joint escrow instructions of Buyer and Seller to Escrow Holder,** which Escrow Holder is to use along with any related counter offers and addenda, and any additional mutual instructions to close the escrow: 1, 2, 4, 12, 13B, 14E, 18, 19, 24, 25B and C, 26, 28, 29, 32A, 33 and paragraph D of the section titled Real Estate Brokers on page 8. If a Copy of the separate compensation agreement(s) provided for in paragraph 29 or 32A, or paragraph D of the section titled Real Estate Brokers on page 8 is deposited with Escrow Holder by Broker, Escrow Holder shall accept such agreement(s) and pay out from Buyer's or Seller's funds, or both, as applicable, the Broker's compensation provided for in such agreement(s). The terms and conditions of this Agreement not set forth in the specified paragraphs are additional matters for the information of Escrow Holder, but about which Escrow Holder need not be concerned. Buyer and Seller will receive Escrow Holder's general provisions directly from Escrow Holder and will execute such provisions upon Escrow Holder's request. To the extent the general provisions are inconsistent or conflict with this Agreement, the general provisions will control as to the duties and obligations of Escrow Holder only. Buyer and Seller will execute additional instructions, documents and forms provided by Escrow Holder that are reasonably necessary to close the escrow.

B. A Copy of this Agreement shall be delivered to Escrow Holder within **3** business days after Acceptance (or ☐ _____). Buyer and Seller authorize Escrow Holder to accept and rely on Copies and Signatures as defined in this Agreement as originals, to open escrow and for other purposes of escrow. The validity of this Agreement as between Buyer and Seller is not affected by whether or when Escrow Holder Signs this Agreement.

C. Brokers are a party to the escrow for the sole purpose of compensation pursuant to paragraphs 29, 32A and paragraph D of the section titled Real Estate Brokers on page 8. Buyer and Seller irrevocably assign to Brokers compensation specified in paragraphs 29 and 32A, respectively, and irrevocably instruct Escrow Holder to disburse those funds to Brokers at Close Of Escrow or pursuant to any other mutually executed cancellation agreement. Compensation instructions can be amended or revoked only with the written consent of Brokers. Escrow Holder shall immediately notify Brokers: **(i)** if Buyer's initial or any additional deposit is not made pursuant to this Agreement, or is not good at time of deposit with Escrow Holder; or **(ii)** if Buyer and Seller instruct Escrow Holder to cancel escrow.

D. A Copy of any amendment that affects any paragraph of this Agreement for which Escrow Holder is responsible shall be delivered to Escrow Holder within **2** business days after mutual execution of the amendment.

29. BROKER COMPENSATION FROM BUYER:
If applicable, upon Close Of Escrow, **Buyer** agrees to pay compensation to Broker as specified in a separate written agreement between Buyer and Broker.

30. TERMS AND CONDITIONS OF OFFER:

This is an offer to purchase the Property on the above terms and conditions. All paragraphs with spaces for initials by Buyer and Seller are incorporated in this Agreement only if initialed by all parties. If at least one but not all parties initial, a counter offer is required until agreement is reached. Seller has the right to continue to offer the Property for sale and to accept any other offer at any time prior to notification of Acceptance. Buyer has read and acknowledges receipt of a Copy of the offer and agrees to the above confirmation of agency relationships. If this offer is accepted and Buyer subsequently defaults, Buyer may be responsible for payment of Brokers' compensation. This Agreement and any supplement, addendum or modification, including any Copy, may be Signed in two or more counterparts, all of which shall constitute one and the same writing.

Buyer's Initials (_____)(_____)
Seller's Initials (_____)(_____)

RPA-CA REVISED 10/02 (PAGE 7 OF 8)

Reviewed by _____ Date _____

EQUAL HOUSING OPPORTUNITY

MASTER COPY

CALIFORNIA RESIDENTIAL PURCHASE AGREEMENT (RPA-CA PAGE 7 OF 8)

Property Address: _____ Date: _____

31. EXPIRATION OF OFFER: This offer shall be deemed revoked and the deposit shall be returned unless the offer is Signed by Seller and a Copy of the Signed offer is personally received by Buyer, or by _____, who is authorized to receive it by 5:00 PM on the third calendar day after this offer is signed by Buyer (or, if checked, ☐ by _____ (date), at _____ AM/PM).

Date _____ Date _____

BUYER _____ BUYER _____

_____ _____
(Print name) **(Print name)**

_____
(Address)

32. BROKER COMPENSATION FROM SELLER:
 A. Upon Close Of Escrow, **Seller** agrees to pay compensation to Broker as specified in a separate written agreement between Seller and Broker.
 B. If escrow does not close, compensation is payable as specified in that separate written agreement.

33. ACCEPTANCE OF OFFER: Seller warrants that Seller is the owner of the Property, or has the authority to execute this Agreement. Seller accepts the above offer, agrees to sell the Property on the above terms and conditions, and agrees to the above confirmation of agency relationships. Seller has read and acknowledges receipt of a Copy of this Agreement, and authorizes Broker to deliver a Signed Copy to Buyer.
 ☐ (If checked) **SUBJECT TO ATTACHED COUNTER OFFER, DATED** _____.

Date _____ Date _____

SELLER _____ SELLER _____

_____ _____
(Print name) **(Print name)**

_____
(Address)

(____/____) **CONFIRMATION OF ACCEPTANCE:** A Copy of Signed Acceptance was personally received by Buyer or Buyer's authorized
(Initials) agent on (date) _____ at _____ AM/PM. **A binding Agreement is created when a Copy of Signed Acceptance is personally received by Buyer or Buyer's authorized agent whether or not confirmed in this document. Completion of this confirmation is not legally required in order to create a binding Agreement; it is solely intended to evidence the date that Confirmation of Acceptance has occurred.**

REAL ESTATE BROKERS:
A. Real Estate Brokers are not parties to the Agreement between Buyer and Seller.
B. Agency relationships are confirmed as stated in paragraph 27.
C. If specified in paragraph 2A, Agent who submitted the offer for Buyer acknowledges receipt of deposit.
D. COOPERATING BROKER COMPENSATION: Listing Broker agrees to pay Cooperating Broker **(Selling Firm)** and Cooperating Broker agrees to accept, out of Listing Broker's proceeds in escrow: **(i)** the amount specified in the MLS, provided Cooperating Broker is a Participant of the MLS in which the Property is offered for sale or a reciprocal MLS; or **(ii)** ☐ (if checked) the amount specified in a separate written agreement (C.A.R. Form CBC) between Listing Broker and Cooperating Broker.

Real Estate Broker (Selling Firm) _____
By _____ Date _____
Address _____ City _____ State _____ Zip _____
Telephone _____ Fax _____ E-mail _____

Real Estate Broker (Listing Firm) _____
By _____ Date _____
Address _____ City _____ State _____ Zip _____
Telephone _____ Fax _____ E-mail _____

ESCROW HOLDER ACKNOWLEDGMENT:
Escrow Holder acknowledges receipt of a Copy of this Agreement, (if checked, ☐ a deposit in the amount of $ _____),
counter offer numbers _____ and _____
_____, and agrees to act as Escrow Holder subject to paragraph 28 of this Agreement, any supplemental escrow instructions and the terms of Escrow Holder's general provisions.

Escrow Holder is advised that the date of Confirmation of Acceptance of the Agreement as between Buyer and Seller is _____

Escrow Holder _____ Escrow # _____
By _____ Date _____
Address _____
Phone/Fax/E-mail _____
Escrow Holder is licensed by the California Department of ☐ Corporations, ☐ Insurance, ☐ Real Estate. License # _____

SURE TRAC
The System for Success™
Published by the
California Association of REALTORS®

RPA-CA REVISED 10/02 (PAGE 8 OF 8)

MASTER COPY

Reviewed by _____ Date _____

EQUAL HOUSING OPPORTUNITY

CALIFORNIA RESIDENTIAL PURCHASE AGREEMENT (RPA-CA PAGE 8 OF 8)

Property Address: _____ Date: _____

III. AGENT'S INSPECTION DISCLOSURE
(To be completed only if the Seller is represented by an agent in this transaction.)

THE UNDERSIGNED, BASED ON THE ABOVE INQUIRY OF THE SELLER(S) AS TO THE CONDITION OF THE PROPERTY AND BASED ON A REASONABLY COMPETENT AND DILIGENT VISUAL INSPECTION OF THE ACCESSIBLE AREAS OF THE PROPERTY IN CONJUNCTION WITH THAT INQUIRY, STATES THE FOLLOWING:

☐ Agent notes no items for disclosure.
☐ Agent notes the following items: _____
_____
_____
_____

Agent (Broker Representing Seller) _____ By _____ Date _____
                                    (Please Print)   (Associate-License or Broker Signature)

IV. AGENT'S INSPECTION DISCLOSURE
(To be completed only if the agent who has obtained the offer is other than the agent above.)

THE UNDERSIGNED, BASED ON A REASONABLY COMPETENT AND DILIGENT VISUAL INSPECTION OF THE ACCESSIBLE AREAS OF THE PROPERTY, STATES THE FOLLOWING:

☐ Agent notes no items for disclosure.
☐ Agent notes the following items: _____
_____
_____

Agent (Broker Obtaining the Offer) _____ By _____ Date _____
                                    (Please Print)   (Associate-License or Broker Signature)

V. BUYER(S) AND SELLER(S) MAY WISH TO OBTAIN PROFESSIONAL ADVICE AND/OR INSPECTIONS OF THE PROPERTY AND TO PROVIDE FOR APPROPRIATE PROVISIONS IN A CONTRACT BETWEEN BUYER AND SELLER(S) WITH RESPECT TO ANY ADVICE/INSPECTIONS/DEFECTS.

I/WE ACKNOWLEDGE RECEIPT OF A COPY OF THIS STATEMENT.

Seller _____ Date _____ Buyer _____ Date _____

Seller _____ Date _____ Buyer _____ Date _____

Agent (Broker Representing Seller) _____ By _____ Date _____
                                                     (Associate-License or Broker Signature)

Agent (Broker Obtaining the Offer) _____ By _____ Date _____
                                                     (Associate-License or Broker Signature)

SECTION 1102.3 OF THE CIVIL CODE PROVIDES A BUYER WITH THE RIGHT TO RESCIND A PURCHASE CONTRACT FOR AT LEAST THREE DAYS AFTER THE DELIVERY OF THIS DISCLOSURE IF DELIVERY OCCURS AFTER THE SIGNING OF AN OFFER TO PURCHASE. IF YOU WISH TO RESCIND THE CONTRACT, YOU MUST ACT WITHIN THE PRESCRIBED PERIOD.

A REAL ESTATE BROKER IS QUALIFIED TO ADVISE ON REAL ESTATE. IF YOU DESIRE LEGAL ADVICE, CONSULT YOUR ATTORNEY.

Published and Distributed by:
REAL ESTATE BUSINESS SERVICES, INC.
a subsidiary of the CALIFORNIA ASSOCIATION OF REALTORS®
525 South Virgil Avenue, Los Angeles, California 90020

Reviewed by
Broker or Designee _____ Date _____

EQUAL HOUSING OPPORTUNITY

TDS-11 REVISED 10/01 (PAGE 3 OF 3)

MASTER COPY

REAL ESTATE TRANSFER DISCLOSURE STATEMENT (TDS-11 PAGE 3 OF 3)